Documents from the
History of Lutheranism,
1517–1750

Documents from the History of Lutheranism, 1517–1750

edited by
Eric Lund

Fortress Press

Minneapolis

Cover art: The altar triptych by Lucas Cranach the elder, Church of St. Marien, Wittenberg, Germany, is used by permission of Bridgeman Art Library. The background text (Romans 1) is from a German Bible published in Philadelphia, c.1866.
Cover design: Zan Ceeley
Interior design: Beth Wright

The publisher gratefully acknowledges the following for reprint permission: Westminster John Knox Press for the excerpt on pages 46–47, from *Luther and Erasmus: Free Will and Salvation*; Pickwick Publications for the excerpt on pages 53–54, from *Zwingli's Writings*, vol. 2; Modern Library, a division of Random House, Inc., for the excerpt on pages 55–56, from *Great Debates of the Reformation*; Pearson Education, Inc., Upper Saddle River, N.J., for the excerpt on page 173, from *Renaissance and Reformation, 1300–1648*; and Concordia Publishing House for the excerpts on pages 227–34, from *The Two Natures in Christ, The Lord's Supper*, and *Examination of the Council of Trent: Part 1*.

Library of Congress Cataloging-in-Publication Data

Documents from the history of Lutheranism, 1517–1750 / edited by Eric Lund.
  p.   cm.
  Includes bibliographical references and index.
  ISBN 0-8006-3440-3 (alk. paper)
    1. Lutheran Church—History. I. Lund, Eric, 1948–

BX8018 .D63 2001
284.1′09—dc21

2001054315

Manufactured in the U.S.A.   AF 1-3440
06   05   04   03   02   1   2   3   4   5   6   7   8   9   10

Contents

The Peasants' Revolt 39

The Conflict with Erasmus 45

The Sacramentarian Controversy 50

Negotiations with the Emperor 56

The Assaults of the Devil 66

Pietist Hymns 308

Preface

The Protestant Reformation was one of the major turning points in the intellectual and social development of Western civilization, and Martin Luther was one of the most influential and fascinating figures in the history of that period. For these reasons, many anthologies of primary source documents have been produced for the study of the early sixteenth century and the life and thought of Luther. The fact remains, however, that anyone seeking to acquire an accurate understanding of the Christian reform movement Luther initiated, an ecclesiastical tradition that has endured down to the present day as Lutheranism, cannot confine attention to so narrow a focus. Some of the most distinctive and durable features of Lutheran thought and practice had not yet been fully worked out by the time of the reformer's death, and Luther himself was not the only significant force in the formation of the religious identity of his followers. There is a need for resources that facilitate the acquisition of a wider perspective, and so in this book I have brought together primary source documents from the first two and a half centuries of Lutheran history, illustrating how it evolved from its start in the Reformation to the next major period of revolutionary change in Europe, the Enlightenment.

It is my hope that both theologians and historians will welcome the broader scope of this volume. For those who are interested primarily in issues of religious thought, it covers not only the theology of Luther but also the further clarification of the confessional stance of Lutheranism achieved by the consensus reached in the Formula of Concord of 1577 and the important debates about doctrine and ethics that took place between Orthodox Lutherans, Catholics, Calvinists, and Lutheran Pietists during the seventeenth century. The wider focus of this document collection also fits with a trend among historians of early modern Europe toward study of the more long-term transformations of society that took place between 1500 and 1750. It is common for historians today to speak of a process of "confessionalization," which involved a gradual shift of attention within Protestant movements from the goal of removing burdensome religious and moral strictures toward the reassertion of social discipline and the enforcement of conformity to certain norms of belief. Some of the documents in this book are also relevant to the investigation of this process.

Unfortunately, historians and theologians who analyze the extended evolution of early modern religious movements often diverge considerably in the kind of documents they study. Some historians see little enduring significance in the subtle theological debates among Lutheran clergy and focus instead on changes in popular attitudes and social structures. Some theologians concentrate attention on the development of ideas with little awareness of or interest in the social circumstances that exerted pressures on those who contributed to the formulation of Lutheran doctrine. To bridge the gap between these discrepant preoccupations, each of which offers only a partial picture of

Lutheranism, this anthology also attempts to integrate the study of theology and church history. It brings together both a substantial number of texts focusing on theological arguments and a wide range of others, written at the same time, that reveal the characteristics of religious experience and social behavior.

The documents in this anthology fall into the following general categories:

1) texts providing biographical information about influential Lutheran leaders in their own words or those of their contemporaries;

2) documents presenting firsthand accounts of major events and trends in the institutional development of the Lutheran tradition;

3) significant statements of theological beliefs, including both official confessional documents and excerpts from influential treatises or books by individual theologians;

4) primary source materials illustrating features of popular religious life, including information about the experiences and perceptions of the "common" people and the ways they participated in the Lutheran churches through worship, personal devotion, and the administration of church discipline; and

5) texts describing how outsiders viewed the Lutheran tradition in its various stages of development and how the Lutherans viewed other religious groups with whom they coexisted.

I had two general criteria for the selection of texts. First, I sought to highlight the elements that have promoted unity and a common sense of identity among Lutherans across the centuries. Second, I wanted to acknowledge the presence of significant diversity within Lutheranism, both at any given moment in its history and in successive stages of its development. Certain theological topics will appear repeatedly throughout the chapters of this book, revealing a perennial Lutheran preoccupation with issues such as the authority of the Bible, the proper distinction between law and gospel, the benefits of the saving work of Christ, the relation of faith and good works, the nature of Christ's presence in the Lord's Supper, and the appropriate roles of clergy and laity. Readers will perceive much continuity in the treatment of these themes by writers across the centuries but will also see that these same issues have been perennial causes of sometimes mild and sometimes severe conflicts among Lutherans. In the current day, when dealing with diversity in both church and society has become so central an issue, it is interesting for historian and theologian alike to observe how Lutherans have wrestled with this issue in the past both among themselves and in their relations with other Christian church traditions.

There is a basic chronological order to the organization of the chapters of this book, although there is some overlap of time periods from chapter to chapter because of an additional thematic division. Some chapters are quite clearly theological in focus, while others are more oriented toward the description of historical events and the evolution of religious institutions. Although the complexity of historical development will be discerned more richly by reading these chapters together, anyone who is looking more exclusively for texts related to religious ideas or the role of religion in social life can fairly easily pick out the chapters that are most pertinent to his or her interests.

Each chapter begins with an essay intended to provide necessary background information and explanations of how all of the primary source documents on a particular topic relate to each other. Read together, these eight essays also provide a concise overview of the history of Lutheranism from the Reformation to the Enlightenment for those who are approaching the topic with little prior knowledge. Because so many different kinds of material are included and so broad a period of time is covered in one volume, it has been necessary, more often than not, to provide excerpts rather than complete documents. There is, of course, a danger that selectivity of this sort will distort the reader's impressions of the available historical evidence. Nevertheless, I believe there is a justifiable trade-off in the adoption of this method. For general readers and for most students, many excerpted documents make it possible to gain an appreciation of multiple facets of the history of Lutheranism without being overwhelmed by less important details. For those who are inspired to read the complete texts (and have the skills to do so in the original languages), source information has been included with each selection, and a bibliography has been supplied at the end to facilitate further research.

Chapter one, which concerns Martin Luther and the early decades of the Lutheran movement, contains texts that are, with a few exceptions, available in the fifty-five-volume American edition of *Luther's Works* (jointly published by Fortress Press and Concordia Publishing House). This chapter has the greatest overlap with other anthologies about the Reformation and Luther's theological writings, but I have tried to organize the material in a different way. I have more or less condensed the whole corpus of the American edition into one long chapter in order to show the various ways Luther communicated his innovative religious ideas, and I have placed the selected documents in a sequence that shows how specific events and controversies stimulated his writings. A few of the best-known Luther texts, such as the "Ninety-five Theses against Indulgences" and the three reform treatises of 1520, have been excluded or very minimally excerpted because they are so widely available in other document collections. Instead, the reader will find several lesser known texts that cover some of the same topics. In addition to primary source materials revealing Luther's personal development and the gradual emergence of his reform proposals, several documents demonstrate the perspectives of his Catholic opponents.

Chapters two and three direct attention to the many individuals besides Luther himself who were responsible for the successful development of his reform movement. I have included texts that show how Luther's close associates, such as Philip Melanchthon, Johann Bugenhagen, Nikolaus von Amsdorf, Justus Jonas, Johannes Brenz, and Urbanus Rhegius, contributed to the implementation of reform proposals in various localities in Germany. Supporters of Luther, ranging from well-educated scholars to simple laymen and women, used a wide range of genres to disseminate evangelical ideas and refute criticisms of his intentions or the implications of his beliefs. In the chapter on the dissemination of reform ideas, the reader will be able to see interesting contrasts among the subtleties of formal academic theology, the simpler messages contained in widely circulated pamphlet literature *(Flugschriften)*, and the crude visual propaganda produced to leave an impression in the minds of even the illiterate. The chapter on the implementation of reform proposals consists primarily of excerpts from a variety of church orders *(Kirchenordnungen)*. By translating some of the more interesting passages from these generally neglected resources, I wish both to draw attention to the fact that Lutheranism was embodied in several independent territorial churches and to give readers a feel for the kinds of issues that came up in local parishes during the formative period of Lutheranism.

Chapter four sets the stage for study of the developments that took place after Luther's death by reviewing a hundred years of political developments from the Schmalkald War to the Thirty Years War. The documents reveal an often-troubled social context that needs to be kept in mind in order to understand the attitudes of Lutherans and their religious rivals during the Late Reformation and the Age of Orthodoxy. The next two chapters cover roughly the same time period but show two very different aspects of Lutheranism. Chapter five concentrates on the scholarly Lutherans who were interested in the clarification and defense of true doctrine, and chapter six focuses on more practical writings that offered guidance to a wider audience about the implications of Lutheran teachings for conduct in daily life. The juxtaposing of texts from seventeenth-century dogmatic theologians and devotional writers reveals the diversity of orientations that coexisted within Lutheranism during the Age of Orthodoxy. This should also raise questions about some of the caricaturing that still prevails in the all-too-brief summaries historians often provide concerning post-Reformation religious life.

The final chapter shows how tensions developing within Lutheranism during the Age of Orthodoxy led to the Pietist reform movement. It could be argued that the analysis of Pietism should be extended to show how it related to the Enlightenment, but every book must have its limits. The chronological cut-off point for this collection is the deaths of Johann Albrecht Bengel, the Württemberg Pietist, in 1752 and of his Orthodox critic, Valentin Löscher, in 1749. As a future project, I may assemble another collection of primary source documents that starts with the Enlightenment challenges to traditional religion and traces the development of modern Lutheranism in Europe, North America, and the rest of the world. A case could also be made for including a chapter on the early history of Lutheranism in Scandinavia and Eastern Europe, but in order to keep the book at an appropriate length, I decided to limit the scope of this work to documents from Germany, where most of the major new currents in Lutheranism began.

Many of the documents in this book, except for those in the first chapter, have never been available before in English translation. In a few cases nineteenth-century translations already existed, but I replaced them with new versions because their style was too archaic to appeal to students of the current generation. I tried, as a general rule, to stick closely to the actual wording and syntax of the original texts, but there were many times when I felt it was necessary to subdivide long sentences and follow the spirit rather than the letter in order to make the text more readable. I am grateful for the willingness of several of my colleagues at St. Olaf College to give me advice on matters of translation. In particular, I wish to thank Karl Fink and William Poehlmann for reviewing some of my German documents and Anne Groton and James May for helping me with difficult Latin passages. I take full responsibility, however, for any defects that remain in the final versions.

Students in a course I teach at St. Olaf College, "The Lutheran Heritage," were exposed to ever-expanding versions of this book during the years it was in preparation.

Some of them deserve my thanks for helpful suggestions they offered. I am also appreciative of the assistance and feedback given to me by Jonathan Kibler during the two years he collaborated with me as a student worker. Finally, I owe a debt of gratitude to my wife, Cynthia, and my children, Karsten and Hannah, who tolerated the time I devoted to this project, especially during the summers, when other activities often seemed more tempting to pursue.

Abbreviations and Short Titles

Arndt WC   Arndt, Johann. *Sechs Bücher von wahren Christenthum.* Halle: Gebauer, 1760.

BC   *The Book of Concord: The Confessions of the Evangelical Lutheran Church.* Edited by Robert Kolb and Timothy J. Wengert. Minneapolis: Fortress Press, 2000.

CR   *Corpus Reformatorum Philippi Melanthonis Opera Quae Supersunt Omnia.* 28 vols. Halle and Braunschweig: Schwetschke, 1834–60.

LBW   *Lutheran Book of Worship*

LCC   Library of Christian Classics

LW   *Luther's Works.* American ed. 55 vols. Philadelphia: Fortress; St. Louis: Concordia, 1955–86.

Richter   Richter, Aemilius. *Die evangelischen Kirchenordnungen des sechszehn-ten Jahrhunderts.* 2 vols. Nieuwkoop: De Graaf, 1967. Reprint.

Spener TB   Spener, Philip Jacob. *Theologische Bedencken.* Halle: Waysen-Hauses, 1707.

WA   Luther, Martin. *Luthers Werke: Kritische Gesamtausgabe. [Schriften.]* 65 vols. Weimar: H. Böhlau, 1883–1993.

WABr   Luther, Martin. *Luthers Werke: Kritische Gesamtausgabe. Briefwechsel.* 18 vols. Weimar: H. Böhlau, 1930–85.

Walch   Walch, Johann Georg. *Dr. Martin Luthers Sämmtliche Schriften.* 23 vols. St. Louis: Concordia, 1880–1910.

The Life of Martin Luther: A Chronology

✥

Childhood and Early Education (1483–1505)

1483   Born to Hans and Margaret Luther in Eisleben, where his father is a copper smeltermaster

1484   The family moves to Mansfeld; Luther first attends school there in 1492

1497   Sent away to school in Magdeburg at age thirteen

1498   Transfers to St. George's School in Eisenach; lives in the home of Ursula Cotta

1501   Enters University of Erfurt to study liberal arts

1502   Is awarded baccalaureate degree with class rank of thirteen out of fifty-seven students

1505   Completes work in trivium and quadrivium for master's degree; ranks two out of seventeen

        July 2: caught in thunderstorm in Stotternheim, shortly after beginning study of law; makes vow

Monastic Period (1505–12)

1505   July 17: joins the Reformed Congregation of Augustinian Hermits in Erfurt

1506   After the probationary period as a novice, takes his monastic vows in September

1507   Is ordained as a priest and celebrates his first mass on May 2; more study of theology

1508   At age twenty-five is sent to the University of Wittenberg to lecture on moral philosophy

1509   Wittenberg awards him the Biblical Baccalaureate and Erfurt the Master of the Sentences degree

1510   Makes forty-day journey to Rome to help settle a dispute between two branches of his Order

1511   Transfers to the Augustinian cloister in Wittenberg and continues his studies

University Professor (1512–17)

1512   Earns his doctorate of theology from Wittenberg and joins the theological faculty at age twenty-eight

1513   Lectures at the university on the Psalms

1515   Lectures on Paul's letter to the Romans

1516   Lectures on Paul's letter to the Galatians

The Appeals for Church Reform (1517–21)

1517   September 4: disputation against Scholastic Theology—critique of synergistic theology

	October 31: posts the "Ninety-five Theses against Indulgences" and sends copy to Archbishop Albrecht
1518	April: defends his theology at plenary meeting of the Augustinian Order in Heidelberg
	August: publishes "Explanation of the Ninety-five Theses"; charged with heresy by the Archbishop
	October: is summoned to Augsburg for interrogation by Cardinal Cajetan
1519	June–July: Leipzig Debate—Luther and Karlstadt versus Dominican theologian Johannes Eck
	October: coronation of new emperor, Charles V, a lifelong opponent of Luther
1520	June 24: papal bull *Exsurge Domine* gives Luther sixty days to recant or be excommunicated
	August: "Appeal to the German Nobility" reform proposals and critique of hierarchical polity
	October: "The Babylonian Captivity of the Church," a critique of Catholic view of sacraments
	November: "The Freedom of a Christian" explanation of relation of grace, faith, and good works
	December: burns the papal bull and books of canon law in a public ceremony
1521	January: The Diet of Worms—is given a final hearing before emperor and refuses to recant
	"Decet Romanum Pontificem" papal excommunication decree goes into effect
	May 3: is "kidnapped" and hidden away in Wartburg Castle near Eisenach

Controversies in the Early Development of the Evangelical Churches (1521–29)

1521	December: writes "On Monastic Vows," a strong critique of monasticism
	Translates the whole New Testament into German in eleven weeks
1522	March: returns to Wittenberg to calm turmoil when Karlstadt pushes for rapid changes
	Preaches the Invocavit sermons calling for moderation, patience, and love
	December: publishes "Temporal Authority: To What Extent It Should Be Obeyed" on politics
1523	Publishes *Formula Missae*—worship reforms including greater role of the sermon
	"That Jesus Was Born a Jew" calls for compassion toward Jews, hopes for their conversion
1524	Writings on the Lord's Supper defend the real presence of Christ versus more radical view of Karlstadt
1525	The Peasants' Revolt—"Admonition to Peace" criticizes the princes, warns the peasants
	May: "Against the Robbing and Murdering Horde of Peasants" calls for suppression of revolt
	June: marries Katharina von Bora, a former Cistercian nun
	His prince, Elector Friedrich, dies, succeeded by his brother Johann

	December: publishes "On the Bondage of the Will"; in contrast to Erasmus argues salvation is act of God alone
1526	Writes "The Sacrament of the Body and Blood Christ—Against the Fanatics," which attacks the Swiss reformers
	Writes "The German Mass," a book of liturgical reform calling for worship in German
	Formation of the League of Torgau, an alliance of the pro-Luther princes (Saxony, Hesse)
1527	In this year or the next, writes the famous hymn "A Mighty Fortress Is Our God"
	Collapses under a burden of anxiety—temptation to despair and blasphemy
1528	The first "Visitation" in Saxony gathers information on the state of religious life
1529	May: publishes the Small Catechism to correct the weaknesses revealed by the Visitation
	October: Marburg Colloquy at which he rejects Zwingli's views about the Lord's Supper

Efforts at Reconciliation and Polemics against Various Enemies (1530–46)

1530	Writes in support of public education for both girls and boys
	Stops preaching for a while in disgust over people's laxity and neglect of the poor
	April: The Diet of Augsburg, at which Catholics and Lutherans try to end religious division
	June: Philip Melanchthon submits the Augsburg Confession as summary of Lutheran beliefs
1531	Hope for reconciliation fails; Lutheran princes form Schmalkald League for self-protection
	Faced by threat of Catholic suppression, he gives more support to resistance by force
1532	Elector Johann of Saxony dies and is succeeded by his son, Johann Friedrich
	Is frequently ill with dizziness, hypertension, a weak heart, leg sores, and kidney stones
	The Elector gives him the Augustinian cloister and its lands as his private residence
	Serves as dean of the theological faculty of the university
1534	Publishes his German translation of the Old Testament
	Speaks out against radical reformers, especially the fanatical Anabaptists in Münster
1535	Lectures on Genesis—continues until 1545
	Participates in various doctrinal disputations at the University of Wittenberg
	Is bluntly critical of Catholic church when visited by papal ambassador Vergerio
1536	Writes the Schmalkald Articles as a personal summary of his beliefs

The Wittenberg Concord seems to heal divisions between German and Swiss reformers

1537   The Antinomian Controversy versus Johann Agricola—he defends preaching of both law and gospel

1539   Plans for a Catholic council prompt him to write "On the Councils and the Church"

1540   Supports the bigamy of Duke Philip of Hesse as alternative to his divorce

1541   Writes "Against Hans Wurst," a crude polemic versus Duke Heinrich of Braunschweig-Wolfenbüttel

Colloquy of Regensburg: Melanchthon and Catholic theologians agree on a view of justification

Flatly rejects the conciliatory language worked out in the Regensburg document

1542   Daughter, Magdalena, dies after a painful illness; he is heartbroken

Drafts his will, stating "I desire a good hour of passing on to God. . . . Nothing more is in me."

1543   "On the Jews and Their Lies" advocates action against Jews who reject Christianity

1545   Writes "On the Papacy at Rome, an Institution of the Devil"

1546   Travels to Eisleben to mediate dispute between the Counts of Mansfeld

February 18: writes his final words: "We are beggars, that is true"; dies at age sixty-two

February 22: buried in the Castle Church in Wittenberg

A Chronology of Lutheran History (1517–1750)

The Reformation

1517   October 31: Martin Luther posts the Ninety-five Theses; Archbishop Albrecht sends a copy to Rome

1518   October: Luther is interrogated by Cardinal Cajetan in Augsburg
November: Pope Leo issues bull *"Cum postquam"* clarifying teachings on indulgences

1519   June: Charles V is elected Holy Roman Emperor after death of Maximilian I
July: Luther defends himself versus Johannes Eck at Leipzig Debate

1520   June: promulgation of the bull *"Exsurge Domine"* threatening Luther with excommunication

1521   January: Luther's excommunication is formally pronounced in Rome
January–May: meeting of the Diet of Worms
April: Luther's final defense
May: Charles V publishes the Edict of Worms declaring Luther an outlaw

1523   King Gustav Vasa of Sweden appoints a Lutheran sympathizer, Laurentius Andreae, as chancellor

1524–25 The Peasants' War: Luther condemns violent revolution

1526   Olaus Petri leads disputation of evangelical preachers with Catholic clergy in Sweden
Hans Tausen is appointed court chaplain and begins spread of Lutheranism to Denmark
Diet of Speyer lets German princes deal with religious issues until a general council is convened

1527   Marburg University is founded as first Lutheran university by Philip of Hesse
Charles V's imperial army sacks Rome; destruction of relics by some Lutheran knights
Västeras Diet in Sweden exiles Catholic bishops and secularizes church properties

1529   League of Speyer: "Protestant" princes reject efforts to annul decisions of the Diet of Speyer
Marburg Colloquy: conflict between Luther and Ulrich Zwingli over the Lord's Supper
Ørebro Synod led by Laurentius Andreae introduces changes in worship in Sweden

1530   Diet of Augsburg: Catholic leaders reject the Lutheran Augsburg Confession

1531   Lutheran princes in Germany form the Schmalkald League to protect their interests

	Laurentius Petri becomes first Lutheran archbishop of Uppsala in Sweden
1532	Johann Friedrich succeeds his father as Elector of Saxony
1533	Peace of Nürnberg (Nuremberg): temporary truce between Catholics and Protestants
	Danish Civil War ends: Catholic bishops ousted; church properties seized by King Christian III
1534–35	Anabaptist revolution in Münster enhances suspicions of more radical Protestants
1536	Lutheran reforms in Sweden delayed; Petri brothers resist king's effort to control the church
	New church order establishes Lutheranism in Denmark
	Wittenberg Concord: agreement between Lutherans and south German reformers on the sacraments
1539	Lutheran practices introduced into territories of Electoral Brandenburg and Albertine Saxony
	Ørebro Diet gives king full supremacy over Swedish church and introduces a reformed church order
1540–41	Colloquies of Hagenau, Worms, and Regensburg: continuing Catholic/Protestant dialogues
1541	Early Lutheranism in Hungary: clergy create a confession of faith based on Augsburg Confession
1544	Founding of a Lutheran university in Königsberg
1544–47	Council of Trent: internal reform of the Catholic church begins; discussion of justification

The Late Reformation Period

1546	Death of Luther; beginning of the Schmalkald War: emperor attacks Lutheran territories
1547	Lutheran princes defeated at Mühlberg; Charles V makes Duke Moritz the Elector of Saxony
1548	Emperor imposes the Augsburg Interim; partial recatholicization of worship and doctrine
	Lutheran resistance to the Augsburg Interim; Melanchthon's counterproposal: Leipzig Interim
1549–77	Philippist versus Gnesio-Lutheran controversies over doctrine and church practices
1550	Beginning of Jesuit recatholicization efforts in the Holy Roman Empire
1551–52	Second Meeting of the Council of Trent: rejection of Lutheran views of the sacraments
1552	Second Schmalkald War: Duke Moritz rejoins Lutheran princes to resist the emperor
1555	The Peace of Augsburg: legal recognition of Lutheranism as a religious option
1558	Founding of a Lutheran university in Jena
	Death of Charles V; Ferdinand I becomes Holy Roman Emperor

1560–74	Crypto-Calvinist controversy in Saxony
1561–63	Third Meeting of the Council of Trent
1561	Electoral Palatinate (Kurpfalz) becomes a Calvinist territory
1564	Maximilian II crowned Holy Roman Emperor; milder policy toward Protestants
1566	Martin Chemnitz publishes the major Lutheran critique of the Council of Trent
1568	Lutheranism introduced in territory of Braunschweig-Wolfenbüttel
1571	New Lutheran church order enacted in Sweden
1574	The Swabian Concord: Jakob Andreae attempts to heal Philippist versus Gnesio-Lutheran divisions
	The Swabian-Saxon Concord: Martin Chemnitz brings reconciliation efforts to north Germany
1575	Founding of a Lutheran university in Helmstedt
1576	Rudolf II crowned Holy Roman Emperor
1577	Lutheran doctrinal consensus reached in the Formula of Concord

The Age of Orthodoxy

1580	The Book of Concord assembles the confessional documents of Lutheranism
1583	Papacy stops effort of Archbishop of Cologne to protestantize his lands
1592	Dispute between Catholic and Protestant claimants to the Duchy of Jülich-Cleves
1593	Uppsala convocation requires subscription to Augsburg Confession in Sweden
1601	Calvinism introduced into formerly Lutheran territory of Hesse
1605	Earliest edition of Johann Arndt's influential devotional guide *True Christianity*
1606	Johann Gerhard publishes the Latin version of his *Sacred Meditations*
1607	Controversial recatholicization of the imperial city of Donauwörth after religious clashes
1608	Formation of the Protestant Union after conflicts at the Diet of Regensburg
1610	Johann Gerhard publishes *Loci theologici*, the most influential Orthodox systematic theology
1612	Matthias I succeeds Rudolf II as Holy Roman Emperor; stricter Catholicism influenced by Jesuits
1613	Elector of Brandenburg converts to Calvinism
1618–24	The Thirty Years War begins with defenestration of Prague (The Bohemian Phase)
1619	Ferdinand II elected Holy Roman Emperor after death of Matthias I
1625–29	Danish Phase of the Thirty Years War—King Christian IV supports German Protestants
1630–35	Swedish Lutherans lead Protestant resurgence in third phase of the Thirty Years War
1632	King Gustavus Adolphus II of Sweden dies in the battle of Lützen near Leipzig Johann Gerhard publishes *Confessio Catholica*, a comprehensive apology for Lutheranism
1635–48	French support Protestants; the war ends with the Peace of Westphalia

1645	Georg Calixtus attacked by Orthodox Lutherans for his "syncretistic" ecumenical theology
1647	Beginning of Paul Gerhardt's productive years as a Lutheran hymnwriter
1653	Heinrich Müller becomes professor at Rostock, starts career as influential devotional writer
1670	Christian Scriver begins publication of his most influential devotional writings

Period of the Conflict between Pietism and Orthodoxy

1670	Philip Jacob Spener forms conventicles (small group meetings) in Frankfurt
1675	First publication of Spener's Pietist manifesto, *Pia Desideria*
1685	Johann Quenstedt's "Didactic and Polemical Theology," a major expression of high Orthodoxy
1686	Spener becomes court preacher for Elector of Saxony in Dresden
1687	Conversion or religious awakening of August Hermann Francke in Leipzig
1691	Spener becomes head of the consistory in Berlin
1692	August Hermann Francke becomes pastor in Glaucha and then professor at University of Halle
1695	Beginning of Francke's charitable institutions and educational enterprises in Halle
1699	Gottfried Arnold publishes *Impartial History of Church and Heresy*, a critique of dogmatism
1705	First Lutheran missionaries, educated at Halle, are sent to India, sponsored by Danish king
1713	Death of David Hollaz, the last great systematic theologian of the Age of Orthodoxy
1722	Count Nikolaus von Zinzendorf, a Lutheran Pietist, founds Herrnhut colony for Moravian refugees
1730	Strong support for Pietism in Denmark under King Christian VI
1737	Zinzendorf accepts ordination as a Moravian bishop
1740	Friedrich II, King of Prussia, favors rationalism; decline of Pietist influence at Halle
1742	Johann Albrecht Bengel's *Gnomon of the New Testament* sets principles of textual criticism
1744	Bengel writes critique of Zinzendorf and Moravian piety
1749	Death of Valentin Löscher, leading Orthodox Lutheran critic of Pietism
1752	Death of Johann Albrecht Bengel, noted biblical scholar and Pietist leader in southern Germany

Chapter One

Crises and Controversies during Martin Luther's Lifetime (1483–1546)

The Lutheran church is one of the few branches of Christianity commonly identified by the name of its founder. This was not as Martin Luther wished: He did not set out to create a new church. Soon after his reform efforts had produced a separate organization outside of the Roman Catholic Church, he even stated: "I ask that men make no reference to my name; let them call themselves Christians, not Lutherans. What is Luther? After all, the teaching is not mine" (doc. #18). Nevertheless, Luther's personality was so forceful and his ideas were so innovative for his era that the early development of this religious movement cannot be understood without a careful study of how this one individual responded to a series of crises and controversies during his lifetime.

Martin Luther was born on November 10, 1483, in Eisleben, the chief town of the territories ruled by the counts of Mansfeld. His pious parents, Hans and Margarete, presented him for baptism at their parish church on the following day and named him after Martin of Tours, the saint who is traditionally commemorated on that date. Although his ancestors were simple peasant farmers, Luther's ambitious father spent his life working in the copper mining industry, for which that region was especially noted. Within a year of Martin's birth, Hans moved the family to the town of Mansfeld, where he became a respected owner of mining shafts and smelting furnaces. Hans Luther, who apparently had never attended school himself, wished a better life for his son and sent Martin to schools in Mansfeld, Magdeburg, and Eisenach. In 1501 at the age of seventeen, Martin matriculated at the highly respected University of Erfurt, where he earned his baccalaureate in the liberal arts and his master's degree in four years.

After graduating second in a class of seventeen, Luther followed his father's advice and began to study for an advanced degree in law. On July 2, 1505, while he was returning to Erfurt from a visit to his parents, an incident took place that drastically redirected his life. Caught in a thunderstorm near the village of Stotternheim, Luther was terrified by the possibility of sudden death and prayed for help to St. Anne, the patron saint of miners. Attempting to strike a kind of bargain with God, he also vowed that he would become a monk. To the great disappointment of his father, Luther followed through on this impetuous promise, abandoned his plan to become a lawyer, and entered the monastery of the Augustinian Hermits in Erfurt within two weeks. He took his monastic vows in the fall of 1506 and committed himself wholeheartedly to the challenging regimen of monastic life. In addition, he prepared to become a priest and was ordained, at the age of twenty-three, on April 3, 1507.

Luther developed a reputation as an exemplary monk, but severe fears and doubts about the state of his spiritual life repeatedly tormented him. His response to the thunderstorm was only one example of his perpetual anxiety about death and the prospect of facing the judgment of God. His decision to become a monk was predicated on the commonly held belief that this mode of life offered a safer path to salvation, yet all his ascetic practices and devotional activities failed to assure him that he was measuring up to the standards of holiness demanded by a just God. When he celebrated his first mass, he was overwhelmed by a sense of how unworthy he was to make Christ present in the Eucharist. He was also tortured by the thought that his decision to devote his life to serving God as a monk and a priest was in fact a violation of the fourth commandment that called for obedience to one's parents. Frequent recourse to the sacrament of confession brought no lasting relief to his troubled mind. It even seemed to have the effect of intensifying his consciousness of moral imperfections.

Despite these symptoms of almost morbid sensitivity, Luther impressed his superior, Johannes von Staupitz, by his dedication and his intellectual gifts. In 1508 he was sent to the recently established University of Wittenberg in the principality of Electoral Saxony to spend a year lecturing on Aristotelian ethics. At Wittenberg and Erfurt, he continued his studies toward a doctorate in theology and received the degrees that qualified him to lecture on the Bible and the standard medieval text for the study of doctrine, Peter Lombard's *Book of the Sentences*. During the winter of 1510, Luther was sent to Rome to participate in negotiations prompted by a dispute between two branches of his religious order. In addition to defending the stricter standards commended by the Observant Augustinians, he took advantage of the opportunity to perform meritorious acts of piety at the holy places typically visited by pilgrims and to say mass in some of Rome's most famous churches for the sake of his relatives in purgatory. Shortly after his return, he was sent once again to Wittenberg, which would remain his home for the rest of his life. In 1512, at the age of twenty-eight, Luther received his doctor's degree and in the following year began his work as professor of biblical theology at the University of Wittenberg. He would continue in this role throughout all the tumultuous events of the following years and serve, in addition, as regular preacher at the city church.

Luther's intense involvement in the study of the Bible for the sake of his lectures on the Psalms (1513–15), Romans (1515–16), Galatians (1516–17), and Hebrews (1517–18) was both an enlightening and a disturbing experience for him. He continued to suffer his spiritual trials *(Anfechtungen)* as he struggled with the passages that spoke of the righteousness *(justitia)* of God revealed in both the law and the gospel. His despair over his own lack of righteousness drove him to feel anger toward God for setting such unattainable standards of holiness (doc. #5). As he studied the letters of the apostle Paul, however, he gradually developed a different understanding of how God relates to a sinful humanity. Struck by the phrase, "He who through faith is righteous shall live" (Rom. 1:17), Luther came to believe that the righteousness of God is revealed, not in his justly giving sinners what they deserve, but in setting things right by offering the gift of mercy and forgiveness through Christ. His personal spiritual crisis was resolved when he reached the conclusion that those who trust in God's saving activity and live by faith find favor with God even though the influence of sin persists in their daily lives. The focus of Luther's attention shifted from what God expects of humanity to how God has graciously rescued sinners who cannot save themselves.

Although Luther in later life sometimes spoke of a moment of breakthrough, seemingly around the time he began to lecture on the Psalms for a second time in 1518 (doc. #5), there is evidence that he was on his way to his so-called Reformation Discovery over a period of several years. It gradually dawned on him that there were discrepancies between the presuppositions of the scholastic theology he had been taught and the primary themes that caught his attention in the Psalms and the letters of Paul. In his lectures on Romans, Luther emphasized the depth of human sinfulness and disputed the common late-medieval claim that a person can, by his or her own power, love God above all things. He began to speak of the Christian as a sinner who is, nevertheless, at the same time righteous through faith

Martin Luther

by God's imputation (doc. #1). By September 1517 the foolishness of the "pig-theologians" so agitated Luther that he arranged for a public debate about the scholastics' teachings concerning human nature and the process of salvation. In his "Disputation against Scholastic Theology" (doc. #2), he contended that the nominalist theologians of his day were deceived by the philosophy of Aristotle and simply wrong in their estimates of human ability to avoid sin or prepare for the reception of God's grace. Despite the bluntness of Luther's critique, this challenge to prevailing opinion did not get him into any immediate trouble.

Quite the opposite was the case with his effort in the following month to stimulate discussion about the church's practice of offering indulgences for the remission of the penalty of sins. This issue more than any other stirred up the controversies that led to the eventual formation of a separate Lutheran church. In 1517 Pope Leo X had issued a bull authorizing an indulgence campaign to raise money for the building of a new church in Rome dedicated to St. Peter (doc #3). Those who made a donation to the church for this cause were promised the benefits of the treasury of merit, which the pope as holder of the keys of the kingdom felt authorized to dispense for the sake of both the living and the dead in purgatory. Archbishop Albrecht (Albert) of Mainz was persuaded to allow the indulgence preachers to circulate in Germany by being offered a share of the revenue, which he welcomed to help pay off the debts he had incurred when he had gained a papal dispensation allowing him to serve simultaneously as bishop of more than one diocese. When Luther became aware of how the Dominican friar, Johann Tetzel, was conducting the indulgence campaign in the region near Wittenberg, he reached the conclusion that the sale of indulgences was detrimental to the encouragement of true Christian piety (doc. #4). As a professor, Luther's first response was to call for an academic debate about this practice. He prepared "Ninety-five Theses" in Latin for this purpose and also brought them to the attention of Archbishop Albrecht in a letter he sent on October 31, 1517 (doc. #6). The archbishop and other church leaders became especially concerned when they learned of the circulation of the theses among a wider lay audience in a printed German translation. They suspected Luther of heresy and called for a more thorough investigation of his beliefs.

Pope Leo X ordered the head of the Augustinian order to make inquiries about this young monk, so Luther was asked to travel to Heidelberg in April 1518 to conduct a disputation for his monastic colleagues. The theses he prepared for this occasion (doc. #8) did not directly address the indulgence controversy. They focused instead on some of the same issues he had raised earlier in his "Disputation against Scholastic Theology" (doc. #2). In the next few months, Sylvester Prieras and several other theologians published defenses of church practice in response to the "Ninety-five Theses," prompting Luther in turn to elaborate on the reasons why he questioned the motives of the pope and doubted the pope's authority to offer indulgences (docs. #7, 9, and 10). In October 1518 Luther journeyed to Augsburg for an interview with Cardinal Cajetan (doc. #11). He was asked to declare his loyalty to the pope, but he asserted his belief that the popes were not infallible teachers of theology and morals. He would not acknowledge that their decrees were as authoritative as the Bible. In July 1519 Luther addressed similar issues in a public debate in Leipzig with the Dominican theologian Johannes Eck (doc. #13). Informed of Luther's stubborn defiance, Pope Leo X repeated his defense of the papal right to offer indulgence in the bull *"Cum Postquam"* and, finally, in June 1520 in the bull *"Exsurge Domine"* threatened Luther with excommunication if he failed to recant within sixty days (docs. #12 and 14). This ultimatum did not reach Luther until December 1520. In the meantime, he had boldly pressed forward with his efforts to reform the church by publishing three major treatises addressing the deeper issues that had surfaced in the debates of the past three years. In his "Appeal to the German Nobility," published in August 1520, Luther attacked the hierarchical polity of the church and presented a long list of abuses he wanted to see corrected (doc. #15). Frustrated by the response he was getting from the pope and the clergy, Luther proclaimed "the priesthood of all believers" and justified the involvement of the laity in efforts to reform the church. "The Babylonian Captivity of the Church" (October 1520) thoroughly addressed issues of sacramental piety, and "The Freedom of a Christian" (November 1520) clarified Luther's objections to the synergistic theology of the scholastics and explained the role of faith and good works in the Christian life (doc. #31).

In April 1521 the emperor, Charles V, offered Luther a final hearing at the Diet of Worms. Refusing to violate his conscience by denying what he firmly believed to be a correct interpretation of Christian teachings, Luther defied the threats of both the civil and ecclesiastical authorities. Thus, at the age of thirty-seven, he was declared guilty of treason and excommunicated from the church (docs. #16 and 17). Luther, however, escaped the usual fate of heretics and outlaws as a result of the intervention of his prince, Elector Friedrich the Wise, who hid him away in the remote Wartburg castle near Eisenach. For the next year, Luther occupied himself with the task of preparing a German translation of the Bible.

Although the most powerful church leaders felt threatened by Luther's reform proposals, many people in Saxony and other regions of Germany welcomed his new vision of church and society. While Luther was in hiding, individuals who believed they were acting in accordance with Luther's wishes advocated a rapid reorganization of religious life. Luther's university colleague, Andreas Bodenstein von Karlstadt, abruptly changed the mode of worship in the churches of Wittenberg. "Prophets" from the town of Zwickau, claiming direct guidance by the Holy Spirit, arrived in Wittenberg and began to strip the churches of religious artwork. Disturbed by this violence and the possible confusion generated by hasty change, Luther came out of hiding in 1522 and attempted to impose a measure of restraint on the reform process. He disassociated himself from the activities of the insurrectionists and in his "Invocavit Sermons" called for the use of persuasion rather than force to change people's minds (docs. #18, 20, and 21). Continuing to stress the Bible as the foundation of the church's teachings, he charged that the revelations claimed by the "prophets" were actually from Satan and condemned their indiscriminate iconoclasm (docs. #19 and 22).

Katharina von Bora

Having checked the influence of these radical reformers, Luther proceeded to introduce changes more slowly and cautiously. In 1523 he restored the custom of distributing both bread and wine at the Lord's Supper but waited until 1526 to make German the language of the liturgy. Although he had rejected the value of monasticism as early as 1521, he continued to wear his monastic habit until 1524. Luther had spoken out against the requirement of clerical celibacy since 1520, but he did not marry until 1525, when at the age of forty-two he wedded Katharina von Bora, a twenty-six-year-old former nun.

The problem of radical reformers who used force to implement religious and social change surfaced once again in the Peasants' War, which affected several regions of Germany in 1524 and 1525. Extending the implications of Christian freedom about which Luther had often spoken, the leaders of the peasants demanded greater political rights and economic privileges (doc. #23). Some of them, such as Thomas Müntzer, a former associate of Luther, viewed the uprising as a holy war ordained by God and appealed to the Bible to justify the use of force against oppressive landowners (docs. #24 and 25). Once again, Luther counseled restraint. In his "Admonition to Peace," he acknowledged the legitimacy of some of the peasants' complaints about tyrannical lords but completely rejected their violent tactics and their use of religious rhetoric to support their cause (doc. #26). When the strife continued and worsened, Luther abandoned his initial, moderate approach and called upon the ruling authorities to use every means necessary to punish the peasants (doc. #27). He feared for the future of his religious reform movement if it got the reputation of stimulating social revolution. His sober estimates of human nature also convinced him that chaos was a greater danger than tyranny. With Luther's blessing, the princes suppressed the rebellion and put several thousand peasants to death.

During this tumultuous period, Luther also engaged in a battle of words with one of the great intellectuals of his day, the Dutch humanist Desiderius Erasmus (1469–1536).

Although Erasmus had initially felt sympathy for some of the reforms Luther sought to introduce, he was offended by the reformer's confrontational personality and increasingly disturbed by some of his theological teachings. For several years, Catholic church officials had urged Erasmus to speak out against Luther, but he had tried to avoid being drawn into a public debate. Finally, however, in 1524 he published his "Diatribe on Free Will" after reading what Luther had written about this issue. In Latin and German refutations of the papal bull *"Exsurge Domine,"* Luther had denied that the human will had the power to cooperate in any significant manner in the attainment of salvation (doc. #28). Erasmus claimed that Luther failed to recognize the complexity of this issue and could not reconcile his position with the presence in the Bible of many moral exhortations (doc. #29). In 1525 Luther vehemently responded to Erasmus in his lengthy treatise "On the Bondage of the Will." He attacked the humanist for trying to avoid taking a clear stance on this important doctrinal issue, questioned his interpretation of many biblical passages, and argued that each individual's salvation is solely determined by the hidden will of God (doc. #30).

During the 1520s the interpretation of the Lord's Supper also became a topic of extended debate. Luther had rejected the Catholic doctrine of transubstantiation but was alarmed by his encounters with other reformers who went further and denied that Christ was really present "in, with, and under" the bread and wine of the Lord's Supper (docs. #31 and 32). This was one of several issues that had led to a falling out between Luther and his colleague Karlstadt in 1523. Efforts to promote cooperation between reformers in Germany and Switzerland were also stymied by this issue. Ulrich Zwingli in Zurich and Johann Oecolampadius in Basel argued for a figurative or symbolic interpretation of the words of institution. In their minds it was impossible for Christ's body to be present with the elements of the Lord's Supper because he had ascended to heaven. It was also inconceivable to them that Christ's body could be present in more than one place at the same time, which Luther's view seemed to require (docs. #34 and 36). In several polemical treatises written during the 1520s, Luther attacked the arguments of these "fanatics" and castigated them for making reason the criterion for deciding what God could and could not make happen. He argued for a more literal interpretation of the eucharistic phrase "Take, eat, this is my body" and asserted that, by virtue of the union of Christ's divine and human natures, it was possible for his body to exist in both circumscribed and ubiquitous modes (docs. #32, 33, and 35). A final meeting between Luther and Zwingli at the Marburg Colloquy in October of 1529 failed to produce an agreement on this issue, thus dashing any hopes that the German and Swiss reformers could form a united front to face their Catholic enemies.

In the same year as the Marburg Colloquy, the second Diet of Speyer took place. The emperor, Charles V, had returned from a seven-year stay in Spain and, having emerged victorious from his war with France, was finally beginning to devote his attention to the religious divisions that had developed in the Holy Roman Empire. At the first Diet of Speyer of 1526, dealing with the threat of a Turkish invasion had seemed more urgent than enforcement of the Edict of Worms. In 1529, however, the emperor persuaded the majority of the estates to annul the Recess of the preceding diet, thereby requiring the

Lutherans to conform to Catholic theology and church practices (doc. #37). The Elector of Saxony, the Landgrave of Hesse, and the other princes who supported Luther's reform movement sent a strong statement of protest to the emperor and made a secret agreement to form a "Protestant" union for their mutual defense (docs. #38 and 39). The use of the term "Protestant" to identify the churches that grew out of the sixteenth-century reform movements derives from this new development in 1529. Luther expressed reservations about the formation of such a union, especially if it included parties with divergent theological views (doc. #40). The need to raise money from the princes to finance a new war against the Turks prompted the emperor to summon the Diet of Augsburg in 1530, at which he gave the Protestants another opportunity to work toward a religious settlement. The Elector of Saxony asked Luther and his associates to prepare a document for this diet, summarizing the Lutheran position on various disputed issues (doc. #41). Luther's closest colleague, Philip Melanchthon, carried out this assignment on their behalf and produced the so-called Augsburg Confession, which emphasized the similarities between Catholic and Lutheran beliefs more than the differences (doc. #42). Despite its conciliatory tone, the emperor and the Catholic estates pronounced this confession of faith unacceptable and demanded that the Lutherans return to the Catholic church by April 1531. Faced with new indications of the emperor's readiness to crush the reform movement, the Lutheran princes took the additional step of banding together with Strassburg, Ulm, and some other south German cities to form a defensive military alliance, the Schmalkald League. In this new and dangerous situation, Luther modified his opposition to armed resistance and argued that it was not sedition or rebellion for the princes to defend themselves against the "murderous and bloodthirsty papists" (doc. #43).

The future looked grim, and Luther in his final years often felt that he was living through the troubles that the Bible associated with the end of the world (doc. #44). Already struggling with a number of chronic illnesses, he now confronted new quarrels and complicated problems that seemed at times to wear out his patience and impair his good judgment. There were encouraging moments of progress such as the Peace of Nürnberg of 1532, in which the emperor made temporary concessions to the Lutherans, and the Wittenberg Concord of 1536, an agreement between the south and north German reformers about the Lord's Supper and the other sacraments (doc. #45), but Luther was angered and frustrated by controversies involving some of his closest theological and political allies. Influenced by the distinction Luther made between law and gospel (doc. #46), Johann Agricola, one of his colleagues in Wittenberg, began to argue that it was no longer necessary to preach the law to people who had been converted by the gospel. Beginning in 1537 Luther conducted several disputations on this question and stressed that as long as Christians lived in this world they should hear the preaching of the law in order to prevent the rise of complacency (docs. #47 and 48). Luther worked to block Agricola's appointment as rector of the University of Wittenberg and was permanently alienated from him because of this Antinomian controversy. Shortly thereafter, in 1540, Luther faced the dilemma of deciding how to counsel the Landgrave Philip of Hesse, who felt caught in an unhappy marriage and was carrying on an affair with another woman.

Considering bigamy preferable to adultery, Luther gave his approval to a second marriage between this influential ruler and his mistress, as long as it was kept secret. Later, however, he regretted this action when the arrangement came to the attention of the emperor and raised questions about the moral values of the reformers (doc. #49).

Throughout all these troubled years, Luther maintained some hope for an eventual reconciliation between his reform movement and the Catholics. The pope repeatedly postponed the general council that Luther had long requested, but delegations of Catholic and Protestant theologians resumed discussions of disputed issues. In 1541 the most conciliatory participants at the Colloquy of Regensburg, including Philip Melanchthon, the representative of the Lutherans, thought they had produced a statement on the doctrine of justification that spoke of faith and works in a manner acceptable to all sides, but both Luther and the pope considered the formula too ambiguous and rejected it (docs. #50, 51, and 52).

Luther's deep mistrust of the church leaders in Rome reflected his growing conviction that the pope, the Turks, the Jews, and the radical reformers were all enemies of God, being used by Satan in a final battle against the true church of Christ (doc. #55). He condemned the Muslims for honoring Muhammad above Christ and argued that the true god of the Turks was the devil (doc. #53). Luther had expected that his efforts to reform the church would remove the obstacles that stood in the way of Jewish conversions to Christianity. When this did not take place, he became convinced that the Jews were incorrigible. In 1543 in his worst display of intemperance, Luther responded to rumors of Jewish proselytizing among Christians by recommending the destruction of their synagogues and the silencing of their rabbis (doc. #54).

At the age of sixty-two Luther described himself as "old, decrepit, [and] bereft of energy." Nevertheless, he kept up a hectic schedule of teaching, preaching, and consulting with his associates in order to advance and stabilize the reform movement he had created. In the middle of the winter and despite his frail health, he traveled eighty miles to Eisleben, his birthplace, to help settle a feud between the two counts of Mansfeld. There, on February 18, 1546, he died of an apparent heart attack. His body was returned to Wittenberg and buried in front of the pulpit in the Castle Church, where it remains to this day.

THE CALL FOR REFORM

1. Luther: Lectures on Romans (1515–16)

Luther's lectures on Romans were not published during his lifetime. They are known from his own handwritten manuscript and from a number of student notebooks. Luther dictated explanatory comments on words and phrases (glosses), which the students wrote into their copies of the biblical text. He occasionally added more extended discussions of passages *(scholia)* such as the following, which shows some of his early criticisms of scholastic theology.

From *LW* 25:260–63, trans. J. A. O. Preus; cf. WA 56:274–75.

Scholia on Romans 4:7, "Blessed are they whose iniquities are forgiven."

. . . Therefore, act of sin (as it is called by the theologians) is more correctly sin in the sense of the work and fruit of sin, but sin itself is the passion, the tinder *(fomes),* and the concupiscence, or the inclination, toward evil and the difficulty of doing good. . . .

Experience bears witness that in whatever good work we perform, this concupiscence toward evil remains, and no one is ever cleansed of it, not even the one-day-old infant. But the mercy of God is that this does remain and yet is not imputed as sin to those who call upon him and cry out for his deliverance. For such people easily avoid also the error of works, because they so zealously seek to be justified. Thus in ourselves we are sinners, and yet through faith we are righteous by God's imputation. For we believe him who promises to free us, and in the meantime we strive that sin may not rule over us but that we may withstand it until he takes it from us.

It is similar to the case of a sick man who believes the doctor who promises him a sure recovery and in the meantime obeys the doctor's order in the hope of the promised recovery and abstains from those things that have been forbidden him, so that he may in no way hinder the promised return to health or increase this sickness until the doctor can fulfill his promise to him. Now is this sick man well? The fact is that he is both sick and well at the same time. He is sick in fact, but he is well because of the sure promise of the doctor, whom he trusts and who has reckoned him as already cured, because he is sure that he will cure him; for he has already begun to cure him and no longer reckons to him a sickness unto death. In the same way Christ, our Samaritan, has brought his half-dead man into the inn to be cared for, and he has begun to heal him, having promised him the most complete cure unto eternal life, and he does not impute his sins, that is, his wicked desires, unto death, but in the meantime in the hope of the promised recovery he prohibits him from doing or omitting things by which his cure might be impeded and his sin, that is, his concupiscence, might be increased. Now, is he perfectly righteous? No, for he is at the same time both a sinner and a righteous man: a sinner in fact, but a righteous man by the sure imputation and promise of God that he will continue to deliver him from sin until he has completely cured him. And thus he is entirely healthy in hope, but in fact he is still a sinner; but he has the beginning of righteousness, so that he continues more and more always to seek it, yet he realizes that he is always unrighteous. But now if this sick man should like his sickness and refuse every cure for his disease, will he not die? Certainly, for thus it is with those who follow their lusts in this world. Or if a certain sick man does not see that he is sick but thinks he is well and thus rejects the doctor, this is the kind of operation that wants to be justified and made well by its own works.

Since this is the case, either I have never understood, or else the scholastic theologians have not spoken sufficiently clearly about sin and grace, for they have been under the delusion that original sin, like actual sin, is entirely removed, as if these were items that can be entirely removed in the twinkling of an eye, as shadows before a light, although the ancient fathers Augustine and Ambrose spoke entirely differently and in the way Scripture does. But those men speak in the manner of Aristotle in his *Ethics*,[1] when he bases sin and righteousness on works, both their performance and omission. But blessed Augustine says very clearly that "sin, or concupiscence, is forgiven in Baptism, not in the sense that it no longer exists, but in the sense that it is not imputed." [*de nuptiis et concupiscentia* 1.25] . . .

For this reason it is plain insanity to say that man of his own powers can love God above all things and can perform the works of the Law according to the substance of the act, even if not according to the intentions of him who gave the commandment, because he is not in the state of grace.[2] O fools, O pig-theologians (*Sawtheologen*)! By your line of reasoning grace was not necessary except because of some new demand above and beyond the law. For if the law can be fulfilled by our powers, as they say, then grace is not necessary for the fulfilling of the law, but only for the fulfilling of some new exaction imposed by God above the law. Who can endure these sacrilegious notions? . . .

All of these monstrosities have come from the fact that they did not know what sin is nor forgiveness. For they reduced sin to some very minute activity of the soul, and the same was true of righteousness. For they said that since the will has this *synteresis*, "it is inclined," albeit weakly, "toward the good." And this minute motion toward God (which man can perform by nature) they imagine to be an act of loving God above all things! But take a good look at man, entirely filled with evil lusts (notwithstanding that minute motion). The law commands him to be empty, so that he may be taken completely into God. Thus Isaiah in 41:23 laughs at them and says, "Do good or evil if you can!" This life, then, is a life of being healed from sin; it is not a life of sinlessness, with the cure completed and perfect health attained. The church is the inn and the infirmary for those who are sick and in need of being made well. But heaven is the palace of the healthy and the righteous. . . .

2. Luther: Disputation against Scholastic Theology (1517)

Luther convinced many of his colleagues that there were discrepancies between the teachings of Paul and the scholastic theologians who made extensive use of Aristotelian philosophy. On May 18, 1517, Luther reported in a letter to Johann Lang, prior of the Erfurt monastery: "Our theology and St. Augustine are progressing well, and with God's help rule at our University. Aristotle is gradually falling from his throne, and his final doom is only a matter of time" (*LW* 31:42; WABr 1:99). Luther publicly challenged scholasticism in the following set of theses, written for one of his students to defend on September 4, 1517, to complete the requirements of his Bachelor of Bible degree. (The total document contains ninety-seven theses.)

From *LW* 31:9–16, trans. Harold Grimm; cf. WA 1:221–28.

5. It is false to state that man's inclination is free to choose between either of two oppo-

sites. Indeed, the inclination is not free, but captive. This is said in opposition to common opinion.

6. It is false to state that the will can by nature conform to correct precept. This is said in opposition to Scotus and Gabriel.[3]

7. As a matter of fact, without the grace of God the will produces an act that is perverse and evil.

8. It does not, however, follow that the will is by nature evil, that is, essentially evil, as the Manichaeans maintain.[4]

9. It is nevertheless innately and inevitably evil and corrupt.

10. One must concede that the will is not free to strive toward whatever is declared good. This in opposition to Scotus and Gabriel.

17. Man is by nature unable to want God to be God. Indeed, he himself wants to be God, and does not want God to be God.

20. An act of friendship is done, not according to nature, but according to prevenient grace. This in opposition to Gabriel.

21. No act is done according to nature that is not an act of concupiscence against God.

22. Every act of concupiscence against God is evil and a fornication of the spirit.

29. The best and infallible preparation for grace and the sole disposition toward grace is the eternal election and predestination of God.

30. On the part of man, however, nothing precedes grace except indisposition and even rebellion against grace.

39. We are not masters of our actions, from beginning to end, but servants. This in opposition to the philosophers.

40. We do not become righteous by doing righteous deeds but, having been made righteous, we do righteous deeds. This in opposition to the philosophers.

41. Virtually the entire *Ethics* of Aristotle is the worst enemy of grace. This in opposition to the scholastics.

44. Indeed, no one can become a theologian unless he becomes one without Aristotle.

50. Briefly, the whole Aristotle is to theology as darkness is to light. This in opposition to the scholastics. . . .

In these statements we wanted to say and believe we have said nothing that is not in agreement with the Catholic Church and the teachers of the church.

3. Pope Leo X's Indulgence Bull (1517)

This excerpt notes the particular reasons for the beginning of a new indulgence campaign. The lengthy papal bull goes on to specify in great detail which sins can and cannot be covered by the indulgence.

From Walch 15:232–43.

Bishop Leo, a servant of the servants of God, to all Christian believers who will read this letter: salvation and apostolic greetings!

After we, despite our unworthiness, succeeded by divine grace to the apostolic sovereignty, in addition to the other things that we constantly made it our concern to achieve and strove diligently to accomplish and that we longed for from the ground of our heart for the sake of those of lower degree, we were also attentive to the salvation of Christ-believing souls and the completion of the building of the cathedral of the prince of the apostles in the city [of Rome]. Although it is a good shepherd's chief duty to make the flock entrusted to him blessed, as well as to build the heavenly court, it was also considered highly necessary to rebuild the church that is the head of all churches and the throne of the Apostolic See. Pope Julius II, of blessed memory, had always thought that he might accomplish both, and for that reason he bestowed a plenary indulgence and many spiritual gifts to stimulate Christian believers to do works of piety and to offer a helping hand to the building.

We follow, then, in the footsteps of our remembered predecessor, and it is plentifully known by all Christians that St. Peter was made Prince of the Apostles by our Savior, the Lord Jesus Christ. The power to bind and loose souls was given over to him through divine grace, by these words: "You are Peter and on this rock I will build my church. I will give you the keys of the kingdom, and whatever you bind on earth will also be bound in heaven and whatever you loose on earth will also be loosed in heaven" [Matt. 16:18-19]. And so we, despite our unworthiness, have become a successor to the selfsame possessor of the heavenly keys, and sit in his place in the holy church of God. Therefore although we are empowered by the divinely commanded apostolic office to care for all churches throughout the entire world, such that the churches as houses of God are not only erected but also where necessary repaired, we consider ourselves especially obligated to exert greater care and diligence for the cathedral of St. Peter, the Prince of the Apostles, which has been mostly demolished and needs to be rebuilt and enlarged in a suitable fashion. . . .

Moreover, since the church, the holy mother, has so many necessary costs to bear and does not have the resources for the completion of such a building, and since the building cannot be brought to its wished end without the holy and ample contributions of Christian believers, we have out of concern for the salvation of Christ-believing souls . . . concluded in a fatherly manner that we will, trusting in the grace of almighty God and saints Peter and Paul, his apostles and the merits of all the saints and with good knowledge, forethought, and fullness of apostolic power, announce an indulgence for the full forgiveness of all sins for all Christian believers, both male and female, from whatever class, degree, rank, order, office, or dignity they may be and for the monks of all orders and other seculars in all lands and islands who repent and confess within one year of the announcement of our present letter. . . . This indulgence shall be as extensive as the indulgence announced in a holy year, and they will attain as much indulgence for the forgiveness of sins as if they fasted every day and visited all churches in Rome and other cities that Christians are accustomed to visit for their prayers. . . .

Since the salvation of souls is promoted the more they receive the help of others and some may not be able to procure this assistance, we also permit the benefits of the treasury of the church, the holy mother, to be granted to the souls in purgatory who have departed from this world united through love with Christ and who have merited during their lifetimes that such help might come to them. Because we want sympathetically to help such souls as much as we can, out of divine grace and the fullness of apostolic power we declare that if some parents, friends, or other Christians contribute alms to the commissioners for the work of this building out of mercy for the souls in purgatory, the plenary indulgence shall be an aid to these souls for their deliverance from the penalties required by divine justice. . . .

4. Luther's Memory of the Indulgence Controversy (1541)

Luther offered these recollections in 1541 in the context of his polemical treatise, "Against Hans Wurst."

From *LW* 41:231–33, trans. Eric Gritsch; cf. WA 51:538.

... It happened in the year 1517 that a preaching monk called Johann Tetzel, a great ranter, made his appearance. He had previously been rescued in Innsbruck by Duke Friedrich from a sack—for Maximilian had condemned him to be drowned in the river Inn (presumably on account of his great virtue)—and Duke Friedrich reminded him of it when he began to slander us Wittenbergers; he also freely admitted it himself. This same Tetzel now went around with indulgences, selling grace for money, as dearly or as cheaply as he could, to the best of his ability. At that time I was a preacher here in the monastery and a fledgling doctor fervent and enthusiastic for Holy Scripture.

Now when many people from Wittenberg went to Jüterbog and Zerbst for indulgences, and I (as truly as my Lord Christ redeemed me) did not know what the indulgences were, as in fact no one knew, I began to preach very gently that one could probably do something better and more reliable than acquiring indulgences. I had also preached before in the same way against indulgences at the castle and had thus gained the disfavor of Duke Friedrich because he was very fond of his religious foundation.[5] Now I—to point out the true cause of the Lutheran rumpus—let everything take its course. However, I heard what dreadful and abominable articles Tetzel was preaching, and some of them I shall mention now; namely:

That he had such grace and power from the pope that even if someone seduced the holy Virgin Mary and made her conceive, he could forgive him, provided he placed the necessary sum in the box. . . .

Again, that if St. Peter were here now, he would not have greater grace or power than he [Tetzel] had. . . .

Again, that if anyone put money in the box for a soul in purgatory, the soul would fly to heaven as soon as the coin clinked on the bottom.

Title Page of *Against Hans Wurst*

Again, that the grace from indulgences was the same grace as that by which a man is reconciled to God.

Again, that it was not necessary to have remorse, sorrow, or repentance for sin, if one bought (I ought to say, acquired) an indulgence or a dispensation; indeed, he sold also for future sins.[6]

He did an abominable amount of this, and it was all for the sake of money. I did not know at that time who would get the money. Then a booklet appeared, magnificently ornamented with the coat of arms of the bishop of Magdeburg, in which the sellers of indulgences were advised to preach some of these articles. It became quite evident that Bishop Albrecht had hired this Tetzel because he was a great ranter; for he was elected bishop of Mainz with the agreement that he was himself to buy (I mean acquire) the pallium at Rome. . . .

Thus the bishop devised this scheme, hoping to pay the Fuggers (for they had advanced the money for the pallium) from the purse of the common man. And he sent this great fleecer of men's pockets into the provinces; he fleeced them so thoroughly that a pile of money began to come clinking and clattering into the boxes. He did not forget himself in this either. And in addition the pope had a finger in the pie as well, because one half was to go toward the building of St. Peter's Church in Rome. Thus these fellows went about their work joyfully and full of hope, rattling their boxes under men's purses and fleecing them. But, as I say, I did not know that at the time. . . .

Then I wrote a letter with the Theses to the bishop of Magdeburg, admonishing and beseeching him to stop Tetzel and prevent this stupid thing from being preached, lest it give rise to public discontent—this was a proper thing for him to do as Archbishop. I can still lay my hands on that letter, but I never received an answer. . . .

5. Luther's Memory of a Moment of Insight (Preface to Latin Writings, 1545)

From *LW* 34:329–38, trans. Lewis Spitz Sr.; cf. WA 54:179–87.

. . . When in the year 1517 indulgences were sold (I wanted to say promoted) in these regions for most shameful gain—I was then a preacher, a young doctor of theology, so to speak—and I began to dissuade the people and to urge them not to listen to the clamors of the indulgence hawkers; they had better things to do. I certainly thought that in this case I should have a protector in the pope, on whose trustworthiness I then leaned strongly, for in his decrees he most clearly damned the immoderation of the quaestors, as he called the indulgence preachers.

Soon afterward I wrote two letters [doc. #6], one to Albrecht, the archbishop of Mainz, who got half of the money from the indulgences, the pope the other half—something I did not know at the time—the other to the ordinary (as they call them) Jerome, the bishop of Brandenburg. I begged them to stop the shameless blasphemy of the quaestors. But the poor little brother was despised. Despised, I

Martin Luther as a Monk

published the Theses and at the same time a German Sermon on Indulgences [doc. #7], shortly thereafter also the Explanations [doc. #9], in which, to the pope's honor, I developed the idea that indulgences should indeed not be condemned, but that good works of love should be preferred to them.

This was demolishing heaven and consuming the earth with fire. I am accused by the pope, am cited to Rome, and the whole papacy rises up against me alone. All this happened in the year 1518, when Maximilian held the diet at Augsburg. In it, Cardinal Cajetan served as the pope's Lateran legate. The most illustrious Duke Friedrich of Saxony, Elector Prince, approached him on my behalf and brought it about that I was not compelled to go to Rome, but that he himself should summon me to examine and compose the matter. Soon the diet adjourned.

The Germans in the meantime, all tired of suffering the pillagings, traffickings, and endless impostures of Roman rascals, awaited with bated breath the outcome of so great a matter, which no one before, neither bishop nor theologian, had dared to touch. In any case that popular breeze favored me, because those practices and "Romanizations," with which they had filled and tired the whole earth, were already hateful to all.

So I came to Augsburg, afoot and poor, supplied with food and letters of commendation from Prince Friedrich to the senate and to certain good men. I was there three days before I went to the cardinal, though he cited me day by day through a certain orator [Urbanus of Serralonga], for those excellent men forbade and dissuaded me most strenuously, not to go to the cardinal without a safe conduct from the emperor. The orator was rather troublesome to me, urging that if I should only revoke, everything would be all right [doc. #11]! But as great as the wrong, so long is the detour to its correction. . . .

Maximilian [the emperor] died in the following year, 1519, in February, and according to the law of the empire Duke Friedrich was made deputy. Thereupon the storm ceased to rage a bit and gradually contempt of excommunication or papal thunderbolts arose. For when Eck and Caraccioli [a papal legate] brought a bull from Rome condemning Luther and revealed it, the former here, the latter there to Duke Friedrich, who was at Cologne at the time together with other princes in order to meet Charles who had been recently elected [emperor], Friedrich was most indignant. He reproved that papal rascal with great courage and constancy, because in his absence he and Eck had disturbed his and his brother Johann's dominion. He jarred them so magnificently with incredible insight, caught on to the devices of the Roman Curia and knew how to deal with them in a becoming manner, for he had a keen nose and smelled more and farther than the Romanists could hope or fear. . . .

The gospel advanced happily under the shadow of that prince and was widely propagated. His authority influenced very many, for since he was a very wise and most keen-sighted prince, he could incur the suspicion only among the hateful that he wanted to nourish and protect heresy and heretics. This did the papacy great harm.

That same year the Leipzig debate was held, to which Eck had challenged us two, Karlstadt and me [doc. #13]. But I could not, in spite of all my letters, get a safe conduct from Duke Georg [of Albertine Saxony]. Accordingly, I came to Leipzig not as a prospective debater, but as a spectator under the safe conduct granted to Karlstadt. Who stood in my way I do not know, for till then Duke Georg was not against me. This I know for certain.

Here Eck came to me in my lodgings and said he had heard that I refused to debate. I replied, "How can I debate, since I cannot get a safe conduct from Duke Georg?" "If I cannot debate with you," he said, "neither do I want to with Karlstadt, for I have come here on your account. What if I obtain a safe conduct for you? Would you then debate with me?" "Obtain," said I, "and it shall be." He left and soon a safe conduct was given me too and the opportunity to debate. . . .

Meanwhile, I had already during that year returned to interpret the Psalter anew. I had confidence in the fact that I was more skillful, after I had lectured in the university on St. Paul's Epistles to the Romans, to the Galatians, and the one to the Hebrews. I had indeed been captivated with an extraordinary ardor for understanding Paul in the Epistle to the Romans. But up till then it was not the cold blood about the heart, but a single word in chapter 1[:17], "In it the righteousness of God is revealed," that had stood in my way. For I hated that word "righteousness of God," which, according to the use and custom of all the teachers, I had been taught to understand philosophically regarding the formal or active righteousness, as they called it, with which God is righteous and punishes the unrighteous sinner.

Though I lived as a monk without reproach, I felt that I was a sinner before God with an extremely disturbed conscience. I could not believe that he was placated by my satisfaction. I did not love, yes, I hated the righteous God who punishes sinners, and secretly, if not blasphemously, certainly murmuring greatly, I was angry with God, and said, "As if, indeed, it is not enough, that miserable sinners, eternally lost through original sin, are crushed by every kind of calamity by the law of the Decalogue, without having God add pain to pain by the gospel and also by the gospel threatening us with his righteousness and wrath!" Thus I raged with a fierce and troubled conscience. Nevertheless, I beat importunately upon Paul at that place, most ardently desiring to know what St. Paul wanted.

At last, by the mercy of God, meditating day and night, I gave heed to the context of the words, namely, "In it the righteousness of God is revealed, as it is written, 'He who through faith is righteous shall live.'" There I began to understand that the righteousness of God is that by which the righteous lives by a gift of God, namely by faith. And this is the meaning: the righteousness of God is revealed by the gospel, namely, the passive righteousness with which merciful God justifies us by faith, as it is written, "He who through faith is righteous shall live." Here I felt that I was altogether born again and had entered paradise itself through open gates. There a totally other face of the entire Scripture showed itself to me. Thereupon I ran through the Scriptures from memory. I also found in other terms an analogy, as, the work of God, that is, what God does in us, the power of God, with which he makes us strong, the wisdom of God, with which he makes us wise, the strength of God, the salvation of God, the glory of God.

And I extolled my sweetest word with a love as great as the hatred with which I had before hated the word "righteousness of God." Thus that place in Paul was for me truly the gate of paradise. Later I read Augustine's *The Spirit and the Letter,* where contrary to hope I found that he too interpreted God's righteousness in a similar way, as the righteousness with which God clothes us when he justifies us. Although this was heretofore said imperfectly and he did not

explain all things concerning imputation clearly, it nevertheless was pleasing that God's righteousness with which we are justified was taught. . . .

I relate these things, good reader, so that, if you are a reader of my puny works, you may keep in mind, that, as I said above, I was all alone and one of those who, as Augustine says of himself, have become proficient by writing and teaching. I was not one of those who from nothing suddenly become the topmost, though they are nothing, neither have labored, nor been tempted, nor become experienced, but have with one look at the Scriptures exhausted their entire spirit.

To this point, to the years 1520 and 1521, the indulgence matter proceeded. Upon that followed the sacramentarian and the Anabaptist affairs. . . .

6. Luther's Letter to Archbishop Albrecht (October 31, 1517)

From *LW* 48:46–49, trans. Gottfried Krodel; cf. WABr 1:110–11.

. . . Under your most distinguished name, papal indulgences are offered all across the land for the construction of St. Peter. Now, I do not so much complain about the quacking of the preachers, which I haven't heard, but I bewail the gross misunderstanding among the people that comes from these preachers and that they spread everywhere among common men. Evidently the poor souls believe that when they have bought indulgence letters they are then assured of their salvation. They are likewise convinced that souls escape from purgatory as soon as they have placed a contribution into the chest. Further, they assume that the grace obtained through these indulgences is so completely effective that there is no sin of such magnitude that it cannot be forgiven—even if (as they say) someone should rape the Mother of God, were this possible. Finally they also believe that man is freed from every penalty and guilt by these indulgences.

O great God! The souls committed to your care, excellent Father, are thus directed to death. For all these souls you have the heaviest and a constantly increasing responsibility. Therefore, I can no longer be silent on this subject. No man can be assured of his salvation by any episcopal function. He is not even assured of his salvation by the infusion of God's grace, because the Apostle [Paul] orders us to work out our salvation constantly "in fear and trembling" [Phil. 2:12-13]. Even "the just will hardly be saved" [1 Pet. 4:18]. Finally the way that leads to life is so narrow that the Lord, through the prophets Amos and Zechariah, calls those that will be saved "a brand plucked out of the fire." And everywhere else the Lord proclaims the difficulty of salvation. How can the [indulgence agents] then make the people feel secure and without fear [concerning salvation] by means of those false stories and promises of pardon? After all, the indulgences contribute absolutely nothing to the salvation and holiness of souls; they only compensate for the external punishment that—on the basis of Canon Law—once used to be imposed.

Works of piety and love are infinitely better than indulgences, and yet [the indulgence preachers] do not preach them with an equally big display and effort. What is even worse, [the preachers] are silent about them because they have to preach the sale of indulgences. The first and only duty of the bishops, however, is to see that the people learn the gospel and the love of Christ. For on no occasion has Christ ordered that indulgences should be preached, but he forcefully commanded the gospel to be preached. What a horror, what a danger for a

Archbishop Albrecht of Mainz

bishop to permit the loud noise of indulgences among his people, while the gospel is silenced, and to be more concerned about the sale of indulgences than with the gospel! Will not Christ say to [such bishops], "You strain out a gnat but swallow a camel" [Matt. 23:24]?

Added to this, my Most Reverend Father in the Lord, is the fact that in the Instruction for the indulgence agents that is published under Your Highness's name, it is written (certainly without your full awareness and consent, Most Reverend Father) that one of the principal graces [bestowed through the indulgences] is that inestimable gift of God by which man is reconciled with God and by which all the punishments of purgatory are blotted out. It is also written there that contrition is not necessary on the part of those who buy off their souls or acquire *confessionalia*.

What can I do, excellent Bishop and Most Illustrious Sovereign? I can only beg you, Most Reverend Father, through the Lord Jesus Christ, to deign to give this matter your fatherly attention and totally withdraw that little book and command the preachers of indulgences to preach in another way. If this is not done, someone may rise and, by means of publications, silence those preachers and refute the little book. This would be the greatest disgrace for Your Most Illustrious Highness. I certainly shudder at this possibility, yet I am afraid it will happen if things are not quickly remedied.

I beg Your Most Illustrious Grace to accept this faithful service of my humble self in a princely and episcopal—that is, in the most kind—way, just as I am rendering it with a most honest heart and in absolute loyalty to you, Most Reverend Father. For I, too, am a part of your flock. May the Lord Jesus protect you, Most Reverend Father, forever. Amen.

Were it agreeable to you, Most Reverend Father, you could examine my disputation theses, so that you may see how dubious is this belief concerning indulgences, which these preachers propagate as if it were the surest thing in the whole world.

Your unworthy son,
Martin Luther
Augustinian, called Doctor of Sacred Theology

7. Luther's Sermon on Indulgence and Grace (March 1518)

From WA 1:243.

First, you should know that some modern teachers such as the Master of the Sentences [Peter Lombard], St. Thomas [Aquinas], and their followers suppose penance to have three parts, namely contrition, confession, and satisfaction. Although it will be discovered that their view of this differentiation is hardly or not at all based on Holy Scripture or on the ancient holy Christian teachers, we will let that rest for now and speak according to their way.

Second, they say that the indulgence removes not the first or second part, that is contrition or confession, but the third part, namely satisfaction.

Third, satisfaction is further divided into three parts: praying, fasting, almsgiving. Praying includes all kinds of work that pertains to the soul, such as reading, meditating, hearing God's word, preaching, teaching, and the like. Fasting includes all kinds of work for the mortification of one's flesh, such as vigils, labors, a hard bed, matters of clothing, and so on. Almsgiving encompasses all kinds of good works of love and mercy toward one's neighbors.

Fourth, it is doubtless in all of their minds that the indulgence takes the place of the same works of satisfaction that are owed or imposed because of sins; so that if the indulgence were to take the place of all of these works, no good work would remain for us to do.

Fifth, for many there has been an important and still unresolved issue whether the indulgence also removes something more than such imposed good works, namely whether the indulgence also removes the suffering that God's righteousness demands for sins. . . .

Ninth, I say, even if the Christian church would today decide and declare that the indulgence removes more than the works of satisfaction, it would still be a thousand times better if no Christian would buy or desire the indulgence but would rather do the works and endure the suffering. For the indulgence is and cannot be anything other than a release from good works and wholesome suffering that one should rather welcome than avoid (in spite of the fact that some modern preachers have invented two kinds of suffering: remedial and satisfactory, that is, some suffering for satisfaction and some for improvement). But we have more freedom to scorn the likes of such babble (God be praised) than they have to invent it. For all suffering—yes, everything God imposes—is beneficial and salutary to Christians. . . .

Thirteenth, it is a great error for anyone to think that he can make satisfaction for his own sins since God always freely forgives them out of his priceless grace and desires nothing more than that a person live rightly thereafter. Christianity actually does demand something. Therefore it can and also should remit the same and impose nothing difficult or unbearable.

Fourteenth, the indulgence is allowed for the sake of imperfect and indolent Christians who do not want to be bold in good works or are insufferable. The indulgence helps no one improve but tolerates and allows for imperfection. Therefore one should not speak against the indulgence, but one should also not speak in favor of it. . . .

Seventeenth, the indulgences are not commanded and also not advised. Rather, it is counted among those things that are permitted and allowed. Therefore it is not a work of obedience and also not meritorious but, instead, a flight from obedience. Therefore, while no one should prevent anyone from buying the same, still one should draw all Christians away from the indulgence and stir them up and strengthen them for the good works and suffering that they remit.

Eighteenth, whether souls are drawn out of purgatory through the indulgence, I do not know. I do not yet believe it, despite the fact that some modern doctors say so, because they cannot prove it, and the church has not yet established it. Therefore to be more secure, it is much better that you pray for them yourself and do your work, for this is more valuable and certain. . . .

Twentieth, some may now rebuke me as a heretic, for such truth is very damaging to their treasury. I do not pay much attention to their bawling since that can only be done by some darkened minds that never got a whiff of Scripture, never read the Christian teachers, never understood their own teachers, but prefer to rot in their riddled and ripped up opinions. If they had understood these, they would know they ought to defame no man unheard and

unvanquished. Still, may God give them and us right understanding. Amen.

8. Luther: The Heidelberg Disputation (May 1518)

From *LW* 31:39–70, trans. Harold Grimm; cf. WA 1:354f.

THESIS 3

Although the works of man always seem attractive and good, they are nevertheless likely to be mortal sins.

Human works appear attractive outwardly, but within they are filthy, as Christ says concerning the Pharisees in Matthew 23[:27]. For they appear to the doer and others [as] good and beautiful, yet God does not judge according to appearances but searches "the minds and hearts" [Ps. 7:9]. For without grace and faith it is impossible to have a pure heart. Acts 15[:9]: "He cleansed their hearts by faith."

The thesis is proven in the following ways: If the works of righteous men are sins, as Thesis 7 of this disputation states, this is much more the case concerning the works of those who are not righteous. But the just speak on behalf of their works in the following ways: "Do not enter into judgment with thy servant, Lord, for no man living is righteous before thee" [Ps. 143:2]. The Apostle speaks likewise in Galatians 3[:10], "All who rely on the works of the law are under the curse." But the works of men are the works of the law, and the curse will not be placed upon venial sins. Therefore they are mortal sins. . . .

THESIS 13

Free will, after the fall, exists in name only, and as long as it does what it is able to do, it commits a mortal sin.

The first part is clear, for the will is captive and subject to sin. Not that it is nothing, but that it is not free except to do evil. According to John 8[:34, 36], "Every one who commits sin is a slave to sin. . . . So if the Son makes you free, you will be free indeed." Hence St. Augustine says in his book *The Spirit and the Letter,* "Free will without grace has the power to do nothing but sin," and in the second book of *Against Julian,* "You call the will free, but in fact it is an enslaved will," and in many other places. . . .

THESIS 16

The person who believes that he can obtain grace by doing what is in him adds sin to sin so that he becomes doubly guilty.

On the basis of what has been said, the following is clear: While a person is doing what is in him, he sins and seeks himself in everything. But if he should suppose that through sin he would become worthy of or prepared for grace, he would add haughty arrogance to his sin and not believe that sin is sin and evil is evil, which is an exceedingly great sin. As Jeremiah 2[:13] says, "For my people have committed two evils: they have forsaken me, the fountain of living waters, and hewed out cisterns for themselves, broken cisterns, that can hold no water," that is, through sin they are far from me, and yet they presume to do good by their own ability.

Now you ask, "What then shall we do? Shall we go our way with indifference because we can do nothing but sin?" I would reply, By no means. But, having heard this, fall down and pray for grace and place your hope in Christ in whom is our salvation, life, and resurrection. For this reason we are so instructed—for this reason the law makes us aware of sin so that, having recognized our sin, we may seek and receive grace. Thus God "gives grace to the humble" [1 Pet. 5:5], and "whoever humbles himself will be exalted" [Matt. 23:12]. The law humbles, grace exalts. The law effects fear and wrath; grace effects hope and mercy. "Through the law comes knowledge of sin" [Rom. 3:20];

through knowledge of sin, however, comes humility; and through humility grace is acquired. Thus an action that is alien to God's nature results in a deed belonging to his very nature: He makes a person a sinner so that he may make him righteous.

THESIS 25

He is not righteous who does much, but he who, without work, believes much in Christ.

For the righteousness of God is not acquired by means of acts frequently repeated, as Aristotle taught, but is imparted by faith, for "He who through faith is righteous shall live" (Romans 1[:17]), and "Man believes with his heart and so is justified" (Romans 10[:10]). Therefore I wish to have the words "without work" understood in the following manner: Not that the righteous person does nothing, but that his works do not make him righteous, rather that his righteousness creates works. For grace and faith are infused without our works. After they have been imparted, the works follow. Thus Romans 3[:20] states, "No human being will be justified in his sight by works of the law," and, "For we hold that man is justified by faith apart from works of law" (Romans 3[:28]). In other words, works contribute nothing to justification. Therefore man knows that works he does by such faith are not his but God's. For this reason he does not seek to become justified or glorified through them but seeks God. His justification by faith in Christ is sufficient to him. Christ is his wisdom, righteousness, etc., as 1 Corinthians 1[:30] has it, that he himself may be Christ's action and instrument.

THESIS 26

The law says, "do this," and it is never done. Grace says, "believe in this," and everything is already done.

The first part is clear from what has been stated by the Apostle and his interpreter, St. Augustine, in many places. And it has been stated often enough above that the law works

Castle Church in Wittenberg

wrath and keeps all men under the curse. The second part is clear from the same sources, for faith justifies. "And the law (says St. Augustine) commands what faith obtains." For through faith Christ is in us, indeed, one with us. Christ is just and has fulfilled all the commands of God, wherefore we also fulfill everything through him since he was made ours through faith.

9. Luther's Explanation of the Ninety-five Theses (August 1518)

Luther wrote this conciliatory treatise over several months in response to what he considered to be misinterpretations of the original theses by his opponents. At this time he had still not completely rejected belief in purgatory, the treasury of merits or the special authority of the pope.

From *LW* 31:154–231, trans. Carl Folkemer.

Thesis 25

That power that the pope has in general over purgatory corresponds to the power that any bishop or curate has in a particular way in his own diocese or parish.

. . . I doubt and dispute whether the popes have the power of jurisdiction over purgatory. As much as I have read and perceive up to this moment, I hold fast to the negative position. I am prepared, however, to maintain the affirmative after the church has decided upon it. Meanwhile, I speak here concerning the power of energies, not of laws—the power of working, not of commanding—so that the meaning is this: The pope has absolutely no authority over purgatory, nor does any other bishop. If, however, he does have some authority, he certainly has only the same kind in which his subordinates also share.

Moreover, this is an authority by which the pope and any Christian who so wishes can intercede, pray for, fast, etc., on behalf of departed souls—the pope in a general way, the bishops in a particular way, and the Christian in an individual way. Therefore it is evident that the thesis is absolutely true. For just as the pope, at one time and with the whole church, may intercede for souls (as is done on All Souls' Day), so every bishop who wishes may do it with his own diocese, also the curate in his own parish (as is done at funerals and anniversaries), and any Christian who wishes in his own private devotion. Either one denies that such aid is an intercession or else concedes that each and every prelate, along with his subordinates, can intercede for souls. . . .

Thesis 28

It is certain that when money clinks in the money chest, greed and avarice can be increased; but when the church intercedes, the result is in the hands of God alone.

It is strange that my opponents do not preach the most precious gospel of Christ with as great a desire and loud wailing as they do other things. The fact that they seem to think more of profit than of piety makes me suspicious of this business. Perhaps, however, they may be justifiably excused by the fact that they do not know the gospel of Christ. Therefore, since indulgences possess no piety, no merit, and are not a command of Christ, but only something that is permitted, even though it may be a pious work that redeems people, it certainly appears that profit rather than piety is increased by indulgences. For these indulgences are promoted so extensively and exclusively that the gospel is treated as an inferior thing and is hardly mentioned. . . .

THESIS 41

Papal indulgences must be preached with caution, lest people erroneously think that they are preferable to other good works of love.

I would say this to people: Look, brothers, you ought to know that there are three types of good works that can be done by expending money. The first and foremost consists of giving to the poor or lending to a neighbor who is in need and in general of coming to the aid of anyone who suffers, whatever may be his need. This work ought to be done with such earnestness that even the building of churches must be interrupted and the taking of offerings for the purchase of holy vessels and for the decoration of churches be discontinued. After this has been done and there is no longer anyone who is in need, then should follow the second type, namely contributing to the building of our churches and hospitals in our country, then to buildings of public service. However, after this has been done, then, finally, if you so desire, you may give, in the third place, for the purchase of indulgences. The first type of good work has been commanded by Christ; there is no divine command for the last type.

If you should say, "With that type of preaching very little money would be collected through indulgences," I answer, I believe that. But what is so strange about that, since popes by means of indulgences do not seek money

but the salvation of souls, as is evident in those indulgences that they bestow at the consecration of churches and altars? So they do not wish through their indulgences to hinder the better things but rather to promote charity.

I say very frankly that whoever teaches people otherwise and reverses this order is not a teacher but a seducer of people, unless people because of their sins at times do not deserve to hear the truth rightly preached.

THESIS 62

The true treasure of the church is the most holy gospel of the glory and grace of God.

The gospel of God is something that is not very well known to a large part of the church. Therefore I must speak of it at greater length. Christ has left nothing to the world except the gospel. Also he has handed down to those who have been called to be his servants no such things as *minae,* talents, riches, and *denarii,* in order to show by these terms that speak of temporal treasures that the gospel is the true treasure. And Paul says that he himself lays up treasures for his children [2 Cor. 12:14]. Christ speaks of the gospel as a treasure that is hidden in a field [Matt. 13:44]. And because it is hidden, it is at the same time also neglected.

Moreover, according to the Apostle in Romans 1[:3-6], the gospel is a preaching of the incarnate Son of God, given to us without any merit on our part for salvation and peace. It is a work of salvation, a word of grace, a word of comfort, a word of joy, a voice of the bridegroom and the bride, a good word, a word of peace. Isaiah says, chapter 52[:7], "How beautiful . . . are the feet of those who bring good tidings, who publish peace, who preach good tidings." But the law is a word of destruction, a word of wrath, a word of sadness, a word of grief, a voice of the judge and the defendant, a word of restlessness, a word of curse. For according to the Apostle, "The law is the power of sin" [cf. 1 Cor. 15:56], and "the law brings wrath" [Rom. 4:15]; it is a law of death [Rom. 7:5, 13]. Through the law we have nothing except an evil conscience, a restless heart, a troubled breath because of our sins, which the law points out but does not take away. And we ourselves cannot take it away. Therefore for those of us who are held captive, who are overwhelmed by sadness and in dire despair, the light of the gospel comes and says, "Fear not" [Isa. 35:4], "comfort, comfort my people" [Isa. 40:1], "encourage the fainthearted" [1 Thess. 5:14], "behold your God" [Isa. 40:9], "behold the Lamb of God who takes away the sin of the world" [John 1:29]. Behold that one who alone fulfills the law for you, whom God has made to be your righteousness, sanctification, wisdom, and redemption, for all those who believe in him [1 Cor. 1:30]. When the sinful conscience hears this sweetest messenger, it comes to life again, shouts for joy while leaping about full of confidence, and no longer fears death, the types of punishment associated with death, or hell. Therefore those who are still afraid of punishments have not yet heard Christ or the voice of the gospel, but only the voice of Moses.

Therefore the true glory of God springs from this gospel. At the same time we are taught that the law is fulfilled not by our works but by the grace of God, who pities us in Christ, and that it shall be fulfilled not through works but through faith, not by anything we offer God, but by all we receive from Christ and partake of in him. "From his fullness have we all received" [John 1:16], and we are partakers of his merits. I have spoken of this more extensively on other occasions.

LUTHER ON TRIAL

10. Prieras's Dialogue concerning the Power of the Pope (December 1517)

Sylvester Mazzolini, also known as Prieras (1456–1523) was a Dominican theologian at the papal court who was commissioned by Pope Leo X to respond to Luther's "Ninety-five Theses."

From *Dialogus de potestate papae* in *Dokumente zur Causa Lutheri*, Teil 1, ed. Peter Fabisch and Erwin Iserloh (Münster: Aschendorffsche, 1988), 1:52–56.

THE FIRST FUNDAMENTAL PROPOSITION:
The universal church is essentially the assembly in divine worship of all believers in Christ. Indeed for all practical purposes the universal church is the Roman Church, the head of all churches, and its Supreme Pontiff. The Roman Church is to be found, by representation, in the college of cardinals but is, in effect, the highest Pontiff, who is head of the church, although in a different sense than Christ is head.

THE SECOND FUNDAMENTAL PROPOSITION:
Just as the universal church is not able to err in determining faith or morals, so also a true council when it does its best to discern the truth is not able to err. On first glance it may appear fallible, and while in the process of inquiring about the truth, it may err to some degree, but in the end it will be able to discern the truth through the Holy Spirit. Similarly, neither the Roman Church nor its Supreme Pontiff, when acting in his official capacity as pope, is able to err when he does his best to discern the truth.

THE THIRD FUNDAMENTAL PROPOSITION:
Whoever does not accept the doctrine of the Roman Church and of the Roman pontiff as the infallible rule of faith from which sacred

Scripture draws its strength and authority is a heretic.

THE FOURTH FUNDAMENTAL PROPOSITION:

The Roman Church is able to decide something concerning faith and morals by action as well as by word. Nor are these different except that words are more adaptable than actions. By this reasoning, custom obtains the strength of law because the will of a ruler is expressed either by permission given to others or practically by things done. Consequently, in the same way that a person is a heretic who thinks wrongly about the truth of Scripture, so also that person is a heretic who thinks wrongly about the teachings and actions of the church concerning faith and morals.

THE COROLLARY:

Whoever says concerning indulgences that the Roman Church is not able to do what in fact she does is a heretic. Act now, Martin, and report your conclusions out in the open.

II. Proceedings at Augsburg (Luther's Interview with Cardinal Cajetan, October 1518)

Luther published this account after his return from three days of discussion with the cardinal at the Diet of Augsburg.

From *LW* 31:263, 284–85, trans. Harold Grimm; cf. WA 2:6–26.

. . . I, with notary and witnesses who had been brought to the meeting, testified formally and personally by reading in the presence of the most reverend legate the following:

"Above all, I, brother Martin Luther, Augustinian, declare publicly that I cherish and follow the holy Roman Church in all my words and actions—present, past, and future. If I have said or shall say anything contrary to this,

I wish it to be considered as not having been said.

"The Most Reverend Cardinal Cajetan by command of the pope has asserted, proposed, and urged that with respect to the above disputation that I held on indulgences I do these three things: first, to come to my senses and retract my error; second, to pledge not to repeat it in the future; and third, to promise to abstain from all things that might disturb the church. . . . Today, I declare publicly that I am not conscious of having said anything contrary to Holy Scripture, the church fathers, or papal decretals or their correct interpretation. All that I have said today seems to me to have been sensible, true, and catholic. . . ."

. . . Jurists may emphasize their traditions, whereas we theologians preserve the purity of Scripture. We do this particularly because we in our time see evil flatterers appear who elevate the pope over the councils. The consequence is that one council is condemned by another until nothing certain remains for us and finally one man, the pope, can crush all things under foot since he is at the same time above the council and within it. He is above it since he can condemn it, within it since he accepts from the council as from a higher power authority by means of which he becomes higher than the council. There are also those who brazenly state in public that the pope cannot err and is above Scripture. If these monstrous claims were admitted, Scripture would perish and consequently the church also, and nothing would remain in the church but the word of man. These flatterers actually seek to arouse hatred in all things. I resist only those who in the name of the Roman Church strive to erect a Babylon for us and wish that whatever occurs to them—if only they could move the tongue enough to mention the Roman Church—be accepted as the interpretation of the Roman Church, as if Holy Scripture no longer existed, according to which (as

Augustine says) we must judge all things, and against which the Roman Church certainly never teaches or acts. . . .

12. Papal Bull *"Cum Postquam"* (On Indulgences, November 9, 1518)

From Walch 25:626–31.

It has come to our attention that some monks in Germany who are ordained for the preaching of the word of God have imprinted errors on many hearts through public sermons about the indulgences that we and preceding Roman popes have dispensed from time immemorial. This was difficult and distressing to learn. . . .

So that no one will be able to plead ignorance of the doctrine of the Roman Church concerning such indulgences and their efficacy or make excuses under the pretext of ignorance or seek the aid of fabricated protestations, and so that those who try to do so may be judged guilty of notorious lying and justifiably condemned, we have decided that you should be informed by our representatives among you that the Roman Church, which all other churches are bound to follow as their mother, has handed down that the Roman pontiff is the successor of Peter, bearer of the keys, and the vicar of Jesus Christ on earth. By the power of the keys that are able to open the kingdom of heaven and remove impediments in the faithful of Christ (namely the guilt and punishment owed for actual sins, the guilt remedied by the sacrament of penance, and the temporal punishment due for actual sins according to divine justice remedied by the indulgence of the church), [the pontiff] can for reasonable causes grant indulgences from the superabundant merits of Christ and the saints to the same faithful of Christ. Through

the bond of love, they are members of Christ's body whether they be in this life or in purgatory; thus, the pontiff by apostolic authority dispenses the treasury of the merits of Jesus Christ and the saints by granting the indulgence to both the living and the dead. He has been accustomed to confer the same indulgence by means of absolution or to transfer it by means of suffrage. And therefore all who have truly attained such indulgences, be they living or dead, are freed from temporal punishments that are owed by divine justice for their actual sins, to the amount equivalent to the distributed and acquired indulgence. We determine by apostolic authority and in accordance with these present writings that this ought to be preached and all should uphold it or else bear the penalty of a sentence of excommunication, which cannot be absolved (except in cases when death immediately threatens) by anyone other than the Roman pontiff. . . .

13. Luther's Letter to Spalatin on the Leipzig Debate (July 20, 1519)

Johannes Eck (1486–1543) was a theologian from the University of Ingolstadt who wrote an early critical response to Luther's theses. After this debate at Leipzig, he traveled to Rome and helped draft the papal bull *"Exsurge Domine"* (doc. #14).

From *LW* 31:320–23, trans. Harold Grimm; cf. WABr 1:420–24.

. . . Eck and Karlstadt at first debated for seven days over the freedom of the will. With God's help Karlstadt advanced his arguments and explanations excellently and in great abundance from books that he had brought with him. Then when Karlstadt had also been given the opportunity of rebuttal, Eck refused to debate unless the books were left at home. Andreas [Karlstadt] had used the books to demonstrate to Eck's face that he had correctly quoted the words of Scripture and the church fathers, that he had not done violence to them as Eck was now shown to have done. This marked the beginning of another uproar until at length it was decided to Eck's advantage that the books should be left at home. . . .

The next week, Eck debated with me, at first very acrimoniously, concerning the primacy of the papacy. His proof rested on the words, "You are Peter" [Matt. 16:18], "Feed my sheep, . . . follow me" [John 21:17, 22], and "strengthen your brethren" [Luke 22:32], adding to these passages many quotations from the church fathers. What I answered you will soon see. Then, coming to the last point, he rested his case entirely on the Council of Konstanz, which had condemned Huss's article alleging that papal authority derived from the emperor instead of from God.[7] Then Eck stamped about with much ado as though he were in an arena, holding up the Bohemian before me and publicly accusing me of the heresy and support of the Bohemian heretics, for he is a sophist, no less impudent than rash. These accusations tickled the Leipzig audience more than the debate itself.

In rebuttal I brought up the Greek Christians during the past thousand years and also the ancient church fathers, who had not been under the authority of the Roman pontiff, although I did not deny the primacy of honor due the pope.[8] Finally we also debated the authority of a council. I publicly acknowledged that some articles had been wrongly condemned [by the Council of Konstanz], articles that had been taught in plain and clear words by Paul, Augustine, and even Christ himself. At this point the adder swelled up, exaggerated my crime, and nearly went insane in his adulation of the Leipzig audience. Then I proved by the words of the council itself that

not all the articles that it condemned were actually heretical and erroneous. So Eck's proof had accomplished nothing. There the matter rested.

The third week Eck and I debated penance, purgatory, indulgences, and the power of a priest to grant absolution, for Eck did not like to debate with Karlstadt and asked me to debate alone with him. The debate over indulgences fell completely flat, for Eck agreed with me in nearly all respects, and his former defense of indulgences came to appear like mockery and derision, whereas I had hoped that this would be the main topic of the debate. He finally acknowledged his position in public sermons so that even the common people could see that he was not concerned with indulgences. He also is supposed to have said that if I had not questioned the power of the pope, he would readily have agreed with me in all matters. . . .

He conceded one thing in the disputation hall but taught the people the opposite in church. When confronted by Karlstadt with the reason for his changeableness, the man answered without blinking an eye that it was not necessary to teach the people that which was debatable. . . .

14. Papal Bull *"Exsurge Domine"* (The Threat of Excommunication, June 15, 1520)

From *Bullarum, diplomatum et privilegium sanctorum romanorum pontificum taurinensis editio* (Turin: Franco, Dalmazzo, 1860) 5:748–57, and Walch 25:1426–57.

. . . Rise up, Lord, and judge your cause. Be mindful of the slander that the foolish spread about all day long [Ps. 74:22]. Incline your ear

Luther's "Game of Heresy" broadsheet

to our prayers. Foxes have arisen and have attempted to ruin the vineyard [Song of Sol. 2:15], whose wine-press you alone have trodden [Isa. 63:3]. When you ascended to your Father in heaven, you commended the care, management, and administration of this vineyard to Peter as its head and as your representative and also to his successors, as the church triumphant. A wild boar of the woods has attempted to destroy this vineyard, and a wild beast wishes to devour it [Ps. 80:13].

Rise up, Peter, and in accordance with the pastoral care entrusted to you by God, attend to this cause of the holy Roman Church, the mother of all churches, the mistress of the faith, which you by God's command have sanctified with your blood and against which, as you have said before [2 Peter 2:1], teachers of lies have arisen, introducing pernicious sects. . . .

Rise up, we also pray, Paul, who by your teaching and likewise your martyrdom enlightened this church. . . . Finally, rise up, all you saints and the whole remaining universal church. . . . Rise up, I say, and, together with the most blessed apostles, make intercession that almighty God, after purging all errors from his flock and driving out all heresies from the domain of the faithful, might deign to preserve the peace and unity of his holy church. . . .

We can scarcely mention the reports and rumors brought to us by trustworthy and reputable sources without feeling anguish and pain. Unfortunately, with our own eyes we have also seen and read about many and various errors that have been stirred up and disseminated recently by certain thoughtless teachers in the renowned nation of Germany. Some of these errors have already been condemned by councils and the decrees of our predecessors and clearly replicate the heresies of the Greeks and the Bohemians. Others are truly heretical or false or scandalous ideas that offend the ears of the pious yet seduce the simple-minded. These are spread about by false caretakers of the faith, who have an arrogant desire for worldly honor and, in opposition to the teachings of the apostle Paul [1 Thess. 2:7], want to be wiser than is appropriate. . . .

Therefore, by reason of the pastoral office laid upon us by divine grace, we can in no way tolerate or ignore the poisonous virus of these errors any longer without marring the Christian religion or doing injury to the orthodox faith. We have drawn up a list of some of these errors [41 in toto], which are as follows:

5. That the threefold division of penance into contrition, confession, and satisfaction is not based on either holy Scripture or the writings of the ancient and holy Christian teachers.

10. That no sins are remitted unless, when the priest pronounces absolution, a person believes that they are remitted. . . .

13. That in the sacrament of penance or the remission of guilt, the pope or the bishop does no more than the lowliest priest, and furthermore, that where there is no priest, any Christian whatsoever could do the same—even a woman or a child.

15. That they are greatly in error who approach the Eucharist relying on the fact that they have confessed, are not conscious of

any mortal sin, and have performed their prayers and preparations: all these eat and drink to their own judgment. But if they believe and are confident that they will find grace there, this faith alone makes them pure and worthy.

16. That the church has apparently determined by a general council that the laity should receive communion in both kinds; so, the Bohemians, who commune in both kinds, are not heretics—but schismatics.

17. That the treasures of the church from which the pope grants indulgences are not the merits of Christ and the saints. . . .

19. That even those indulgences that are sincerely attained have no power for the remission of the penalties that are owed for actual sins according to divine justice. . . .

25. That the Roman pontiff, successor of Peter, is not the vicar of Christ over all churches throughout the whole world, ordained as such by Christ himself in blessed Peter.

26. That the word of Christ to Peter: "Whatever you loose on earth," etc. [Matt. 16:19], applies only to what Peter himself bound. . . .

28. That if the Pope, together with a large part of the church, holds this or that opinion—and even one that is not an error, it is still neither a sin nor heresy to hold a contrary view, especially on matters that are not necessary for salvation, up to the time when a universal council will have condemned one view and approved the other. . . .

31. That in every good work a righteous person sins.

35. That, on account of the most secret vice of pride, no one can be certain of not sinning mortally all the time.

36. That free will after sin is a thing in name only, and that when it does the best it can, it sins mortally.

37. That purgatory cannot be proved from the sacred Scriptures that are in the canon. . . .

Since these errors, and many others, are found in the writings or pamphlets of Martin Luther, . . . we condemn, reject, and denounce these pamphlets and all the writings and sermons of this Martin, whether they appear in Latin or any other form. . . .

Pertaining to this same Martin: good God!, what haven't we not let go by, what haven't we done, what fatherly love did we not exercise in order that we might call him back from these kinds of errors? After we had cited him, wanting to deal with him most gently, we appealed to him through many treatises by our legates and admonished him by our writings to depart from his errors. . . . But he dared to show contempt for our citation and each and every one of our appeals, enduring a censure with a hardened heart for more than a year and remaining defiant until the present day. . . .

Therefore, we solemnly appeal to this same Martin and his associates, his protectors and supporters, . . . to stop disturbing the peace, unity, and truth of the church for which the Savior fervently prayed to the Father [John 17:11] . . . and to abstain entirely from proclaiming such pernicious errors. . . .

If love of righteousness and virtue will not draw him back and the hope of pardon will not bring him again to repentance, then fear of the pain of punishment might influence him. Therefore, we order him and his accomplices . . . to desist from preaching, publishing, or asserting his errors within sixty days (three periods of twenty days) of the affixing of this bull at the places mentioned below. . . . This same Martin is to retract his errors and such assertions entirely, and this revocation should be transmitted to us within another sixty days in the form of a legal, public document sealed by the hands of two prelates. Or, if he wishes, he should come to us under a safe-conduct, which we will now grant, to inform us in person. This would be preferable in order to leave no doubt of his true obedience. . . .

If, however, this Martin, his supporters, accomplices, associates, and protectors should act contrary to these orders and fail to fulfill each and every one of these conditions within the stipulated period of time, we shall, in keeping with the teachings of the Apostle, who advises that we should shun a heretic after a first and second admonition [Titus 3:10], declare this Martin, his supporters, adherents, accomplices, and protectors . . . to be notorious and obstinate heretics. . . .We shall seize and subject each and every one of them to legal penalties. . . .

15. Luther's Appeal to the German Nobility (August 1520)

The following excerpt summarizes some of Luther's major reform proposals.

From *LW* 44:115–217, trans. Charles M. Jacobs, rev. James Atkinson; cf. WA 6:404–69.

. . . The Romanists have very cleverly built three walls around themselves. Hitherto they have protected themselves by these walls in such a way that no one has been able to reform them. As a result, the whole of Christendom has fallen abominably. . . .

Let us begin by attacking the first wall. It is pure invention that pope, bishop, priests, and monks are called the spiritual estate while princes, lords, artisans, and farmers are called the temporal estate. This is indeed a piece of deceit and hypocrisy. Yet no one need be intimidated by it, and for this reason: all Christians are truly of the spiritual estate, and there is no difference among them except that of office. Paul says in 1 Corinthians 12[:12-13] that we are all one body, yet every member has its own work by which it serves the other. . . .

Therefore, just as those who are now called "spiritual," that is, priests, bishops, or popes, are neither different from other Christians nor superior to them, except that they are charged with the administration of the word of God and the sacraments, which is their work and office, so it is with the temporal authorities. They bear the sword and rod in their hand to punish the wicked and protect the good. A cobbler, a smith, a peasant—each has the work and office of his trade, and yet they are all alike consecrated priests and bishops. . . .

The second wall is still more loosely built and less substantial. The Romanists want to be the only masters of Holy Scripture, although they never learn a thing from the Bible all their life long. They assume the sole authority for themselves, and quite unashamed they play about with words before our very eyes, trying to persuade us that the pope cannot err in matters of faith, regardless of whether he is righteous or wicked. . . .

They cannot produce a single letter [of Scripture] to maintain that the interpretation of Scripture or the confirmation of its interpretation belongs to the pope alone. They themselves have usurped this power. . . .

We ought not to allow the spirit of freedom (as Paul calls him [2 Cor. 3:17]) to be frightened off by the fabrications of the popes, but we ought to march boldly forward and test all that they do or leave undone by our believing understanding of the Scriptures. We must compel the Romanists to follow not their own interpretation but the better one. . . .

The third wall falls of itself when the first two are down. When the pope acts contrary to the Scriptures, it is our duty to stand by the Scriptures, to reprove him and constrain him. . . .

The Romanists have no basis in Scripture for their claim that the pope alone has the right to call or confirm a council. This is just their own ruling, and it is only valid as long as it is not harmful to Christendom or contrary to the laws of God. Now when the pope deserves punishment, this ruling no longer obtains, for

Title Page of Luther's *On Good Works*

not to punish him by authority of a council is harmful to Christendom. . . .

Therefore, when necessity demands it, and the pope is an offense to Christendom, the first man who is able should, as a true member of the whole body, do what he can to bring about a truly free council. No one can do this so well as the temporal authorities, especially since they are also fellow-Christians, fellow-priests, fellow-members of the spiritual estate, fellow-lords over all things. . . .

Now, although I am too insignificant a man to make propositions for the improvement of this dreadful state of affairs, nevertheless I shall sing my fool's song through to the end and say, so far as I am able, what could and should be done, either by the temporal authority or by a general council. . . .

9. The pope should have no authority over the emperor, except the right to anoint and crown him at the altar just as a bishop crowns a king. . . .

12. Pilgrimages to Rome should either be abolished or else no one should be allowed to make such a pilgrimage for reasons of curiosity or his own pious devotion, unless it is first acknowledged by his parish priest, his town authorities, or his overlord that he has a good and sufficient reason for doing so. . . .

13. . . . It is the bittersweet truth that the further building of mendicant houses should not

be permitted. God help us, there are already too many of them. . . . My advice is to join together ten of these houses or as many as need be and make them a single institution for which adequate provision is made so that begging will not be necessary. . . . The pope must also be forbidden to found or endorse any more of these orders; in fact he must be ordered to abolish some and reduce the number of others. Inasmuch as faith in Christ, which alone is the chief possession, exists without any kind of orders, there is no little danger that men will be easily led astray to live according to many and varied works and ways rather than to pay heed to faith. . . .

14. . . . The Roman See has interfered and out of its own wanton wickedness made a universal commandment forbidding priests to marry. . . . My advice is, restore freedom to everybody and leave every man free to marry or not to marry. . . .

18. All festivals should be abolished, and Sunday alone retained. If it were desired, however, to retain the festivals of Our Lady and of the major saints, they should be transferred to Sunday, or observed only by a morning mass, after which all the rest of the day should be a working day. Here is the reason: since the feast days are abused by drinking, loafing, and all manner of sin, we anger God more on holy days than we do on other days. . . .

20. . . . Although the canonization of saints may have been a good thing in former days, it is certainly never good practice now. Like many other things that were good in former times, feast days, church holdings, and ornaments now are scandalous and offensive. For it is evident that through the canonization of saints neither God's glory nor the improvement of Christians is sought, but only money and reputation.

22. It is also to be feared that the many masses that were endowed in ecclesiastical foundations and monasteries are not only of

little use, but arouse the great wrath of God. It would therefore be profitable not to endow any more of these masses, but rather to abolish many that are already endowed. It is obvious that these masses are regarded only as sacrifices and good works, even though they are sacraments just like baptism and penance, which profit only those who receive them and no one else. But now the custom of saying masses for the living and the dead has crept in, and all hopes are built upon them. . . .

25. The universities, too, need a good, thorough reformation. . . . What are they but places where loose living is practiced, where little is taught of the Holy Scriptures and Christian faith, and where the blind, heathen teacher Aristotle rules far more than Christ? . . . Above all, the foremost reading for everybody, both in the universities and in the schools, should be Holy Scripture—and for the younger boys, the Gospels. And would to God that every town had a girls' school as well, where the girls would be taught the gospel for an hour every day either in German or in Latin. . . .

16. Luther's Answer at the Diet of Worms (April 18, 1521)

From *LW* 32:109–13, trans. Roger Hornsby; cf. WA 7:814–57.

. . . Most Serene Emperor, Most Illustrious Princes, concerning those questions proposed to me yesterday on behalf of Your Serene Majesty, whether I acknowledge as mine the books enumerated and published in my name and whether I wished to persevere in their defense or to retract them, I have given to the first question my full and complete answer, in which I still persist and shall persist forever. These books are mine and they have been pub-

lished in my name by me, unless in the meantime, either through the craft or the mistaken wisdom of my emulators, something in them has been changed or wrongly cut out. For plainly I cannot acknowledge anything except what is mine alone and what has been written by me alone, to the exclusion of all interpretations of anyone at all.

In replying to the second question, I ask that Your Most Serene Majesty and Your Lordships may deign to note that my books are not all of the same kind.

For there are some in which I have discussed religious faith and morals simply and evangelically, so that even my enemies themselves are compelled to admit that these are useful, harmless, and clearly worthy to be read by Christians. Even the bull, although harsh and cruel, admits that some of my books are inoffensive, and yet allows these also to be condemned with a judgment that is utterly monstrous. Thus, if I should begin to disavow them, I ask you, what would I be doing? Would not I, alone of all men, be condemning the very truth upon which friends and enemies equally agree, striving alone against the harmonious confession of all?

Another group of my books attacks the papacy and the affairs of the papists as those who both by their doctrines and very wicked examples have laid waste the Christian world with evil that affects the spirit and the body. For no one can deny or conceal this fact, when the experience of all and the complaints of everyone witness that through the decrees of the pope and the doctrines of men the consciences of the faithful have been most miserably entangled, tortured, and torn to pieces. Also, property and possessions, especially in this illustrious nation of Germany, have been devoured by an unbelievable tyranny and are being devoured to this time without letup and by unworthy means. [Yet the papists] by their decrees warn that the papal laws and doctrines that are contrary to the gospel or the opinions of the fathers are to be regarded as erroneous and reprehensible. If, therefore, I should have retracted these writings, I should have done nothing other than to have added strength to this [papal] tyranny and I should have opened not only windows but doors to such great godlessness. . . .

I have written a third sort of book against some private and (as they say) distinguished individuals—those, namely, who strive to preserve the Roman tyranny and to destroy the godliness taught by me. Against these I confess I have been more violent than my religion or profession demands. But then, I do not set myself up as a saint; neither am I disputing about my life, but about the teachings of Christ. It is not proper for me to retract these works, because by this retraction it would again happen that tyranny and godlessness would, with my patronage, rule and rage among the people of God more violently than ever before. . . .

Since then Your Serene Majesty and Your Lordships seek a simple answer, I will give it in this manner, neither horned nor toothed: Unless I am convinced by the testimony of the Scriptures or by clear reason (for I do not trust either in the pope or in councils alone, since it is well known that they have often erred and contradicted themselves), I am bound by the Scriptures I have quoted and my conscience is captive to the Word of God. I cannot and I will not retract anything, since it is neither safe nor right to go against conscience.

I cannot do otherwise, here I stand, may God help me, Amen.

17. The Edict of Worms (May 26, 1521)

From *Deutsche Reichstagsakten: Jüngere Reihe*, vol. 2 (Göttingen: Vandenhoeck & Ruprecht, 1962), 645–55.

. . . Although, after the delivery of the papal bull and the last condemnation of Luther, we proclaimed this admonition in many places in the German nation . . . , Martin Luther has ignored it and has failed to correct and revoke his errors. He has not sought absolution from his Papal Holiness and a return to the grace of the holy Christian church. Not only that, he has spread abroad much evil fruit and the effect of his perverted heart and mind, like a madman attempting an apparent suppression of the holy church. Through many books in Latin and German, containing both new and old heresies and blasphemies, he has destroyed, overturned, and shown disrespect for the number, order, and practice of the seven sacraments upheld for so many years by the holy church. . . .

He not only deprecates the priestly office but also prompts the worldly laypeople to wash their hands in priestly blood. He uses slanderous and shameful words to speak of the foremost priest of our Christian faith, the successor of St. Peter and the true vicar of Christ on earth, and attacks him with many unprecedented hostile writings and insults.

He also affirms from the heathen poets that there is no free will, believing that all things stand fast by a certain fixed law. He writes that having a mass celebrated for someone brings no benefit, and he overturns the custom of fasting and prayer that has been established by the holy church and maintained until now. Most notably, he scorns the authority of the holy fathers who have been honored by the church. He does away with obedience and authority altogether, and whatever he writes prompts nothing but revolt, division, war, manslaughter, robbery, arson, and the total degradation of the Christian faith. . . .

Seeing how this matter has turned out and how Martin Luther perseveres with his manifestly heretical opinions . . . we have recourse to the following remedies against this severe, poisonous disease:

First, to the praise of the Almighty and for the defense of the Christian faith and the proper honor of the Roman bishop, we, by the power of our imperial dignity and authority, . . . pronounce judgment and declare Martin Luther a member severed from the church of God, whom each and everyone should regard as an obstinate schismatic and an indisputable heretic. . . .

We strictly order . . . that particularly after the expiration of the appointed twenty days, which end on the fourteenth day of the present month of May, you shall refuse to give the aforementioned Martin Luther lodging, food, or drink, or offer him any help, support, or assistance, by word or deed, either secretly or openly. Wherever you might happen to meet him, you shall take him prisoner, if you have sufficient force, and deliver him to us, or arrange to have this done, or at least let us know promptly where he may be captured. In the meantime, you shall keep him imprisoned until you receive further notice from us about what to do, according to the direction of the law. You shall receive suitable compensation for such holy work and for your effort and expense. . . .

Furthermore, we order that no one shall buy, sell, read, keep, copy, print, or have printed any of the writings of the aforementioned Martin Luther, which have been condemned by Our Holy Father the Pope, or any other writings in German, Latin, or any other language that he has produced or will produce in the future, since they are evil and suspect

and proceed from an evident, stiff-necked heretic.

The Threat of Radical Reformers

18. Luther: Admonition against Insurrection (March 1522)

After hearing rumors about unrest, Luther made a secret visit to Wittenberg. He wrote this treatise shortly after his return to the Wartburg castle.

From *LW* 45:65–71, trans. W. A. Lambert, rev. Walter Brandt; cf. WA 8.

. . . Those who read and rightly understand my teaching will not start an insurrection; they have not learned that from me. If some incite to insurrection, however, and make use of our name, what can we do about it? How much are the papists doing in the name of Christ that Christ has not only forbidden but that tends to destroy Christ? Must we keep our company so pure that among us there may not even be a stumbling St. Peter? Why, among the papists there are none but Judases and Judas-like deceit—still they are not willing to have their teachings ascribed to the devil. But, as I say, the devil thus tries in every way to find an occasion for slandering our teaching. If there were anything worse he could do, he would do it. But he is checkmated and, God willing, must take his punishment now that he has been reduced to such lame, futile, and rotten schemes. He will not and shall not succeed in stirring up the insurrection he so much desires.

Therefore, I beseech all who would glory in the name of Christ to be guided by what St. Paul says in 2 Corinthians 3 [6:3], that we give our opponents no occasion to find fault with our teaching. For we see how apt the papists are to ignore the log in their own eyes and how zealously they hunt and scratch to find a tiny speck in our eyes. We are not supposed to reproach them with the fact that among them there is hardly anything good, but if even a single one of us is not wholly spiritual and a perfect angel, our entire cause is supposed to be wrong. Then they rejoice, then they dance, then they sing as if they had won the victory. Therefore, we must guard against giving them any occasion for slander, of which they are full to overflowing. . . .

Get busy now; spread the holy gospel, and help others spread it; teach, speak, write, and preach that man-made laws are nothing; urge people not to enter the priesthood, the monastery, or the convent, and hinder them from so doing; encourage those who have already entered to leave; give no more money for bulls, candles, bells, tablets, and churches; rather tell them that a Christian life consists of faith and love. Let us do this for two years, and you shall see what will become of pope, bishops, cardinals, priests, monks, nuns, bells, towers, masses, vigils, cowls, hoods, tonsures, monastic rules, statutes, and all the swarming vermin of the papal regime; they will all vanish like smoke. . . .

There are some who, when they have read a page or two or have heard a sermon, go at it slam bang, and do no more than overwhelm others with reproach and find fault with them and their practices as being unevangelical, without stopping to consider that many of them are plain and simple folk who would soon learn the truth if it were told them. This also I have taught no one to do, and St. Paul has strictly forbidden it [Rom. 14:1—15:1; 1 Cor. 4:5-6]. Their only motive in doing it is the desire to come up with something new and to be regarded as good Lutherans. But they are perverting the holy gospel to make it serve their own pride. You will never bring the gospel into the hearts of men in that way. You are much more apt to

frighten them away from it, and then you will have to bear the awful responsibility of having driven them away from the truth. You fool, that's not the way; listen, and take some advice.

In the first place, I ask that men make no reference to my name; let them call themselves Christians, not Lutherans. What is Luther? After all, the teaching is not mine [John 7:16]. Neither was I crucified for anyone [1 Cor. 1:13]. St. Paul, in 1 Corinthians 3, would not allow the Christians to call themselves Pauline or Petrine but Christian. How then should I—poor stinking maggot-fodder that I am—come to have men call the children of Christ by my wretched name? Not so, my dear friends; let us abolish all party names and call ourselves Christians, after him whose teachings we hold. The papists deservedly have a party name, because they are not content with the teaching and name of Christ, but want to be papists as well. Let them be papists then, since the pope is their master. I neither am nor want to be anyone's master. I hold, together with the universal church, the one universal teaching of Christ, who is our only master [Matt. 23:8]. . . .

19. Luther's Letter to Melanchthon on the "Prophets" (January 13, 1522)

From *LW* 48:365–67, trans. Gottfried Krodel; cf. WABr 2:424–27.

. . . Now, let me deal with the "prophets." Before I say anything else, I do not approve of your timidity, since you are stronger in spirit and learning than I. First of all, since they bear witness to themselves, one need not immediately accept them; according to John's counsel, the spirits are to be tested. If you cannot test them, then you have the advice of Gamaliel that you postpone judgment. Thus far I hear of

Martin Luther as Junker Jorg

approached hell" [Ps. 88:3]. . . . Therefore, examine [them] and do not even listen if they speak of the glorified Jesus, unless you have first heard of the crucified Jesus. . . .

20. Luther's Letter to Elector Friedrich of Saxony (March 7 or 8, 1522)

From *LW* 48:394–97, trans. Gottfried Krodel; cf. WABr 2:459–62.

nothing said or done by them that Satan could not also do or imitate. Yet find out for me whether they can prove [that they are called by God], for God has never sent anyone, not even the Son himself, unless he was called through men or attested by signs. In the old days the prophets had their authority from the law and the prophetic order, as we now receive authority through men. I definitely do not want the "prophets" to be accepted if they state that they were called by mere revelation, since God did not even wish to speak to Samuel except through the authority and knowledge of Eli. This is the first thing that belongs to teaching in public.

In order to explore their individual spirit, too, you should inquire whether they have experienced spiritual distress and the divine birth, death, and hell. If you should hear that all [their experiences] are pleasant, quiet, devout (as they say), and spiritual, then don't approve of them, even if they should say that they were caught up to the third heaven. The sign of the Son of Man is then missing, which is the only touchstone of Christians and a certain differentiator between the spirits. Do you want to know the place, time, and manner of [true] conversations with God? Listen: "Like a lion has he broken all my bones" [Isa. 38:13]; "I am cast out from before your eyes" [Ps. 31:22]; "My soul is filled with grief, and my life has

. . . Most Serene, Noble Sovereign and Most Gracious Lord: I have very carefully considered that it truly would be a burden for Your Electoral Grace if I would return to Wittenberg again without Your Electoral Grace's wish and permission, particularly since it seems that this would cause great danger for Your Electoral Grace, the whole country, and all the people, but especially for myself, banned and condemned by papal and imperial law as I am, and expecting death at any moment.

What should I do? There is urgent reason for my return, and God compels and calls me. Therefore it has to be this way and will be so; so let it be in the name of Jesus Christ, the Lord of life and death. . . .

The first reason [for my return]: I am called by the whole congregation at Wittenberg in a letter filled with urgent begging and pleading. Since no one can deny that the [present] commotion has its origin in me, and since I must confess that I am a humble servant of the congregation to which God has sent me, I had no way of refusing [this call] without rejecting Christian love, trust, and obedience. . . .

The second reason [for my return]: on account of my absence Satan has intruded into my fold at Wittenberg. The whole world shouts it abroad—and it certainly is true—that Satan has injured some [sheep] that I cannot heal with any writing. I have to deal with them personally via mouth and ear. My conscience will no longer allow me to yield or procrastinate. . . .

The third reason [for my return]: I am rather afraid (and I worry that unfortunately I may be only too right) that there will be a real rebellion in the German territories, by which God will punish the German nation. For we see that this gospel is excellently received by the common people, but they receive it in a fleshly sense; that is, they know that it is true but do not want to use it correctly. Those who should calm such rebellion only aid it. They attempt to put out the light by force, not realizing that they are only embittering the hearts of men by this and stimulating them to revolt. They behave as if they wanted themselves, or at least their children, destroyed. No doubt God sends this as a punishment. . . .

Now God has commanded, through Ezekiel, that we set ourselves before him as a wall of protection for the people [Ezek. 13:5; 22:30]. Therefore I—and my friends—have considered it necessary to act upon this, to see whether we might turn away or defer God's judgment. . . .

21. Luther's Invocavit Sermons 1 and 2 (March 1522)

From *LW* 51:69–78, trans. John Doberstein; cf. WA 10.

FIRST SERMON ON INVOCAVIT SUNDAY

. . . In the first place, we must know that we are the children of wrath, and all our works, intentions, and thoughts are nothing at all. . . .

Second, that God has sent us his only-begotten Son that we may believe in him and that whoever trusts in him shall be free from sin and a child of God, as John declares in his

"Friedrich the Wise" by Albrecht Dürer

first chapter, "To all who believed in his name, he gave power to become children of God" [John 1:12]. . . .

Third, we must also have love and through love we must do to one another as God has done to us through faith. For without love faith is nothing, as St. Paul says (1 Corinthians 2 [13:1]): If I had the tongues of angels and could speak of the highest things in faith and have not love, I am nothing. And here, dear friends, have you not grievously failed? I see no signs of love among you, and I observe very well that you have not been grateful to God for his rich gifts and treasures. . . . For a faith without love is not enough—rather it is not faith at all, but a counterfeit of faith, just as a face seen in a mirror is not a real face, but merely the reflection of a face [1 Cor. 13:12].

Fourth, we also need patience. For whoever has faith, trusts in God, and shows love to his neighbor, practicing it day by day, must needs suffer persecution. For the devil never sleeps, but constantly gives him plenty of trouble. But patience works and produces hope [Rom. 5:4], which freely yields itself to God and vanishes away in him. Thus faith, by much affliction and persecution, ever increases and is strengthened day by day. A heart thus blessed with virtues can never rest or restrain itself, but rather pours itself out again for the benefit and service of the brethren, just as God has done to it. . . .

What does a mother do to her child? First she gives it milk, then gruel, then eggs and soft food, whereas if she turned about and gave it solid food, the child would never thrive [cf. 1 Cor. 3:2, Heb. 5:12-13]. So we should also deal with our brother, have patience with him for a time, have patience with his weakness and help him bear it; we should also give him mild food, too [1 Pet. 2:2; cf. Rom. 14:1-3], as was done with us, until he too grows strong, and thus we do not travel heavenward alone, but bring our brethren, who are not now our friends, with us. . . . Dear brother, if you have suckled long enough, do not at once cut off the breast, but let your brother be suckled as you were suckled. I would not have gone so far as you have done, if I had been here. The cause is good, but there has been too much haste. For there are still brothers and sisters on the other side who belong to us and must still be won. . . .

All those have erred who have helped and consented to abolish the mass; not that it was not a good thing, but that it was not done in an orderly way. You say it was right according to the Scriptures. I agree, but what becomes of order? For it was done in wantonness, with no regard for proper order and with offense to your neighbor. If beforehand you had called upon God in earnest prayer and had obtained the aid of the authorities, one could be certain that it had come from God. . . .

Take note of these two things: "must" and "free." The "must" is that which necessity requires and which must ever be unyielding; as, for instance, the faith, which I shall never permit any one to take away from me but must always keep in my heart and freely confess before every one. But "free" is that in which I have choice and may use or not, yet in such a way that it profit my brother and not me. Now do not make a "must" out of what is "free," as you have done, so that you may not be called to account for those who were led astray by your loveless exercise of liberty. For if you entice any

one to eat meat on Friday, and he is troubled about it on his deathbed, and thinks, Woe is me, for I have eaten meat and I am lost! God will call you to account for that soul. I, too, would like to begin many things, in which but few would follow me, but what is the use? . . .

Let us, therefore, feed others also with the milk that we received, until they too become strong in faith. For there are many who are otherwise in accord with us and who would also gladly accept this thing, but they do not yet fully understand it—these we drive away. Therefore, let us show love to our neighbors; if we do not do this, our work will not endure. . . .

Second Sermon on Monday

. . . In the things that are "musts" and are matters of necessity, such as believing in Christ, love nevertheless never uses force or undue constraint. Thus the mass is an evil thing, and God is displeased with it, because it is performed as if it were a sacrifice and work of merit. Therefore it must be abolished. Here there can be no question or doubt, any more than you should ask whether you should worship God. Here we are entirely agreed: the private masses must be abolished. As I have said in my writings, I wish they would be abolished everywhere and only the ordinarily evangelical mass be retained. Yet Christian love should not employ harshness here nor force the matter. However, it should be preached and taught with tongue and pen that to hold mass in such a manner is sinful, and yet no one should be dragged away from it by the hair; for it should be left to God, and his Word should be allowed to work alone, without our work or interference. Why? Because it is not in my power or hand to fashion the hearts of men as the potter molds the clay and fashion them at my pleasure [Eccles. 33:13]. I can get no farther than their ears; their hearts I cannot reach. And since I cannot pour faith into their hearts, I cannot, nor should I, force any one to have faith. That is God's work alone, who causes faith to live in the heart. . . .

Once, when Paul came to Athens (Acts 17[:16-32]), a mighty city, he found in the temple many ancient altars, and he went from one to the other and looked at them all, but he did not kick down a single one of them with his foot. Rather he stood up in the middle of the market place and said they were nothing but idolatrous things and begged the people to forsake them; yet he did not destroy one of them by force. When the Word took hold of their hearts, they forsook them of their own accord, and in consequence the thing fell of itself. Likewise, if I had seen them holding mass, I would have preached to them and admonished them. Had they heeded my admonition, I would have won them; if not, I would nevertheless not have torn them from it by the hair or employed any force, but simply allowed the Word to act and prayed for them. For the Word created heaven and earth and all things [Ps. 33:6]; the Word must do this thing and not we poor sinners.

In short, I will preach it, teach it, write it, but I will constrain no man by force, for faith must come freely without compulsion. Take myself as an example. I opposed indulgences and all the papists, but never with force. I simply taught, preached, and wrote God's Word; otherwise I did nothing. And while I slept [cf. Mark 4:26-29], or drank Wittenberg beer with my friends Philip and Amsdorf, the Word so greatly weakened the papacy that no prince or emperor ever inflicted such losses upon it. I did nothing; the Word did everything. Had I desired to foment trouble, I could have brought great bloodshed upon Germany; indeed, I could have started such a game that even the emperor would not have been safe. But what would it have been? Mere fool's play. I did nothing; I let the Word do its work. . . .

22. Luther: Against the Heavenly Prophets (February 1525)

From *LW* 40:91, 128, trans. Bernhard Erling; cf. WA 18.

. . . I would release and free consciences and the soul from sin, which is a truly spiritual and evangelical pastoral function, while Karlstadt seeks to capture them with law and burden them with sin without good cause. And yet he does this not with a law of God, but with his own conceit and mischief, so that he is not only far from the gospel, but also not even a Mosaic teacher. And yet he continually praises the "Word of God, the Word of God," just as if it were therefore to become God's Word as soon as one could say the Word of God. Usually those who make great ado in praising God's Word do not have much to back them up, as unfortunately we have previously experienced under our papistical tyrants.

However, to speak evangelically of images, I say and declare that no one is obligated to break violently images even of God, but everything is free, and one does not sin if he does not break them with violence. One is obligated, however, to destroy them with the Word of God, that is, not with the law in a Karlstadtian manner, but with the gospel. This means to instruct and enlighten the conscience that it is idolatry to worship them, or to trust in them, since one is to trust alone in Christ. Beyond this let the external matters take their course. God grant that they may be destroyed, become dilapidated, or that they remain. It is all the same and makes no difference, just as when the poison has been removed from a snake.

Now I say this to keep the conscience free from mischievous laws and fictitious sins and not because I would defend images. Nor would I condemn those who have destroyed them, especially those who destroy divine and idolatrous images. But images for memorial and witness, such as crucifixes and images of saints, are to be tolerated. . . .

The pope commands what is to be done, Dr. Karlstadt what is not to be done. Thus through them Christian freedom is destroyed in two ways: on the one hand, when one commands, constrains, and compels what is to be done, which is nevertheless not commanded or required by God; on the other hand, when one forbids, prevents, and hinders one from doing that which is neither prohibited nor forbidden by God. For my conscience is ensnared and misled just as much when it must refrain from doing something, which it is not necessary to refrain from doing, as when it must do something, which it is not necessary to do. When men must refrain from doing that from which they need not refrain and are compelled to do what they need not do, Christian freedom perishes in either case. . . .

THE PEASANTS' REVOLT

23. The Twelve Articles of the Peasants (March 1525)

From Heinrich Böhmer, *Urkunden zur Geschichte des Bauernkrieges* (Berlin: de Gruyter, 1933), 4–10.

THE FIRST ARTICLE

First, it is our humble request and desire, the wish and intention of us all, that from now on we should have authority and power as a whole community to choose and select a pastor for ourselves. We should also have the authority to dismiss him if he should conduct himself improperly. . . .

THE SECOND ARTICLE

Second, since the duty to tithe is established in the Old Testament and perfected in the New Testament, we are quite willing to pay the tithe of grain—as long as it is a fair amount. The tithe is given to God to be passed on to his servants, so it is appropriate that a pastor who preaches according to the Word of God should receive it. Yet, in the future we would like the church wardens appointed by our community to collect and receive this tithe. The pastor, chosen by our entire community, should be given a suitable and adequate living for himself and his family, in accordance with the determination of the whole community, and what is left over should be distributed to the poor who are present in our own village, in accordance with their needs as determined by the whole community. . . .

THE THIRD ARTICLE

Third, it has been the custom until now for lords to hold us as their own property. This is pitiful, considering that Christ has redeemed and purchased us all by the shedding of his precious blood, both the lowly shepherd as well as the highest noble, excepting no one. We find in Scripture that we are free, and we wish to be so. However, God does not teach us that we should be so entirely free that we do not recognize any authority over us. We should live orderly lives and not in fleshly wantonness. We should love God as our Lord and apprehend him in our neighbor. . . .

THE FOURTH ARTICLE

Fourth, it has been the custom until now that no poor man has had permission to catch wild game or fowl, or fish in flowing water. This seems to us quite improper and unbrotherly. It is selfish and not in accordance with God's Word. . . .

THE FIFTH ARTICLE

Fifth, we are also troubled about the cutting of wood because our lords have appropriated all the woods for themselves alone. . . .

THE SIXTH ARTICLE

Our sixth complaint concerns the hard burden of labor demanded of us [by our lords], which is increasing from day to day. . . .

THE SEVENTH ARTICLE

Seventh, we will not allow the lords to overburden us any more in the future. The lords should devise an appropriate way for leaseholds to be possessed by the terms of an agreement between lord and peasant. . . .

THE EIGHTH ARTICLE

Eighth, we are burdened because many of us have lands that cannot yield enough to pay the required rent. The peasants suffer loss in this way and are ruined. We ask the lords to appoint honorable persons to inspect these lands and assign a fair rent. . . .

THE NINTH ARTICLE

Ninth, we are burdened by the constant making of new laws concerning serious crimes. Punishments are not administered in accordance with the nature of the case, but sometimes out of spite and other times out of partiality. . . .

THE TENTH ARTICLE

Tenth, we are troubled that certain individuals have claimed meadows and fields as their own that at one time belonged to the community. . . .

THE ELEVENTH ARTICLE

Eleventh, we want the custom called Todfall[9] [the servile death tax] to be totally abolished. . . .

CONCLUSION

Twelfth, it is our conclusion and final intention, that if one or more of the articles set forth here should not be in conformity with the Word of God, which we do not believe to be the case, we will give it up once we are shown from the Word of God that it is improper. . . .

24. Müntzer's Letter to the People of Allstedt (April 26 or 27, 1525)

Müntzer was an early supporter of Luther who put a greater stress on the guidance of the inner voice of God. He blamed Luther for allowing "spiritless, soft living" in Wittenberg. One month after he wrote this letter, he was captured and executed.

From Günther Franz, ed., *Müntzer Schriften* (Gütersloh: Gerd Mohn, 1968), 454–55.

May the pure fear of God prevail, dear brothers. How long will you sleep; how long will you go on without acknowledging the will of God because, in your estimation, he has forsaken you? Alas, how many times have I told you how it must be, how God cannot reveal himself in any other way, and that you must remain undisturbed? If you fail to do so, then your heart-breaking sacrifice, your heart-wounding suffering is to no avail. You might then have to begin your suffering all over again. I will tell you this, that if you do not want to suffer according to God's will, then you will have to be martyrs for the devil. So watch out, don't be faint-hearted or negligent and no longer flatter the perverted fools, the godless evildoers. Get going and fight the fight of the Lord! It is high time. Keep your brothers all at it, so that they do not scorn the divine witness, or else they will all perish. The entire lands of Germany, France, and Italy are awake; the master wants to play the game and the evildoers must be in it too. At Fulda, during Easter week, four abbeys were laid waste; the peasants in the Klettgau and the Hegau in the Black Forest have risen, three thousand strong, and the more time passes, the larger their number grow. My only worry is that the foolish people will consent to a false treaty, because they do not yet recognize the extent of the wrong that has been done.

Even if there are only three of you who submit to God and seek his name and honor alone, you need not fear a hundred thousand. So go onward, onward, onward! Now is the time, since the evildoers have lost heart, like [scared] dogs! Arouse your brothers, so that they may come to peace and bear witness to their commitment. It is extremely urgent! Go onward, onward, onward! Show no pity, even if Esau offers kind words to you, Genesis 33. Pay no heed to the cries of the godless. They will plead with you so amicably, weeping and begging like children. Show them no pity, as God commanded through Moses, Deuteronomy 7[:1-5], and has revealed the same to us. Arouse the villages and towns and especially the mine-workers and other good comrades who can do us some good. We must sleep no longer. . . .

25. Müntzer's Letter to Albrecht of Mansfeld (May 12, 1525)

From Franz, ed., *Müntzer Schriften*, 469–70.

To brother Albrecht von Mansfeld, written for his conversion.

Let all who do evil fear and tremble, Romans 2[:9]. It disturbs me that you terribly misuse the epistle of Paul. You want to support the wicked authorities in whatever they do, just like the pope, who has made Peter and Paul into jailers. Do you think that the Lord God cannot stir up his simpleminded people to depose the tyrants in his wrath? Hosea 13[:11] and 8[:4]. Didn't the mother of Christ speak through the Holy Spirit of you and your sort when she prophesied in Luke 1[:52]: "He has cast the mighty down from their thrones and raised up the lowly (whom you despise)"? Have you been unable to find in your Lutheran

Thomas Müntzer

gruel and your Wittenberg soup what Ezekiel prophesied in his thirty-seventh chapter [verse 4]? You, in your Martinian peasant muck, have also been unable to taste what the same prophet goes on to say in the thirty-ninth chapter, how God commands all the birds of the air to consume the flesh of the princes, and how the dumb beasts are to drink the blood of the high and mighty, as Revelation chapters 18 and 19[:18] describe? Do you suppose that God is not more concerned about his people than he is about you tyrants? Under the name of Christ, you want to act like a pagan while using Paul as a cover-up. But your path will be blocked, that is for sure. If you will acknowledge Daniel 7[:27], according to which God has given power to the common man, and if you are willing to appear before us and retract your stance, then we will gladly accommodate you and accept you as our common brother. But if you do not, then we will not pay attention to your lame, weak tricks but will take up the fight against you as against an arch-enemy of the Christian faith; that is for sure.

From Frankenhausen on the Friday after Jubilate in the year 1525

Thomas Müntzer with the sword of Gideon.

26. Luther's Admonition to Peace (April 1525)

From *LW* 46:19–43, trans. Charles M. Jacobs and Robert C. Schultz; cf. WA 18:279–34.

TO THE PRINCES AND LORDS

We have no one on earth to thank for this disastrous rebellion, except you princes and lords and especially you blind bishops and mad priests and monks, whose hearts are hardened even to the present day. You do not cease to rant and rave against the holy gospel, even though you know that it is true and that you cannot refute it. In addition, as temporal rulers you do nothing but cheat and rob the people so that you may lead a life of luxury and extravagance. The poor common people cannot bear it any longer. The sword is already at your throats, but you think that you sit so firm in the saddle that no one can unhorse you. This false security and stubborn perversity will break your necks, as you will discover. . . .

A great part of God's wrath has already come, for God is sending many false teachers and prophets among us, so that through our error and blasphemy we may richly deserve hell and everlasting damnation. The rest of it is now here, for the peasants are banding together, and, unless our repentance moves God to prevent it, this must result in the ruin, destruction, and desolation of Germany by cruel murder and bloodshed. . . .

To make your sin still greater and guarantee your merciless destruction, some of you are beginning to blame this affair on the gospel and say that it is the fruit of my teaching. Well, well, slander away, dear lords! You did not want to know what I taught or what the gospel is; now the one who will soon teach you is at the door, unless you change your ways. You, and everyone else, must bear witness that I have taught with all quietness, have striven earnestly against rebellion, and have energetically encouraged and exhorted people to obey and respect even you wild and dictatorial tyrants. This rebellion cannot be coming from me. Rather the murder-prophets, who hate me as they hate you, have come among these people and have gone about among them for more than three years, and no one has resisted and fought against them except me. . . .

If it is possible to give you advice, my lords, give way a little to the will and wrath of God. A cartload of hay must give way to a drunken man—how much more ought you to stop your raging and obstinate tyranny and not deal unreasonably with the peasants, as though they were drunk or out of their minds! Do not start a fight with them, for you do not know how it will end. Try kindness first, for you do not know what God will do to prevent the spark that will kindle all Germany and start a fire that no one can extinguish. . . .

TO THE PEASANTS

. . . You say that the rulers are wicked and intolerable, for they will not allow us to have the gospel; they oppress us too hard with the burdens they lay on our property, and they are ruining us in body and soul. I answer: The fact that the rulers are wicked and unjust does not excuse disorder and rebellion, for the punishing of wickedness is not the responsibility of everyone, but of the worldly rulers who bear the sword. Thus Paul says in Romans 13[:4] and Peter in 1 Peter 3 [2:14], that the rulers are instituted by God for the punishment of the wicked. Then, too, there is the natural law of all the world, which says that no one may sit as judge in his own case or take his own revenge. The proverb is true, "Whoever hits back is in the wrong." Or as it is said, "It takes two to start a fight." The divine law agrees with this, and says, in Deuteronomy 32[:35], "Vengeance is mine; I will repay, says the Lord." Now you cannot deny that your rebellion actually involves you in such a way that you make yourselves your own judges and avenge yourselves. You are quite unwilling to suffer any wrong. That is contrary not only to Christian law and the gospel, but also to natural law and all equity. . . .

Be careful, therefore, with your liberty, that you do not run away from the rain and fall in the water. Beware of the illusion that you are winning freedom for your body when you are really losing your body, property, and soul for all eternity. God's wrath is there; fear it, I advise you! The devil has sent false prophets among you; beware of them! . . .

Listen, then, dear Christians, to your Christian law! Your Supreme Lord Christ, whose name you bear, says in Matthew 6 [5:39-41], "Do not resist one who is evil. If anyone forces you to go one mile, go with him two miles. If anyone wants to take your coat, let him have your cloak too. If anyone strikes you on one cheek, offer him the other too." Do you hear this, O Christian association? How does your program stand in light of this law? You do not want to endure evil or suffering, but rather want to be free and experience only goodness and justice. However, Christ says that you should not resist evil or injustice but always yield, suffer, and let things be taken from us. If you will not bear this law, then lay aside the name of Christian and claim another name that accords with your actions, or else Christ himself will tear his name away from you, and that will be too hard for you. . . .

I have never drawn a sword or desired revenge. I began neither conspiracy nor rebellion, but so far as I was able, I have helped the worldly rulers—even those who persecuted the gospel and me—to preserve their power and honor. I stopped with committing the matter to God and relying confidently at all times upon his hand. This is why God has not only preserved my life in spite of the pope and all the tyrants—and this many consider a really great miracle, as I myself must also confess—but he has made my gospel grow and spread. Now you interfere with what I am doing. You want to help the gospel and yet you do not see that what you are doing hinders and suppresses it most effectively. . . .

I shall pray for you, that God may enlighten you and resist your undertaking and not let it succeed. For I see well that the devil, who has not been able to destroy me through the pope, now seeks to exterminate me and swallow me up by means of the bloodthirsty prophets of murder and spirits of rebellion that are among you. Well, let him swallow me! I will give him a bellyful, I know. And even if you win, you will hardly enjoy it. I beg you, humbly and kindly, to think things over so that I will not have to trust in and pray to God against you. . . .

ADMONITION TO BOTH RULERS AND PEASANTS

. . . As I see it, the worst thing about this completely miserable affair is that both sides will sustain irreparable damage; and I would gladly risk my life and even die if I could prevent that from happening. . . .

I, therefore, sincerely advise you to choose certain counts and lords from among the nobility and certain councilmen from the cities and ask them to arbitrate and settle this dispute amicably. You lords, stop being so stubborn! You will finally have to stop being oppressive tyrants—whether you want to or not. Give these poor people room in which to live and air to breathe. You peasants, let yourselves be instructed and give up the excessive demands of your articles. In this way it may be possible to reach a solution of this dispute through human laws and agreements, if not through Christian means.

If you do not follow this advice—God forbid!—I must let you come to blows. But I am innocent of your souls, your blood, or your property. The guilt is yours alone. I have told you that you are both wrong and that what you are fighting for is wrong. . . .

✠   ✠   ✠

27. Luther: Against the Robbing and Murdering Hordes of Peasants (May 1525)

From *LW* 46:49–55, trans. Charles M. Jacobs and Robert C. Schultz; cf. WA 18:344f.

In my earlier book on this matter, I did not venture to judge the peasants, since they had offered to be corrected and to be instructed; and Christ in Matthew 7[:1] commands us not to judge. But before I could even inspect the situation, they forgot their promise and violently took matters into their own hands and are robbing and raging like mad dogs. All this now makes it clear that they are trying to deceive us and that the assertions they made in their Twelve Articles were nothing but lies presented under the name of the gospel. To put it briefly, they are doing the devil's work. . . .

The peasants have taken upon themselves the burden of three terrible sins against God and man; by this they have abundantly merited death in body and soul. In the first place, they have sworn to be true and faithful, submissive and obedient to their rulers, as Christ commands when he says, "Render to Caesar the things that are Caesar's" [Luke 20:25]. . . . In the second place, they are starting a rebellion and are violently robbing and plundering monasteries and castles that are not theirs; by this they have doubly deserved death in body and soul as highwaymen and murderers. . . . In the third place, they cloak this terrible and horrible sin with the gospel, call themselves "Christian brethren," take oaths and submit to them, and compel people to go along with them in these abominations. Thus they become the worst blasphemers of God and slanderers of his holy name. Under the outward appearance of the gospel, they honor and serve the devil, thus deserving death in body

and soul ten times over. I have never heard of a more hideous sin. I suspect that the devil feels that the Last Day is coming and therefore he undertakes such an unheard-of act, as though saying to himself, "This is the end, therefore, it shall be the worst; I will stir up the dregs and knock out the bottom." God will guard us against him! See what a mighty prince the devil is, how he has the world in his hands and can throw everything into confusion, when he can so quickly catch so many thousands of peasants, deceive them, blind them, harden them, and throw them into revolt, and do with them whatever his raging fury undertakes. . . .

Now since the peasants have brought [the wrath] of God and man down upon themselves and are already many times guilty of death in body and soul, and since they submit to no court and wait for no verdict, but only rage on, I must instruct the temporal authorities on how they may act with a clear conscience in this matter.

First, I will not oppose a ruler who, even though he does not tolerate the gospel, will smite and punish these peasants without first offering to submit the case to judgment. He is within his rights, since the peasants are not contending any longer for the gospel, but have become faithless, perjured, disobedient, rebellious murderers, robbers, and blasphemers, whom even a heathen ruler has the right and authority to punish. Indeed, it is his duty to punish such scoundrels, for this is why he bears the sword and is "the servant of God to execute his wrath on the wrongdoer," Romans 13[:4]. . . .

Let whoever can stab, smite, slay. If you die in doing it, good for you! A more blessed death can never be yours, for you die while obeying the divine word and commandment in Romans 13[:1, 2], and in loving service of your neighbor, whom you are rescuing from the bonds of hell and of the devil. And so I beg everyone who can to flee from the peasants as from the devil himself; those who do not flee, I pray that God will enlighten and convert. As for those who are not to be converted, God grant that they may have neither fortune nor success. To this let every pious Christian say, "Amen!" for this prayer is right and good and pleases God; this I know. If anyone thinks this is too harsh, let him remember that rebellion is intolerable and that the destruction of the world is to be expected every hour.

The Conflict with Erasmus

28. Luther: Defense and Explanation of the Condemned Articles (March 1521)

Luther wrote Latin and German treatises in response to the charges against him listed in the papal bull *Exsurge Domine* (doc. #14). The following excerpt on free will is from the German treatise.

From *LW* 32:92–94, trans. Charles Jacobs, rev. George Forell.

The Thirty-Sixth Article

Since the fall of Adam, or after actual sin, free will exists only in name, and when it does what it can it commits sin.

. . . St. Augustine says in his work *On the Spirit and the Letter,* chapter 4, "The free will, without God's grace, can do nothing but sin." What do you say now, pope? Is it freedom to be without power to do anything but evil? You might as well say that a lame man walks straight, though he can only limp and never walk straight. It is just as if I were to call the pope "most holy," though St. Paul calls him a "man of sin and son of perdition" [2 Thess. 2:3], and Christ calls him "the desolating sacri-

lege" [Matt. 24:15], the head of all sin and destruction. The papists have so distorted the meaning of words that they have created a new language and confused everything, just like the builders of the tower of Babel. Now "white" is called "black," and "black," "white," to the unspeakable damage of Christendom. . . .

It is a profound and blind error to teach that the will is by nature free and can, without grace, turn to the spirit, seek grace, and desire it. Actually, the will tries to escape from grace and rages against it when it is present. Whose reason is not shocked to think that although spirit and flesh are the two greatest enemies, yet the flesh is supposed to desire and seek its enemy, the spirit? Surely, every man knows from his own experience how all his powers fight against grace in order to expel and destroy it. My opponents' position suggests that when nobody can control a wild and ravenous beast with chains, you let it go free, and it will chain itself and go into captivity of its own accord. . . .

For this reason I would wish that the words "free will" had never been invented. They are not found in Scripture and would better be called "self will," which is of no use. But if anyone wishes to retain these words, he ought to apply them to the newly created man, so as to understand by them the man who is without sin. He is truly free, as was Adam in Paradise, and it is of him that Scripture speaks when it deals with our freedom. But those who are involved in sins are not free, but prisoners of the devil. Since they may become free through grace you can call them men of free will, just as you might call a man rich, although he is a beggar because he can become rich. But it is neither right nor good to play tricks with words in matters of such great importance. . . .

29. Erasmus: Diatribe on the Freedom of the Will (September 1524)

The following two excerpts reveal both the different temperaments of the two figures in this debate and the differences in their theological beliefs.

From E. Gordon Rupp and A. N. Marlow, *Luther and Erasmus: Free Will and Salvation* (LCC 17; Philadelphia: Westminster, 1969).

. . . I have never sworn allegiance to the words of Luther. So that it should not seem unbecoming to anybody if at any point I differ publicly from him, as a man surely may differ from another man, nor should it seem a criminal offense to call in question any doctrine of his, still less if one engages in a temperate disputation with him for the purpose of eliciting truth. . . .

To be sure, I know that I was not built for wrestling matches: there is surely nobody less practiced in this kind of thing than I, who have always had an inner temperamental horror of fighting and who have always preferred to sport in the wider plains of the Muses rather than to brandish a sword in a hand-to-hand fight.

And, in fact, so far am I from delighting in "assertions" that I would readily take refuge in the opinion of the skeptics, wherever this is allowed by the inviolable authority of the Holy Scriptures and by the decrees of the church, to which I everywhere willingly submit my personal feelings, whether I grasp what it prescribes or not. . . .

As far as I am concerned, I admit that many different views about free choice have been handed down from the ancients about which I have, as yet, no fixed conviction, except that I think there to be a certain power of free choice. For I have read the Assertion of Martin Luther, and read it without prejudice, except that I

have assumed a certain favor toward him, as an investigator may toward an arraigned prisoner. And yet, although he expounds his case in all its aspects with great ingenuity and fervor of spirit, I must say, quite frankly, that he has not persuaded me. . . .

Even though I believe myself to have mastered Luther's argument, yet I might well be mistaken, and for that reason I play the debater, not the judge; the inquirer, not the dogmatist, ready to learn from anyone if anything truer or more scholarly can be brought. Yet I would willingly persuade the man in the street that in this kind of discussion it is better not to enforce contentions that may the sooner harm Christian concord than advance true religion.

For there are some secret places in the Holy Scriptures into which God has not wished us to penetrate more deeply and, if we try to do so, then the deeper we go, the darker and darker it becomes, by which we are led to acknowledge the unsearchable majesty of the divine wisdom, and the weakness of the human mind. . . .

Therefore, in my judgment on this matter of free choice, having learned what is needful to know about this, if we are in the path of true religion, let us go on swiftly to better things, forgetful of the things that are behind, or if we are entangled in sins, let us strive with all our might and have recourse to the remedy of penitence that by all means we may entreat the mercy of the Lord without which no human will or endeavor is effective; and what is evil in us, let us impute to ourselves, and what is good, let us ascribe wholly to divine benevolence, to which we owe our very being, and for the rest, whatever befalls us in this life, whether it be joyful or sad, let us believe it to be sent by him for our salvation, and that no harm can come to us from a God who is by nature just, even if some things happen that seem to us amiss, for none ought to despair of the pardon of a God who is by nature most merciful. This, I say, was in my judgment sufficient for Christian godliness, nor should we through irreverent inquisitiveness rush into those things that are hidden, not to say superfluous: whether God foreknows anything contingently; whether our will accomplishes anything in things pertaining to eternal salvation; whether it simply suffers the action of grace; whether what we do, be it of good or ill, we do by necessity or rather suffer to be done to us. . . .

When I hear that the merit of man is so utterly worthless that all things, even the works of godly men, are sins, when I hear that our will does nothing more than clay in the hands of a potter, when I hear all that we do or will referred to absolute necessity, my mind encounters many a stumbling block. First, why does one so often read that godly men, full of good works, have wrought righteousness and walked in the presence of God, turning neither to the right nor to the left, if the deeds of even the most godly men are sins, and sin of such character that, did the mercy of God not intervene, it would have plunged into hell even him for whom Christ died? How is it that we hear so much about reward if there is no such thing as merit? With what impudence is the obedience of those who obey the divine commands praised, and the disobedience of those who do not obey condemned? Why is there so frequent mention of judgment in Holy Scriptures if there is no weighing of merits? Or are we compelled to be present at the Judgment Seat if nothing has happened through our own will, but all things have been done in us by sheer necessity? There is the further objection: What is the point of so many admonitions, so many precepts, so many threats, so many exhortations, so many expostulations, if of ourselves we do nothing, but God in accordance with his immutable will does everything in us, both to will and to perform the same? He wishes us to pray without ceasing, to watch, to fight, to contend for the

prize of eternal life. Why does he wish anything to be unceasingly prayed for which he has already decreed either to give or not to give, and cannot change his decrees, since he is immutable? Why does he command us to seek with so many labors what he has decided freely to bestow? . . . But I know not how they are to appear consistent who so exaggerate the mercy of God to the godly that as regards others they almost make him cruel. Pious ears can admit the benevolence of one who imputes his own good to us, but it is difficult to explain how it can be a mark of his justice (for I will not speak of his mercy) to hand over others to eternal torments in whom he has not deigned to work good works, when they themselves are incapable of doing good, since they have no free choice or, if they have, it can do nothing but sin. . . .

In my opinion free choice could have been so established as to avoid that confidence in our merits and the other dangers that Luther avoids, . . . and without losing those benefits that Luther admires. . . .

Let us try to express our meaning in a parable. . . . A father lifts up a child who has fallen and has not yet strength to walk, however much it tries, and shows it an apple that lies over against it; the child longs to run, but on account of the weakness of its limbs it would have fallen had not its father held its hand and steadied its footsteps, so that led by its father it obtains the apple, which the father willingly puts in its hand as a reward for running. The child could not have stood up if the father had not lifted it, could not have seen the apple had the father not shown it, could not advance unless the father had all the time assisted its feeble steps, could not grasp the apple had the father not put it into his hand. What, then, can the infant claim for itself? And yet it does something. . . .

30. Luther: The Bondage of the Will (December 1525)

Luther's response was four times the length of Erasmus's original treatise. Luther always considered this one of the best books he ever wrote.

From *LW* 33:19–140, trans. Philip Watson and Benjamin Drewery.

I want to begin by referring to some passages in your Preface, in which you rather disparage our case and puff up your own. I note, first, that just as in other books you censure me for obstinate assertiveness, so in this book you say that you are so far from delighting in assertions that you would readily take refuge in the opinion of the Skeptics wherever this is allowed by the inviolable authority of the Holy Scriptures and the decrees of the Church, to which you always willingly submit your personal feelings, whether you grasp what it prescribes or not. This [you say] is the frame of mind that pleases you.

I take it (as it is only fair to do) that you say these things in a kindly and peace-loving spirit. But if anyone else were to say them, I should probably go for him in my usual manner, and I ought not to allow even you, excellent though your intentions are, to be led astray by this idea. For it is not the mark of a Christian mind to take no delight in assertions; on the contrary, a man must delight in assertions or he will be no Christian. . . .

This is how a Christian will rather speak: So far am I from delighting in the opinion of the Skeptics that, whenever the infirmity of the flesh will permit, I will not only consistently adhere to and assert the sacred writings, everywhere and in all parts of them, but I will also wish to be as certain as possible in things that are not vital and that lie outside of Scripture. For what is more miserable than uncertainty? . . .

I come now to the second passage, which is of a piece with this. Here you distinguish between Christian dogmas, pretending that there are some that it is necessary to know, and some that it is not, and you say that some are [meant to be] obscure and others quite plain. . . .

It is true that for many people much remains abstruse, but this is not due to the obscurity of Scripture, but to the blindness or indolence of those who will not take the trouble to look at the very clearest truth. . . .

It is, you say, irreverent, inquisitive, and superfluous to want to know whether our will does anything in matters pertaining to eternal salvation or whether it is simply passive under the action of grace. Yet now you contradict this by saying that Christian godliness means striving with all one's powers and that without the mercy of God the will is not effective. Here you plainly assert that the will does something in matters pertaining to eternal salvation, when you represent it as striving, though you make it passive when you say it is ineffective apart from mercy. You do not, however, state precisely how this activity and passivity are to be understood, for you take good care to keep us in ignorance of what God's mercy and our will can achieve, even while you are telling us what they actually do. Thus the prudence of yours makes you veer about, determined not to commit yourself to either side, but to pass safely between Scylla and Charybdis; with the result that, finding yourself battered and buffeted by the waves in the midst of the sea, you assert everything you deny and deny everything you assert. . . .

You make the power of free choice very slight and of a kind that is entirely ineffective apart from the grace of God. Do you not agree? Now I ask you, if the grace of God is absent or separated from it, what can that very slight power do of itself? It is ineffective, you say, and does nothing good. Then it cannot do what

God or his grace wills, at any rate if we suppose the grace of God to be separated from it. But what the grace of God does not do is not good. Hence it follows that free choice without the grace of God is not free at all, but immutably the captive and slave of evil, since it cannot of itself turn to the good. . . .

But if we are unwilling to let this term go altogether—though that would be the safest and most God-fearing thing to do—let us at least teach men to use it honestly, so that free choice is allowed to man only with respect to what is beneath him and not what is above him. That is to say, a man should know that with regard to his faculties and possessions he has the right to use, to do, or to leave undone, according to his own free choice, though even this is controlled by the free choice of God alone, who acts in whatever way he pleases. On the other hand in relation to God, or in matters pertaining to salvation or damnation, a man has no free choice, but is a captive, subject and slave either of the will of God or the will of Satan. . . .

It is an evangelical word and the sweetest comfort in every way for miserable sinners, where Ezekiel [18:23, 32] says: "I desire not the death of a sinner, but rather that he may turn and live," like Psalm 28 [30:5]: "For his anger is but for a moment and his favor is for a lifetime." But just as free choice is not proved by other words of mercy or promise or comfort, so neither is it proved by this one: "I desire not the death of a sinner," etc.

This word, therefore, "I desire not the death of a sinner," has as you see no other object than the preaching and offering of divine mercy throughout the world, a mercy that only the afflicted and those tormented by the fear of death receive with joy and gratitude, because in them the law has already fulfilled its office and brought the knowledge of sin. Those, however, who have not yet experienced the office of the law and neither recognize sin nor feel death have no use for the mercy promised by that word. But why some are touched by the law and others are not, so that the former accept and the latter despise the offered grace, is another question and one not dealt with by Ezekiel in this passage. For he is here speaking of the preached and offered mercy of God, not of the hidden and awful will of God whereby he ordains by his own counsel which and what sort of persons he wills to be recipients and partakers of his preached and offered mercy. . . .

Diatribe [Erasmus's book], however, deceives herself in her ignorance by not making any distinction between God preached and God hidden, that is, between the Word of God and God himself. God does many things that he does not disclose to us in his Word; he also wills many things that he does not disclose himself as willing in his Word. Thus he does not will the death of a sinner, according to his word, but he wills it according to that inscrutable will of his. It is our business, however, to pay attention to the Word and leave that inscrutable will alone, for we must be guided by the Word and not by that inscrutable will. After all, who can direct himself by a will completely inscrutable and unknowable? It is enough to know simply that there is a certain inscrutable will in God, and as to what, why, and how far it wills, that is something we have no right whatever to inquire into, hanker after, care about, or meddle with, but only to fear and adore.

It is therefore right to say, "If God does not desire our death, the fact that we perish must be imputed to our own will." It is right, I mean, if you speak of God as preached; for he wills all men to be saved [1 Tim. 2:4], seeing he comes with the word of salvation to all, and the fault is in the will that does not admit him, as he says in Matthew 23[:37]: "How often would

I have gathered your children, and you would not!" But why that majesty of his does not remove or change this defect of our will in all men, since it is not in man's power to do so, or why he imputes this defect to man, when man cannot help having it, we have no right to inquire; and though you may do a lot of inquiring, you will never find out. . . .

THE SACRAMENTARIAN CONTROVERSY

31. Luther: The Babylonian Captivity of the Church (October 1520)

This long treatise addressed issues of theology and practice related to all of the seven traditional sacraments. This excerpt notes the three major problems that Luther associated with the medieval Catholic view of the Lord's Supper.

From *LW* 36:20–49, trans. A. T. W. Steinhaeuser, rev. Frederick Ahrens and Abdel Wentz; cf. WA 6:497–573.

. . . [The first captivity of the sacrament of the Lord's Supper: the withholding of the cup from the laity]

Christ gave the whole sacrament to all his disciples. That Paul delivered both kinds is so certain that no one has ever had the temerity to say otherwise. Add to this that Matthew [26:27] reports that Christ did not say of the bread, "eat of it, all of you," but of the cup, "drink of it all of you." . . . The sacrament does not belong to the priests but to all men. The priests are not lords but servants in duty bound to administer both kinds to those who desire them, as often as they desire them. . . .

[The second captivity of this sacrament: the doctrine of transubstantiation]

. . . My one concern at present is to remove all scruples of conscience, so that no one may fear being called a heretic if he believes that real bread and real wine are present on the altar, and that every one may feel at liberty to ponder, hold, and believe either one view or the other without endangering his salvation. However, I shall now set forth my own view. . . .

[W]hat is true in regard to Christ is also true in regard to the sacrament. In order for the divine nature to dwell in him bodily [Col. 2:9], it is not necessary for the human nature to be transubstantiated and the divine nature contained under the accidents of the human nature. Both natures are simply there in their entirety, and it is truly said: "This man is God, this God is man." Even though philosophy cannot grasp this, faith grasps it nonetheless. And the authority of God's Word is greater than the capacity of our intellect to grasp it. In like manner, it is not necessary in the sacrament that the bread and the wine be transubstantiated and that Christ be contained under their accidents in order that the real body and real blood may be present. But both remain there at the same time, and it is truly said: "This bread is my body, this wine is my blood," and vice versa. . . .

[The third captivity of this sacrament: viewing the mass as a good work and a sacrifice]

. . . What we call the mass is a promise of the forgiveness of sins made to us by God, and such a promise as has been confirmed by the death of the Son of God. . . . If the mass is a promise, as has been said, then access to it is to be gained not with any works, or powers, or merits of one's own, but by faith alone. . . . By them we have been carried away out of our own land as into a Babylonian captivity and despoiled of all our precious possessions. This has been the fate of the mass: it has been converted by the teaching of godless men into a good work. They themselves call it an *opus operatum,* and by it they presume themselves to be all-powerful with God. . . . It is a manifest and wicked error to offer or apply the mass for sins, for satisfactions, for the dead, or for any needs whatsoever of one's own or of others. . . . Each one can derive personal benefit from the mass only by his own personal faith. It is absolutely impossible to commune on behalf of anyone else. . . .

32. Luther: The Adoration of the Sacrament (April 1523)

From *LW* 36:276–84, trans. Abdel Wentz; cf. WA 11:417–56.

. . . In the first place, there have been some who have held that in the sacrament there is merely bread and wine, such as people otherwise eat and drink. They have taught nothing more than that the bread signifies the body and the wine signifies the blood of Christ, just as if one were to take a figure from the Old Testament and say: the bread from heaven that the Jews ate in the wilderness *signifies* the body of Christ or the gospel, but the bread from heaven *is* not the gospel or the body of Christ. . . .

Now beware of such a view. Let go of reason and intellect; for they strive in vain to understand how flesh and blood can be present, and because they do not grasp it they refuse to believe it. Lay hold on the word that Christ speaks: "Take, this is my body, this is my blood." One must not do such violence to the words of God as to give to any word a meaning other than its natural one, unless there is clear and definite Scripture to do that. This is what is done by those who without any basis in Scripture take the word "is" and forcibly twist it to mean the same as the word "signifies."

They sneer at Christ's statement: "This is my body," and say it is equivalent to: "This signifies my body," and so forth. But we should and will simply stick to the words of Christ—he will not deceive us—and repel this error with no other sword than the fact that Christ does not say: "This signifies my body," but "This is my body." . . .

The second error involves the perversion also of the two phrases "my body" and "my blood." Indeed, it gives the whole passage a different meaning. It does this by claiming that when Christ says: "This is my body," he means: If you take this bread and wine, you will have a share in my body. Thus the sacrament is nothing else than a participation in the body of Christ, or, better, an incorporation into his spiritual body. To implement this process of incorporation he presumably instituted this bread and wine, as a sure sign that the spiritual incorporation is taking place and that the spiritual body is being realized. This is a clever sophistry. It is based on the fact that the Scriptures ascribe to Christ two kinds of body: one a natural body, which is born physically of Mary, just as all other men have bodies; the other a spiritual body, which is the whole Christian church, of which Christ is the head—just as husband and wife are one body and the husband is the head of the wife, of which Paul writes in Romans 12[:5] and in 1 Corinthians 12[:27] and in many other passages. . . .

Since, therefore, the words of Christ "This is my body that is given for you" stand so clearly in the way and so directly contradict such an interpretation, we should by no means follow this understanding of the sacrament. For even Paul himself, after he has spoken in the tenth chapter [1 Cor. 10:16] about the participation in the body, nevertheless in the eleventh chapter [1 Cor. 11:23-24] comes back to the words and speaks just as Christ himself spoke, and says: "I have delivered to you what I have received, that the Lord Jesus on the night when he was betrayed took bread, gave thanks, broke it, and said: 'Take and eat, this is my body that is given for you; do this in remembrance of me.'" Here the words are plain and clear, that it is not the spiritual body of Christ that is present, but his natural body. . . .

33. Luther: The Sacrament of the Body and Blood of Christ—Against the Fanatics (1526)

From *LW* 36:336–41, trans. Frederick Ahrens; cf. WA 19:471–523.

. . . If anyone wishes to pursue a true course and not come to grief, let him beware of the clever idea, inspired by the devil in this matter everywhere, that he may suck the egg dry and leave us the shell, that is, remove the body and blood of Christ from the bread and wine, so that it remains no more than mere bread, such as the baker bakes. In accordance with this clever idea our opponents mock us at their pleasure, charging that we are eaters of flesh and drinkers of blood and that we worship a baked God. . . . Such are the tricks that the devil is playing against us nowadays everywhere.

Now God is the sort of person who likes to do what is foolish and useless in the eyes of the world, as Paul says in 1 Corinthians 1[:23]: "We preach Christ crucified, a stumbling block to the Jews and folly to the Gentiles." And again: "For since, in the wisdom of God, the world did not know God through wisdom, it pleased God through the folly of what we preach to save those who believe in him" [1 Cor. 1:21]. Well then, if anyone does not believe this, let him believe accordingly that it is mere bread or a batch of bread. Anyone who has failed to grasp the faith may thenceforth believe whatever he likes; it makes no difference. Just as

when someone is on the point of drowning, whether he drowns in a brook or in the middle of a stream, he is drowned just the same. So I say of these fanatics: if they let go of the word, let them believe whatever they like and squabble as long as they like. It has already happened that six or seven sects have arisen over the sacrament, but all of them under the delusion that Christ's flesh and blood are not present. . . .

Again, I preach the gospel of Christ, and with my bodily voice I bring Christ into your heart, so that you may form him within yourself. If now you truly believe, so that your heart lays hold of the word and holds fast within it that voice, tell me, what have you in your heart? You must answer that you have the true Christ, not that he sits in there, as one sits on a chair, but as he is at the right hand of the Father. How that comes about you cannot know, but your heart truly feels his presence, and through the experience of faith you know for a certainty that he is there. . . .

But what happens when I bring Christ into the heart? Does it come about, as the fanatics imagine, that Christ descends on a ladder and climbs back up again? Christ still sits on the right hand of the Father and also in your heart, the one Christ who fills heaven and earth. I preach that he sits on the right hand of God and rules over all creatures, sin, death, life, world, devils, and angels; if you believe this, you already have him in your heart. Therefore your heart is in heaven, not in an apparition or dream, but truly. For where he is, there you are also. So he dwells and sits in your heart, yet he does not fall from the right hand of God. Christians experience and feel this clearly. But those people see none of these things, great as it is that Christ dwells thus in the heart and imparts himself completely in every heart and is distributed through the Word. Therefore, whoever can believe this does not find it difficult to believe also that his body and blood are in the sacrament. For if you try in this way to measure

Martin Luther Serving Communion

that wondrous sign with the measuring-rod of thought and reason, you will at last reach the point where you must also say that Christ does not dwell in the hearts of the faithful. . . .

34. Zwingli: Friendly Exegesis—That Is, Exposition of the Matter of the Eucharist to Martin Luther (February 1527)

From *Zwingli's Writings*, vol. 2, ed. E. J. Furcha, trans. H. Preble, rev. W. Pipkin (Allison Park, Pa.: Pickwick, 1984), 333–41.

. . . We know that you would show him (Christ) in the bread, but Scripture does not support you. Prove, therefore, by unequivocal passages of Scripture that he is in the bread, as we do that he is in heaven. And that the human side of Christ (that we may not maintain anything not perfectly supported by Scripture) is so circumscribed or situated that it must be in one place only, we prove this: Christ himself has circumscribed his body in very many passages, not a few of which I have already cited, first by its going away or sitting at the right hand, and he has done it so thor-

oughly that no teacher could by any philosophy better show that it was circumscribed. Second, Christ has also made manifest where he is to be until the day of universal judgment, and has nowhere hinted that he should have his place anywhere else than where he has shown he will be. . . .

Third, we prove that Christ's body is finite and circumscribed because it even rose from the dead, as the angel said to the women, "You see Jesus the crucified. He is risen; he is not here" [Matt. 28:6]. On this passage enough has been said above. Nor can we say that he is by turns sometimes everywhere, sometimes not, for the infinite cannot draw itself together so as not to be infinite and then spread itself out so as to be infinite again. Fourth, all the appearances by which he manifested himself after the resurrection prove our point. Raised from the dead, he determined to present himself in visible and tangible shape to his disciples, but he never appeared thus in different places at once, as we may see in the last chapter of Luke [24], in John 20, and in 1 Corinthians 15, where we read that all his appearances took place in a successive series. And what is written in the last chapter of John, how he stood upon the shore when the disciples had been drawing an empty net all night even unto the dawn, is a mark of circumscription. Fifth, passages like "Where I am, there shall my servant be also" point to the same conclusion. If they are where he is, in virtue of his humanity, namely, then, as they are circumscribed, so must he also be circumscribed. . . .

He uses these words, "I go away, I leave the world, I shall now not be in the world." So too the apostles: "He was parted from them"; "While they beheld, he was taken up"; "A cloud received him out of their sights"; "He was received up into heaven"; "He sits at the right hand." What will be sacred among us, my dear Luther, if we do violence to these words? . . .

[To clarify the issues further, Zwingli makes a point by point contrast of his view and Luther's:]

LUTHER: We must believe that the body of Christ is eaten here. They that believe do thereby eat.

ZWINGLI: . . . In saying we must believe that it is eaten here because the words say so, they sin twice: they bid us understand words wrongly that they have not understood, and without authorization they set up for our belief what we have nowhere been directed to believe. For we have nowhere been taught to believe that the body of Christ is to be eaten in a bodily sense, however much Christ must be eaten, that is, must have our trust put in him. Strange how they *ekperdikizosi* ("flutter away like partridges") from what is taught in John 6 under the figurative form of eating the body. May the Lord give them knowledge of himself and of themselves. Amen. . . .

35. Luther: Confession concerning Christ's Supper (March 1528)

From *LW* 37:206–23, trans. Robert H. Fischer; cf. WA 26:240–509.

. . . Whoever will take a warning, let him beware of Zwingli and shun his books as the prince of hell's poison. For the man is completely perverted and has entirely lost Christ. Other sacramentarians settle on one error, but this man never publishes a book without spewing out new errors, more and more all the time. But anyone who rejects this warning may go his way, just so he knows that I warned him, and my conscience is clear. . . .

If they prove conclusively that God's power and wisdom extends no farther than the range of our sight, and that he is able to do no more than we can physically see and judge with our eyes or touch with our fingers, then you should join their side. Then I too will believe that God

knows of no other way whereby Christ can be at the same time in heaven and his body in the Supper. Demand and insist on this. They are bound to do it. Their teachings cannot be established until they have made this clear and certain, for on this their teaching rests. . . .

Again, since they do not prove that the right hand of God is a particular place in heaven, the mode of existence of which I have spoken also stands firm, that Christ's body is everywhere because it is at the right hand of God, which is everywhere, although we do not know how that occurs. For we also do not know how it occurs that the right hand of God is everywhere. It is certainly not a mode by which we see with our eyes that an object is somewhere, as the fanatics regard the sacrament. But God no doubt has a mode by which it can be somewhere, and that's the way it is until the fanatics prove the contrary. . . .

My grounds, on which I rest in this matter, are as follows: The first is this article of our faith, that Jesus Christ is essential, natural, true, complete God and man in one person, undivided and inseparable. The second, that the right hand of God is everywhere. The third, that the Word of God is not false or deceitful. The fourth, that God has and knows various ways to be present at a certain place, not only the single one of which the fanatics prattle, which the philosophers call "local." . . .

Because we prove from Scripture, however, that Christ's body can exist in a given place in other modes than his corporeal one, we have by the same token sufficiently argued that the words "This is my body" ought to be believed as they read. For it is contrary to no article of faith, and moreover it is scriptural, in that Christ's body is held to have passed through the sealed stone and the closed door. Since we can point out a mode of existence other than the corporeal, circumscribed one, who will be so bold as to measure and span the power of

Ulrich Zwingli

God, as if he knows of no other modes? Yet the position of the fanatics cannot be maintained unless they can prove that the power of God can be measured and spanned, for their whole argument rests on the assertion that the body of Christ can exist in a given place only in a corporeal and circumscribed manner. . . .

And now to come to my own position: Our faith maintains that Christ is God and man, and the two natures are one person, so that this person may not be divided in two; therefore, he can surely show himself in a corporeal, circumscribed manner at whatever place he will, as he did after the resurrection and will do on the Last Day. But above and beyond this mode he can also use the second, uncircumscribed mode, as we have proved from the gospel, that he did at the grave and the closed door.

. . . The one body of Christ has a threefold existence, or all three modes of being at any given place. First, the circumscribed corporeal mode of presence, as when he walked bodily on earth, when he occupied and yielded space according to his size. . . . Second, the uncircumscribed, spiritual mode of presence according to which he neither occupies nor yields space but passes through everything created as he wills. . . . Third, since he is one person with God, the divine, heavenly mode, according to

which all created things are indeed much more permeable and present to him than they are according to the second mode.

36. The Marburg Colloquy (1529)

From *Great Debates of the Reformation*, trans. Donald Ziegler (New York: Random House, 1969), 93–94, 97–98.

OECOLAMPADIUS: Every body can only be in one place, confined within limits.

LUTHER: Mathematical hairsplitting I will not listen to. God—this even the Aristotelians grant—can make a body be in one place alone or in several places at the same time or in no place at all, and he can make several be in one place at the same time. Therefore I wish to avoid distressing argumentation about whether the presence is real or not. This is no concern of mine. It is not arguments of this nature, based upon reason, but scriptural passages of clarity and certainty that are called for. Nevertheless, if everybody wants this, I shall argue mathematics into the ground with you at the appointed time. I have already declared, however, that such argumentation will contribute nothing to this question. Here it is scriptural evidence that is needed. . . .

ZWINGLI: We speak too of a "sacramental" presence of the body of Christ, and by this we mean that the body of Christ is "represented" in the Lord's Supper.

LUTHER: You seek to describe a continuous presence of Christ's body in such a way as to remove the substance of the body from the bread, leaving us merely the empty form, even though the words of Christ read quite differently: "This is my body."

ZWINGLI: Oecolampadius and I further grant that God can of course make a body be in different places. But that he does this in the Lord's Supper, this is what we want proved. The Holy Scriptures always show us Christ in one particular place, as in the manger, in the temple, in the desert, on the cross, in the tomb, at the right hand of the Father. For this reason, I believe that he must always be in one particular place.

OSIANDER: With these references one can do no more than prove that Christ was in particular places at various times. That, however, he always and eternally is, indeed must be, in one particular place or certain spot, and that he cannot be nowhere or in many places in ways that are natural and unnatural, as you say—this will never be proved by these passages.

ZWINGLI: I have proved that Christ was in one place. You prove in return that he is nowhere at all or in many places.

LUTHER: You expressed your willingness at the outset to prove that this cannot be, and that our understanding was false. It is your obligation to do this and not to demand proof of us, for we are not obligated to you.

ZWINGLI: It would be outrageous if we affirmed, taught, and defended such an important article and yet were neither able nor willing to point to a single passage of Scripture!

LUTHER (raising the tablecloth): "This is my body!" Right here is our Scripture. You haven't torn it away from us yet like you promised to do. We need none other. My esteemed lords, as long as the text of my Lord Jesus Christ is there—*Hoc est corpus meum*—then truly I cannot pass over it, but must confess and believe that Christ's body is there. . . .

Negotiations with the Emperor

37. The Imperial Proposition at the Diet of Speyer (March 15, 1529)

From *The Augsburg Confession,* trans. M. Reu (Chicago: Wartburg, 1930), 32–33.

. . . [Your] Imperial Majesty has not little grief and trouble due to the fact that in the German nation, during your reign, such evil, grave, perilous, and pernicious doctrines and errors in our holy faith have arisen and are not daily increasing more and more. Not only (though this is the most serious result) are the Christian and laudable laws, customs, and usages of the church, in consequence, brought into contempt and disgrace to the reproach and dishonor of God our Maker, but also to that of Your Imperial Majesty and the Empire. Worse still, the German nation, its estates, subjects, and allies are by these errors roused and inflamed to grievous and pitiful revolts, tumults, war, misery, and bloodshed; while the recesses of the Empire are regarded so lightly, or rather, in so many ways treated with such bold opposition and contempt, that Your Majesty is greatly displeased, and not minded (as becomes the Head of Christendom) to tolerate or permit them any longer. . . .

7. And whereas an article was included in the Recess of the Diet of Speyer in 1526, which states that "the Electors, Princes, and Estates of the Empire, and their ambassadors unanimously agreed and resolved, that while waiting for the Council, with our subjects, each one would so live, govern, and carry himself, in matters concerning the edict published by His Imperial Majesty at the Diet held at Worms, as he hopes and trusts to answer to God and His Imperial Majesty"; and whereas, from this article, as it has hitherto been understood, expounded, and explained according to their

pleasure, by several of the Estates of the Holy Empire, great trouble and misunderstanding has arisen against our holy Christian faith, as also against the Magistrates through the disobedience of their subjects, and much other disadvantage, over which Your Imperial Majesty is greatly astonished; and to the end that in the future, this article may not be interpreted by every man according to his pleasure, and that the consequences, which in the past have proved so disastrous to our holy faith, may be averted, Your Majesty hereby repeals, revokes, and annuls the article contained in the Recess mentioned above, now as then and then as now, all out of your own Imperial absolute power. . . .

38. The Protestation at the Diet of Speyer (April 19, 1529)

From _The Augsburg Confession_, trans. M. Reu, 489–90.

. . . Although we know that our ancestors, brothers, and we have at all times exercised perfect, faithful, voluntary, and eager obedience in all matters in which we owed allegiance to the Roman Emperors—the deceased as well as the now reigning Emperor—and have always sought to further His Imperial Majesty's and the Empire's glory, prosperity, and welfare and have been so eager to do this that without boasting and without minimizing the services of any others we yield first place in this respect to no one, and although we are, with God's help, henceforth till our dying day willing and ready to offer all due and possible obedience to His Imperial Roman Majesty, as our most gracious Lord, without sparing body or property, and to show all friendliness, favor, and impartiality to Your

Royal Highness and Your Honors, our dearly beloved and gracious uncles, cousins, brothers-in-law, friends, and other Estates of the Holy Empire, yet, as Your Royal Highness and Your Honors know, these are matters that concern the glory of God and that affect the salvation of each and every one of us; here we must, by the command of God and for the sake of our consciences, by virtue of our baptism and his holy divine Word, acknowledge our Lord and God as the highest King and the Lord of lords, and we confidently trust that Your Royal Highness, Your Honors, and the other Estates will kindly, graciously, and benevolently hold us excused (as we petitioned before) if we do not agree with Your Royal Highness, Your Honors, and the Others in reference to the above-mentioned article and if we do not obey the majority in this respect, because we are convinced that the former decree of Speyer, which states explicitly that it has been adopted unanimously and not only by a unanimous vote, cannot be properly and legally annulled except by a unanimous vote; furthermore, because in matters pertaining to the glory of God and the salvation of our souls, every man must himself give an answer to God for his conduct so that in this respect no man can conceal himself behind other people's acts or behind majority resolutions; and for numerous other good and well-founded reasons. . . .

(signed by the Elector of Saxony, Margrave of Brandenburg, Duke of Braunschweig-Lüneburg, the Landgrave of Hesse and the Prince of Anhalt)

39. The Secret Agreement: The Protestant Union (April 22, 1529)

From *The Augsburg Confession*, trans. M. Reu, 34-37.

Articles of agreement discussed at a gracious and secret conference that was held today by the Elector of Saxony and Philip, Landgrave of Hesse and also the aforementioned three cities of Strassburg, Nürnberg, and Ulm, for the purpose of arriving at a definite understanding. . . .

Since matters everywhere and especially at the present Diet have taken such a turn that it has become highly doubtful that peace and unity in the Empire will be furthered, therefore at the above-mentioned meeting the problem shall be discussed how and in what form in case of emergency, which God may graciously prevent, the one shall offer help and assistance to any or all of the others if, on account of the divine Word, they should be attacked, violated, or molested. . . .

In the event that the opposing party suddenly and unexpectedly attacks or invades the territory of the Elector, or the Landgrave, or both, then the cities, at their own expense, shall furnish the Elector and the Landgrave with . . . armed soldiers who may be used for defensive purposes as is necessary in the judgment of the assembled councilors.

Similarly, if one or more of the above-mentioned cities are attacked, then the said Elector and Landgrave shall, at their expense, furnish . . . mounted horsemen to be employed in the defense of the cities as noted above. . . .

It is likewise agreed that this Christian, secret union shall be in force for six years, beginning at the time of its definite acceptance, and that at the end of the fifth year, a conference shall be held in reference to the further continued existence of this union. . . .

40. Luther's Letter to Elector Johann of Saxony (May 22, 1529)

From *LW* 49:224-26, trans. Gottfried Krodel; cf. WABr 5:76-77.

. . . Master Philip has brought to me from the diet, among other [news], the word that supposedly a new alliance has come into being, in particular between my gracious lord, the Landgrave of Hesse, and some cities, which disturbed me not a little. . . .

First of all, it is certain that such an alliance is neither made by God nor by trust in God, but rather by human ambition and for the sole purpose of seeking human aid and depending upon it. [Such an alliance] does not have a good foundation, and in addition cannot bring forth any good fruit, in view of the fact that such an alliance is unnecessary. For the papistic crowd neither is in a position nor has the courage to do so much as even begin something [against us]—and God has already protected us against them with the wall of his might. The result of such an alliance is simply that the opponents are led also to make an alliance; perhaps, in addition, for the sake of defense and protection, they might do what they would otherwise have left undone. . . .

Second, the worst thing is that in such an alliance we are forced to include those who work against God and the sacrament [of the altar] as wanton enemies of God and his Word. In so doing we are forced to load upon us, participate in, and fight for all their vice and blasphemy, so that certainly no more dangerous alliance could be made to blaspheme and impede the gospel and to condemn us, both soul and body. Unfortunately this is what the devil is after.

41. Letter from Elector Johann of Saxony to Luther, Jonas, Bugenhagen, and Melanchthon (March 14, 1530)

From WABr 5:264–65.

. . . It is our gracious opinion that you should not be left unaware of an order we have received from His Imperial Majesty, our most gracious Lord, summoning us, together with the other Estates of the Holy Empire, to a diet in Augsburg on the eighth day of this coming April, where it is said that His Imperial Majesty intends to be present in person. We are sending the contents of this order to you in the enclosed transcript.

Among the foremost matters that are to be discussed at this diet, one pertains to the division in our Christian religion, and it is expressly said that this important matter is to be discussed and resolved in the following manner. Namely, the viewpoints, opinions, and ideas among the Estates themselves are to be heard, understood, and considered with love and kindness; the divisions are to be reconciled and brought toward one united Christian truth; all things on either side that are not rightly explained or practiced are to be abolished; one single, true religion is to be accepted and adhered to by us all; and, since we are all under one Christ, we are all to live in one communion, church, and unity and, finally, promote harmony and peace. Since this diet will perhaps take the place of a council or national assembly, we have thought it over and concluded that it is necessary for us to have all the articles causing divisions (those concerning both matters of faith and external church usages and ceremonies) gathered and written up in some form so that before the diet begins we may be firmly and thoroughly in agreement about the scope and form of discussion that we and the other Estates who have accepted pure doctrine can allow with good reason and in good conscience before God without causing troublesome annoyance.

Since, however, the matters are to be taken up in such a way (we cannot interpret the aforementioned announcement of the diet otherwise), no one can more competently, thoroughly, or faithfully reflect on or offer advice about them than you. Thus, we hereby graciously ask you to do this and especially request that you will let all other matters and business rest and attend to this task so that you can finish between now and Oculi Sunday and come to us here at Torgau on that date. Considering that the time until the diet is very short and we must get going without delay, we leave the matter entirely to you. . . .

42. The Augsburg Confession (1530)

Philip Melanchthon is the author of this confession, but it is based on Luther's Schwabach Articles of 1529. Both Latin and German texts were prepared for presentation to the emperor at the Diet of Augsburg. The following translation is based on the German version. This document was the most important statement of Lutheran beliefs from Luther's lifetime. It has continued to be a defining element of Lutheran identity worldwide to the present day.

From BC 36–58.

[I. CONCERNING GOD]

In the first place, it is with one accord taught and held, following the decree of the Council of Nicea, that there is one divine essence which is named God and truly is God. But there are three persons in the same one essence, equally powerful, equally eternal: God the Father, God the

Son, and God the Holy Spirit. All three are one divine essence, eternal, undivided, unending, of immeasurable power, wisdom, and goodness, the creator and preserver of all visible and invisible things. What is understood by the word "person" is not a part nor a quality in another but that which exists by itself, as the fathers once used the word concerning this issue.

Rejected, therefore, are all the heresies that are opposed to this article, such as the Manichaeans, who posited two gods, one good and one evil; the Valentinians, the Arians, the Eunomians, the Mohammedans, and all others like them; also the Samosatenians, old and new, who hold that there is only one person and create a deceitful sophistry about the other two, the Word and the Holy Spirit, by saying that the two need not be two distinct persons since "Word" means an external word or voice and the "Holy Spirit" is a created motion in all creatures.

[II. CONCERNING ORIGINAL SIN]

Furthermore, it is taught among us that since the fall of Adam, all human beings who are born in the natural way are conceived and born in sin. This means that from birth they are full of evil lust and inclination and cannot by nature possess true fear of God and true faith in God. Moreover, this same innate disease and original sin is truly sin and condemns to God's eternal wrath all who are not in turn born anew through baptism and the Holy Spirit.

Rejected, then, are the Pelagians and others who do not regard original sin as sin in order to make human nature righteous through natural powers, thus insulting the suffering and merit of Christ.

[III. CONCERNING THE SON OF GOD]

Likewise, it is taught that God the Son became a human being, born of the pure Virgin Mary, and that the two natures, the divine and the human, are so inseparably united in one person that there is one Christ. He is true God and true human being who truly "was born, suffered, was crucified, died, and was buried"

in order both to be a sacrifice not only for original sin but also for all other sins and to conciliate God's wrath. Moreover, the same Christ "descended into hell, truly rose from the dead on the third day, ascended into heaven, is sitting at the right hand of God" in order to rule and reign forever over all creatures, so that through the Holy Spirit he may make holy, purify, strengthen, and comfort all who believe in him, also distribute to them life and various gifts and benefits, and shield and protect them against the devil and sin. Finally, the same Lord Christ "will come" in full view of all "to judge the living and the dead . . . ," according to the Apostles' Creed. Rejected are all heresies that are opposed to this article.

[IV. CONCERNING JUSTIFICATION]

Furthermore, it is taught that we cannot obtain forgiveness of sin and righteousness before God through our merit, work, or satisfactions, but that we receive forgiveness of sin and become righteous before God out of grace for Christ's sake through faith when we believe that Christ has suffered for us and that for his sake our sin is forgiven and righteousness and eternal life are given to us. For God will regard and reckon this faith as righteousness in his sight, as St. Paul says in Romans 3[:21-26] and 4[:5].

[V. CONCERNING THE OFFICE OF PREACHING]

To obtain such faith God instituted the office of preaching, giving the gospel and the sacraments. Through these, as through means, he gives the Holy Spirit who produces faith, where and when he wills, in those who hear the gospel. It teaches that we have a gracious God, not through our merit but through Christ's merit, when we so believe.

Condemned are the Anabaptists and others who teach that we obtain the Holy Spirit without the external word of the gospel through our own preparation, thoughts, and works.

[VI. CONCERNING THE NEW OBEDIENCE]

It is also taught that such faith should yield good fruit and good works and that a person must do such good works as God has commanded for God's sake but not place trust in them as if thereby to earn grace before God. For we receive forgiveness of sin and righteousness through faith in Christ, as Christ himself says [Luke 17:10]: "When you have done all [things] . . . , say, 'We are worthless slaves.'" The fathers also teach the same thing. For Ambrose says: "It is determined by God that whoever believes in Christ shall be saved and have forgiveness of sins, not through works but through faith alone, without merit."

[VII. Concerning the Church]

It is also taught that at all times there must be and remain one holy, Christian church. It is the assembly of all believers among whom the gospel is purely preached and the holy sacraments are administered according to the gospel.

For this is enough for the true unity of the Christian church that there the gospel is preached harmoniously according to a pure understanding and the sacraments are administered in conformity with the divine Word. It is not necessary for the true unity of the Christian church that uniform ceremonies, instituted by human beings, be observed everywhere. As Paul says in Ephesians 4[:4-5]: "There is one body and one Spirit, just as you were called to the one hope of your calling, one Lord, one faith, one baptism."

[VIII. What Is the Church?]

Likewise, although the Christian church is, properly speaking, nothing else than the assembly of all believers and saints, yet because in this life many false Christians, hypocrites, and even public sinners remain among the righteous, the sacraments—even though administered by unrighteous priests—are efficacious all the same. For as Christ himself indicates [Matt. 23:2-3]: "The scribes and the Pharisees sit on Moses' seat. . . ."

Condemned, therefore, are the Donatists and all others who hold a different view.

[IX. Concerning Baptism]

Concerning baptism it is taught that it is necessary, that grace is offered through it, and that one should also baptize children, who through such baptism are entrusted to God and become pleasing to him.

Rejected, therefore, are the Anabaptists, who teach that the baptism of children is not right.

[X. Concerning the Lord's Supper]

Concerning the Lord's Supper it is taught that the true body and blood of Christ are truly present under the form of bread and wine in the Lord's Supper and are distributed and received there. Rejected, therefore, is also the contrary teaching.

[XI. Concerning Confession]

Concerning confession it is taught that private absolution should be retained and not abolished. However, it is not necessary to enumerate all misdeeds and sins, since it is not possible to do so. Psalm 19[:12]: "But who can detect their errors?"

[XII. Concerning Repentance]

Concerning repentance it is taught that those who have sinned after baptism obtain forgiveness of sins whenever they come to repentance and that absolution should not be denied them by the church. Now properly speaking, true repentance is nothing else than to have contrition and sorrow, or terror about sin, and yet at the same time to believe in the gospel and absolution that sin is forgiven and grace is obtained through Christ. Such faith, in turn, comforts the heart and puts it at peace. Then improvement should also follow, and a person should refrain from sins. For these should be the fruits of repentance, as John says in Matthew 3[:8]: "Bear fruit worthy of repentance."

Rejected here are those who teach that whoever has once become righteous cannot fall again.

However, also condemned are the Novatians, who denied absolution to those who had sinned after baptism.

Also rejected are those who do not teach that a person obtains forgiveness of sin through faith but through our own satisfactions.

Also rejected are those who teach that "canonical satisfactions" are necessary to pay for eternal torment or purgatory.

[XIII. CONCERNING THE USE OF SACRAMENTS]
Concerning the use of sacraments it is taught that the sacraments are instituted not only to be signs by which people may recognize Christians outwardly, but also as signs and testimonies of God's will toward us in order thereby to awaken and strengthen our faith. That is why they also require faith and are rightly used when received in faith for the strengthening of faith.

Rejected, therefore, are those who teach that the sacraments justify *ex opere operato* without faith and who do not teach that this faith should be added so that the forgiveness of sin (which is obtained through faith and not through work) may be offered there.

[XIV. CONCERNING CHURCH GOVERNMENT]
Concerning church government it is taught that no one should publicly teach, preach, or administer the sacraments without a proper [public] call.

[XV. CONCERNING CHURCH REGULATIONS]
Concerning church regulations made by human beings, it is taught to keep those that may be kept without sin and that serve to maintain peace and good order in the church, such as specific celebrations, festivals, and so forth. However, people are also instructed not to burden consciences with them as if such things were necessary for salvation. Moreover, it is taught that all rules and traditions made by human beings for the purpose of appeasing God and of earning grace are contrary to the gospel and the teaching concerning faith in Christ. That is why monastic vows and other traditions concerning distinctions of foods, days, and the like, through which people imagine they can earn grace and make satisfaction

for sin, are good for nothing and contrary to the gospel.

[XVI. CONCERNING PUBLIC ORDER AND SECULAR GOVERNMENT]
Concerning public order and secular government it is taught that all political authority, orderly government, laws, and good order in the world are created and instituted by God and that Christians may without sin exercise political authority; be princes and judges; pass sentences and administer justice according to imperial and other existing laws; punish evildoers with the sword; wage just wars; serve as soldiers; buy and sell; take required oaths; possess property; be married; and so forth.

Condemned here are the Anabaptists, who teach that none of the things indicated above is Christian.

Also condemned are those who teach that Christian perfection means physically leaving house and home, spouse and child, and refraining from the above-mentioned activities. In fact, the only true perfection is true fear of God and true faith in God. For the gospel teaches an internal, eternal reality and righteousness of the heart, not an external, temporal one. The gospel does not overthrow secular government, public order, and marriage but instead intends that a person keep all this as a true order of God and demonstrate in these walks of life Christian love and true good works according to each person's calling. Christians, therefore, are obliged to be subject to political authority and to obey its commands and laws in all that may be done without sin. But if a command of the political authority cannot be followed without sin, one must obey God rather than any human beings (Acts 5[:29]).

[XVII. CONCERNING THE RETURN OF CHRIST TO JUDGMENT]
It is also taught that our Lord Jesus Christ will return on the Last Day to judge, to raise all the dead, to give eternal life and eternal joy to

those who believe and are elect, but to condemn the ungodly and the devils to hell and eternal punishment.

Rejected, therefore, are the Anabaptists, who teach that the devils and condemned human beings will not suffer eternal torture and torment.

Likewise rejected are some Jewish teachings, which have also appeared in the present, that before the resurrection of the dead, saints and righteous people alone will possess a secular kingdom and will annihilate all the ungodly.

[XVIII. CONCERNING FREE WILL]

Concerning free will it is taught that a human being has some measure of free will, so as to live an externally honorable life and to choose among the things reason comprehends. However, without the grace, help, and operation of the Holy Spirit a human being cannot become pleasing to God, fear or believe in God with the whole heart, or expel innate evil lusts from the heart. Instead, this happens through the Holy Spirit, who is given through the Word of God. For Paul says (1 Cor. 2[:14]): "Those who are natural do not receive the gifts of God's Spirit."

In order that it may be recognized that nothing new is taught here, these are the clear words of Augustine concerning free will, quoted here from the third book of the Hypognosticon: "We confess that there is a free will in all human beings. For all have a natural, innate mind and reason—not that they can act in matters pertaining to God, such as loving or fearing God with their whole heart—but they do have the freedom to choose good or evil only in the external works of this life. By 'good' I mean what can be done by nature: whether to work in the field or not, whether to eat and drink, whether to visit a friend or not, to dress or undress, to build a home, to marry, to engage in a trade, and to do whatever may be useful and good. To be sure, all of this neither exists nor endures without God, but everything is from him and through him. On the other hand, a human being can by personal choice do evil, such as to kneel before an idol, commit murder, and the like."

Rejected here are those who teach that we can keep the commandments of God without grace and the Holy Spirit. For although we are by nature able to do the external works of the commandments, yet we cannot do the supreme commandments in the heart, namely, truly to fear, love, and believe in God.

[XIX. CONCERNING THE CAUSE OF SIN]

Concerning the cause of sin it is taught among us that although almighty God has created and preserves all of nature, nevertheless the perverted will causes sin in all those who are evil and despise God. This, then, is the will of the devil and of all the ungodly. As soon as God withdrew his hand, it turned from God to malice, as Christ says (John 8[:44]): "When [the devil] lies, he speaks according to his own nature."

[XX.] CONCERNING FAITH AND GOOD WORKS

Our people are falsely accused of prohibiting good works. But their writings concerning the Decalogue and other writings demonstrate that they have given good and useful account and admonition concerning proper Christian walks of life and works, about which little had been taught before our time. Instead, for the most part childish, unnecessary works—such as rosaries, the cult of the saints, joining religious orders, pilgrimages, appointed fasts, holy days, brotherhoods, and the like—were emphasized in all sermons. Our opponents also no longer praise such unnecessary works as highly as they once did. Moreover, they have also learned to speak now of faith, about which they did not preach at all in former times. Rather, they now teach that we do not become righteous before God by works alone, but they add faith in Christ, saying that faith and works make us righteous before God. Such talk may offer a little more comfort than the teaching that one should rely on works alone.

Because at present the teaching concerning faith, which is the principal part of the Christian life, has not been emphasized for such a long time, as all must admit, but only a doctrine of works was preached everywhere, our people have taught as follows:

In the first place, our works cannot reconcile us with God or obtain grace. Instead, this happens through faith alone when a person believes that our sins are forgiven for Christ's sake, who alone is the mediator to reconcile the Father. Now all who imagine that they can accomplish this by works and can merit grace despise Christ and seek their own way to God contrary to the gospel.

This teaching about faith is publicly and clearly treated in Paul at many places, especially in Ephesians 2[:8-9]: "For by grace you have been saved through faith, and this is not your own doing; it is the gift of God—not the result of works, so that no one may boast. . . ."

That no new interpretation is introduced here can be demonstrated from Augustine, who diligently deals with this matter and also teaches that we obtain grace and become righteous before God through faith in Christ, and not through works. His whole book *On the Spirit and the Letter* proves it.

Now although untested people despise this teaching completely, it is nevertheless the case that it is very comforting and beneficial for timid and terrified consciences. For the conscience cannot find rest and peace through works but by faith alone, when it concludes on its own with certainty that it has a gracious God for Christ's sake, as Paul says (Rom. 5[:1]): "Therefore, since we are justified by faith, we have peace with God."

In former times people did not emphasize this comfort in sermons but instead drove the poor consciences to their own works. As a result, all sorts of works were undertaken. For the conscience forced some into monasteries, in the hope of obtaining grace there through the monastic life. Some devised other works as a way of earning grace and making satisfaction for sins. Many of them discovered that a person could not obtain peace by such means. That is why it became necessary to preach this teaching concerning faith in Christ and diligently to emphasize it, so that each person may know that God's grace is grasped by faith alone, without merit.

We must also explain that we are not talking here about the faith possessed by the devil and the ungodly, who also believe the story that Christ suffered and was raised from the dead. But we are talking about true faith, which believes that we obtain grace and forgiveness of sin through Christ.

All who know that in Christ they have a gracious God call upon him and are not, like the heathen, without God. For the devil and the ungodly do not believe this article about the forgiveness of sin. That is why they are enemies of God, cannot call upon him, and cannot hope for anything good from him. Moreover, as has now been indicated, Scripture talks about faith but does not label it knowledge such as the devil and the ungodly have. For Hebrews 11[:1] teaches that faith is not only a matter of historical knowledge, but a matter of having confidence in God to receive his promise. Augustine also reminds us that we should understand the word "faith" in Scripture to mean confidence in God—that God is gracious to us—and not merely such knowledge of these stories as the devils also have.

Further, it is taught that good works should and must be done, not that a person relies on them to earn grace, but for God's sake and to God's praise. Faith alone always takes hold of grace and forgiveness of sin. Because the Holy Spirit is given through faith, the heart is also moved to do good works. For before, because it lacks the Holy Spirit, the heart is too weak. Moreover, it is in the power of the devil who drives our poor human nature to many sins, as we observe in the philosophers who tried to live honestly and blamelessly, but then failed to do so and fell into many great, public sins. That is what happens to human beings when they are separated from true faith, are without the Holy Spirit, and govern themselves through their own human strength alone.

That is why this teaching concerning faith is not to be censured for prohibiting good works. On the contrary, it should be praised for teaching the performance of good works and for offering help as to how they may be done. For without faith and without Christ human nature and human power are much too weak to do good works: such as to call on God, to have patience in suffering, to love the neighbor, to engage diligently in legitimate callings, to be obedient, to avoid evil lust, and so forth. Such lofty and genuine works cannot be done without the help of Christ, as he himself says in John 15[:5]: "Apart from me you can do nothing."

[XXI. CONCERNING THE CULT OF THE SAINTS]
Concerning the cult of the saints our people teach that the saints are to be remembered so that we may strengthen our faith when we see how they experienced grace and how they were helped by faith. Moreover, it is taught that each person, according to his or her calling, should take the saints' good works as an example. For instance, His Imperial Majesty, in a salutary and righteous fashion, may follow the example of David in waging war against the Turk. For both hold a royal office that demands defense and protection of their subjects. However, it cannot be demonstrated from Scripture that a person should call upon the saints or seek help from them. "For there is only one single reconciler and mediator set up between God and humanity, Jesus Christ" (1 Tim. 2[:5]). He is the only savior, the only high priest, the mercy seat, and intercessor before God (Rom. 8[:34]). He alone has promised to hear our prayers. According to Scripture, in all our needs and

concerns it is the highest worship to seek and call upon this same Jesus Christ with our whole heart. "But if anyone does sin, we have an advocate with the Father, Jesus Christ, the righteous . . ." [1 John 2:1].

43. Luther's Warning to His Dear German People (1531)

From *LW* 47:18–20, trans. Martin Bertram; cf. WA 30/3:276f.

. . . It is not fitting for me, a preacher, vested with the spiritual office, to wage war or to counsel war or incite it, but rather to dissuade from war and to direct to peace, as I have done until now with all diligence. All the world must bear witness to this. However, our enemies do not want to have peace, but war. If war should come now, I will surely hold my pen in check and keep silent and not intervene as I did in the last uprising [the Peasants' Revolt of 1525]. I will let matters take their course, even though not a bishop, priest, or monk survives and I myself also perish. For their defiance and boasting are intolerable to God; their impenitent heart is carrying things too far. They were begged, they were admonished, they were implored for peace beyond all reasonable measure. They insist on forcing the issue with flesh and blood; so I, too, will force the issue with them through the Spirit and through God and henceforth set not one or two papists but the entire papacy against me, until the Judge in heaven intervenes with signs. I will not and cannot be afraid of such miserable enemies of God. I disdain their defiance, and I laugh at their wrath. They can do no more than deprive me of a sack of ailing flesh. But they shall soon discover of what I am able to deprive them.

Furthermore, if war breaks out—which God forbid—I will not reprove those who defend themselves against the murderous and bloodthirsty papists, nor let anyone else rebuke them as being seditious, but I will accept their action and let it pass as self-defense. I will direct them in this matter to the law and to the jurists. For in such an instance, when the murderers and bloodhounds wish to wage war and to murder, it is in truth no insurrection to rise against them and defend oneself. Not that I wish to incite or spur anyone on to such self-defense, or to justify it, for that is not my office; much less does it devolve to me to pass judgment or sentence on him. A Christian knows very well what he is to do—namely, to render to God the things that are God's and to Caesar the things that are Caesar's [Matt. 22:21], but not to render to the bloodhounds the things that are not theirs. I want to make a distinction between sedition and other acts and to deprive the bloodhounds of the pretext of boasting that they are warring against rebellious people and that they were justified according to both human and divine law; for so the little kitten is fond of grooming and adorning itself. Likewise, I do not want to leave the conscience of the people burdened by the concern and worry that their self-defense might be rebellious. For such a term would be too evil and too harsh in such a case. It should be given a different name, which I am sure the jurists can find for it.

We must not let everything be considered rebellious that the bloodhounds designate as such. For in that way they want to silence the lips and tie the hands of the entire world, so that no one may either reprove them with preaching or defend himself with his fist, while they keep their mouth open and their hands free. Thus they want to frighten and ensnare all the world with the name "insurrection," and at the same time comfort and reassure themselves. No, dear fellow, we must submit to you a different interpretation and definition of that

term. To act contrary to law is not rebellion; otherwise every violation of the law would be rebellion. No, he is an insurrectionist who refuses to submit to government and law, who attacks and fights against them, and attempts to overthrow them with a view of making himself ruler and establishing the law, as Müntzer did; that is the true definition of a rebel. *Alius est invasor, aliud transgressor.* In accordance with this definition, self-defense against the bloodhounds cannot be rebellious. For the papists are deliberately starting the war; they refuse to keep the peace, they do not let others rest who would like to live in peace. Thus the papists are much closer to the name and the quality that is termed rebellion. . . .

THE ASSAULTS OF THE DEVIL

44. Luther's Letter to Duke Johann Friedrich of Saxony (February/March 1530)

From *Luther's Correspondence*, vol. 2, trans. Preserved Smith (Philadelphia: Lutheran, 1913), 516.

The world runs and hastens so diligently to its end that it often occurs to me forcibly that the last days will break before we can completely turn the Holy Scriptures into German. For it is certain from the Holy Scriptures that we have no more temporal things to expect. All is done and fulfilled: the Roman Empire is at an end; the Turk has reached his highest point; the pomp of the papacy is falling away, and the world is cracking on all sides almost as if it would break and fall apart entirely. It is true that this same Roman Empire now under our Emperor Charles is coming up a bit and is becoming mightier than it has been for a long time, but I think that that shows it is the last

Duke Johann Friedrich

phase, and that before God it is just as when a light or wisp of straw is burnt up and about to go out, then it gives forth a flame as if it was going to burn brightly and even at the same moment goes out—even so Christendom now goes with the light of the gospel.

45. The Wittenberg Concord (May 1536)

The South German reformers were torn between the views of Zwingli and Luther on the Lord's Supper. Martin Bucer, however, continued to work to unify the Protestant position on this hotly disputed issue. In the following agreement resulting from negotiations in Wittenberg, the South Germans accepted two important points Luther had insisted on: the presence of Christ with the bread and the reception of Christ by all, worthy and unworthy alike.

From Walch 27:2087–88.

On The Lord's Supper
The First Article

We confess, in accordance with the words of Irenaeus, that there are two things in this holy sacrament: one heavenly and one earthly. Therefore we hold the belief and teach that with the bread and the wine the body and blood of Christ are truly and essentially present and are distributed and received.

The Second Article

And although they hold the belief that there is no transubstantiation and also do not believe that the body of Christ is locally present, that is enclosed spatially in the bread or persistently united with it apart from the eating of the holy sacrament, they still confess and hold the belief that through sacramental union the bread is the body of Christ. They hold and believe that the body of Christ is truly present with the bread and is truly received. For apart from the use, when the bread is laid aside or enclosed in the monstrance or tabernacle or carried about and displayed in procession, the body of Christ is not present.

The Third Article

They hold the belief that it is the institution of this sacrament through Christ that makes it efficacious for Christianity, and it does not depend on the worthiness of the one who distributes or receives it. For, as Paul says, the unworthy also receive the sacrament. Thus, they also hold the belief that the body and blood of Christ are truly distributed to the unworthy and that where Christ the Lord's words of institution are observed, the unworthy truly receive it. But, as Paul says, they receive it to their judgment for they misuse the holy sacrament because they receive it without true repentance and faith. Therefore, the holy sacrament is instituted to attest that all who repent and console themselves through faith in Jesus Christ the Lord receive the grace and benefits of Christ, are incorporated into Christ, and are washed through the blood of Christ. . . .

Signed by Wolfgang Capito, Martin Bucer, Martin Luther, Justus Jonas, Johann Bugenhagen, Philip Melanchthon, et alia.

46. Luther's Commentary on Galatians 4:3 (1535)

One of the hallmarks of Luther's theology was the careful distinction he made between law and gospel, between commandments and promises. He developed this understanding especially from his favorite Pauline epistle, Galatians, on which he published commentaries in 1519 and 1535. Remarks such as the following inspired the Antinomian position of Agricola.

From *LW* 26:365–66, trans. Jaroslav Pelikan; cf. WA 40.

GALATIANS 4:3

If you permit the law to dominate in your conscience instead of grace, then when the time comes for you to conquer sin and death in the sight of God, the law is nothing but the dregs of all evils, heresies, and blasphemies; for all it does is to increase sin, accuse, frighten, threaten with death, and disclose God as a wrathful Judge who damns sinners. If you are wise, therefore, you will put Moses, that lisper and stammerer, far away with his law; and you will not let his terrors and threats affect you in any way at all. Here he should be as suspect to you as an excommunicated and condemned heretic, worse than the pope and the devil, and therefore not to be listened to at all.

Apart from the matter of justification, on the other hand, we, like Paul, should think reverently of the law. We should endow it with the highest praises and call it holy, righteous, good, spiritual, divine, etc. Apart from our conscience we should make a god of it; but in our conscience it is truly a devil, for in the slightest trial it cannot encourage or comfort the conscience but does the very opposite, frightening and saddening it and depriving it of confidence in righteousness, of life, and of everything good. This is why Paul calls the law "weak and beggarly ele-

ments" later on (Gal. 4:9). Therefore let us not permit it to dominate our conscience in any way, especially since it cost Christ so much to remove the tyranny of the law from the conscience. . . .

47. The Antinomian Theses on Law and Gospel Reported by Luther at the First Disputation against the Antinomians (December 1537)

Ever since 1527 Johann Agricola had been upset with Melanchthon's emphasis on the need for the law to arouse repentance prior to the declaration of God's promise of forgiveness through the gospel. Johann Agricola extended Luther's antithesis between law and gospel to the point that he spoke of the continued preaching of the law as unnecessary and even incompatible with the gospel. Luther considered this a misunderstanding of his position and called for a series of disputations on the topic. The following theses summarize the position attributed to Agricola.

From WA 39/1:342–44 and Walch 20:1625.

1. Repentance should be learned not from the Ten Commandments or any law of Moses but through the gospel from consciousness of our violation of the Son.

2. For Christ says in the last chapter of Luke [24:26, 46, 47]: Thus must Christ die and in this way enter into his glory so that repentance and forgiveness of sins might be preached in his name.

3. Christ also says in John [16:8] that the Spirit convicts the world of sin, not the law.

4. The last sermon of Christ teaches the same: Go, preach the gospel to all creatures.

5. When Paul says to the Philippians [2:5, 12]: "Have this mind among yourselves which

also is in Christ Jesus" so that you work out your salvation in fear and trembling, he clearly establishes that repentance (which is called fear and trembling) should be taught from the remembrance of Christ, not from the law.

6. From the preaching of Paul and Barnabas it is also quite clear that the work of the law is in no way a part of justification [Rom. 3:20f., Acts 13:38f.]. . . .

14. Whoever improperly adds to the words of Christ and teaches that first the law and then the gospel should be taught contorts the words of Christ for they do not hold to the simple understanding of Christ's words.

15. For just as one must uphold the simple sense of these words: "This is my body," so must we also uphold the simple sense of these words: "Go and preach the gospel, baptizing, etc."

16. The law merely exposes sin and to be sure without the Holy Spirit; so that it exposes to damnation.

17. But now such a teaching is needed that not only damns with great power but also at the same time saves. The gospel is such a teaching that teaches together repentance and the forgiveness of sins.

18. For the gospel of Christ teaches the wrath of God from heaven and also justification before God, Rom. 1:17. For it is a preaching of repentance conjoined with a promise that reason does not comprehend by nature but by divine revelation.

OTHER ANTINOMIAN THESES

1. The law is not worthy of being called the Word of God. . . .

4. The Ten Commandments belong in the town hall, not the pulpit. . . .

6. We should not prepare people for the gospel through the preaching of the law. God, whose work it is, must do that.

7. In the gospel, one should not deal with the violation of the law but with the violation of the Son.

8. To hear the Word and live according to it is the result of the law.

9. To hear the Word and feel it in the heart is the actual essence of the gospel; that is our method.

48. Luther: Third Disputation against the Antinomians (September 6, 1538)

In the latter part of his life, Luther increasingly expressed disappointment at the lack of moral discipline among people who claimed to be Christians. This feeling was especially stimulated by the information gathered from a systematic visitation of the parishes in Saxony. In 1529 he wrote, "Now that the gospel has been restored, they have mastered the fine art of abusing liberty." This concern surfaced in his response to Agricola's view of the law.

From WA 39/1:571–74.

It is true that at the start of this movement we began to teach the gospel vigorously and make use of these words that the Antinomians now use. But the situation at that time was very different from what it is today. Then the world was terrified to such a degree that the pope or the angry look of a single priest caused the whole of Olympus to tremble, not to mention earth and hell, over which that man of sin had usurped all power to himself. When consciences were so oppressed, terrified, miserable, anxious, and afflicted, there was no need to inculcate or teach the law. Rather, the need then was to present the other part of the teaching of Christ where he commands us to preach the remission of sin in his name, so that those who were already terrified enough might learn not to despair, but to flee to the grace and mercy promised in Christ. Now, however, when the times are very dissimilar from those under the pope, our Antinomians, sweet theologians that they are, retain our words, our doctrine, the joyful promise concerning Christ, but, what is worse, wish to preach this alone. They do not observe that people are other than they were under that hangman pope and have become secure, harsh, wicked violators—yes, even Epicureans who respect neither God nor men. They affirm and comfort such people by their doctrine. In those days we were so terrified that we trembled even at the sound of a leaf falling from a tree. On account of which, I tell you, we also initially taught repentance from love of righteousness, that is, from the gospel, because people in that period were exceedingly crushed and were almost brought to despair. Moreover, they were already twisting round and round in the middle of hell so that unless you wanted them to utterly perish, it was necessary to lead them quickly back from the depths. But now, our Antinomians, not wanting to follow unless they can sing sweet songs, pay no attention to the fact that these times are much more perverse than they were before. They make people secure who are of themselves already so secure that they fall away from grace. So, this is how I respond to their argument that penitence should be taught by or should begin with love of righteousness: this is right for those who are and were afflicted and crushed as we were in that time under the pope, when we fled from the monstrous terrors and fears that worthless man inspired. I know how much anxious sweat that brought about for me, and I escaped it only little by little. Even today I cannot look at my Lord Jesus with as cheerful a face as he would like after having been inculcated with that pestilent doctrine, which depicted a God who was angry with us and a judgmental Christ. All the demagogues were mute concerning faith in Christ and the gratuitous

remission of sins on account of Christ, and there was pure silence about this in the writings of all the canonists and schoolmen, although they were disposed by profession to heal consciences. Now these Antinomians want us to continue preaching forever the speeches appropriate to a despondent age. To do that is certainly not to divide the word of God rightly [2 Tim. 2:15] but to tear it apart and scatter it and, thus, to destroy souls. Our sound judgment has been and will continue to be this: if you see the afflicted and crushed, preach grace as much as you can. But do not do the same to the secure, the slothful, the fornicators, the adulterers, and blasphemers. If you will not do this, you will be answerable for their shameful conduct. There are two types of people in the world: the poor and infirmed, that is, the pious ones or those desiring to be pious, and the rich and healthy, that is, those impious and secure, worthless fellows. Therefore, people remain the same at all times, but it is proper when the word of God is rightly divided that not all things be taught to all without discrimination. The healthy have no need of a physician. . . .

49. Luther's Letter on Philip of Hesse's Bigamy (June 10, 1540)

This letter to Elector Johann Friedrich of Saxony expresses Luther's afterthoughts about the controversial bigamy of his important political supporter, Philip of Hesse.

From WABr 9:133–34.

Most illustrious, noble Elector, gracious Lord! I hear that Your Grace has been unjustly tormented by the court of Dresden [Albertine Saxony] concerning the case of the Landgrave

[Philip of Hesse]. Your Grace wishes to know what opinion to express to the clever men of Meissen. . . .

This is the situation: Martin Bucer brought a letter and reported that the Landgrave was not able to stay chaste, due to some deficiencies in his wife. He has lived until now in a way that is not good but would like to be Evangelical and at one with the foremost leaders of the church. He has declared before God and his conscience that he would not be able to avoid such vice in the future unless he were allowed to take another wife. We were deeply alarmed at this narration and at the obvious scandal that would result. We pleaded with his Grace not to do as he wished, but we were told again that he would not agree to this. He said that if we would not allow it, he would disregard us and obtain what he wanted from the Emperor or Pope. So that this would not happen, we humbly requested that if his Grace would not or could not, in good conscience and before God (as he said), do otherwise, he should at least keep it a secret, because, although he felt compelled by necessity, this act was not defensible before the world and the imperial laws. This, then, is what he said he would do. For our part, we agreed to help him before God and exculpate him as much as possible by noting examples such as Abraham [Genesis 16]. This all happened as though in the confessional, and no one can blame us, as if we acted voluntarily or willingly or with pleasure or joy. It was hard enough for our hearts, but because we could not prevent it; we thought we should set free his conscience as best we could. . . .

But if I had known that the Landgrave had been satisfying his desires for a long time and could well satisfy them with others, as I have now just learned that he did with the woman of Eschwege, certainly no angel could have induced me to give such advice. I was taking into consideration the unavoidable necessity and his weakness and the perilous state of his

Philip of Hesse

conscience, as Bucer has explained it to us. Much less would I have advised that there should be a public marriage, to which a young princess and young countess would come. He didn't tell us about this fact, which cannot be tolerated and is insufferable to the whole empire. Nevertheless, I understood and hoped, as long as he was inclined in the common way to gratify the weakness of the flesh with sin and shame, that he would perhaps take some honorable maiden in secret marriage. Even though this would have seemed illegitimate before the world, it would have overridden the great need of his conscience. Such has happened many times to other great lords. In a similar fashion, I advised certain priests in the lands of Duke Georg [of Albertine Saxony] and the [Catholic] bishops to marry their cooks secretly.

This was my confessional advice. I would much rather have kept silence if the need had not forced it, but I could not do that. The men at Dresden speak as though I had taught the same for thirteen years, and yet they give us to understand what a friendly heart they have toward us and what great desire they have for love and unity. They act as if there were no scandal nor sin in their lives that are ten times worse before God than anything I ever advised, but the world must confidently fret about the splinter in its neighbor's eye and forget the beam in its own eye. If I must defend all I have said or done in former years, especially at the beginning, I must ask the pope to do the same, for if they defend their former deeds (I will keep silent about their present ones) they would belong to the devil more than to God.

I am not ashamed of my advice, even if it should come to the attention of the whole world, but due to the aversion it aroused, I would, rather, if possible, have kept it secret.

50. The Regensburg Book of 1541

This theological document, prepared primarily by the South German reformer Martin Bucer and the Catholic theologian Johannes Gropper, formed the basis for the negotiations at the Colloquy of Regensburg. Attempting to honor Protestant preoccupation with justifying faith and Catholic concern for the works of faith, it presented the controversial formula of "double justification."

From CR 4:199–201; cf. Walch 17:594–97.

CHAPTER FIVE: ON JUSTIFICATION

. . . It is steadfast and sound doctrine that the sinner is justified by a living and efficacious faith, for through such we are made acceptable to God and accepted on account of Christ. We call this living faith a movement of the Holy Spirit by which those who truly repent of their old life are directed to God and truly grasp the mercy that is promised in Christ so that they truly feel that they have forgiveness of sins and reconciliation with God on account of the merits of Christ, accept the grace and benefits of God, and cry to God: Abba, dear Father. Nevertheless, this is obtained by no one unless at the same time love is poured in and heals a

person's will so that after the will has been made well, as Augustine says, it begins to fulfill the law. This living faith grasps the mercy of God and believes that the righteousness that is in Christ is imputed to us gratuitously and at the same time receives the promise of the Holy Spirit and love. This faith that justifies is the same faith that is active through love. However, it is true that by this faith we are justified (that is, made acceptable and reconciled to God) because this same faith grasps the mercy and righteousness that is imputed to us on account of Christ and his merits, not on account of our worthiness or the perfection of righteousness that has been initiated in us by Christ.

Although the person who is reckoned righteous through Christ receives a righteousness within, as St. Paul says: "You were washed, you were sanctified, you were justified" [1 Cor. 6:11] and for this reason the old fathers have used the word "justified" for the reception of this righteousness that we have within us, nevertheless the faithful soul should not rest on this but only on the righteousness of Christ that is given to us and without which there neither is nor can be any righteousness. And thus we are justified or reckoned so through faith in Christ, which is made acceptable to God through his merits, not on account of our own worthiness or works. Yet on account of the righteousness within us, we are said to be righteous because we do good works, according to 1 John 3:7: "Whoever does right, is righteous."

And although the reborn should always grow in the fear of God, repentance, humility, and other virtues, since their renewal is not yet perfected and great weakness clings to them, nevertheless one should teach that those who are truly penitent should believe and have no doubt that they are always acceptable and pleasing to God on account of Christ the mediator. For Christ is the propitiator, the high priest and intercessor for us whom the

Father has sent to us and along with him, all good things.

Even though certainty is not perfect in the midst of this weakness, and there are many weak and anxious consciences that often wrestle with grave doubt, still no one should be excluded from the grace of God because of this weakness. Rather, such people should be diligently admonished to set the promises of Christ bravely against their doubts and with steady prayer to ask for an increase of their faith. As the Apostle prays, "Lord, increase our faith" [Luke 17:5].

All Christians ought to learn that grace and new birth are not given to us so that we should remain idle in this beginning stage, but that we should grow in all things through Christ who is our head. Therefore, one should teach people to be diligent and to strengthen themselves with good works, internal and external, as God has commanded and recommended. For such, God has clearly and openly promised, in many places in the Gospels, a reward through Christ, namely, benefits for body and soul in this life according to his divine will and a reward in heaven after this life. Therefore, although the inheritance of eternal life is due to the reborn on account of the promise, as soon as they are reborn in Christ God will no less abundantly reward good works that are good, not in their essence or as they come from us, but insofar as they are done in faith and are from the Holy Spirit that dwells in us and acts together with the free will as coworker.

The blessedness of those who do more and greater works will be fuller and greater because through such exercises faith and love increases in them.

Therefore, whoever says "we are justified by faith alone" should also convey the teaching of repentance, fear of God, the judgment of God, and good works so that the summary of our preaching is complete. As Christ says: "Preach repentance and the forgiveness of sins in my name" [Luke 24:47]. Furthermore, this way of speaking should not be understood in any way other than as it was previously stated.

51. Melanchthon's Reply concerning the Book and the Articles Accepted and Rejected during the Colloquy (1541)

Philip Melanchthon was temperamentally more conciliatory than Luther, but even he had some reservations about the compromise represented by the Regensburg Book. He prepared this reply on behalf of the Protestant princes.

From *Great Debates of the Reformation*, ed. Donald J. Ziegler (New York: Random House, 1969), 152–60.

Unquestionably, Your Imperial Majesty's intentions in publishing the book were benevolent and kindly, for we have indeed noted its author's attempts to moderate and correct several abuses. And if those on the other side were to show themselves reasonable, then a way toward settlement would be achieved. Therefore we express our most humble appreciation to Your Imperial Majesty for this disposition and willingness to put an end to strife and misunderstanding in the church through discussion by learned men and by peaceful means, as befits the church of Christ. . . .

We have considered the articles on which agreement has been reported, such as those on original sin, justification, church discipline, and several others. These articles require further elaboration in several places, which we intend to point out subsequently. Yet if we want to maintain an honest and at the same time a respectable and reasonable disposition toward the matter, whatever shortcomings those places might still have, we know that we cannot condemn the views and judgments of the disputants. It was most certainly our intention, however, that sound, uncorrupted teaching, the grace of Christ, and the justification of faith be extended throughout the church. Therefore, since this teaching is treated with some brevity in the articles presented in the book, a more detailed exposition of these articles might be added that truly contributes to the salvation of souls and to Christian unity, thereby avoiding the doubts and fresh controversies that might arise from the brevity. For we interpret these articles in the sense that they are found in our confession and apology. Moreover, we have not wanted to confuse anything, because neither God nor the church would be served by articles that are puzzling and questionable in nature. They might be stretched by opponents into misconceptions and absurdities, quite like putting one oversized shoe on either foot. For this reason we have taken great pains wherever possible to achieve clear and accurate understanding of our views, which we have no doubt are in accord with the judgment and belief of the universal church. So if we are indeed to effect a reconciliation, we request in view of the importance of this matter that the articles be further explained and clarified. . . .

POINTS THAT REQUIRE FURTHER COMMENT
. . . In the article on justification, where it speaks of an efficacious faith, it is our understanding that some have turned this around to mean that an efficacious faith is a workable faith and consequently to understand by this article that man is justified by faith along with works. For it is the common view of several on the other side that Paul's statement that we are justified by faith is to be taken as if he had intended to say we are made ready for justification, that is, for love, through faith. At this point we become acceptable to God and are

justified before him—not through faith for the sake of Christ. If this article is to be corrupted and perverted in such a manner then we must of necessity oppose it. For when our representatives stated here that we acquire piety and blessedness through a living and efficacious faith, they intended to be understood as speaking, not about faith that is mere knowledge of history, but about the kind of faith that is trust, that helps us for the sake of Christ to grasp the mercy of God and that lifts up frightened souls. It was in this sense that our representatives spoke of the efficacy of faith, through which faith itself is a burning stimulus from the Holy Spirit to take heart by abandoning oneself to Christ and acquire life. As declared in the subsequent passage about faith in the book's article on justification, and in the words of the prophet, the just shall live by faith. Therefore, in order to avoid fresh disputes arising from the dual meaning, either this declaration should be appended or else the word (efficacious) should be deleted. . . .

52. Letter from Luther and Bugenhagen to Elector Johann Friedrich (May 10 or 11, 1541)

From WABr 9:406–9.

Grace and peace in Christ. Illustrious, noble Prince, gracious Lord! We have received the writing Your Gracious Lord sent and have diligently read it all. First of all, you have rightly judged that the document of agreement is a diffuse and patched-together thing. For we have also observed from the writing that Master Philip sent us how it has gone, namely, that Master Philip first set forth a right document, noting how we are justified by faith alone without works. They could not tolerate this and have presented another, that faith is active through love. This Master Philip also rejected. Finally they harmonized and glued both of these documents together. Thus this detailed and pieced-together document has come about according to which they are right and we are also right.

Now if Doctor Eck will confess (as he will not do) that they were previously not so learned, then might such an agreement superficially endure for awhile. But if he boasts (as he most certainly will) and stands on the statement in Galatians 5: "Faith is active," saying that they have always taught this, then the agreement is like Christ said in Matthew 9: "No one sews a new piece of cloth on an old cloak because the tear will be made worse." For with such false, dissimilar people there can be no other agreement, since they will cry that they have retained the correct view. In opposition to this our side says that they have protected well against them with their new patch and clarification that is in the document, and they especially make clear that they have given up nothing from their confession.

Thus, we are further divided than before and their false, roguish stratagem that they have masterfully hidden in their document will come to light, as we intend. That will soon happen when they come to another article that flows forth from and is grounded in this chief article. Our side has sniffed this out and has simply confessed already that where no agreement can take place in other articles, so it must also be with this document because they observe falsehood within it. Thus, we must and will return to our original, pure document or form which is expressed in Romans 3: "We are justified without merit," and in the same place, "We hold that one is justified through faith without the works of the law." That is our document and form with which we will remain, and which is short and clear. The devil, Eck,

the archbishop of Mainz, and Duke Heinrich may storm against it and will not stand for it, but we will see who will win.

The saying in Galatians 5 does not speak about justification but about the life of the justified. There is much difference between being and acting, as the boys in school learn: the active and the passive verb. It is exact to speak of them differently (which Eck and his part cannot allow or understand). It is one thing to ask through what means one is justified before God; it is entirely another question to ask what the justified do or cause to happen. Becoming and doing are two different things; becoming a tree and bearing fruit are two different things. . . .

But the papist trick is this (it can be found in the following articles) that one will be or is justified, not only through faith but also through works, or through love and grace, what they call inherent (which is much the same thing). That is all false and where they have that, they have it entirely and completely, and we have nothing of the sort. For nothing is worthy before God but only and merely his dear son, Jesus Christ, who is entirely pure and holy in himself, whom God sees and in whom he is well pleased, Luke 3[:22]. Now the Son is grasped and taken hold of in the heart, not through works but only through faith without all works. Then God says, "The heart is holy. and my son will dwell therein through faith." . . .

53. Luther: On War against the Turk (April 1529)

From *LW* 46:170–77, trans. Charles Jacobs and Robert Schultz; cf. WA 30/2.

. . . Since the Turk is the rod of the wrath of the Lord our God and the servant of the raging devil, the first thing to be done is to smite the devil, his lord, and take the rod out of God's hand, so that the Turk may be found only, in his own strength, all by himself, without the devil's help and without God's hand. If the Turk's god, the devil, is not beaten first, there is reason to fear that the Turk will not be easy to beat. . . .

I have some parts of Muhammad's Koran, which in Germany might be called a book of sermons or doctrines of the kind that we call pope's decretals. When I have time I must translate it into German so that everyone may see what a foul and shameful book it is.

In the first place, he greatly praises Christ and Mary as being the only ones without sin, and yet he believes nothing more of Christ than that he is a holy prophet, like Jeremiah or Jonah, and denies that he is God's Son and true God. Furthermore, he does not believe that Christ is the Savior of the world who died for our sins, but that he preached to his own time and completed his work before his death, just like any other prophet.

On the other hand, Muhammad highly exalts and praises himself and boasts that he has talked with God and the angels, and that since Christ's office of prophet is now complete, he has been commanded to bring the world to his faith, and if the world is not willing, to compel it or punish it with the sword; there is much glorification of the sword in it. Therefore, the Turks think that their Muhammad is much higher and greater than Christ, for the office of Christ has come to an end and Muhammad's office is still in force.

From this anyone can easily see that Muhammad is a destroyer of our Lord Christ and his kingdom, and if anyone denies the articles concerning Christ, that he is God's Son, that he died for us and still lives and reigns at the right hand of God, what has he left of Christ? Father, Son, Holy Ghost, baptism, the sacrament, gospel, faith, and all Christian doctrine and life are gone, and instead of Christ only Muhammad with his doctrine of works and especially of the sword is left. That is the chief doctrine of the Turkish faith, in which all abominations, all errors, all devils are piled up in one heap. . . .

54. Luther: On the Jews and Their Lies (1543)

In 1523 Luther had written a treatise, "That Jesus Christ Was Born a Jew," in which he said, "I hope that if one deals in a kindly way with the Jews and instructs them carefully from Holy Scripture, many of them will become genuine Christians." Twenty years later, Luther was irritated by their failure to accept his interpretation of Scripture and wrote the following treatise in a very different tone.

From *LW* 47:137–272, trans. Martin Bertram; cf. WA 53:417f.

. . . Grace and peace in the Lord. Dear sir and good friend, I have received a treatise in which a Jew engages in dialogue with a Christian. He dares to pervert the scriptural passages that we cite in testimony to our faith, concerning our Lord Christ and Mary his mother, and to interpret them quite differently. With this argument he thinks he can destroy the basis of our faith.

This is my reply to you and to him. . . .

They have failed to learn any lesson from the terrible distress that has been theirs for over fourteen hundred years in exile. Nor can they obtain any end or definite terminus of this, as they suppose, by means of the vehement cries and laments to God. If these blows do not help, it is reasonable to assume that our talking and explaining will help even less.

Therefore, a Christian should be content and not argue with the Jews. But if you have to or want to talk with them, do not say any more than this: "Listen, Jew, are you aware that Jerusalem and your sovereignty, together with your temple and priesthood, have been destroyed for over 1,460 years?" For this year, which we Christians write as the year 1542 since the birth of Christ, is exactly 1,468 years, going on fifteen hundred years, since Vespasian and Titus destroyed Jerusalem and expelled the Jews from the city. Let the Jews bite on this nut and dispute this question as long as they wish.

For such ruthless wrath of God is sufficient evidence that they assuredly have erred and gone astray. Even a child can comprehend this. For one dare not regard God as so cruel that he would punish his own people so long, so terribly, so unmercifully, and in addition keep silent, comforting them neither with words nor with deeds, and fixing no time limit and no end of it. Who would have faith, hope, or love toward such a God? Therefore this work of wrath is proof that the Jews, surely rejected by God, are no longer his people, and neither is he any longer their God. . . .

They were never able to tolerate a prophet and always persecuted God's word and declined to give ear to God. That is the complaint and lament of all the prophets. And as their fathers did, so they still do today, nor will they ever mend their ways. If Isaiah, Jeremiah, or other prophets went about among them today and proclaimed what they proclaimed in their day, or declared that the Jews' present circumcision and hope for the Messiah are futile, they would again have to die at their hands as happened then. Let him who is endowed with reason, to say nothing of Christian understanding, note how arbitrarily they pervert and twist the prophets' books with their confounded glosses, in violation of their own conscience (on which we can perhaps say more later). For now that they can no longer stone or kill the prophets physically or personally, they torment them spiritually, mutilate, strangle, and maltreat their beautiful verses so that the human heart is vexed and pained. For this forces us to see how, because of God's wrath, they are wholly delivered into the devil's hands. In brief, they are a prophet-murdering people; since they can no longer murder the living ones, they must murder and torment the ones that are dead. . . .

What shall we Christians do with this rejected and condemned people, the Jews? Since they live among us, we dare not tolerate their conduct, now that we are aware of their lying and reviling and blaspheming. If we do, we become sharers in their lies, cursing, and blasphemy. Thus we cannot extinguish the unquenchable fire of divine wrath, of which the prophets speak, nor can we convert the Jews. With prayer and the fear of God, we must practice a sharp mercy to see whether we might save at least a few from the glowing flames. We dare not avenge ourselves. Vengeance a thousand times worse than we could wish them already has them by the throat. I shall give you my sincere advice:

First, to set fire to their synagogues or schools and to bury and cover with dirt whatever will not burn, so that no man will ever again see a stone or cinder of them. This is to be done in honor of our Lord and of Christendom, so that God might see that we are Christians, and do not condone or knowingly tolerate such public lying, cursing, and blaspheming of his Son and of his Christians. . . .

Second, I advise that their houses also be razed and destroyed. For they pursue in them the same aims as in their synagogues. Instead, they might be lodged under a roof or a barn, like the gypsies. . . .

Third, I advise that all their prayer books and Talmudic writings, in which such idolatry, lies, and cursing, and blasphemy are taught, be taken from them.

Fourth, I advise that their rabbis be forbidden to teach henceforth on pain of loss of life and limb. . . .

Fifth, I advise that safe-conduct on the highways be abolished completely for the Jews. For they have no business in the countryside, since they are not lords, officials, tradesmen, or the like. Let them stay at home. I have heard it is said that a rich Jew is now traveling across the country with twelve horses—his ambition is to become a Kokhba—devouring princes, lords, lands, and people with his usury, so that the great lords view it with jealous eyes. . . .

Sixth, I advise that usury be prohibited to them, and that all cash and treasure of silver and gold be taken from them and put aside for safekeeping. . . . Whenever a Jew is sincerely converted, he should be handed one hundred, two hundred, or three hundred florins, as personal circumstances may suggest. . . .

Seventh, I recommend putting a flail, an ax, a hoe, a spade, a distaff, or a spindle into the hands of young, strong Jews and Jewesses and letting them earn their bread in the sweat of their brow, as was imposed on the children of Adam (Genesis 3[:29]). For it is not fitting that they should let us accursed Goyim toil in the sweat of our faces, while they, the holy people, idle away their time behind the stove, feasting and farting, and on top of all, boasting blasphemously of their lordship over the Christians by means of our sweat. . . .

55. Luther's Sermon for the Feast of the Holy Angels (September 1544)

This sermon illustrates Luther's apocalyptic state of mind and the combination of discouragement and confidence that characterized his final years.

From WA 49:583.

TEXT: REVELATION 12:7-12

". . . But woe to you, O earth and sea, for the devil has come down to you in great wrath, because he knows that his time is short!"

. . . The devil, especially in this last time, prepares new heretics and rotten spirits in surprising ways; for he wants at all times to possess the heavenly realm and to be lord in Christendom. He does not ask much of the Turks or the papists since they are already his. However, he does struggle through them against the church, because he wants to sit and rule in the pure, holy Temple of God.

Now, how should we act toward him? We can cheerfully ponder this, especially when the Word of God guides us, even though we have no hope for peace. Imagine that we are his soldiers who must be situated in the field; yes, always standing on guard so that when one battle stops we can go quickly on to another. For we are called through Christ and already enrolled—through baptism—in the army that fights under Christ against the devil. . . .

Christ is the God who is a prince of war or a proper duke who leads his regiment in the strife, not above in heaven among the holy angels, where no struggle is needed, but here on earth in the midst of his church. Yes, even though he sits at the right hand of the Father, he himself is at the head of his army against the enemy that no human power or weapon can resist, to steer and defend them through the Word he has given them.

Such strife arises because the Christians hear, believe, and preach the Word of this Lord. The devil cannot suffer this to take place in the world. Therefore, he sets himself against them with all his power, through both lies and murder in order to eradicate it. Therefore, Christ must gather his church as a counter-force and fight against the hellish army of the dragon, the pope, the Turks, the Jews, the rotten spirits, so that faith and the confession of Christ will remain pure. For he is God's Son, born of a virgin, our Lord and Savior, who saved and made us holy through his blood, as our confession says. Satan wants to rip this confession entirely out of the hearts and mouths of all people and seeks in every way, now in Baptism, now in the sacrament, now in the text of the gospel to falsify the faith and seduce people. . . .

This text gives us, as I have said, both the teaching and the consolation that Christ, God's Son, truly is with his church that possesses and believes his Word and through it wants to prove his power against the devil, so that through its belief and confession it will be preserved and will be victorious over the devil, as he said in Matt. 16:18, "that the gates of hell shall not overpower the church," which stands, believes, and confesses on this ground that he is the living Son of God. . . .

Chapter Two

The Dissemination of the Reform Message

The controversies described in chapter one continuously shifted Martin Luther's attention from one issue to another, but his response to each crisis consistently reflected his enduring concern for certain theological beliefs that he viewed as crucial components of the Christian message. The preoccupation of the Lutheran movement can be summarized, most simply, by the three *"solas"*: *sola scriptura* (scripture alone), *sola gratia* (grace alone), and *sola fide* (faith alone) and by its emphasis on the priesthood of all believers, the clear differentiation between law and gospel, and Christ's presence "in, with, and under" the bread and the wine of the Lord's Supper. While vigorously defending these ideas against opponents whom he thought were delaying or misdirecting the reform of the church, Luther also worked steadily to make them understandable to every level of society, from the educated elites who could provide future religious or political leadership to the much larger number of simple believers who were unlikely to grasp the subtleties of most theological disputes.

Luther became well known throughout all of Europe primarily as a result of the publication of his writings. He traveled occasionally to participate in negotiations or to serve as a mediator in disputes, but for the most part he spent his whole life in Wittenberg, continuing to carry out his ordinary duties as preacher and university professor. In both of these roles, he worked to promote greater familiarity with the contents of the Bible.

Luther thought that neglect of the Bible had caused the church's decline and that reform of the church could only take place if the Bible were more widely distributed and studied with greater care. One of Luther's most memorable contributions to this process was his effort to make the Bible available in the vernacular language of the German people. His translation of the New Testament first appeared in 1524, and he completed his version of the Old Testament by 1534. For the rest of his life, he worked with others on a comprehensive revision of this monumental work.

To equip pastors for their work in the church, Luther also regularly lectured on individual books of the Bible in the theological faculty of the university. Before the indulgence controversy, he had lectured on the Psalms, Romans, Galatians, and Hebrews. In later years, he presented a decade-long series of lectures on Genesis, worked through several other Old Testament books, and focused once again on Galatians, the letter of Paul that had so powerfully influenced his understanding of justification by grace through faith. During these same years, Luther also filled in several times as pastor of the city church while Johannes Bugenhagen (1485–1558) was absent for extended periods to help set up Lutheran churches in other territories. When his health was good, Luther would often preach as many as seventy times a year.

Luther's lectures and sermons emphasized similar themes (docs. #56 and 57), but stylistically they were often quite different. In the lectures, Luther analyzed each biblical verse at great length. In most of his sermons, he presented a briefer exposition of his text and ended with practical suggestions for daily living. Even among the sermons, there is considerable stylistic variety. Some, such as the Invocavit Sermons of 1522 (see doc. #21, cf. doc. #7), directly addressed a particular topic or problem and reflected on it with the help of a variety of biblical texts. His later sermons more frequently concentrated on the interpretation of the biblical passage assigned by the lectionary for a specific day of the church calendar. Luther's best-known published sermon collection, the Church Postil (doc. #56), bears only slight resemblance to the sermons that Luther actually preached, without a written text, to an assembled congregation. These sermons, published between 1522 and 1525 were carefully prepared expositions of the biblical text that were designed to provide guidance for other preachers. Luther recognized that these sermons were generally too lengthy to serve as exact models for preaching, but he still remarked in 1527 that this postil was the best book he had ever written.[1]

Although the lectures and sermons can now be studied in written form, it is important to remember that they were initially communicated orally. The overall literacy rate in the Holy Roman Empire may have been as low as 5 percent, and at most only 30 percent of the population in the urban areas was able to read. Luther was well aware of this fact and therefore emphasized the great value of the effectively crafted and well-delivered sermon. Noting that Christ himself wrote nothing, Luther stated in 1521 that the gospel should be seen first and foremost as "a proclamation that is spread not by pen but by word of mouth."[2]

In addition to encouraging simple believers to attend worship services where the gospel was preached, Luther advocated the development of short summaries of basic beliefs that even the illiterate could be expected to memorize. Most notable among these were his two catechisms. Luther had preached sermons on the Ten Commandments, the Creed, the Lord's Prayer, and the sacraments, and when the first systematic visitation of the parishes in Saxony in 1528 revealed widespread ignorance of Christian teachings among both rural clergy and the common people, he reorganized the contents of these sermons as the Large Catechism, primarily for the instruction of pastors. At the same time, he prepared a shorter version, the Small Catechism, for laypeople and published it as an illustrated booklet in 1529 (doc. #58). Luther hoped that families would voluntarily review the contents of the Small Catechism in their homes, but since this ideal never became a widespread reality, the Lutheran churches also instituted scheduled occasions when the congregation would hear its contents reviewed. Pastors read the catechism aloud from the pulpit and preached series of sermons on its sections. In many schools, teachers required students to recite it weekly as part of their regular lessons, and children were expected to have memorized it before their first communion.

Hymns provided another way for people to share in the recitation of basic teachings. Luther advocated congregational singing as a way to involve the laity along with the clergy in the act of worship. He also recognized the power of rhymed phrases and rhythmic melodies to move people's hearts and to help them remember what they had been taught. The first Lutheran hymnal, the Eight Song Book, was published in 1524. It contained four hymns by Luther, three by Paul Speratus, and one by an unnamed composer. Another hymnal arranged to follow the liturgical calendar appeared in 1529 and was reissued in revised form at least five more times before Luther's death. Luther wrote over thirty hymns. Some were German paraphrases of well-known Latin canticles, while others were new compositions, often based on the Psalms (doc. #59:a and b). Luther also versified parts of the catechism, such as the Ten Commandments and the Apostles' Creed (doc. #59:c and d). Luther, Speratus, and many other Lutheran hymnwriters repeatedly stressed the sinner's need for God's grace and consoled believers with the promise of salvation through Christ (doc. #59:e).

As decisive as his own voice was during the formative period of the Lutheran church, Luther also required the assistance of many coworkers in the task of disseminating the reform message. Many others preached sermons and produced catechisms or hymns. Some of Luther's associates were also better equipped than he was to achieve certain goals. Luther's more theologically sophisticated writings were almost all prompted by specific controversies. The task of providing a more systematic summary of his teachings was left to Philip Melanchthon (1497–1560), his colleague at the university in Wittenberg. Melanchthon had come to the university in 1518 to teach Greek. Although he quickly developed a reputation as an exceptional scholar, he never attained a doctorate and had little formal training in theology. Nevertheless, he became the master interpreter of Luther's theology. Melanchthon's superior philological skills were valuable to Luther as he worked on the translation of the Bible. Melanchthon also represented Luther at many of the diets and colloquies with other religious parties that Luther could not attend because of his outlaw status or his precarious health. The Augsburg Confession, which became the official summary of Lutheran teaching (see doc. #42), faithfully represents Luther's viewpoint, but Melanchthon was the actual author of the document. Melanchthon also prepared the more elaborate Apology for the Augsburg Confession (doc. #60) as a rebuttal to the Catholic arguments that convinced the emperor to reject this confession at the diet in 1530.

Melanchthon published the first Lutheran systematic theology in Latin in 1521. The *Loci Communes*, often translated as Commonplaces or Fundamental Theological Themes, carefully defined the central concepts of Lutheran doctrine and defended them, one by one, with extensive support from biblical exegesis. Melanchthon revised and expanded this dogmatic summary several times during his career, and other coworkers made it available in a German edition (doc. #61). The evolution of this major work also reveals that Melanchthon was an independent thinker. In later editions, he began to explicate topics such as good works, free will, or the Lord's Supper in ways that were uncharacteristic of Luther (doc. #62). This would later provoke the controversies discussed in chapter five.

While Melanchthon defended Lutheran teachings against attacks by highly educated critics, other writers directed their efforts to the persuasion of simple laypeople. They wrote numerous short pamphlets or *Flugschriften* in German, which were often made attractive by decoration with woodcuts and could be purchased relatively inexpensively (for the equivalent of the cost of a chicken or a third of an artisan's daily wage).[3] It is estimated that more than four thousand different broadsheets were printed in the early decades of the Reformation and that their influence extended beyond a literate audience because they were frequently read aloud to an assembled group.[4] One of the most prolific and influential of these pamphleteers was Johann Eberlin von Günzburg (1455–1534), a Franciscan friar from southern Germany who left his order after reading Luther's reform treatises of 1520. Eberlin published a series of pamphlets called "The Fifteen Comrades," which attacked corruption in the Catholic church. Other pamphlets, such as "A Beautiful Mirror of the Christian Life," assembled numerous biblical quotes to support a simpler mode of piety in keeping with the central themes of Luther's teachings (doc. #63).

Other pamphleteers were laypeople who, though theologically untrained, were often audacious defenders of Luther's cause. Their writings appeared in many forms such as letters, dialogues, poems, and polemical satires. Argula von Grumbach (c.1490–c.1564) is notable for being one of several lay women writers. The wife of a minor court official, she was prompted to write four pamphlets by the arrest of a young instructor at the University of Ingolstadt for the possession of Lutheran writings. In her letter to the Duke of Bavaria, published in 1523, she argued that Luther's teachings were consistent with the Bible and that rulers ought to honor the Bible more than the judgments of the corrupt clergy (doc. #64). Erasmus Alber (1500–1553), a schoolteacher in Hesse, provides an example of a more satirical piece. His letter from Lucifer to Luther, published in 1524, fits into a genre that dates from the fourteenth century. Many writers portrayed the pope as an instrument of the devil (doc. #65).

Lutherans had no monopoly on satirical propaganda. Catholics and Protestants published attacks on each other that were often both vicious and entertaining. The crudeness of some of these writings may, in fact, have enhanced their appeal among simple people. Thomas Murner (1475–1537), a Franciscan friar, was the premier Catholic satirist. In 1522, he published a long poem called "The Great Lutheran Fool," which associated the Lutheran movement with all sorts of nonsensical and destructive activities. Murner portrays himself in the poem as an exorcist of many fools who had been placed in the body of the Great Fool by the devil (doc. #66). Johannes Cochlaeus (1479–1552) portrayed Luther as an inconsistent and increasingly dangerous teacher in a 1529 treatise titled "The Seven-Headed Luther" (doc. #67). Later he also wrote a lengthy biography of Luther that once again made reference to this image.

Woodcuts accompanying these writings enhanced their impact. Even those who could not read could be strongly influenced by the associations communicated by visual images. Lutherans also participated in the production of such visual propaganda. Andreas Osiander (1496–1552), an important Lutheran reformer in Nürnberg, published a series of woodcuts in 1527 that portrayed the popes as immoral and power-hungry enemies of God (doc. #68). In 1545 Luther himself commissioned an even cruder set of images that also associated the pope with the devil and encouraged the simple people, by the portrayal of scatological gestures, to relinquish any residual respect they had for the leaders of the church in Rome (doc. #69).

The character and motivations of Luther were issues in much of this literature as frequently as questions about the truth or effects of his teachings. Catholics often portrayed Luther as a degenerate schemer, so Luther's defenders were intent on refuting this caricature. Once again, this task was undertaken by both lay Lutherans and influential pastors or theologians. For example, Haug Marschalck (1491–1535), an army paymaster in Augsburg, published a pamphlet in 1522 that memorably associated positive qualities with each of the letters of Luther's name. Johannes Mathesius (1504–65), a pastor in Bohemia, preached and published a famous set of sermons that reviewed all the details of Luther's life and praised his accomplishments. Mathesius refrained from placing Luther explicitly in the same category as the prophets and apostles but left the impression that Luther deserved close to the same recognition. While acknowledging that Luther did not claim direct messages from God, Mathesius credited him with prophetic insights. Luther did not perform miracles like the apostles, but Mathesius considered it a divine miracle that Luther had been so successful in introducing so many reforms into the churches of Germany.

The biographies of Luther presented by Cochlaeus and Mathesius could hardly have been more dissimilar. Each author, however, had a long-standing influence on how Catholics and Lutherans evaluated the man and his message.

LUTHER'S SERMONS AND LECTURES

56. Church Postil (1522): Sermon for the Sunday after Christmas on Galatians 4:1-7

A postil is a book of sermons on the Gospel and epistle texts assigned for each Sunday and festival in the church year. Luther began work on this postil while in hiding at the Wartburg castle; hence it is also referred to at times as the Wartburg Postil. Later, Veit Dietrich published another Luther postil known as the House Postil. This latter collection, intended to be read in homes, was mostly based on Gospel sermons Luther had preached in his own home between 1532 and 1534.

WA 10/1:1, 324–48.

. . . You should know that there is one way to speak when teaching about good works and another when teaching about justification; just as someone's nature or person is one thing and someone's actions or works are another. Justification relates to the person and not to the works. It is the person, not the work, that is justified and saved, or sentenced and condemned. So, it can be concluded that no one is justified by works; you must first be justified by other means. As Moses says in Genesis 4[:4-5], "God looked with favor upon Abel and his offering." First, he looked with favor on Abel the person and then on his offering. First the person was pious, just, and acceptable and then also his offering. The sacrifice was accepted because of the person, and not the person because of the sacrifice. "But on Cain and his offering he did not look with favor." God did not have favor toward Cain the person and therefore also not his offering. From this text it can be determined that it is not possible for any work to be good in God's sight unless beforehand the person is good and acceptable. On the other hand, it is not possible for any work to be evil in God's sight unless the person is already evil and unacceptable. We have said enough now and can conclude that there are two kinds of good works; some come before and others come after justification. The ones that come before appear to be good but are useless; the others are truly good. . . .

So then you ask: "What shall I do? How does my person become good and acceptable? How will I obtain justification? The gospel answers: "You must hear Christ, have faith in him, utterly deny yourself, and believe that you will be changed from a Cain to an Abel, and then present your offerings." This faith is preached apart from all your work or merit, so it will also be given out of grace apart from any of your merits. This same faith justifies the person and is also justification itself. Because of it God remits and forgives all sins, the entire Adam and Cain in our nature, according to the will of Christ his beloved Son, whose name is synonymous with faith. He also gives his Holy Spirit, who changes the person into a new creature that has a different reason and will, now inclined to the good. This person performs purely good works, and what is done is good. Therefore, nothing else is necessary for justification besides hearing and believing in Jesus Christ as our Savior. But both of these are not natural to us; they are works of grace. Whoever proposes to attain justification by works only hinders the gospel, faith, grace, Christ, God, and everything. On the other hand, good works belong to nothing but justification (for none but the justified do good, and all that is done when one is justified is good without distinction of works). The order of salvation is first, before all things, to hear the Word of God. Thereafter comes faith and then works. This is how one is saved. Whoever reverses or changes this order is certainly not of God. . . .

Now, look at the common way of thinking and acting among the people. They are accustomed to saying, "I still want to become pious. Yes, one must be pious." But if one asks them what a person must do in order to become pious, they begin to say, "One must pray, fast, go to church, abstain from sin, etc." This one runs off to the Carthusians, that one joins another monastic order. One becomes a priest, another puts on a hair shirt. This one whips himself, that one tortures himself in another way. See, that is to act just like Cain and to do Cain's work. The person remains unchanged, and there is no justification because there is only an outward change, a change of work, clothing, place, or demeanor. They are really apes who adopt the demeanor of the saints but are still not holy. Not thinking about faith, they rush forth with only their [supposed] good works, torturing themselves to get to heaven. . . .

So, you may say, "If it is true that we are justified not by works, but by hearing and believing that Christ gave himself for us, what need and use do the commandments have? Why has God made such hard demands? To answer that, we come now to this epistle lesson that tells us why the commandments are given. The Galatians first learned the Christian faith from Paul but were afterwards turned around by certain false teachers so that they fell back on their works and imagined that they must become righteous through the works of the law. In our lesson, Paul calls them back from their works to faith, and with many strong words proves that there are the two kinds of works of the law. He concludes that the works preceding justification or faith have no value and make us only servants. However, faith makes us children or sons of God and truly good works must follow from that. One must note Paul's customary use of words when he distinguishes between the servant and the child. The sanctimonious,

about whom he has much to say, he calls servants. The believer in Christ, who is and will be justified by faith alone without works, he calls a child. All this is because the sanctimonious one does not serve in the same way as the child who is heir to his own inheritance. The service of the sanctimonious is like that of a day-laborer who works on another's property. Although the works of the two seem alike or of the same sort, they are differentiated by the spirit of each doer, by conscience and faith. . . .

The apostle wants to say, and this is true, that without faith, the law with all its works makes us merely servants. Only faith can make us children. Neither the law, nor the works of the law, nor human nature can give us this faith; only the gospel brings it. For the hearer, this gospel is a word of grace, and the Word is accompanied by the Holy Spirit when preached and quietly heard. Acts 10 proves this, for Cornelius and his family receive the Holy Spirit through listening to St. Peter. The law was not given except to show man that without grace he has the mind of the servant, not the child. Without faith and trust, he serves God unwillingly. If they were to confess further, they would have to admit that they would rather be without the law, and they do not live under it willingly. What they do is a faithless thing, done out of compulsion, and through the law they are not able to make any progress. They should learn from the law that they are like servants and not like children. Therefore, to change from the condition of servant to that of a child, they must regard their efforts as worthless, for it is only through faith and the grace of God that they may attain their rightful place in life. . . .

Now, if, unfortunately, Cain . . . does not learn to see himself this way through the law but remains impenitent and blind in his works, not acknowledging his inner wickedness, then he will maliciously judge the whole world in

Title Page of Luther's 1534 Bible

general and despise sinners as the Pharisee did in the Gospel [Luke 18:11-13], thinking himself to be pious, unlike other people. . . .

But those who will be like Abel and become children learn to know themselves by the law and recognize that their hearts are averse to the law. Relinquishing their overconfidence, letting go both hand and foot, they become as nothing in their own eyes through this knowledge. Then the gospel comes. There God gives grace to the humble, and they grasp the testament and believe. In and with this faith they receive the Holy Spirit, who gives them a new heart that delights in the law, hates sin, and does what is good freely and cheerfully. There are no more works of the law but now the heart of the law. This is the time when the father decides that the heir should no longer be a servant nor under a guardian. . . .

Paul says that after Christ has come and been recognized, the person is no longer a servant. As we have said, one cannot be both a child and a servant at the same time because the mind of each is so different. The child is willing and free; the servant is unwilling and constrained. The child goes forth in faith; the servant in works. Once more, we see here that no one can acquire anything related to salvation by works before God. Before works are done, salvation must be obtained and pos-

sessed so that the works that follow are done freely for the honor of God and for the benefit of the neighbor. . . .

57. Lecture on Galatians 4 (1535)

Paul's letters to the Romans and Galatians were of utmost importance in the formation of Luther's theology. The reformer completed an early commentary on Galatians in 1519. The following excerpt is from the later lectures, which he delivered orally at the university in 1531 and which were transcribed and prepared for publication in 1535 by George Rörer. See another excerpt from this lecture in chapter 1 (doc. #46).

From *LW* 26:359–91, trans. Jaroslav Pelikan.

CHAPTER 4

1. I mean that the heir, as long as he is a child, is no better than a slave, though he is the owner of all the estate;

2. but he is under guardians and trustees until the date set by the father.

. . . Ordinary people are caught more easily by analogies and illustrations than by difficult and subtle discussions; they would rather look at a well-drawn picture than a well-written book. Therefore after the analogy of the human testament and about the prison [Galatians 3] and the custodian, [Paul] also cites this very familiar one about the heir, in order to convince them. . . .

3. So with us; when we were children, we were slaves to the elements of this world.

. . . We were indeed heirs, having the promise of a future inheritance to be granted through Abraham's offspring, Christ, who was to bless all nations. But because the time had not yet fully come, Moses, our guardian, manager, and custodian, came and held us confined and captive, to prevent us from taking the upper hand and gaining control and possession of our inheritance. Meanwhile, however, just as an heir is nourished by the hope of his coming freedom, so Moses nourished us with hope in the promise to be revealed in due time, namely, when Christ came. Before his coming it was the time of the law; when he came, this was finished, and the time of grace is at hand. . . .

. . . The law was dominant over us and oppressed us with harsh slavery as serfs and captives. In the first place, it was a political restraint upon uncivilized and carnal men to keep them from rushing headlong into all sorts of crimes. The law threatens transgressors with punishment; and if they were not afraid of this, they would do nothing but commit evil. Those who are restrained by the law this way are dominated by the law. In the second place, the law accused, terrified, killed, and condemned us before God spiritually or theologically. This was the chief dominion of the law over us. Therefore just as an heir who is subject to guardians is whipped and forced to obey their rules and to carry out their orders carefully, so consciences before Christ are oppressed by the harsh tyranny of the law; that is, they are accused, terrified, and condemned by the law. Now this dominion, or rather tyranny, of the law is not permanent but is supposed to last only until the time of grace. Therefore, the function of the law is indeed to denounce and to increase sin, but for the purpose of righteousness; and to kill, but for the purpose of life. For the law is the custodian until Christ comes. . . .

I am not saying this with the intention that the law should be held in contempt. Paul does not intend this either, but that it should be held in esteem. But because Paul is dealing here with the issue of justification—a discussion of justification is something vastly differ-

ent from a discussion of the law—necessity demands that he speak of the law as something very contemptible. When we are dealing with this argument, we cannot speak of it in sufficiently vile and odious terms either. For here the conscience should consider and know nothing except Christ alone. Therefore we should make every effort that in the question of justification we reject the law from view as far as possible and embrace nothing except the promise of Christ. . . .

4. But when the time had fully come, God sent forth his Son, born of woman, born under the law,

5. to redeem those who were under the law.

. . . This passage testifies that when the time of the law was completed, Christ did not establish a new law to follow the old law of Moses but abrogated it and redeemed those who were being oppressed by it. Therefore it is a very wicked error when the monks and sophists portray Christ as a new lawgiver after Moses, not unlike the error of the Turks, who proclaim that their Muhammad is the new lawgiver after Christ. Those who portray Christ this way do him a supreme injury. He did not come to abrogate the old law with the purpose of establishing a new one; but, as Paul says here, he was sent into the world by the Father to redeem those where were being held captive under the law. These words portray Christ truly and accurately. . . .

We adults, who are imbued with the noxious doctrine of the papists, which we absorbed into our very bones and marrow, acquired an opinion of Christ altogether different from the one that Paul sets forth here. No matter how much we declared with our mouths that Christ had redeemed us from the tyranny and slavery of the law, actually we felt in our hearts that he was a lawgiver, a tyrant, and a judge more fearful than Moses himself. Even today, in the great light of the truth, we cannot completely banish this wicked opinion from our minds. So stubbornly do things to which we have been accustomed since youth cling to us! You young people, who are still unspoiled and have never been infected by this wicked notion, have less difficulty in teaching purely about Christ than we adults have in banishing these blasphemous illusions about him from our minds, yet you have not altogether escaped the wiles of the devil. For even if you have not yet been imbued with this wicked idea of Christ as a lawgiver, you still have the same source of this idea in you, namely, the flesh, the reason, and the wickedness of our nature, which cannot think of Christ in any other way than as a lawgiver. Therefore you must contend with all your might, in order that you may learn to acknowledge and regard Christ as Paul portrays him in this passage. . . .

But in what manner or way has Christ redeemed us? The manner was as follows: He was born under the law. When Christ came, he found us all captive under guardians and trustees, that is, confined and constrained under the law. What did he do? He himself is Lord of the law; therefore the Law has no jurisdiction over him and cannot accuse him, because he is the Son of God. He who was not under the law subjected himself voluntarily to the law. The law did everything to him that it did to us. It accused us and terrified us. It subjected us to sin, death, and the wrath of God; and it condemned us with its judgment. And it had a right to do all this, for we have all sinned. But Christ "committed no sin, and no guile was found on his lips" [1 Pet. 2:22]. Therefore he owed nothing to the law. And yet against him—so holy, righteous, and blessed—the law raged as much as it does against us accursed and condemned sinners and even more fiercely. It accused him of blasphemy and sedition; it found him guilty in the sight of God of all the sins of the entire world; finally it so sad-

dened and frightened him that he sweat blood [Luke 22:44]; and eventually it sentenced him to death, even death on a cross [Phil. 2:8].

This was truly a remarkable duel, when the law, a creature, came into conflict with the Creator, exceeding its every jurisdiction to vex the Son of God with the same tyranny with which it vexed us, the sons of wrath [Eph. 2:3]. Because the law has sinned so horribly and wickedly against its God, it is summoned to court and accused. Here Christ says: "Lady Law, you empress, you cruel and powerful tyrant over the whole human race, what did I commit that you accused, intimidated, and condemned me in my innocence?" Here the law, which once condemned and killed all men, has nothing with which to defend and to cleanse itself. Therefore it is condemned and killed in turn, so that it loses its jurisdiction not only over Christ—whom it attacked and killed without any right anyway—but also over all who believe in him. . . .

Therefore the law is guilty of stealing, of sacrilege, and of the murder of the Son of God. It loses its rights and deserves to be damned. Whenever Christ is present or is at least named, it is forced to yield and to flee this name as the devil flees the cross. Therefore we believers are free of the law through Christ, who "triumphed over it in him" [Col. 2:15]. This glorious triumph, accomplished for us through Christ, is grasped not by works but by faith alone. Therefore faith alone justifies. . . .

7. So through God you are no longer a slave but a son.

. . . To be a slave, according to what Paul says here, means to be sentenced and imprisoned under the law, under the wrath of God, and under death; it means to acknowledge God not as God or as Father but as a tormentor, an enemy, a tyrant. This is truly to live in slavery and in a Babylonian captivity and to be cruelly tormented in it. For the more someone performs works under the law, the more he is oppressed by its slavery. That slavery, he says, has ended; it does not strain and oppress us any longer. . . .

Therefore do not let Moses—much less the pope—enter the bridegroom's chamber to lie there, that is, to reign over the conscience that Christ has delivered from the law to make it free of any slavery. Let the slaves remain in the valley with the ass, and let Isaac ascend the mountain along with Abraham, his father. That is, let the law have its dominion over the flesh and the old self; let this be under the law; let this permit the burden to be laid upon it; let this permit itself to be disciplined and vexed by the law; let the law prescribe to this what it should do and accomplish, how it should deal with other men. But let the law not pollute the chamber in which Christ alone should take his rest and sleep; that is, let it not disturb the conscience, which should live only with Christ, its Bridegroom, in the realm of freedom and sonship. . . .

COMMUNAL AFFIRMATIONS OF THE GOSPEL MESSAGE

58. Luther's Small Catechism (1529)

In the preface to this document, Luther wrote: "The deplorable conditions that I recently encountered when I was a visitor [to the congregations of Electoral Saxony] constrained me to prepare this brief and simple catechism or statement of Christian teachings. Good God, what wretchedness I beheld! The common people, especially those who live in the country, have no knowledge whatever of Christian teaching, and unfortunately many pastors are quite incompetent and unfitted for teaching." He summarized Christian beliefs first in a

series of five charts and soon after in the following handbook form.

BC 351–63.

THE TEN COMMANDMENTS . . .

The First [Commandment]

You are to have no other gods.

What is this? Answer:

We are to fear, love, and trust God above all things.

The Second [Commandment]

You are not to misuse the name of your God.

What is this? Answer:

We are to fear and love God, so that we do not curse, swear, practice magic, lie, or deceive using God's name, but instead use that very name in every time of need to call on, pray to, praise, and give thanks to God.

The Third [Commandment]

You are to hallow the day of rest.

What is this? Answer:

We are to fear and love God, so that we do not despise preaching or God's Word, but instead keep that Word holy and gladly hear and learn it.

The Fourth [Commandment]

You are to honor your father and your mother.

What is this? Answer:

We are to fear and love God, so that we neither despise nor anger our parents and others in authority, but instead honor, serve, obey, love, and respect them.

The Fifth [Commandment]

You are not to kill.

What is this? Answer:

We are to fear and love God, so that we neither endanger nor harm the lives of our neighbors, but instead help and support them in all of life's needs.

The Sixth [Commandment]

You are not to commit adultery.

What is this? Answer:

We are to fear and love God, so that we lead pure and decent lives in word and deed, and each of us loves and honors his or her spouse.

The Seventh [Commandment]

You are not to steal.

What is this? Answer:

We are to fear and love God, so that we neither take our neighbors' money or property nor acquire them by using shoddy merchandise or crooked deals, but instead help them to improve and protect their property and income.

The Eighth [Commandment]

You are not to bear false witness against your neighbor.

What is this? Answer:

We are to fear and love God, so that we do not tell lies about our neighbors, betray or slander them, or destroy their reputations. Instead we are to come to their defense, speak well of them, and interpret everything they do in the best possible light.

The Ninth [Commandment]

You are not to covet your neighbor's house.

What is this? Answer:

We are to fear and love God, so that we do not try to trick our neighbors out of their inheritance or property or try to get it for ourselves by claiming to have a legal right to it and the like, but instead be of help and service to them in keeping what is theirs.

The Tenth [Commandment]

You are not to covet your neighbor's wife, male or female servant, cattle, or whatever is his.

What is this? Answer:

We are to fear and love God, so that we do not entice, force, or steal away from our neighbors their spouses, household workers, or livestock, but instead urge them to stay and fulfill their responsibilities to our neighbors.

What then does God say about all these commandments? Answer:

God says the following: "I, the Lord your God, am a jealous God. Against those who hate me I visit the sin of the fathers on the children up to the third and fourth generation. But I do good to those who love me and keep my commandments to the thousandth generation."

What is this? Answer:

God threatens to punish all who break these commandments. Therefore we are to fear his wrath and not disobey these commandments. However, God promises grace and every good thing to all those who keep these commandments. Therefore we also are to love and trust him and gladly act according to his commands.

THE CREED:

In a very simple way in which the head of a house is to present it to the household

The First Article: On Creation

I believe in God, the Father almighty, Creator of heaven and earth.

What is this? Answer:

I believe that God has created me together with all that exists. God has given me and still preserves my body and soul: eyes, ears, and all limbs and senses; reason and all mental faculties. In addition, God daily and abundantly provides shoes and clothing, food and drink, house and farm, spouse and children, fields, livestock, and all property—along with all the necessities and nourishment for this body and life. God protects me against all danger and shields and preserves me from all evil. And all this is done out of pure, fatherly, and divine goodness and mercy, without any merit or worthiness of mine at all! For all of this I owe it to God to thank and praise, serve and obey him. This is most certainly true.

The Second Article: On Redemption

And [I believe] in Jesus Christ, his only Son, our Lord, who was conceived by the Holy Spirit, born of the Virgin Mary, suffered under Pontius Pilate, was crucified, died, and was buried; he descended into hell. On the third day he rose [again]; he ascended into heaven, seated at the right hand of God, the almighty Father, from where he will come to judge the living and the dead.

What is this? Answer:

I believe that Jesus Christ, true God, begotten of the Father in eternity, and also a true human being, born of the Virgin Mary, is my Lord. He has redeemed me, a lost and condemned human being. He has purchased and freed me from all sins, from death, and from the power of the devil, not with gold or silver but with his holy, precious blood and with his innocent suffering and death. He has done all this in order that I may belong to him, live under him in his kingdom, and serve him in eternal righteousness, innocence, and blessedness, just as he is risen from the dead and lives and rules eternally. This is most certainly true.

The Third Article: On Being Made Holy

I believe in the Holy Spirit, one holy Christian church, the community of the saints, forgiveness of sins, resurrection of the flesh, and eternal life. Amen.

What is this? Answer:

I believe that by my own understanding or strength I cannot believe in Jesus Christ my Lord or come to him, but instead the Holy Spirit has called me through the gospel, enlightened me with his gifts, made me holy and kept me in the true faith, just as he calls, gathers, enlightens, and makes holy the whole Christian church on earth and keeps it with Jesus Christ in the one common, true faith. Daily in this Christian church the Holy Spirit abundantly forgives all sins—mine and those of all believers. On the Last Day the Holy Spirit will raise me and all the dead and will give to me and all believers in Christ eternal life. This is most certainly true.

THE LORD'S PRAYER:

In a very simple way in which the head of a house is to present it to the household

Our Father, you who are in heaven.

What is this? Answer:

With these words God wants to entice us, so that we come to believe he is truly our Father and we are truly his children, in order that we may ask him boldly and with complete confidence, just as loving children ask their loving father.

The First Petition

May your name be hallowed.

What is this? Answer:

It is true that God's name is holy in itself, but we ask in this prayer that it may also become holy in and among us.

How does this come about? Answer:

Whenever the Word of God is taught clearly and purely and we, as God's children, also live holy lives according to it. To this end help us, dear Father in heaven! However, whoever teaches and lives otherwise than the Word of God teaches profanes the name of God among us. Preserve us from this, heavenly Father!

The Second Petition

May your kingdom come.

What is this? Answer:

In fact, God's kingdom comes on its own without our prayer, but we ask in this prayer that it may also come to us.

How does this come about? Answer:

Whenever our heavenly Father gives us his Holy Spirit, so that through his grace we believe his Holy Word and live godly lives here in time and hereafter in eternity.

The Third Petition

May your will come about on earth as in heaven.

What is this? Answer:

In fact, God's good and gracious will comes about without our prayer, but we ask in this prayer that it may also come about in and among us.

How does this come about? Answer:

Whenever God breaks and hinders every evil scheme and will—as are present in the will of the devil, the world, and our flesh—that would not allow us to hallow God's name and would prevent the coming of his kingdom, and instead whenever God strengthens us and keeps us steadfast in his Word and in faith until the end of our lives. This is his gracious and good will.

The Fourth Petition

Give us today our daily bread.

What is this? Answer:

In fact, God gives daily bread without our prayer, even to all evil people, but we ask in this prayer that God cause us to recognize what our daily bread is and to receive it with thanksgiving.

What then does "daily bread" mean? Answer:

Everything included in the necessities and nourishment for our bodies, such as food, drink, clothing, shoes, house, farm, fields, livestock, money, property, an upright spouse, upright children, upright members of the household, upright and faithful rulers, good government, good weather, peace, health, decency, honor, good friends, faithful neighbors, and the like.

The Fifth Petition

And remit our debts, as we remit what our debtors owe.

What is this? Answer:

We ask in this prayer that our heavenly Father would not regard our sins nor deny these petitions on their account, for we are worthy of nothing for which we ask, nor have we earned it. Instead we ask that God would give us all things by grace, for we daily sin much and indeed deserve only punishment. So, on the other hand, we, too, truly want to forgive heartily and to do good gladly to those who sin against us.

The Sixth Petition

And lead us not into temptation.

What is this? Answer:

It is true that God tempts no one, but we ask in this prayer that God would preserve and keep us, so that the devil, the world, and our flesh may not deceive us or mislead us into false belief, despair, and other great shame and vice, and that, although we may be attacked by them, we may finally prevail and gain the victory.

The Seventh Petition

But deliver us from evil.

What is this? Answer:

We ask in this prayer, as in a summary, that our Father in heaven may deliver us from all kinds of evil—affecting body or soul, property or reputation—and at last, when our final hour comes, may grant us a blessed end and take us by grace from this valley of tears to himself in heaven.

Amen.

What is this? Answer:

That I should be certain that such petitions are acceptable to and heard by our Father in heaven, for he himself commanded us to pray like this and has promised to hear us. "Amen, amen" means "Yes, yes, it is going to come about just like this."

THE SACRAMENT OF HOLY BAPTISM:

In a simple way in which the head of a house is to present it to the household

First

What is baptism? Answer:

Baptism is not simply plain water. Instead it is water enclosed in God's command and connected with God's Word.

What then is this Word of God? Answer:

Where our Lord Christ says in Matthew 28[:19], "Go into all the world, teach all nations, and baptize them in the name of the Father and of the Son and of the Holy Spirit."

Second

What gifts or benefits does baptism grant? Answer:

It brings about forgiveness of sins, redeems from death and the devil, and gives eternal salvation to all who believe it, as the words and promise of God declare.

What are these words and promise of God? Answer:

Where our Lord Christ says in Mark 16[:16], "Whoever believes and is baptized will be saved, but whoever does not believe will be damned."

Third

How can water do such great things? Answer:

Clearly the water does not do it, but the Word of God, which is with and alongside the water, and faith, which trusts this Word of God in the water. For without the Word of God the water is plain water and not a baptism, but with the Word of God it is a baptism, that is, a grace-filled water of life and a "bath of the new birth in the Holy Spirit," as St. Paul says to Titus in chapter 3[:5-8], "through the bath of rebirth and renewal of the Holy Spirit, which he richly poured out over us through Jesus Christ our Savior, so that through that very grace we may be righteous and heirs in hope of eternal life. This is surely most certainly true."

Fourth

What then is the significance of such a baptism with water? Answer:

It signifies that the old creature in us with all sins and evil desires is to be drowned and die through daily contrition and repentance, and on the other hand that daily a new person is to come forth and rise up to live before God in righteousness and purity forever.

Where is this written? Answer:

St. Paul says in Romans 6[:4], "We were buried with Christ through baptism into death, so that, just as Christ was raised from the dead through the glory of the Father, we, too, are to walk in a new life."

HOW SIMPLE PEOPLE ARE TO BE TAUGHT TO CONFESS

What is confession? Answer:

Confession consists of two parts. One is that we confess our sins. The other is that we receive the absolution, that is, forgiveness, from the confessor as from God himself and by no means doubt but firmly believe that our sins are thereby forgiven before God in heaven.

Which sins is a person to confess?

Before God one is to acknowledge the guilt for all sins, even those of which we are not aware, as we do in the Lord's Prayer. However, before the confessor we are to confess only those sins of which we have knowledge and which trouble us.

Which sins are these?

Here reflect on your walk of life in light of the Ten Commandments: whether you are father, mother, son, daughter, master, mistress, servant; whether you have been disobedient, unfaithful, lazy; whether you have harmed anyone by word or deed; whether you have stolen, neglected, wasted, or injured anything. Please provide me with a brief form of confession! Answer:

You are to say to the confessor:

"Honorable, dear sir, I ask you to listen to my confession and declare to me forgiveness for God's sake."

"Proceed."

"I, a poor sinner, confess before God that I am guilty of all my sins. In particular I confess in your presence that although I am a manservant, maidservant, etc., I unfortunately serve my master unfaithfully, for in this and that instance I did not do what they told me; I made them angry and caused them to curse; I neglected to do my duty and allowed harm to occur. I have also spoken and acted impudently. I have quarreled with my equals; I have grumbled about and sworn at my mistress, etc. I am sorry for all this and ask for grace. I want to do better."

A master or mistress may say the following:

"In particular I confess to you that I have not faithfully cared for my child, the members of my household, my spouse to the glory of God. I have cursed, set a bad example with indecent words and deeds, done harm to my neighbors, spoken evil of them, overcharged them, and sold them inferior goods and short-changed them," and whatever else he or she has done against the commands of God and their walk of life, etc.

However, if some individuals do not find themselves burdened by these or greater sins, they are not to worry, nor are they to search for or invent further sins and thereby turn confession into torture. Instead mention one or two that you are aware of in the following way: "In particular I confess that I cursed once, likewise that one time I was inconsiderate in my speech, one time I neglected this or that, etc." Let that be enough.

If you are aware of no sins at all (which is really quite unlikely), then do not mention any in particular, but instead receive forgiveness on the basis of the general confession, which you make to God in the presence of the confessor.

Thereupon the confessor is to say:

"God be gracious to you and strengthen your faith. Amen."

Let the confessor say [further]:

"Do you also believe that my forgiveness is God's forgiveness?"

[Answer:] "Yes, dear sir."

Thereupon he may say:

"'Let it be done for you according to your faith.' And I by the command of our Lord Jesus Christ forgive you your sin in the name of the Father and of the Son and of the Holy Spirit. Amen. Go in peace."

A confessor, by using additional passages of Scripture, will in fact be able to comfort and encourage to faith those whose consciences are heavily burdened or who are distressed and under attack. This is only to be an ordinary form of confession for simple people.

The Sacrament of the Altar:

In a simple way in which the head of a house is to present it to the household

What is the Sacrament of the Altar? Answer:

It is the true body and blood of our Lord Jesus Christ under the bread and wine, instituted by Christ himself for us Christians to eat and to drink.

Where is this written? Answer:

The holy evangelists, Matthew, Mark, and Luke, and St. Paul write thus:

"Our Lord Jesus Christ, on the night in which he was betrayed, took the bread, gave thanks, and broke it and gave it to his disciples and said, 'Take; eat; this is my body which is given for you. Do this in remembrance of me.' "In the same way he also took the cup after the supper, gave thanks, and gave it to them and said, 'Take, and drink of it, all of you. This cup is the New Testament in my blood, which is shed for you for the forgiveness of sins. Do this, as often as you drink it, in remembrance of me.'"

What is the benefit of such eating and drinking? Answer:

The words "given for you" and "shed for you for the forgiveness of sins" show us that forgiveness of sin, life, and salvation are given to us in the sacrament through these words, because where there is forgiveness of sin, there is also life and salvation.

How can bodily eating and drinking do such a great thing? Answer:

Eating and drinking certainly do not do it, but rather the words that are recorded: "given for you" and "shed for you for the forgiveness of sins." These words, when accompanied by the physical eating and drinking, are the essential thing in the sacrament, and whoever believes these very words has what they declare and state, namely, "forgiveness of sins."

Who, then, receives this sacrament worthily? Answer:

Fasting and bodily preparation are in fact a fine external discipline, but a person who has faith in these words, "given for you" and "shed for you for the forgiveness of sins," is really worthy and well prepared. However, a person who does not believe these words or doubts them is unworthy and unprepared, because the words "for you" require truly believing hearts.

[Following sections concern morning and evening prayers, grace at table, and a table of duties for different groups in society.]

59. Early Lutheran Hymns (1523–29)

The following four hymns were written by Martin Luther. The first one is inspired by Psalm 130, but the sentiments also seem to echo Luther's personal religious experience. The second one is the most familiar of Luther's hymns. For this one and several others, he also wrote the hymn tune. The third and fourth selections are less well known but clearly illustrate Luther's desire to use hymns as teaching tools.

a. *Aus tiefer Not schrei ich zu dir* (1523)
(*LBW* 295, trans. Gracia Grindal)

Out of the depths I cry to you;
O Father, hear me calling.
Incline your ear to my distress
In spite of my rebelling.
Do not regard my sinful deeds.
Send me the grace my spirit needs;
Without it I am nothing.

All things you send are full of grace;
You crown our lives with favor.
All our good works are done in vain
Without our Lord and Savior.
We praise the God who gives us faith
And saves us from the grip of death;
Our lives are in his keeping.

It is in God that we shall hope,
And not in our own merit.
We rest our fears in his good Word
And trust his Holy Spirit.
His promise keeps us strong and sure;

We trust the holy signature
Inscribed upon our temples.

My soul is waiting for the Lord
As one who longs for morning;
No watcher waits with greater hope
Than I for his returning.
I hope as Israel in the Lord;
He sends redemption through his Word.
We praise him for his mercy.

b. *Ein feste Burg ist unser Gott* (1527/28)
(*LBW* 229)

A mighty fortress is our God,
A sword and shield victorious;
He breaks the cruel oppressor's rod
And wins salvation glorious.
The old evil foe,
Sworn to work us woe,
With dread craft and might
He arms himself to fight.
On earth he has no equal.

No strength of ours can match his might!
We would be lost, rejected.
But now a champion comes to fight,
Whom God himself elected.
Ask who this may be:
Lord of hosts is he!
Jesus Christ, our Lord,
God's only Son, adored.
He holds the field victorious.

Though hordes of devils fill the land,
All threat'ning to devour us,
We tremble not, unmoved we stand;
They cannot overpow'r us.
This world's prince may rage,
In fierce war engage.
He is doomed to fail;
God's judgment must prevail!
One little word subdues him.

God's Word forever shall abide,
No thanks to foes, who fear it;
For God himself fights by our side
With weapons of the Spirit.
If they take our house,
Goods, fame, child, or spouse,
Wrench our life away,
They cannot win the day.
The Kingdom's ours forever!

c. *Mensch, willst du leben seliglich*
[Hymn on the Ten Commandments]
(**LW 53:281, trans. George McDonald**)

Man, wouldst thou live all blissfully
And dwell with God eternally,
Thou shalt observe the Ten Commands
Written by God with his hands.
Kyrioleis

Thy God and Lord I am alway;
No other god shall make thee stray;
Thy heart must ever trust in me;
Mine own kingdom shalt thou be.
Kyrioleis

My name to honor thou shalt heed
And call on me in time of need.
Thou shalt hallow the sabbath day
So in thee I work alway.
Kyrioleis

Father and mother thou shalt hold
In honor next to me, thy Lord.
None kill nor yield to anger wild,
And keep thy wedlock undefiled.
Kyrioleis

From any one to steal beware;
'Gainst none thou shalt false witness bear;
Thy neighbor's wife thou shall not eye—
Let his be his willingly.
Kyrioleis

d. *Wir glauben all an einen Gott* (1524)
[Hymn version of the Creed]
(**LW 53:272–73, trans. George McDonald**)

In one true God we all believe,
Maker of the earth and heaven;
Who us as children to receive,
Hath himself as Father given.
Now and henceforth he will feed us,
Soul and body will surround us,
'Gainst mischances he will heed us,
Nought shall meet us that shall wound us.
He watches o'er us, cares, defends;
And ev'rything is in his hands.

And we believe in Jesus Christ,
His own God, our Lord and Master
Who besides the Father highest
Reigns in equal might and glory.
Born of Mary, virgin mother
By the Spirit's operation
He was made our elder brother
That the lost might find salvation;
Slain on the cross by wicked men
And raised by God to life again.

We all confess the Holy Ghost
With the Father and the Savior
Who the fearful comforts most
And the meek doth crown with favor.
All of Christendom he even
In one heart and spirit keepeth.
Here all sins shall be forgiven;
Wake too shall the flesh that sleepeth.
After these suff'rings there shall be
Life for us eternally.

e. *Es ist das Heil uns kommen* (1524)
Paul Speratus (1484–1551), the author of
this hymn that appeared in the first
Lutheran hymnbook, was the dominant
figure in the formation of the Lutheran
church in Prussia. The original German
version has fourteen verses.

(From *Evangelical Lutheran Hymnal of the Evangelical Lutheran Joint Synod of Ohio*, trans. Henry Mills [Columbus: Lutheran Book Concern, 1888].)

To us salvation now has come,
God's wondrous grace revealing;
Works never can avert our doom,
They have no power of healing.
Faith looks to God's beloved Son,
Who has for us deliv'rance won,
He is our great Redeemer!

What God's most holy precept claims
No child of Adam renders;
But from the throne dread vengeance flames,
And speaks the curse in thunders.
The flesh ne'er prompts those pure desires
That 'bove all else the law requires
Relief by law is hopeless!

But all the law must be fulfilled,
Or we must sink despairing;
Then came the Son—so God had willed—
Our human nature sharing,
Who for us all the law obeyed,
And thus his Father's vengeance stayed,
Which over us impended.

Now to the God of matchless grace,
To Father, Son, and Spirit,
We lift our highest songs of praise,
All praise his favors merit.
All he has said he will perform,
And save us by his mighty arm—
His worthy name be hallowed!

Philip Melanchthon's Systematic Theology

60. The Apology of the Augsburg Confession: On Good Works (1530)

Melanchthon wrote this defense of each of the articles of the confession (see doc. #42) as a reply to the Roman Confutation, which the Catholic theologians presented at the Diet of Augsburg. It was published in 1531 and was included in the *Book of Concord* (see chapter five) as an official statement of Lutheran beliefs. This excerpt relates topically to the other selection from Melanchthon's 1559 *Loci* and to Luther's postil sermon and Galatians lecture.

From *BC* 237.

. . . The opponents also include some passages to support their condemnation, and it is worthwhile to examine several of them. They quote from Peter [2 Pet. 1:10], "be all the more eager to confirm your call . . ." Now here you see, dear reader, that our opponents have not wasted any effort in learning logic, for they have learned the art of inferring whatever they like from the Scriptures. "Make your calling sure through good works." Therefore works merit the forgiveness of sins! This is a very good way of arguing, since one could argue this way about a person who stood under the sentence of death and who was then pardoned. "The judge commands that from now on you stop stealing what belongs to another. Therefore, through this you have merited the pardon of the penalty, because you from now on will refrain from taking what belongs to another." To argue this way is to make a cause out of an effect. Peter is talking about the works that follow the forgiveness of sins and teaches why they should be done, namely, in order to confirm their calling, that is, so that they do not fall from their calling by sinning again. Do good works to persevere in your calling and to keep from losing the gifts of your calling, which were given beforehand, not on account of the works that follow, and which are now retained by faith. Faith does not remain in those who lose the Holy Spirit and reject repentance. As we said above, faith exists in repentance.

They add other passages that are no more relevant. Finally, they say that our position was condemned a thousand years ago during the time of Augustine. This, too, is patently false. For the church of Christ has always held that the forgiveness of sins takes place freely. In point of fact, the Pelagians were condemned for contending that grace was given on account of our works. Besides, we have sufficiently shown above that we maintain that good works must necessarily follow faith. For we do not abolish the law, Paul says [Rom. 3:31], but we establish it, because when we receive the Holy Spirit by faith the fulfillment of the law necessarily follows, through which love, patience, chastity, and other fruits of the Spirit continually grow.

61. Outline of the 1521, 1555, and 1559 Versions of the *Loci Communes*

The later editions of the *Loci* are at least four times as long as the original Latin version. The early German versions were translations by George Spalatin and Justus Jonas, but Melanchthon also prepared his own German text after 1535. This document was the starting point for the development of the other systematic theologies examined in chapter six.

From *Melanchthons Werke*, ed. Hans Engelland (Gütersloh: Bertelsmann, 1952–53). 2:1,2.

Outline of the 1521 Latin edition

Locus 1—Of Human Powers or Free Choice
Locus 2—Of Sin
  What Sin Is
  Whence Original Sin Comes
  The Power and Results of Sin
Locus 3—Of the Law
  Of Divine Laws
  Of Counsels
  Of Monastic Vows
  Of Ceremonies
  Of Human Laws
Locus 4—Of the Gospel
  What the Gospel Is
  Of the Power of the Law
  Of the Power of the Gospel
Locus 5—Of Grace
Locus 6—Of Justification and Faith
  Of Efficacious Faith
  Of Charity and Hope
Locus 7—Of the Difference between the Old and New Testaments
  Of the Abrogation of the Law
  Of the Old and New Man
  Of Mortal and Daily Sin
Locus 8—Of Signs
  Of Baptism
  Of Repentance
  Of Private Confession
  Of Participation in the Lord's Supper
Locus 9—Of Love
Locus 10—Of Magistrates
Locus 11—Of Offense or Scandal

Outline of the 1555 German edition

Locus 1—Of God
Locus 2—Of the Three Persons: Father, Son, and Holy Spirit
Locus 3—Of the Article that God Created All Other Things
Locus 4—Of the Origin of Sin
Locus 5—Of Human Powers or Free Choice

OUTLINE OF THE 1559 LATIN EDITION

62. *The Loci Communes* (1559): Why Should Good Works Be Done?

Although Melanchthon defended the doctrine of justification by grace alone, he was also concerned that people might take the moral life less seriously after hearing preaching about freedom from the law. Thus, in the later editions of the *Loci*, he increasingly discussed the "necessity" of good works. Language of this sort provoked the Majorist Controversy discussed in chapter five. In the 1559 version of the *Loci*, written after that controversy had already begun, Melanchthon takes care to articulate the sense in which good works might be said to be "necessary."

From *Melanchthons Werke, Band 2, Teil 1,* ed. Hans Engelland (Gütersloh: Bertelsmann, 1952), 404–9.

FOR WHAT REASONS SHOULD GOOD WORKS BE DONE?

There are multiple reasons: necessity, worthiness, and rewards. Regarding the first, there are many kinds of necessity. There are the necessities of command, of debt, of retaining faith, and of avoiding punishment. For although it is something else to speak of compulsion, there nevertheless remains the eternal and immutable order of God that the creature ought to conform to the will of God. This immutable order is the necessity of command and the necessity of debt, as Paul says [Rom. 8:12], "We are debtors to God, not to the flesh." And Christ says [John 13:34], "This is my command that you love one another." Also 1 Thessalonians 4[:3, 8]: "This is the will of God, your sanctification, that you abstain from fornication, that each possess his vessel, that is the body, in sanctification and honor, not in the passions of lust like the people who do not know God, and that no one injure or defraud a brother in business, because God is an avenger in all these things. For God did not call us to uncleanness but to sanctification." . . .

There is [also] the necessity of retaining our faith, because the Holy Spirit is driven out and disturbed when we commit sins against conscience. As it clearly says in 1 John 3[:7-8], "Let no one deceive you; he who commits sin is of the devil," And Romans 8[:13], "If you put to death the deeds of the flesh by the Spirit, you will live; if you live according to the flesh, you will die." . . .

Thus David banished faith and the Holy Spirit when he seized another man's wife, and indeed he troubled the Holy Spirit in many ways, first in his heart from which he was driven into adultery, and thereafter in many of the saints, for his scandal caused some to sorrow and brought about an occasion for destruction for others. . . .

The necessity of avoiding punishment ought [also] to move our minds, since we see the whole history of the world filled with the most sad events, which certainly are the punishment of sins. But the blindness of men is so great that they think the cause of all these things is accidental. This insanity must be abolished. . . .

We should also resist that cool quibbling by which the benefits that come from fear of punishment are disparaged. The response of the pious is simple for they know that there are many causes and reasons for the same action. They know that things should be done more for the sake of God than because of punishments. But they also know that God wants his will and his wrath to be recognized in punishments and wants present and future punishments to be feared. . . .

The worship of idols brought in by Solomon was the cause of the tearing apart of the kingdom of Israel. This disassembling brought about religious discord and unending wars. God wants us to consider these examples so that we might fear his wrath and consider our own salvation and that of others. . . .

The next cause is worthiness. Here again I remind you that we should not attribute any worthiness to our virtues, as if because of them a person has the remission of sins because they satisfy the law of God, or as if they are the prize of eternal life. But faith should shine forth that causes us to be pleasing to God because of the Son of God, as it was said above. But afterwards, because of this same Mediator, our worship is also pleasing to God who does not will that the whole human race perish. Therefore he also wants there to be the church in which he is acknowledged, invoked, and honored, whose obedience He accepts for the sake of his Son; and those works by which God judges that he is treated with honor he calls sacrifices. . . .

As for rewards, they are given to us freely for the sake of the Son of God in order for us to be certain concerning the remission of sins and reconciliation. They should be received by faith. Again, they would be uncertain matters if they depended on the condition of our merits, but, afterwards, in those who have been reconciled, good works do merit spiritual and physical rewards in this life and after this life, since, as we have said, they are pleasing by faith for the sake of the Mediator. As the parable of the talents clearly shows [Matt. 25:29], "To those who have more shall be given . . ."; also in 1 Timothy 4[:8] it says, "Godliness holds promises for the present life and the life to come." . . .

Individuals cannot keep their faith without practicing it; and doctrine cannot shine brightly or be preserved in the administration of either the church or the government without these spiritual gifts. . . .

GUIDANCE FOR DAILY LIVING

63. Eberlin von Günzburg: A Beautiful Mirror of the Christian Life (1524)

Johann Eberlin von Günzburg spent three years in Wittenberg after leaving the Franciscan Order. He is especially remembered for his ability to express the basic points of Lutheran theology in terms that even the uneducated laity could understand. This pamphlet sets forth a simple form of piety while also emphasizing the burdensome nature of Catholic rules and regulations.

From *Johann Eberlin von Günzburg: Sämtliche Schriften 3*, ed. **Ludwig Enders** (Halle: Max Niemeyer, 1902), 99–106.

Christ says in Matthew, the first chapter [1:21], "You shall call his name Jesus for he will save his people from their sins." John, chapter 1[:29]: "He was called the Lamb of God who took upon himself the sin of the world." Paul says to the Galatians in chapter 2[:16]: "No one is made righteous by the works of the law." Further, he says to the Romans in the third chapter [3:23-24]: "All people are sinners and lack that which finds favor with God but are justified without merit by his grace through the salvation that has taken place through Christ whom God has placed on the mercy seat, through their faith in his blood." Luke 22[:20]: "This is the cup, the new covenant in my blood, which was shed for you."

It follows from this that no angelic or human work (even the totally faultless) can take away the least daily sin.

No penance should be accepted from the priest or undertaken by oneself in order to blot out sin before God since all of that repudiates the blood of Christ and sets one's own works in the place of Christ's. Only the merits of Christ

make us righteous before the angry God, without all of our prior cooperation, as Isaiah says in chapter 64[:6], "All our righteousness is an abomination to God." Therefore, we can neither acquire grace through it nor make ourselves worthy by it. Not we, but God makes us righteous without all our forethought or preparation, according to Ephesians, chapter 1[:4-6], and in the first Epistle of John, chapter 4[:9-10].

In Isaiah, chapter 55[:9], the Lord says, "My thoughts are not as your thoughts, neither are my ways as yours, for as high is the heaven is above the earth, so high are my ways above your ways and my thoughts above yours."

It follows from this that no one knows what pleases God unless he shows this, just as also a person cannot be certain to have pleased another unless that one shows it with words or gestures. And often you make your friend sad, even when you yourself considered what you were doing to be done out of great love. Therefore, if you want to be certain to please God, then hear what he expects of you: you find his will in the Holy Bible and in no other book. Serve God not according to your own will but according to his will.

In Matthew 6[:7] we have: "When you pray you should not use much babbling as the heathen do, who think they will be heard by many words. You should not be like them."

It follows that rosaries, recitations of the psalter, crown prayers, weeklong devotions, etc. should not be called prayers when they are just so much babbling. One supposes God's grace to be obtained more this way than with short prayers. But Christ knew well that the human heart cannot remain two or three hours raised up to God, yet he respected the setting of words in order so that the heart might relate earnestly to God. Therefore he alone rightly teaches how to pray, for prayer is none other than a raising of the mind to God. As soon as the heart falls away, so also does the prayer.

Christ says in John, chapter 4[:21-23]: "Neither on this mountain nor in Jerusalem will you worship the Father. God is a spirit, so whoever would worship him must worship him in spirit and truth." Paul also says in the first Epistle to Timothy, chapter 2[:8]: "I desire that men should pray in all places." He is also against the attributing of special holiness to the temple or churches above other places. Concerning prayer, you have a long text in the seventh chapter of Acts and Matthew, chapter 6[:5]. "When you pray do not as the hypocrites (who seek praise of men by public prayer), but when you pray, go into your bedroom and close yourself up and pray to the Father."

It follows that pilgrimages to this or that place, as if God or his saints would be more gracious there, are not right. It is also not necessary for one to run daily to the church for forgiveness as if prayer within sacred walls is more pleasing to God. Christ knows well who prays well, as he has taught you.

So one should not spend a long time in church with sermons, sacraments, or the common commandments as if the Christians had to do certain things on holy days to avoid offense. On workdays, remain at home at your work, for you have nothing you need to do in the church.

In Deuteronomy, chapter 15, God says there should be no beggars among you.

It follows that up until now the mendicant orders have unrightly been set up and established in the Christian community who foolishly give up many of their own rightful things and shamelessly beg for things belonging to others. Out of this grows uneasiness of the heart, insincere feelings, the destruction of morals, and a common bad example of beggars throughout the world.

In Genesis, chapter 3[:19], God says to the man: "By the sweat of your brow shall you eat your bread." In 2 Thessalonians, chapter 3[:12],

Paul complains of some idlers, restless people, and admonishes them to work quietly, from which they might gain their sustenance. But it follows that the priests and cloisters are in opposition to God, cause offense to others, and contribute to great unrest and idle sophistry. When here there is so much evil desire to acquire goods, concern for such desires grows in all the world. As one says, the religious devise all sorts of foolishness.

The religious say that their work is the service of God in the choir. Christ says in John, chapter 6[:29]: "This is service to God, that you believe in him whom he has sent." And Paul says in Romans 1[:9], in his mind, service to God is to preach the gospel. God knows nothing of this pharisaic worship of the temple servants, much less of the temple itself. The pharisees of our time are more in need of and desirous of human honor than the old ones. So they don't have to read more than three psalms, they ring the bells for a quarter of an hour. Also in the night, they have closed the churches. Why? So that one will think these people are awake in prayer. And so that one will keep no more than a thought of the soul in the mass, one cries out from the pulpit. Matthew 13[:19-22] speaks of such people. And do not talk about your worship, as if it were right. It is not, for only Christ teaches you what is right. Christ says in Matthew 15[:8-9]: "The people praise me with their lips, but their hearts are far from me. In vain you serve me, teaching human teachings."

We have in Matthew 15[:11]: "What goes into the mouth cannot make people impure." Paul in 1 Timothy 4[:3]: From the devil comes the teaching of abstinence from foods. No one should judge you in matters of food and drink.

It follows that no monk or religious prelate may command, on penalty of mortal sin, that you avoid this or that food on a certain day, such as eggs, butter, meat, etc. The devil speaks through whoever does this, and those who believe and follow them are separated from faith and are followers of the devil. First Timothy 4[:3]. But until the error of this seduction is uprooted, the enlightened strong Christians should patiently bear with the weak a long time, also help them and avoid offense. Romans 4 and 1 Corinthians 8 and 10.

Christ says in Matthew 9 [19:10-12?]: Not everyone can abstain from marriage; only those to whom it is given. Paul in 1 Timothy 4[:3]: "To forbid marriage is a teaching of the devil. First Corinthians 7[:9]: "It is better to marry than to burn with passion."

It follows that priests, monks, nuns, etc. who live with such great burning of their flesh and teach that chastity alone is pleasing to God are all separated from faith and are followers of the devil's teaching. If they want to be holy, they must marry, since they cannot abstain. And to remark further of fasts and commandments of the church, prayers, the hearing of the mass, festivals as they are now practiced, nothing about this is written in the Holy Bible in which God reveals everything that pleases him. It follows that one also is not bound by them nor is God's wrath turned from us by them.

Faith in Christ makes us righteous before God and inclines us to love of the neighbor, so that one makes oneself useful for the betterment of the neighbor, each in his proper estate.

In Ephesians 5[:22] we have it that a wife should obey her husband, as the community is subjected to Christ. So should a husband love his wife as Christ the community.

Children should hold their elders in honor. The elders should raise up their children in the teachings and discipline of the Lord.

The servant should serve his temporal master as Christ, with fear and trembling. The master should be friendly toward his servant and consider that he also has a master in heaven, as Christ says. Beware of false prophets, etc.

It follows that Christians should judge teachings, everyone for himself, according to what he hears from others, and according to the measurement of the Holy Bible.

We have in Deuteronomy, chapter 11[:19]: "You shall teach the law of the Lord to your children."

It follows that parents are responsible for teaching their children the fear of God and his commandments, as Abraham did in Genesis, chapter 18. A father is his children's bishop and preacher.

Paul in Romans, chapter 13[:1], and in 1 Corinthians, chapter 7: Christian teaching does not annul temporal duty toward earthly lords, irrespective of whether they demand something just or unjust of us, issuing in good or ill. Christ says in Matthew 5[:40]: "Whoever takes your coat from you, do not quarrel with him, but let him also have your cloak." Therefore a Christian customarily honors taxes, tithes, and festival offerings, so long as such are demanded by the authorities and community. Let no one decide something only according to his own opinion.

St. Paul in his first Epistle to the Corinthians in chapter 1[:30-31] says: "Jesus is made by God our wisdom, righteousness, sanctification, and redemption so that (as it is written), "Whoever boasts, let him boast in the Lord." The knowledge of Christ that God teaches us is salvation and the way also given to us so that we may learn. It follows that all human wisdom, schooling, and teaching cannot compare to it and falls short in the Christian community. Christ is our righteousness, so that all cloisters and foundations through which one undertakes to become righteousness or to be preserved in righteousness are worth nothing. It comes to pass only through God's power from faith as we have it in 1 Peter, chapter 1[:5].

Also, no daily sin can be taken away by holy water. Christ is our blessing or holiness, so it follows that a human blessing does nothing. When the soul is cleansed through faith, the body is also a holy temple of God on account of the faithful soul, as we have it in the first distinction in Corinthians, chapter 6[:19]. And all that a believer uses is pure and holy for him, according to Titus, chapter 1[:15]: all, I say, be it clothes, food, etc., is blessed. Christ is our deliverance from death, the devil, hell, and sin, so may he also alone keep us in the future from the devil's specter, without all means of blessed water, plants, lights, saints, etc.

Still, no one should do any dishonor to common places such as parish churches, churchyards, etc., no less than to a councilroom or any similar common place, and what is used in church for the common order should be considered pure and clean, as an honorable mind may well perceive, as Paul also says in similar language in Romans 14[:20].

Christ is our life, John 14[:6]. Christ is the only mediator between God and us, 1 Timothy 2[:5]. Christ is our advocate, 1 John 2[:1]. Christ is our consolation and sweetness, Romans 5[:1] and 8[:39?]. No saint will take away this honor from Christ, nor should anyone attribute such honor to a saint. As long as Christ is held to honor, all the saints rejoice. If one places this honor entirely or in part on a saint, the saint himself would be angry and all the saints above us, if they knew what we were doing. You cannot give Christ too much honor, but if you place too much honor on a saint by a hair's breadth, you have insulted Christ and the saints, and your ignorance or good intention will not excuse you. God and the saints should not be insulted. Praise God, that he has so highly honored his saints and has shown them such grace and mercy and the saints themselves go and ask God with a right confidence, that he also will bestow such grace

and mercy on you. That is the right way to honor the saints.

Do not do good works in order to acquire God's favor, to do penance for your sins; this you may not do, for Christ alone has done that. But believe that Christ has made the Father gracious toward you, who holds you in his fatherly protection now and forever. Think earnestly about that so that there may grow within you a reciprocal love for God as toward a best friend for whom you are inclined to do everything to please. Now works follow from this as you wish God's love for your neighbors, friends, and foes. Now right contrition also follows, for whatever you have done against the loving God. Faithful one, you please God well through Christ and also all you do and abstain from doing when you do not trust in yourself. Stand at rest until your heart is fortified in trust, for what one does without such trust in God is sin. This distinction is made in Romans 13[:8].

A Christian child is accustomed to seek all things from Christ, to pray to God [for] life, joy, peace, healing, nourishment, wisdom, hope, redemption, and protection from all evil. In short, the Christian is taught to think of Christ as the best, most trustworthy, friendliest friend who is more friendly, loving, and trustworthy than all angels, saints, etc. When one then seeks all things from Christ, all misplaced reverence for the saints will soon be discarded. All love and suffering, however small it is, which God gives you, receive as a fatherly gift to you from your loving God. Then you will have peace and joy. And let God rule the world as he pleases. Stand still and ask God for grace for you and others so you may have peace. Speak of God's word with respect.

PAMPHLET LITERATURE: DEFENSES OF LUTHER'S REFORMATION

64. Von Grumbach: A Christian Writing of an Honorable Noble Woman (1523)

Argula von Grumbach was the daughter of a minor noble who was influenced by a friend in Nürnberg to read Luther's writings. She exchanged letters with Luther and visited with him in Coburg in 1530.

From *Reformatorische Verkündigung und Lebensordnung*, ed. Robert Stupperich (Bremen: Carl Schünemann, 1962), 289–98.

Argula von Grumbach

To the Enlightened, High-Born Sovereign Prince and Lord, Wilhelm, Count Palatine of the Rhine, Duke of Upper and Lower Bavaria—

My Gracious Lord:

I heartily wish grace and peace from God through his Holy Spirit for Your Princely Grace, now and forever. Highborn Prince, Gracious Lord, it has come to pass that now on the eve of our dear lady's birth [September 7], the University of Ingolstadt has, without holding any disputation, forced a young man named Arsacius Seehofer to renounce the holy gospel and Word of God by threatening after long imprisonment to put him to death by burning. Every Christian should take that to heart. Moreover, some boast that this has happened at the very bidding of your Princely Grace. Now, a citizen of Nürnberg has sent me a document that scornfully described how this transpired. I answered as best I could, being of the opinion that the truth about your Gracious Lord was not rightly reported in this case. I know your Princely Grace is so Christian that you would not encroach on God's authority. For no person has the power to forbid the Word of God and to manipulate it. The Word of God alone should and must govern all

things. They may call it "Luther's word," but it is not "Lutheran"; rather, it is God's Word. We have read in John 7[:7]: "The Lord revealed to them their evil, therefore they became an enemy to you." This is also happening now to Luther. The disciple is not above the master; what happened to all apostles has also happened to all those who have confessed Christ, be it Luther or Melanchthon or whoever. And even if it were possible that the devil proclaimed the holy gospel out of hell, it would still be and remain the Word of God. Paul also says to the Galatians [1:8]: "If an angel should come from heaven and teach you another gospel, so should he be cursed." They have excluded nothing; he [Arsacius Seehofer] had to renounce the writings entirely, whether Luther's or Melanchthon's, or go into the fire. Did Martin write the entire Bible or simply translate it into German according to the plain text? Your Princely Grace may judge for himself whether it doesn't amount to renouncing God and his Word, if I renounce evangelical, apostolic, or prophetic writings!

I do not believe that such was Your Princely Grace's command, unless he was not rightly instructed by them concerning this matter. They have taken an eighteen-year-old youth into custody and none of them used the Scriptures [to convict him]. Although I hear that he had to suffer much persecution from them and was placed in prison three times, I thank God that he has been rescued from death out of their bloodstained hands at the command of Your Princely Grace, declared in an oath. God will not let Your Princely Grace go unrewarded, for the blood of the righteous cries out to God. . . .

I also implore your Princely Grace by God's will to never believe their words but to test them before the Spirit according to divine Scripture, as John says in chapter 4 of his first epistle: "Whoever confesses Christ is from God" [1 John 4:2]. It is especially necessary to exercise judgment in the midst of such tyranny, for whoever does not accept those who are Christ's cannot be a Christian. It is not enough for us to say, "I believe what my elders have believed." We must believe in God, not our elders. If our elders determine right belief, then the Jewish way would be best, but Christ says in Matthew 10[:32-33]: "Whoever confesses me before people, I will confess before my Father. Whoever does not confess me I will also not confess." And Luke 9[:26]: "Whoever is ashamed of me and my word, I will also be ashamed of them when I come in my majesty." Such words should at all times stand before my eyes, because my God himself has spoken them. . . .

You should make sure that your authority is not misused, since you have the rule of the gospel just as we do. It does not teach the prohibiting of God's Word or that one should obey such a prohibition; rather it teaches that one should sooner lose body and life. If one wants to be a Christian as we do, then we have the command in chapters 4 and 5 of Acts [5:29] to obey God rather than people. If, through God's help, Your Princely Grace abides by this same Word of God, then the land and people will partake of good fortune and prosperity. Where this does not happen, God will not let it go unpunished. In the divine biblical writings we find that God punished and still threatens to punish us with plagues, for what

he spoke to Jerusalem and the land of Jordan he spoke unto all peoples. Now God says he will give us into the hands of our enemies and subject us to a foreign lord with harsh servitude, estrange us from our fatherland, slay us with the sword, so that no one remains who can bury us, giving our bodies as food to the birds and wild animals and making a great people into a small one. He can suddenly kill us and our cattle through death and pestilence, turn our earth into an infertile desert, send hunger upon us and such anguish that the father devours the son and the son the father, and children die in the arms and at the breasts of their mothers, as we read in 2 Chronicles 2 and 36, Isaiah 30 and 36, Baruch 2, Ezekiel 5 and 7, Hosea 14, and many other places in the Bible. God has said this, not Luther, and the Word of God is a yea without any nay! "Heaven and earth he says will pass away but my Word will never pass away" [Matt. 24:35]. . . .

What does God say in Matthew 7[:15]?: "Protect yourself from false prophets who are clothed in sheep's clothing but inwardly are rapacious wolves." I think God has uncovered some of them: they are priests, monks, and nuns. What prince, indeed, would build robberhouses in the best cities and most beautiful places, if the Empire allowed him to do so? Which count or lord has ever acquired such freedom from your Grace or your Grace's ancestors?

The Lord speaks and calls them robbers, for example, in Isaiah 3[:12], "They have robbed my people and ravished their wives." God says this; if I said it, it would be called Lutheran. Thus they must let it remain.

O God, what sodomitical purity and avaricious poverty! They have the appetite of the flesh just as we do, but they have covered it up with the shame-hiding cowl. It does not help before God. If it helped, we would all wear cowls. Paul says in 1 Corinthians 7[:9]: "Every man should have a wife. Every woman should have a husband. For it is better to marry than to suffer from lust." . . .

The pope has followed the counsel of the devil, has forbidden priests to take wives, but has permitted sleeping with loose women in exchange for money. O Prince, take notice of this lest you be ruined by this. The sword of punishment belongs to you and not to the clergy. It is their task to proclaim the Word of God. Would to God that your eyes would be opened and you would take in hand the sword that God has given you. Matthew 20[:25-28]: "The princes of this world should rule over the people, but it should not be so with you; whichever of you is the greatest should be the least and the servant of all the others, just as the Son of Man did not come to be served, but to serve."

We are guilty due to our sins; all that is called spiritual has been turned around. Princes [of the church] and prelates have the money, the seculars are left with only the sack. Your Princely Grace, help us all and take counsel so that God may not send his wrath upon us as we just now noted. . . .

I have not been able to refrain from writing to your Princely Grace as my brother in Christ. May the Spirit of God judge this, for I mean well. God is my witness that I have joy when Your Princely Grace is fortunate and suffer when Your Princely Grace has misfortune. I cannot forget that after the death of my father and mother, when I was robbed of both within five days, I was commended to Your Princely Grace as my supreme guardian, and at the time I became Your Princely Grace's mother's lady of the bedchamber. I was consoled in my grief by Your Princely Grace with these words: I should not cry because he would be not only my prince but also my father. My husband has also experienced this kindness, and our child has been raised and nurtured in Your Princely

Grace's service. This has obligated me not a little to write to Your Princely Grace to show my thankfulness in part for the benefits I received. It is with me as with St. Peter: "Silver and gold have I none" [Acts 3:6], but to be sure I have love toward God and Your Princely Grace as my neighbor. For the Lord says in Luke 9[:25], "What use is it for a person to gain the whole world and lose his soul? With what will he buy it again?"

Out of Christian duty, I could not keep silent. I have written a letter to the university, a copy of which I am now sending to Your Princely Grace, so that if they falsely slander me, Your Princely Grace might be informed of the truth. What I have written I know by God's grace to be justified, for it is not my word but God's word. Would that Your Princely Grace takes it to heart that God will indeed demand an account of you for the souls under your charge. Would that Your Princely Grace did not put faith in and give authority to the money-grubbers for one sees that they struggle against God out of avarice and hence without power. We would all like to abide by God's Word, but the priests, monks, procurators, advocates, and jurists cannot stand for this. The Lord says: "What you want others to do to you, you should also do to them" [Matt. 7:12]. This law carries a sure judgment. Do not let it happen that generation after generation carries on a process without being able to obtain a judgment. . . .

65. Alber: Declaration of War from Lucifer to Luther (1524)

This satirical letter of challenge *(Fehd-schrift)* was published in Speyer shortly after the Diet of Nürnberg, at which the cardinal legates persuaded Emperor

Charles V to enforce the Edict of Worms. At the time it was written, Erasmus Alber was a schoolteacher in Oberursel in Hesse. Later, from 1528 to 1539, he served as a Lutheran pastor in Sprendlinger. After that, his often harsh polemics forced him to move frequently and to seek refuge occasionally in Wittenberg. Alber also wrote at least twenty-three hymns and published a Lutheran retelling of Aesop's fables.

From *Flugschriften Bd. 3*, ed. Otto Clemen (Nieuwkoop: deGraaf, 1967), 364–67.

We, Lucifer, a lord and possessor of eternal darkness, powerful ruler, and master of the whole world, also of all treasures and kingdoms that are in it, etc., send you, Martin Luther, this announcement of our wrath and disfavor. Our dear, trusted representatives in Rome, the legates Laurentius Campegius and Matthias Lang of Salzburg, both cardinals, together with all our officers who are gathered in Regensburg, have humbly reported and forwarded their message about how you, without reasonable cause, make use of fierce writing and preaching again and again against us, to the detriment of us all and our yearly revenues and income. And they report to us that if your disposition and intention strengthen daily, increase and guide you completely, you yourself might very well intend to drive out and eradicate our servants and officers. We also have found out for ourselves by the inspection of our registers and soul-books, how many in seven years, through your writing, teaching, and preaching, have been turned away from us and directed in another way toward Christ (who sometime previously also powerfully deprived us of our kingdom). This is entirely unsuitable and improper because you have now violated and betrayed the vow and obliga-

tion that you originally made to us as a monk. And in doing this, your unmanly, evil, spiteful, and obstinate mind is revealed and used against us and our servants, and you are able still more to be harmful and detrimental to our kingdom. So, you give preference to the Bible and Gospel books that, by our command and bidding, have not been used much for some hundred years. We, and our appointed councils that we have authorized to assemble in many places and especially most recently at Konstanz, have also earnestly forbidden the basing of preaching and disputing on them. At that time [the Council of Konstanz, 1415], we horribly punished and had burned two criminals and transgressors of this command, Jan Huss and Jerome of Prague (who also in your manner dared to fight against us). Besides that, you inspire monks and nuns in the cloisters to run away to take wives and husbands. They had been honoring us, and not a little, with the sin by which we overcame the people and the five cities of Sodom and Gomorrah. You contend for and deprive us also of the priests and monks, our trusted servants, who hear confessions. They no longer perform so conveniently and boldly the adultery, whoring, and seducing of virgins that they had many opportunities to practice in the past, and they also no longer want to abuse people with our ban. You not only apply yourself against us and our servants in these and the other matters mentioned above, but also against all other evil tricks and stratagems for which we and our servants are daily reviled, disgraced, and scorned by many. Because now (as we have sufficiently ascertained) you have no regard for our amicable requesting, have despised the offering of a great gift and riches, and will not let your hard head be softened through friendly or earnest admonitions, our adherents have not hesitated or abhorred the power and might that we have among worldly princes, in addition to our bishops. So we, with our counselors, after sufficient consideration of all your abuse and harm directed against us, have fully decided to persecute you, and your adherents, helpers, and helper's helpers with true severity. We announce therefore to you and notify your adherents by virtue of this open letter, our enmity, hostility, and disapproval, on behalf of ourselves, our pope, cardinals, bishops, and our other servants and officers who are in our power and service and others who belong to us in other ways. We also intend for you and your crowd and adherents, burning, beheading, drowning, robbing, and deprivation of the body, property, and possessions of you and your children. Moreover, we will do whatever we can and want to advance our horrible undertaking and uphold our devilish honor, as a true war order is capable and accustomed to do, and will not feel guilty for responding to you and your adherents either within or outside the law. We have also earnestly commanded and given full power to all of our servants and officers and especially those who are now assembled at Regensburg, to attack you and all your adherents or protectors further, in our name and for our sake, and to carry out the deed that we have announced here with even greater exuberance. In witness thereof, our hellish seal is pressed to the end of this letter that is sent out from our city of eternal damnation on the last day of September in the year 1524.

Satirical Propaganda

66. Murner: The Great Lutheran Fool (1522)

Thomas Murner's 4,772-line satirical poem against Lutheranism has a meandering and farcical plot. In the early section excerpted here, Murner (portraying himself as a cat-monk because another Lutheran satirist had previously mocked his name by comparing it to *murmawen*, the German verb "to meow") converses with the Great Fool, who represents various Lutheran sympathizers who had criticized Catholic theology and practice, including Eberlin von Günzburg. In a later section, Murner converses with Luther himself, who explicitly admits to all the malevolent and disruptive intentions that the poet thought the Lutherans clandestinely supported. By the end of the poem, all the little fools have been exorcised from the Great Fool, and Luther has died and fallen into a toilet.

From *Satirische Feldzüge wider die Reformation*, ed. Arnold Berger (Darmstadt: Wissenschaftliche Buchgesellschaft, 1967), 44–63.

How the Great Lutheran Fool Must Be Exorcised

. . . As soon as I saw the great, haughty fool draw near, I began to flee into a corner where I hid myself and made the sign of the holy cross, although blessing oneself before a fool is like trying to stand stiff as the wind blows. I expressly shouted out three names: *"Narrabo, narrabis, narrabitis."* As soon as I uttered these names and said "Luthery," my heart and mind were strengthened. I called out, "O God, protect me from this great fool who has come sliding in on a sled." Soon it occurred to my mind that I am a fool-exorcist and have exorcised fools before, though not so great a fool as the one who came sliding in on the snow. . . .

At first, when I began the exorcism, I spit in my hands and set about to consider how I might exorcise the fool. "Stand still and do not lift a limb! You must answer me and not move from your place. Tell me who made you, who your father and mother are, why you were made and why you are so huge. . . .

The Great Lutheran Fool

THE FOOL TELLS WHY HE IS SO LARGE AND SWOLLEN

. . . I must tell you, text and gloss, why I am so huge. I am not swollen up for no reason. Many fools have hidden themselves within me, and many who wish not to be named have buried themselves inside of me. They are all hidden in me and lie there without a care. O God, if they only knew how hard it is to be exorcised, they would be on their guard. . . . I cannot defend myself against this horrible exorcism. The words are too strong: *O narrabo, narrabis, narrabitis!* Each one breaks my heart. . . .

THE GREAT FOOL WARNS THE EXORCIST OF THE FOOLS IN HIS BODY

. . . I was born a poor fool, as were all my ancestors. Therefore you must soon exorcise me. But those who sit within me have great intelligence and foolish wits. If you want to exorcise them and do not speak the words as you should or recite your blessings deliberately, you will be harmed by them. . . .

THE FOOLS THAT SIT IN THE GREAT FOOL'S HEAD

Fools sit in my head whom the devil has allowed in. They plague me so much that I am almost dying. . . . In the head that one uses for thinking sit the learned fools who stand in the pulpit to preach. They will not let go of Luther for they are too partial to him because he speaks of nothing but the gospel and the truth for all the world. . . .

The first thing they preach to you is about how one should harm the pope and how one should understand the words "Peter, feed my sheep" [John 21:15]. From these words it is to be decided whether Christ set up a pope. They propose to do away with the pope, the shepherd of Christendom, and intend to cause his downfall. This would harm the other sheep, for when the shepherd is struck down, no one else can lead the sheep.

After this, they raise the issue of why the pope deprives you of the body of Christ in both kinds, the flesh and the blood, wanting you to understand that this is done mischievously by a hateful clergy who do not want to permit this and have manipulated you by lies to deprive you of it in an unchristian way. Believe me that no one wants to begrudge you the sacrament. . . .

I wish someone would punish these fools with exorcism so that I may sleep more restfully. Yes, I and everyone. They have the greatest guilt. . . .

THE FOOLS THAT SIT IN THE GREAT FOOL'S POCKETS

. . . Fools sit in my pockets who are waiting for goods and money. . . . They have their own gospel about redirecting donations and completely ripping up cloisters. This they preach with great zeal. . . . God will not allow anyone to steal and rob. Why then do you want to take from me what I possess with full right and by true title? They have devised a cloak of pretense that the common people do not understand. They make it out to be a Christian teaching although it is a lie. . . .

THE FOOLS THAT SIT IN THE GREAT FOOL'S BELLY

. . . O dear cousin, you want to know why my belly is so swollen? You would be surprised to know what fools sit together in there and how many would like to remain there. If you would drive them out of me, you would be doing me a service. I cannot bear them any longer. I am hoping that you will figure out how to exorcise them from me. . . .

67. Cochlaeus: The Seven-Headed Luther (1529/49)

In a 1529 treatise and in the woodcut that accompanied it, Johannes Cochlaeus portrayed Luther as degenerating from doctor to fanatic to the equivalent of Barabbas the murderer/insurrectionist (Luke 23:19) released by Pilate instead of Jesus. He commented more generally on this image in the following excerpt from his 1549 commentary on the life of Luther.

From *Commentaria Ioannis Cochlaei de actis et scriptis Martini Lutheri* (1549), 197.

Once Africa brought forth many monstrosities, but now Germany has spawned more marvelous monstrosities. For what is more monstrous than so many heads, so contrary and dissimilar among themselves, residing in one cowl. What, compared to these, is two-faced Janus, three-headed Geryon, triple-throated Cerberus? They are fables of the poets and laughable figments. But the seven-headed cowl, nay rather, that cowled dragon of ours, confounds Germany truly and seriously with

The Seven-Headed Luther

its seven heads, and breathes on it and corrupts it lethally with very bad poison. Who previously has seen, I ask, such a portent anywhere? Indeed, it is astonishing, a mystery full of majesty, sublime and venerable above all sense and intellect that there are three in one God and these three are one; one in substance, three in persons. But in one cowl of one Luther there are seven and these seven are not only one in substance but also one in person. Assuredly, this is an amazing theology, previously unheard of by Jews, Gentiles, and Christians. Of the multitude of those believers in old Christianity, the heart was one and the soul was one. However, in this new gospel of Luther one heart and one flesh are cut up into many hearts and heads, so that not only do different ones think many different things but one [Luther] also arrogates many heads and attitudes to himself. Indeed, we who unwillingly and gravely with weariness and nausea have read the books of Luther, have briefly drawn out the seven. And if one wishes to find more things in these writings, be they monstrosities or heads, let him only search or review a little more diligently, and he will discover beyond a doubt many more amazing things and these indeed so absurd, impious, and blasphemous that a pious and God-fearing man could not endure to express them with the tongue or think and reflect on them with the mind. . . .

Woodcut 5

68. Osiander: Wondrous Prophecy of the Papacy (1527)

Andreas Osiander discovered a book in the libraries of Nürnberg that contained illustrations representing various popes. This book was written to convey prophetic messages about the good and bad popes of the past and the future and was sympathetic toward the Spiritual Franciscans, who had been at odds with the papacy in the fourteenth century. In Osiander's republication of a set of thirty woodcuts based on this book, he ignored some of the details originally associated with the pictures and substituted his own brief commentaries to express Lutheran views about the popes.

From Andreas Osiander, d. Ä. Gesamtausgabe Bd. 2: Schriften und Briefe April 1525 bis Ende 1527, ed. Gottfried Seebaß and Gerhard Müller (Gütersloh: Gerd Mohn, 1977), 403–83.

WOODCUT 5

The pope has already abandoned God's law and still cannot rule without law. Therefore, he must make a new law and that from what is suggested to him by Satan. Therefore, Satan speaks with him from a bush as God spoke with Moses. He also follows that word and makes laws and forbids food and marriage and many other things that holy Paul clearly teaches to be of the devil (1 Tim. 4:1-3).

[Editor's note: The woodcut originally portrayed Pope Benedict XI (1303–4) and associated him with the devil for opposing the Spiritual Franciscans. The fig tree also alluded to the story that he was allegedly killed by eating a poisoned fig.]

Woodcut 8

Woodcut 8

Here the pope sits to judge, thrusts poor Righteousness away from him with his left hand, and wants to give gifts to the rich Unrighteousness. Satan, who hangs on his right hand in the shape of a snake, entices him.

[Editor's note: The woodcut originally portrayed Pope Nicholas IV (1288–92). It censured him for abandoning his "old bride," the Franciscan Order, in order to seek election as pope.]

Woodcut 9

Woodcut 9

Now that the pope has made devilish laws, it follows that he also must use the keys according to the same law that the devil taught him. Therefore the Holy Spirit must languish. And since he imposes the law at risk of mortal sin and entangles the conscience with it, so faith and the gospel must also decline. Therefore the sword of false teaching goes out of his mouth and with it he wounds Christ the Lamb, that is the Word and eternal truth of God. His law and teaching cannot bear to have God's Word nearby, or it will be weakened and wounded by it. With the switch he strikes and torments the conscience that should be consoled and healed.

[Editor's note: The woodcut originally portrayed Pope John XXII (1316–34) and was meant to characterize him as an enemy of Christ, the lamb, and the Franciscan Spirituals, the dove. The dragon with the tiara to the pope's left depicted the antipope Nicholas V.]

Woodcut 10

So that one may see who the monk is, he stands in his cassock and has his sign, the rose in his hand. I believe he is Luther. But because Isaiah says in 40[:6], "All flesh is as grass," he stands with his sickle and cuts down, not grass but flesh and all that is fleshly, for he preaches against that. And when it is uprooted [Matt. 15:13], he will strike the fire iron and rekindle the fire of Christian love, which has been extinguished.

[Editor's note: The woodcut may have referred at one time to Pope Celestine V who was a Benedictine monk but later founded the Celestine Order. He served as pope for six months in 1294 and then abdicated.]

Woodcut 10

69. Luther: Depiction of the Papacy (1545)

In 1545, around the time he wrote a treatise titled "Against the Roman Papacy, an Institution of the Devil," Luther also attacked the pope through the publication of a set of visual caricatures. Lucas Cranach the Elder executed the woodcuts, and Luther provided the accompanying text.

From WA 54:346–73. See woodcuts in Hartmann Grisar, *Luthers Kampfbilder* (Freiburg: Herder, 1921–23).

Contempt for the Pope

LUTHER'S COMMENTS:
Don't frighten us with your ban, and don't be such an angry man. Or else we will defend ourselves against you and show you a pretty view.

EVALUATIONS OF LUTHER

70. Marschalk: On Luther's Name (1523)

Haug Marschalk participated as a soldier in various imperial campaigns against peasant rebels, the French, and the Turks. Although he was not well educated, he published six pamphlets between 1521 and 1525.

From Adolf Laube, Annerose Schneider, Sigrid Loos, eds., *Flugschriften der frühen Reformationsbewegung*, vol. 2. (Berlin: Akademie-Verlag, 1983), 563–66.

It is a wonder that no one can gain their spurs without referring to the Christian Doctor

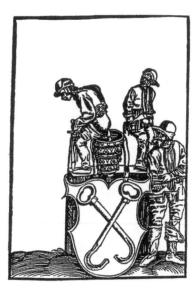

Defiling the Papal Tiara

LUTHER'S COMMENTS:
The pope has treated the kingdom of God just as his crown is here being treated. But if that makes you doubt or despair, note that God has promised a consolation through the Spirit. Revelation 18[:6, "Render to her as she has rendered"].

Luther with anger, scolding, blasphemy, and abuse. But all of this is a certain sign of the truth of the belief that is upheld daily by this renowned doctor, for Christ also had to bear with many false names. The scribes taught in the schools that he had a devil in him and did wonders through the power of the devil. They said he was a perverter of people and accused him of being an evildoer [Matt. 12:24; John 7:12, 18:30]. He was put to judgment with thieves and put to death. When he called to his father at his death, they said he was calling for Elijah [Matt. 27:38, 46, 47]. Christ and his apostles suffered and still suffer from many such insults that the cross proclaims. That is God's Word and the holy gospel.

And now in these last times, the most learned Christian Doctor Martin Luther is incessantly insulted and persecuted not by Christians and the learned but by the heathen and ignorant tyrants who rule the people under the name of the gentle Christ.

First of all, they have thought about deciphering his name (as if his art and teaching were the same as his body and life to them). They say he is not the enlightener *(Lauterer)* but the darkener *(Trüber)*. He darkens the Christian faith that had long been clear without any dissensions or contradictions until Luther now came along, pretending to understand it. He tore apart the bond of the Christian church, made things dark, and shattered all order. And where there is no order, there can be no peace. Paul spoke out against this in 1 Corinthians 14[:40]: "All things should be done according to an order," [supposedly] as the Roman Church ordered it. The unlearned one constantly shouts from the pulpit "heretic," and whoever seeks the true foundation is despised and scorned. Whoever upsets this order or speaks against it, he says, should have his tongue taken out. O, you avenger of all perverters, has Christ taught you that when

he says [Matt. 5:44], "Pray for your enemies, do good to those who do evil to you?"

Secondly they say he is a rascal *(Lotter)*. Those who believe in him and the Scriptures are good-for-nothing and villainous, have fallen away from the old belief, followed their seducer, and have brought other people away from a good, old, long-established belief with empty, rascally babble that the devil speaks through them.

Lastly, they say he is a lurker or secret scoundrel *(Laurer)* who never offers much to the priests but wishes to oppose them. They say that because he is disobedient and fails to respect the ban, he must be a lurker. More could be said about what envious tongues speak, but I will keep silent. . . .

It is not surprising that they should so vehemently misuse Luther's name and treat it so flippantly (as we have noted above). What else would you expect from those who crucify God's Son daily with their sacrifices and forget his testament and promise? I will give a new signification to this name "Luther" (but this will be worth nothing to the unbelievers who are not moved by any word or sign). This name "Luther" is written in German with six letters, which are L.U.T.H.E.R. That signifies

L Pure *(Lautere)* evangelical teaching

U Overflowing *(Überflüssige)* grace of the Holy Spirit

T True *(Treulicher)*, faithful servant of Christ

H Elijah *(Heliam)* [cf. 1 Kings 18]

E Enoch (Jude 14, 15), who revealed the Antichrist

R Rabbi, that is, he who has become master over all profaners of Scripture.

Now see if these six significations do not make this Luther understandable. What teacher in four hundred years has made the Scriptures as clear as day as our Luther has, so that the common man can also understand? . . .

What teacher has completed so many writings, disputations, and sermons and has fought and overcome so many enemies? This would not be possible without a special grace from the Holy Spirit. Have any doctors in our times learned, as our Luther has, that they should distribute the Word of God and the holy sacrament and not seek their own needs, praise, and honor? . . . Hasn't the common rumor circulated for a long time that Enoch and Elijah will destroy the Antichrist, who is concealed under the robe of the pope? And still the antichristian regiment in Rome and the pope's apostles are in training. . . .

Enough has been played out on this name "Luther." I know well that the unbelieving heathen will joke about and ridicule all that our Luther writes and what is written about him. But do not be discouraged because they cannot suppress his teachings or triumph over his name. It will be rectified, for the scolding and blasphemy has gone too far. God give us all his grace. Amen.

71. Mathesius: A Commemorative Sermon (1566)

Johannes Mathesius's book of biographical sermons about Luther was the first important account of the reformer's life published by one of his followers. This excerpt from the last of the sermons was first delivered in 1564 in the form of a funeral sermon on the anniversary of Luther's death.

From *Historien von des Ehrwirdigen Mannes Gottes D. Martin Luthers* (Nürnberg: Gerlach, 1583), 167–83.

On this, the eighteenth day of February, eighteen years ago [1546], our dear, honorable master and father, Doctor Martin Luther

from Eisleben went to his blessed rest, called by the Eternal Mediator in whom he put his trust.

Because we remember the day of his Christian departure, we also want on this anniversary of that day to hold a Christian remembrance of his funeral and his teaching and to thank God from our hearts that this dear teacher awakened us, rescued us from the teaching of the Antichrist, restored pure, holy teaching, and brought it into our church. In the name of Jesus Christ, we ask the eternal Father that he might never let us forget this Christian man and his teaching and that he might preserve our descendants and graciously protect them from all heresy and falsification of the gospel. . . .

Help us, eternal Son of God, who awakened this man through your Spirit, entrusted your word to him, and worked many wonders through him in the power of your word, that we may be reckoned as obedient and thankful disciples and children of your true servant and may praise you in him and his teachings forever and ever. Amen. . . .

Now it is reported to us in the Bible that the true prophets and apostles of the Son of God are called without means and sent out and that what they teach they have heard themselves from the head of the church, the eternal Son of God. Therefore prophets and apostles steadily apply themselves to their calling and teach nothing that was not reported to them by Christ or his Spirit. . . .

Just as prophets and apostles only ground their teachings on what they have heard from the mouth of God's Son, so all ordained church workers preach, write, and dedicate themselves to nothing besides the writings of the prophets and apostles that are the only rule and measure and the only ground and support of all truth that should be taught and believed in Christendom. . . .

Johannes Mathesius

I mention this to you in the beginning so that you might differentiate between messengers of God and know what actually belongs to and is necessary to make one a prophet, apostle, bishop, or true doctor. . . .

God called forth ordained Levites and priests at the foundation of his house who were born into this office, raised up, and publicly established in it. Through the prophets and apostles, with prayer and the laying on of hands, he also selected, ordained, and established witnesses and messengers whom he adorned and confirmed with the gifts and spirit of this office that they might understand, rightly and blessedly clarify, and interpret the writings of the prophets and apostles. They help to make the people blessed through the word of the prophets and apostles, which is actually the voice of the Son of God, when they call the people to repentance and remembrance of their sins, direct them to Christ's blood and sacrifice, and exhort them to good works and new obedience.

Now our dear master and father, Doctor Martin, belongs to this latter group. He did not himself see or hear God and his Son as had the old prophets and apostles. He also often prayed heartily that God would not let an angel speak with him or give him any visions or dreams. He was content and satisfied to have the word of the prophets and apostles and to stand as a called servant of the church and Christian brother according to God's Word. Moreover, he had all the qualities and characteristics that belong to a true and Christian Doctor of Holy Scripture, a witness of Christianity, a blessed servant of the church, and messenger of the Lord Christ.

Matters related to his calling have been reported at length this year [in these sermons]. He was baptized, learned the catechism from his parents, and was then sent to school, but against the wishes of his parents he entered the cloister and became a priest. He submitted himself in obedience to his vicar and the entire order (just as God wondrously led his other saints, placing Moses in the Egyptian school and Daniel in the Babylonian school). At the recommendation of his entire order, his superior appointed him to be first a Reader of the Fathers and then a Doctor of Theology, which also took place with the knowledge, will, and recommendation of his prince. . . .

We have heard, furthermore, how he attained his doctorate. He was legitimately called, selected, and chosen to be a doctor, and as the public record of his matriculation at Wittenberg gives evidence, he was made and approved as a doctor and teacher of theology and as preacher and interpreter of God's Word.

Now we have no more certain writing or teaching from God than what was written down by the prophets and apostles from the mouth of Jesus Christ through the Spirit of God. Therefore his calling and commission required his teaching and testifying to the Word of God. This Word preceded and followed him his whole life long. Therefore, he abandoned the teachings of the sophists, the heathens, the Jews, the Papists, the Turks, and all heretics and enthusiasts and applied himself only to the theology and Word of God. As he often said, "I have started out with the spoken Word of God, which the prophets and apostles wrote down and to which all of Christianity is a witness. I stand and rest on this Word with which I began and which has brought me so far. I will carry it forth to the end with God's help as I have sworn an oath and have publicly pledged my poor soul to our God to do."

The call, mark well, is true. The teaching is also certain, for our doctor placed and grounded his actions and arguments only on the Scriptures. With this, he attacked the papacy, purified many churches, planted pure religion, consoled and made many hearts joyful and blessed, that they might accept his teachings and commit their body and blood to it. . . .

Doctor Luther has preached the teachings that the Son of God brought forth from the bosom of the Father and that was declared and written down through his Spirit in the prophets and apostles and that he strengthened from the beginning with greater miracles according to the prophecy of Moses (Deut. 13:5, 10). Because this doctor brought forth no new teaching but only the established teachings of the old patriarchs, prophets, and apostles, the well-grounded and confirmed Word needed no miraculous signs. . . .

O Lord Christ, thank you for the confirmed Word of the prophets and apostles and protect us from wondrous signs, visions, and dreams, for the day of signs and wonders that was to follow the preaching of the gospel is past and God's Word has been proclaimed and sounded forth in all the world. . . . But should anyone want to see the power, victory, and miracles of Christ among us, then I can point out some to honor Doctor Luther's teachings.

Let this, dear friends, be [considered] a great and unheard of miracle that a little David attacked such a great Goliath, such a giant, and came away unscathed. In this sense, Doctor Martin's teachings are adorned and confirmed with a miracle. . . .

That the great leaders of the world let Doctor Luther come before them, heard his confession and that of his followers, and finally came to Wittenberg and allowed cities and schools to abide by his teachings, let this also be [considered] an uncommon sign and miracle through which God wanted to certify and honor the teachings of this man. . . .

I admonish you this day, dear friends, to remain constant by this man's teachings, witness, true prophecy, and interpretation of Scripture. Persevere until the end, thanking God who sent us this chosen instrument in the last days and sustained him in his calling, against the gates of hell [Matt. 16:18], for twenty-nine years in this land. Do not be diverted or led astray by the rogues and troublemakers who would like to suppress and destroy this man's reputation, position, and confession.

Chapter Three

The Implementation of Reform Proposals

Luther's excommunication in 1521 marked an important turning point in his efforts to reform the Catholic church. Although he had been very harsh in his evaluations of "Romanist" church leaders, his hope initially had been to implement changes by working within the institutional structures that they controlled. The judgment rendered at the Diet of Worms thwarted this plan. The future of Luther's reform efforts now depended on more local efforts to reorganize religious life within those territories of the Holy Roman Empire whose secular rulers were willing to carry out independent initiatives under his guidance.

The major treatises of 1520 had laid out an extensive list of proposals for the reform of church polity, worship, and theology (docs. #15 and 31). Luther and his associates were now forced to think in new ways about what strategy to use to accomplish these goals. Luther claimed neither special expertise nor interest in dealing with the details of organizational planning, but early efforts in Wittenberg to make rapid and radical changes alerted him to certain dangers that he clearly wanted to avoid (doc. #20). When he came out of hiding in 1522, Luther formulated several guidelines that would have a lasting impact on the development of the Evangelical or Lutheran churches.

First of all, Luther paid serious attention to the problem of "the weaker brethren," that is, people who found it difficult to change their way of thinking about beliefs or church practices. Convinced that forcing change upon them would create unnecessary anxiety, confusion, and potentially a backlash against his reform movement, Luther looked to the New Testament for advice about how to deal with this matter. In his letter to the Romans, Paul urged the strong to be patient and even to make temporary concessions to the weak. Paul and Peter compared the process of spiritual development to feeding different kinds of food to a child as it matures. Thus, Luther favored persuasion rather than force and gradual rather than abrupt change (doc. #21).

Second, Luther insisted that the reform process be carried out in an orderly manner. His long-standing convictions about the depths of human sinfulness inclined him to favor the installation of extensive restraints on human behavior. The chaos and destruction produced by more radical reformers in the early 1520s gave him additional incentives to stress the need for called and ordained ministers of the gospel, well-established patterns of worship, and some kind of coordination of the work of the church with the important restraining activities carried out by the secular authorities in society. Here again, Luther found guidance from the New Testament letters of Paul, who insisted that "all things should be done decently and in order" (1 Cor. 14:40) and instructed Christians to maintain peace and unity by submitting to divinely ordained or regularly appointed governing authorities (for example, Rom. 13:1-2).

Third, Luther's experiences of oppressive or burdensome methods of control by Catholic church leaders encouraged him to strike a balance between order and freedom. In his mind, there were too many rules and practices in the church structures of his day that were treated as obligatory although they were not based on commandments in the Bible. In his reforming efforts, Luther wanted there to be clearer distinctions between necessary beliefs or practices and other expressions of religious life that should be considered optional even though they might be commendable. For example, Luther insisted on agreement about the nature of Christ's presence in the Lord's Supper and took a strong stand on the question of how the Supper should be celebrated, but he was inclined to treat more detailed matters of worship, such as the use of vestments and candles or incense, as matters of indifference (doc. #72). Similarly, he showed little interest in requiring uniformity in matters such as the number of religious holy days to be observed and was prepared to let each of the territorial churches reach its own decision about how ceremonies such as marriages should be conducted (docs. #72, 73, 74, and 80). The Augsburg Confession made Luther's intended course of action into a general principle when it stated that it was sufficient for the unity of the church that the gospel be preached and the sacraments administered in accordance with the divine Word. Beyond that, ceremonies need not always be observed in the same manner in every place (doc. #42).

Luther's efforts to change the way worship was conducted provide a clear illustration of these principles in action. Since public worship services in a church building are the most frequent and communal expression of religious practice, it is also not surprising that Luther directed his attention to this matter almost immediately after his return to Wittenberg. He published a new order for worship, the *Formula Missae*, in December 1523 (doc. #72). Clearly intending to differentiate between his approach and the measures taken by Karlstadt and the other radicals in 1521, Luther stated his wish to purify and simplify the liturgy rather than to abolish it altogether. He raised no objection to traditional parts of the Mass, such as the *Gloria*, the *Benedictus*, the *Sanctus*, or the *Agnus Dei*, because they were based on words from the Bible. Luther made no immediate issue of the use of Latin as the language of worship, although he suggested that the vernacular might be used in the future. The major changes consisted of a new emphasis on the necessity of regular preaching from biblical texts and revision of the canon of the Mass, or the words used for the institution of the Lord's Supper. Luther had previously objected to the claim that the priest was making an offering to God in the Eucharist on behalf of the people (doc. #31) and now acted to delete everything that "smack[ed] and savor[ed] of sacrifice." He also made the administration of both the bread and the wine to the laity an essential feature of the celebration of the Lord's Supper.

Luther highly valued both word and sacrament and advocated frequent communion. However, he discontinued the practice of private masses and insisted that the Lord's Supper should not be celebrated on any occasion where there were no people present who wished to commune. Luther also called for careful scrutiny of those who came to receive the Lord's Supper. They should be able to articulate their basic knowledge of the faith and be aware of the full significance of the sacrament. He recommended private confession prior to communion because it allowed the minister to conduct an examination of the beliefs and manner of life of communicants. Similar measures to ensure proper respect for the sacrament would become a standard part of the procedures developed in all of the Lutheran territorial churches (docs. #77 and 78).

In 1522 and 1523, new liturgies incorporating more innovative reforms were being put to use in other localities outside of Wittenberg. When some of Luther's associates expressed concern that this proliferation of divergent models might create a new kind of confusion, Luther published an order of worship using the German language. The *Deutsche Messe*, which appeared in 1526, manifested elements of both continuity and change (doc. #73). Instead of completely substituting German for Latin, Luther expressed his wish that both of these languages, and even Greek and Hebrew, be used for worship on appropriate occasions. He called for flexibility in order to meet the needs and interests of the educated and the exceptionally devout as well as the unlearned lay folk who made up the majority of most congregations. Implementing his belief in the priesthood of all believers, he not only made provisions for changing the language of worship but also encouraged active participation by the laity through the introduction of congregational singing as a substitute for or supplement to the music provided by a trained choir.

To fill in the vacuum created by the abolition of daily private masses, Luther developed a new form of weekday worship: a regular communal gathering for Scripture reading and prayer, modeled after the monastic services of Matins and Vespers. The evening service on Saturday also served the special purpose of preparing people for participation in the Lord's Supper on the following day (cf. doc. #78). To foster the religious development of the young, Luther called for these services in larger towns to be tied closely to the daily schedule of the schools, and he supported the involvement of schoolboys in worship as readers of Scripture or as singers (doc. #73).

During the period when he was reflecting on the reform of worship, Luther also addressed other issues such as the need to establish Christian schools for both boys and girls and to develop new regulations for the administration of the financial affairs in parishes (doc. #89). In 1523 he consulted with the congregation of Leisnig, a city located between Leipzig and Dresden, as it set up a common chest from which payments were dispensed to support church workers and schoolteachers, to maintain church property, and to provide care for the poor and elderly (doc. #88).

By 1525 Luther was convinced of the need for broader and more systematic attention to the reorganization of religious life, especially after receiving reports that in some parishes the laity had stopped providing financial support for their pastors and were neglecting other church obligations. In the past, bishops had traditionally ordered visitations of all parishes within a diocese whenever the need was felt to evaluate the state of religious life. Luther's reform movement had not yet settled on a formal leadership structure so he had to look to the already-established leaders in society for the initiation of such a complicated strategy. He asked his prince, the Elector of Saxony, to appoint visitors to find out what was actually taking place in the church congregations throughout his realm. Luther and Melanchthon prepared a series of articles to guide the visitors as they carried out their task, and the procedure was fully implemented in 1528 (doc. #74). This visitation was initially envisioned as a onetime process of assessment to prepare for the thorough reorganization of the church in Saxony, but the conducting of visitations soon became routine practice within the Lutheran territorial churches (doc. #84). The articles of visitation that called for the visitors to make inquiries about what the people believed, how worship was conducted, and how the work of the church was administered in the parishes also became the model for the many Church Orders that established formal policies to regulate all aspects of religious life in the various Lutheran territories and cities.

Luther received invaluable assistance from a number of his associates when he faced the task of expanding and stabilizing the reform movement. Philip Melanchthon collaborated with him as extensively on matters of church administration as he did in the task of articulating a biblically based theology. Melanchthon was also celebrated as the *Praeceptor Germaniae* (Teacher of Germany) for his contributions to the reform of educational institutions. Among Luther's other coworkers in Wittenberg, two in particular were extensively involved in traveling beyond Saxony to help establish other territorial churches. Justus Jonas (1493–1555), like Luther, had first studied law but under the influence of Erasmus had shifted his interests to the study of the Bible and theology. He served as dean of the theology faculty at the University of Wittenberg for ten years, starting in 1523, and participated in the important religious negotiations at the Marburg Colloquy in 1529 and the Diet of Augsburg in 1530 (docs. #36 and 42). Jonas translated many of Luther's and Melanchthon's Latin writings into German so that they would be accessible to a wider audience, and he assisted them in their translating of the Bible. Jonas worked on new Church Orders for Anhalt, Zerbst, and Ducal Saxony in the 1530s and moved to Halle in 1541, where he served as superintendent and also rewrote its Church Order (docs. #77 and 86). Johannes Bugenhagen (1485–1558), called Dr. Pomeranus by his contemporaries because he came from Pomerania, was a priest who became attracted to Luther's teachings in 1520 and moved to Wittenberg in 1521. He lectured at the university and began his long tenure as pastor of the city church in 1523, the same year in which he received his doctorate in theology. Over several decades, he was the most active and influential organizer of Lutheran churches in northern Germany. He visited and prepared Church Orders for the Hanseatic cities of Hamburg, Braunschweig, and Lübeck and the duchy of Braunschweig-Wolfenbüttel (docs. #79 and 85). Later he helped establish the Lutheran church in Pomerania, served as General Superintendent of the church in Electoral Saxony, and was called to Copenhagen by King Christian III to reform the churches of Denmark and Norway. In southern Germany, Johannes Brenz (1499–1570) was of comparable importance. He introduced Lutheranism to the imperial city of Schwäbisch-Hall, where he served for many years as a preacher. He was also a crucial contributor to the organization of the Lutheran churches in Nürnberg and the Duchy of Württemberg (docs. #76 and 78).

There are several common characteristics of the Church Orders prepared by the reformers to regulate the life of the territorial churches. The documents varied in length and degree of detail, but almost all were divided into three parts. The first section usually concerned *Credenda*, or what ought to be believed. It described the doctrines that were considered normative for the churches and often specified what local church workers ought to do to ensure that the people understood and accepted these teachings. The second section, concerning *Agenda*, or what ought to be done, described the liturgy the churches would follow and set forth other regulations for the celebration of church rites.

The third section, *Administranda*, focused on how the churches ought to be organized. It outlined the duties and qualifications of church workers, clarified how the church should relate to civil government, and related the ministry of the churches to other work such as the educating of the young and care for the poor.

Regarding matters of belief, Luther discovered from the initial visitation in Electoral Saxony that the level of doctrinal knowledge in the parishes was far lower than he had expected, not only among the laypeople but even at times among the clergy. To address this problem, he prepared the Large and Small Catechisms (doc. #58). Until the Book of Concord created a fuller summary of Lutheran beliefs in 1580 (see chapter five), Luther's catechisms were the most common standard used to specify the essential elements of Christian belief. The Church Orders frequently summarized the topics covered by the catechisms and set up procedures for teaching the catechism to all age groups within the congregations (doc. #75).

The Church Orders stated the theological principles that determined how the churches celebrated the sacraments and other church rites, but they also explicitly addressed a variety of problems that might be faced in ordinary parish life. For example, they often outlined the obligations of baptismal sponsors and clarified the responsibilities of a mid-wife in cases when a newborn infant was unlikely to live long enough to be brought to a church for the usual baptismal rite (doc. #76). They offered advice to pastors on how to conduct the rite of confession in cases when parishioners seemed insufficiently repentant of their sins or deeply burdened by their sense of guilt (doc. #77). The Church Orders sometimes specified how often church services ought to be held and the frequency with which the Lord's Supper should be celebrated. They also described the procedures to be followed by clergy to prepare people for worthy reception of the sacrament (doc. #78). Such documents indicated how other rites such as confirmation, marriage, ordination, and funerals ought to be conducted and instructed clergy on how to respond to tradi-tional expressions of piety such as the venerating of religious images or the ringing of church bells to avert harm during periods of bad weather (docs. #77, 78, 79, 80, 81, 82, and 83).

Although Luther asserted the priesthood of all believers in response to the medieval dichotomy that accented the differences between the roles of priests and laity, his model of a reformed church still gave the clergy a prominent role as officeholders who would ensure that the Word was correctly preached and the sacraments correctly celebrated. Likewise, the Church Orders carefully specified the qualifications and duties of the clergy and also other church workers who would assist them in their ministry. The leading pastor in large cities was called a superintendent (or *Superattendent*) and was often assisted by other clergy who were called chaplains or deacons. Rural parishes were served by only one pas-tor or by a deacon who was sent out from the city to conduct services and catechetical instruction (doc. #75). Usually, each parish also had a paid sexton *(Küster)*, who main-tained the church building, rang the church bell to announce services, and sometimes helped teach the catechism to children (doc. #85).

Unlike the Roman Catholic Church, which derived the authority of priests from the bishops who ordained them, Luther showed little concern for the development of an Evangelical episcopacy. Once his movement was severed from the old diocesan structure of the Catholic church, he seemed content to let the princes step into the traditional role of the bishops and preside over the organizing of church districts that corresponded to the boundaries of the territories they ruled. The princes in turn usually allowed the overall church affairs of their realms to be administered by a leading member of the clergy, who was most commonly called a General Superintendent. In actual fact, this church official had many of the responsibilities claimed by an archbishop in the past. Later on, however, he would also be accountable in many Lutheran territories to a consistory, a small council of church and civic leaders that proposed corrections for problems discovered during church visitations and made recommendations to the secular ruler about appointments to church positions.

In the 1540s Luther participated on two occasions in the ordination of a "bishop" in small principalities outside of Saxony. This term was also used in several north German territories for a while as the title for the officials who were elsewhere called General Superintendents. However, by the end of the sixteenth century, there were no longer any Lutheran bishops in Germany. Only the Lutheran churches in Scandinavia retained a formal episcopacy, but even in those territories the monarch claimed ultimate authority over church legislation.\

Neglect of accepted church practice came to be considered a civil crime as well as a spiritual offense. Therefore, Lutheran pastors were obligated as holders of a state office to supervise both the religious and moral conduct of their parishioners. Most of the Lutheran churches set up local consistories, or small commissions of pastors and lawyers, which, like the ecclesiastical courts of the past, could propose punishments for individuals who had committed serious moral offenses or were discovered to hold unacceptable religious beliefs (doc. #86).

Church and state officials also jointly regulated a system of publicly supported schools. Training in doctrine and church practice constituted a major part of the education given to young people, and this type of religious instruction was valued for several reasons. Texts such as the catechism were used both to teach what ought to be believed and to encourage the maintenance of order and discipline in society (doc. #87). In Lutheran areas, the civil community and the church community were viewed as coextensive. Thus, leaders of the church and the civil government also cooperated to ensure that proper attention was given to both the spiritual and physical needs of the poor and the needy. The Lutheran clergy visited the sick regularly as part of their pastoral care, and the lay leaders in Lutheran parishes collected and administered funds to meet the bodily needs of those who were unable to earn an income to support themselves (doc. #88). The common chest legislation, which the town of Leisnig had developed in consultation with Luther, became a model for the social welfare ordinances contained in many of the Church Orders (doc. #89).

72. Luther: Formula of Mass for the Church at Wittenberg *(Formula Missae)* (1523)

From *LW* 53:19–60, trans. Paul Zeller Strodach, rev. Ulrich Leupold.

... We first assert: It is not now nor ever has been our intention to abolish the liturgical service of God completely, but rather to purify the one that is now in use from the wretched accretions that corrupt it and to point out an evangelical use. We cannot deny that the Mass, that is, the communion of bread and wine, is a rite divinely instituted by Christ himself and that it was observed first by Christ and then by the apostles, quite simply and evangelically without any additions. But in the course of time so many human inventions were added to it that nothing except the names of the Mass and communion have come down to us. ...

We will set forth the rite according to which we think that it should be used.

First, we approve and retain the introits for the Lord's days and the festivals of Christ, such as Easter, Pentecost, and the Nativity, although we prefer the Psalms, from which they were taken as of old. ...

Second, we accept the *Kyrie eleison* in the form in which it has been used until now, with the various melodies for different seasons, together with the Angelic Hymn, *Gloria in Excelsis,* which follows it. However, the bishop may decide to omit the latter as often as he wishes. ...

Third, the prayer or collect that follows, if it is evangelical (and those for Sunday usually are), should be retained in its accepted form, but there should be only one. After this the epistle is read. Certainly the time has not yet come to attempt revision here, as nothing unevangelical is read, except that those parts from the Epistles of Paul in which faith is taught are read only rarely, while the exhortations to morality are most frequently read. ... If in the future the vernacular be used in the Mass (which Christ may grant), one must see to it that Epistles and Gospels chosen from the best and most weighty parts of these writings be read in the Mass. ...

(Fourth and Fifth: include the gradual and *Alleluia*; omit the sequences or proses.)

Sixth, the Gospel lesson follows, for which we neither prohibit nor prescribe candles or incense. Let these things be free.

Seventh, the custom of singing the Nicene Creed does not displease us, yet this matter should also be left in the hands of the bishop. ...

Eighth, that utter abomination follows that forces all that precedes in the Mass into its service and is, therefore, called the offertory. From here on almost everything smacks and savors of sacrifice. ... Let us, therefore, repudiate everything that smacks of sacrifice, together with the entire canon, and retain only that which is pure and holy, and so order our Mass.

I. After the Creed or after the sermon let bread and wine be made ready for blessing in the customary manner. I have not yet decided whether or not water should be mixed with the wine. I rather incline, however, to favor pure wine without water. ...

II. The bread and wine having been prepared, one may proceed as follows:

The Lord be with you.

Response: and with thy spirit.

Lift up your hearts.

Response: Let us lift them to the Lord.

It is truly meet and right, just and salutary for us to give thanks to Thee always and everywhere, Holy Lord, Father Almighty, Eternal God, through Christ our Lord. ...

III. Then:

... Who the day before he suffered took bread and, when he had given thanks, broke it, and gave it to his disciples, saying, Take, eat; this is my body, which is given for you.

After the same manner also the cup. . . .

IV. The blessing ended, let the choir sing the *Sanctus*. And while the *Benedictus* is being sung, let the bread and cup be elevated according to the customary rite for the benefit of the weak in faith, who might be offended if such an obvious change in the rite of the Mass were suddenly made. . . .

V. After this, the Lord's Prayer shall be read. . . .

VI. Then let him communicate himself, then the people; in the meanwhile let the *Agnus Dei* be sung. . . .

Thus we think about the Mass. But in all these matters we will want to beware lest we make binding what should be free, or make sinners of those who may do some things differently or omit others. All that matters is that the Words of Institution should be kept intact and everything should be done by faith. . . .

We have passed over the matter of vestments. But we think about these as we do about other forms. We permit them to be used in freedom, as long as people refrain from ostentation and pomp. . . .

The Communion of the People

So far we have dealt with the Mass and the function of the minister or bishop. Now we shall speak of the proper manner of communicating to the people, for whom the Lord's Supper was primarily instituted and given this name. . . .

Here one should follow the same usage as with Baptism, namely, that the bishop be informed of those who want to commune. They should request in person to receive the Lord's Supper so that he may be able to know both their names and manner of life. And let him not admit the applicants unless they can give a reason for their faith and can answer questions about what the Lord's Supper is, what its benefits are, and what they expect to

derive from it. In other words, they should be able to repeat the Words of Institution from memory and to explain that they are coming because they are troubled by the consciousness of their sins, the fear of death, or some other evil, such as temptation of the flesh, the world, or the devil, and now hunger and thirst to receive the word and sign of grace and salvation from the Lord himself through the ministry of the bishop, so that they may be consoled and comforted. . . .

But I think it enough for the applicants for communion to be examined or explored once a year. . . .

Now concerning private confession before communion, I still think as I have held heretofore, namely, that it neither is necessary nor should be demanded. Nevertheless, it is useful and should not be despised. . . . I also wish that we had as many songs as possible in the vernacular that the people could sing during Mass, immediately after the gradual and also after the *Sanctus* and the *Agnus Dei*. . . .

This is enough for now about the Mass and communion. What is left can be decided by actual practice, as long as the Word of God is diligently and faithfully preached in the church. . . .

73. Luther: The German Mass *(Deutsche Messe)* (1526)

From *LW* 53:61–90, trans. Augustus Steimle, rev. Ulrich Leupold.

In the first place, I would kindly and for God's sake request all those who see this order of service or desire to follow it: Do not make it a rigid law or entangle anyone's conscience, but use it in Christian liberty as long, when, where, and how you find it to be practical and useful. For this is being published not as though we meant to lord it over anyone else, or to legislate for him, but because of the widespread demand for German masses and services and the general dissatisfaction and offense that has been caused by the great variety of new masses, for everyone makes his own order of service. . . .

Where the people are perplexed and offended by these differences in liturgical usage, however, we are certainly bound to forego our freedom and seek, if possible, to better rather than to offend them by what we do or leave undone. Seeing then that this external order, while it cannot affect the conscience before God, may yet serve the neighbor, we should seek to be of one mind in Christian love, as St. Paul teaches [Rom. 15:5-6; 1 Cor. 1:10; Phil. 2:2]. As far as possible we should observe the same rites and ceremonies, just as all Christians have the same Baptism and the same sacrament [of the altar], and no one has received a special one of his own from God. . . .

Now there are three different kinds of divine service or Mass. The first is the one in Latin that we published earlier under the title *Formula Missae*. It is not now my intention to abrogate or to change this service. It shall not be affected in the form that we have followed so far, but we shall continue to use it when or where we are pleased and prompted to do so. For in no wise would I want to discontinue the service in the Latin language, because the young are my chief concern. And if I could bring it to pass, and Greek and Hebrew were as familiar to us as Latin and had as many fine melodies and songs, we would hold mass, sing, and read on successive Sundays in all four languages, German, Latin, Greek, and Hebrew. . . .

The second is the German Mass and Order of Service, which should be arranged for the sake of the unlearned lay folk and with which we are now concerned. These two orders of service must be used publicly in the churches for all the people, among whom are many who do not believe and are not yet Christians. Most of them stand around and gape, hoping to see something new, just as if we were holding a service among the Turks or the heathen in a public square or out in a field. That is not yet a well-ordered and organized congregation, in which Christians could be ruled according to the gospel; on the contrary, the gospel must be publicly preached [to such people] to move them to believe and become Christians.

The third kind of service should be a truly evangelical order and should not be held in a public place for all sorts of people. But those who want to be Christians in earnest and who profess the gospel with hand and mouth should sign their names and meet alone in a house somewhere to pray, to read, to baptize, to receive the sacrament, and to do other Christian works. According to this order, those who do not lead Christian lives could be known, reproved, corrected, cast out, or excommunicated, according to the rule of Christ, Matthew 18[:15-17]. Here one could also solicit benevolent gifts to be willingly given and distributed to the poor, according to St. Paul's example, 2 Corinthians 9. Here would be no need of much and elaborate singing. Here one could set up a brief and neat order for Baptism and the sacrament and center everything on the Word, prayer, and love. Here one would need a good short catechism on the Creed, the Ten Commandments, and the Our Father.

In short, if one had the kind of people and persons who wanted to be Christians in earnest, the rules and regulations would soon be ready. But as yet I neither can nor desire to begin such a congregation or assembly or to make rules for it. For I have not yet the people or persons for it, nor do I see many who want it. But if I should be requested to do it and could not refuse with a good conscience, I should gladly do my part and help as best I can. In the meanwhile the two above-mentioned orders of service must suffice. . . .

Concerning the Service

Since the preaching and teaching of God's Word is the most important part of divine service, we have arranged for sermons and lessons as follows: For the holy day or Sunday we retain the customary Epistles and Gospels and have three sermons. At five or six in the morning a few psalms are chanted for Matins. A sermon follows on the epistle of the day, chiefly for the sake of the servants so that they too may be cared for and hear God's Word, since they cannot be present at other sermons. After this an antiphon and the *Te Deum* or the *Benedictus,* alternately, with an Our Father, collects, and *Benedicamus Domino.* At the Mass, at eight or nine o'clock, the sermon is on the Gospel for the day. At Vespers in the afternoon the sermon before the *Magnificat* takes up the Old Testament chapter by chapter. For the Epistles and Gospels we have retained the customary division according to the church year, because we do not find anything especially reprehensible in this use. . . . This we think provides sufficient preaching and teaching for the laypeople. He who desires more will find enough on other days.

Namely, on Monday and Tuesday mornings we have a German lesson on the Ten Commandments, the Creed, Lord's Prayer, baptism, and sacrament, so that these two days preserve and deepen the understanding of the catechism. On Wednesday morning again a German lesson, for which the evangelist Matthew has been appointed so that the day shall be his very own, seeing that he is an excellent evangelist for the instruction of the congregation, records the fine sermon of Christ on the Mount, and strongly urges the exercise of love and good works. But the evangelist John, who so mightily teaches faith, has his own day too, on Saturday afternoon at Vespers, so that two of the evangelists have their own days when they are being read. Thursday and Friday mornings have the weekday lessons from the Epistles of the apostles and the rest of the New Testament assigned to them. Thus enough lessons and sermons have been appointed to give the Word of God free course among us, not to mention the university lectures for scholars.

This is what we do to train the schoolboys in the Bible. Every day of the week they chant a few psalms in Latin before the lesson, as has been customary at Matins hitherto. For as we stated above, we want to keep the youth well versed in the Latin Bible. After the psalms, two or three boys in turn read a chapter from the Latin New Testament, depending on the length. Another boy then reads the same chapter in German to familiarize them with it and for the benefit of any layman who might be present and listening. Thereupon they proceed with an antiphon to the German lesson mentioned above. After the lesson the whole congregation sings a German hymn, the Lord's Prayer is said silently, and the pastor or chaplain reads a collect and closes with the *Benedicamus Domino* as usual.

Likewise at Vespers they sing a few of the Vesper psalms in Latin with an antiphon, as heretofore, followed by a hymn if one is available. Again two or three boys in turn then read a chapter from the Latin Old Testament or half a one, depending on length. Another boy reads the same chapter in German. The *Magnificat* follows in Latin with an antiphon or hymn, the Lord's Prayer said silently, and the collects with the *Benedicamus.* This is the daily service throughout the week in cities where there are schools.

On Sunday for the Laity

Here we retain the vestments, altar, and candles until they are used up or we are pleased to make a change. But we do not oppose anyone who would do otherwise. In the true Mass, however, of real Christians, the altar should not remain where it is, and the priest should always face the people as Christ doubtlessly did in the Last Supper. But let that await its own time. . . .

To begin the service we sing a hymn or a German psalm in the First Tone. . . .

Then follows the *Kyrie eleison* in the same Tone. . . .

He [the priest] should read the epistle facing the people, but the collect facing the altar.

After the epistle a German hymn, either "Now Let Us Pray to the Holy Ghost" or any other, is sung with the whole choir.

Then he reads the Gospel in the Fifth Tone, again facing the people. . . .

After the Gospel the whole congregation sings the Creed in German: "In One True God We All Believe."

Then follows the sermon on the Gospel for the Sunday or festival day. And I think that if we had the postil for the entire year, it would be best to appoint the sermon for the day to be read wholly or in part out of the book—not alone for the benefit of those preachers who can do nothing better, but also for the purpose of preventing the rise of enthusiasts and sects. If we observe the homilies read at Matins, we note a usage similar to this. For unless it is a spiritual understanding and the [Holy] Ghost himself that speaks through the preachers (whom I do not wish hereby to restrict; for the Spirit teaches better how to preach than all the postils and homilies), we shall ultimately get where everyone will preach his own ideas, and instead of the Gospel and its exposition we again shall have sermons on castles in Spain. This is one of the reasons we retain the Epistles and Gospels as they are given in the postils— there are so few gifted preachers who are able to give a powerful and practical exposition of a whole evangelist or some other book of the Bible.

After the sermon shall follow a public paraphrase of the Lord's Prayer and admonition for those who want to partake of the sacrament. . . .

Thereupon the Office and Consecration. . . .

It seems to me that it would accord with [the institution of] the Lord's Supper to administer the sacrament immediately after the consecration of the bread, before the cup is blessed, for both Luke and Paul say: He took the cup after they had supped, etc. [Luke 22:20; 1 Cor. 11:25]. Meanwhile, the German *Sanctus* or the hymn, "Let God Be Blest," or the hymn of Johann Huss, "Jesus Christ, Our God and Savior," could be sung. Then shall the cup be blessed and administered, while the remainder of these hymns are sung, or the German *Agnus Dei*. . . .

We do not want to abolish the elevation, but retain it because it goes well with the German *Sanctus* and signifies that Christ has commanded us to remember him. For just as the sacrament is bodily elevated, and yet Christ's body and blood are not seen in it, so he is also remembered and elevated by the word of the sermon and is confessed and adored in the reception of the sacrament. In each case he is apprehended only by faith; for we cannot see how Christ gives his body and blood for us and even now daily shows and offers it before God to obtain grace for us. . . .

The collect follows with the benediction:

We give thanks to thee, Almighty God, that thou has refreshed us with this salutary gift, and we beseech thy mercy to strengthen us through the same in faith toward thee, and in fervent love among us all; for the sake of Jesus Christ our Lord. Amen.

The Lord bless thee and keep thee.

The Lord make his face shine upon thee, and be gracious unto thee.

The Lord lift up his countenance upon thee, and give thee peace. . . .

This is what I have to say concerning the daily service and instruction in the Word of God, which serves primarily to train the young and challenge the unlearned. For those who itch for new things will soon be sated and tired with it all, as they were heretofore in the Latin service. There was singing and reading in the churches every day, and yet the churches remained deserted and empty. Already they do the same in the German service. Therefore, it is best to plan the services in the interest of the young and such of the unlearned as may happen to come. With the other neither law nor order, neither scolding nor coaxing will help. Allow them to leave those things in the service alone that they refuse to do willingly and gladly. God is not pleased with unwilling services; they are futile and vain.

But on the festivals, such as Christmas, Easter, Pentecost, St. Michael's, Purification, and the like, we must continue to use Latin until we have enough German songs. This work is just beginning: not everything has been prepared that is needed. We must arrive at a common standard to assess and control the profusion of orders.

Lent, Palm Sunday, and Holy Week shall be retained, not to force anyone to fast, but to preserve the Passion history and the Gospels appointed for that season. This, however, does not include the Lenten veil, throwing of palms, veiling of pictures, and whatever else there is of such tomfoolery—nor chanting the four Passions, nor preaching on the Passion for eight hours on Good Friday. Holy Week shall be like any other week save that the Passion history be explained every day for an hour throughout the week or on as many days as may be desirable, and that the sacrament be given to everyone who desires it. For among Christians the whole service should center in the Word and sacrament.

In short, this or any other order shall be so used that whenever it becomes an abuse, it shall be straightway abolished and replaced by another. . . . An order is an external thing. No matter how good it is, it can be abused. Then it is no longer an order, but a disorder. No order is, therefore, valid in itself—as the popish orders were held to be until now. But the validity, value, power, and virtue of any order is in its proper use. Otherwise it is utterly worthless

and good for nothing. God's Spirit and grace be with us all. Amen.

74. Melanchthon: Instructions for the Visitors of Parish Pastors in Electoral Saxony (1528)

Luther wrote the preface to this document. Philip Melanchthon, drew up the instructions based on ideas derived from Luther.

From *LW* 40:269–320, trans. Conrad Bergendoff.

Preface

. . . Now that the gospel through the unspeakable grace and mercy of God has again come to us or in fact has appeared for the first time, and we have come to see how grievously the Christian church has been confused, scattered, and torn, we would like to have the true episcopal office and practice of visitation re-established because of the pressing need. . . . We have respectfully appealed to the illustrious and noble prince and lord, Johann, Duke of Saxony, First Marshall and Elector of the Roman Empire, Landgrave of Thuringia, Margrave of Meissen, our most gracious lord and prince, constituted of God as our certain temporal sovereign, that out of Christian love (since he is not obligated to do so as a temporal sovereign) and by God's will for the benefit of the gospel and the welfare of the wretched Christians in his territory, His Electoral grace might call and ordain to this office several competent persons. To this His Electoral Grace through the goodness of God has graciously consented. . . .

Contents of the Instructions
The Doctrine

In regard to doctrine we observe especially this defect that, while some preach about the faith by which we are to be justified, it is still not clearly enough explained how one shall attain to this faith, and almost all omit one aspect of the Christian faith without which no one can understand what faith is or means. For Christ says in the last chapter of Luke [24:47] that we are to preach in his name repentance and forgiveness of sins.

Many now talk only about the forgiveness of sins and say little or nothing about repentance. There neither is forgiveness of sins without repentance nor can forgiveness of sins be understood without repentance. It follows that if we preach the forgiveness of sins without repentance that the people imagine that they have already obtained the forgiveness of sins, becoming thereby secure and without compunction of conscience. This would be a greater error and sin than all the errors hitherto prevailing. . . .

Therefore we have instructed and admonished pastors that it is their duty to preach the whole gospel and not one portion without the other. For God says in Deuteronomy 4[:2]: "You shall not add to the Word . . . nor take from it. . . ."

THE TEN COMMANDMENTS

The preachers are to proclaim and explain the Ten Commandments often and earnestly, yet not only the commandments but also how God will punish those who do not keep them and how he often has inflicted temporal punishment. . . .

So too they are to point out and condemn various specific vices, as adultery, drunkenness, envy, and hate, and how God has punished these, indicating that without doubt after this life he will punish still more severely if there is not improvement here.

The people are thus to be urged and exhorted to fear God, to repent and show contrition, lest their ease and life of false security be punished. Therefore Paul says in Romans 3[:20]:

"Through the law comes (only) knowledge of sin." True repentance is nothing but the acknowledgment of sin.

Then it is important that faith be preached. Whoever experiences grief and contrition over his sins should believe that his sins are forgiven, not on account of his merits, but on account of Christ. When the contrite and fearful conscience experiences peace, comfort, and joy on hearing that his sins are forgiven because of Christ, then faith is present—the faith that makes him righteous before God. . . .

These two are the first elements of Christian life: repentance or contrition and grief, and faith through which we receive the forgiveness of sins and are righteous before God. Both should grow and increase in us. The third element of Christian life is the doing of good works: to be chaste, to love and help the neighbor, to refrain from lying, from deceit, from stealing, from murder, from vengefulness, and avenging oneself, etc.

Therefore again and again the Ten Commandments are to be assiduously taught, for all good works are therein comprehended. . . .

TRUE CHRISTIAN PRAYER

[section omitted]

TRIBULATION

To the third part of Christian life, that is, the doing of good works, belongs also the knowledge of how one shall meet tribulation.

First, we are to teach the people that all tribulation, not only of the spirit but also of the body, is sent from God, whether it is poverty or illness, danger to children, peril of possessions, or hunger. God would thereby admonish us and awaken us to penitence. As we read in 1 Corinthians 11[:32]: "But when we are judged by the Lord, we are chastened so that we may not be condemned along with the world."

Now it is not enough to know that God sends such experiences. We must also teach that in the midst of these tribulations we are to call upon him and confidently believe that he will help. . . .

The Sacrament of Baptism

. . . The common people are to be taught what great benefits Baptism brings, namely that God will care for and protect the child and receive it as his own.

It is well that we use the German language in Baptism so that they who witness the act may understand the prayer and the word in Baptism.

Occasionally also it should be explained to the people in preaching on the sacrament that Baptism does not only mean that God wills to receive children when they are small, but throughout life. Therefore, not only is Baptism a sign to children, but also to the older people it is an incitement and exhortation to repentance. For the water in Baptism signifies penitence, contrition, and sorrow. So Baptism should awaken the faith that those who repent of their sins are cleansed and forgiven. This kind of faith is a complete Baptism. . . .

The Sacrament of the Body and Blood of the Lord

These three articles concerning the sacrament of the true body and blood of our dear Lord Jesus Christ shall be explained to the people.

First, they are to believe that the true body of Christ is in the bread and the true blood of Christ is in the wine. . . .

Second, the people are to be taught that it is right to receive both bread and wine. For now the holy gospel (God be praised) has been restored and we have clear witness that both elements are to be offered and received. . . .

Inasmuch, however, as no one is to be forced to believe, or driven by command or force from his unbelief, since God likes no forced service and wants only those who are his servants by their own free will, and in view of the fact that the people are confused and uncertain, it has been and still is impossible to establish a rule concerning persons to whom both kinds are to be offered and from whom

they are to be withheld according to the teaching of Christ. . . .

We have therefore recommended that the following method and instruction, based on God's counsel, be tried until the Holy Spirit leads us to a better understanding.

First, as indicated above, in every way and manner the doctrine itself shall be firmly held and positively preached and made known that according to the institution of Christ both kinds are to be used in the sacrament. This teaching shall be presented without compromise to everyone, including the weak and the obstinate.

Second, where there are weak Christians, who as yet have not heard or been sufficiently instructed and strengthened by the word of the gospel, and so out of weakness and terror of conscience rather than obstinacy cannot receive both kinds, one may allow these to take communion in one kind for the time being and where they ask for it the pastor or preacher may so administer it. . . .

Third, as for the obstinate who will neither learn nor practice this doctrine, one should simply offer them neither kind, but let them go. . . .

The third article, and the most fundamental, is that one teach the reason for the use of the sacrament and how one shall be properly prepared.

First, the pastor needs to instruct the people how great a sin it is to dishonor the sacrament and to misuse it. . . .

Second, no one shall be admitted to the sacrament unless he has previously been to the pastor who shall inquire if he rightly understands the sacrament, or is in need of further counsel, etc.

Also, it shall be taught that they alone are worthy to receive the sacrament who show true repentance and sorrow for their sins and are terror-stricken in their consciences. Rough, fearless persons will not be admitted. . . .

True Christian Penance

Formerly, it has been taught that penance consists of three parts: contrition, confession, and satisfaction. We have said of the first part that contrition and sorrow imply the acknowledgment of sin and mortification of the flesh. It is well we use these words, contrition and sorrow, for they are clear and easily understood.

True Christian Confession

The papal kind of confession is not commanded, namely, the recounting of all sins. This, furthermore, is impossible, as we read in Psalm 19[:12], "But who can discern his errors? Clear thou me from hidden faults." Yet there are many reasons why we should exhort the people to confession, especially in those cases where they need counsel and wherein they are most troubled.

No one should be allowed to go to communion who has not been individually examined by his pastor to see if he is prepared to go to the holy sacrament. . . .

True Christian Satisfaction for Sin

It is not in us to make satisfaction for our sins, for Christ alone has made satisfaction for our sins. This part of penance belongs to the forgiveness of sins and faith—we know and believe that our sins are forgiven us on account of Christ. This is the way we ought to teach this article. . . .

Thus we should instruct the people: First, we should awaken the people to fear. . . .

Second, we should awaken the people to faith, even if we have deserved nothing else than condemnation. . . .

The Human Order of the Church

. . . Holy days such as Sunday shall be observed and as many others as the respective pastors have been accustomed to observe. For the people must have certain set times to come together to hear the Word of God.

Pastors should not make an issue of the fact that one observes a holy day and another does not. Let each one peacefully keep to his custom. Only do not do away with all holy days. It would be well if there were some uniformity. The days of Annunciation, Purification, Visitation of the Virgin Mary, St. John the Baptist, St. Michael's, Apostles' Day, Magdalene—these have already been discarded and could not conveniently be restored. We should keep especially Christmas, Circumcision, Epiphany, Easter, Ascension, Pentecost, though leaving out the unchristian legends and songs associated with them. These days have been instituted because it is not possible to teach all parts of the gospel at one time. . . .

Beyond such regulations, which were made for the sake of good order, are others, such as regular fasts and abstaining from meat on Fridays, which were instituted in the thought that they would be a special service to God, to appease God and secure his grace. Now Christ teaches in Matthew 15[:9] that it is futile to appease God by the observance of such regulations, for he says: "In vain do they worship me, teaching as doctrines the precepts of men. . . ."

Paul also says in Colossians 2[:20] that no one shall submit to such regulations. We should not make such regulations and should not teach that it is sin to break them. Nor should one teach that it is a service to God to keep these rules.

The people should be taught the difference between Church Order and secular government. Every secular authority is to be obeyed not because it sets up a new service to God but because it makes for orderly life in peace and love. Therefore it is to be obeyed in everything except when it commands what is contrary to the law of God, for example, if the government ordered us to disregard the gospel or some of its parts. . . .

Memorial masses and other paid masses shall no longer be held. For if there were any value in memorial masses, vigils, and the like, it would be possible to atone for sin through works. But as St. John the Baptist testified (John 1[:29]), Christ alone is the Lamb of God that takes away the sin of the world. . . .

Some sing the Mass in German, some in Latin, either of which is permissible. It would be reasonable and useful if we used German where most of the people do not understand Latin. . . .

On high festivals such as Christmas, Easter, Ascension, Pentecost, or the like, it would be well to use some Latin hymns in the Mass, if they are in accordance with Scripture. For it is in poor taste to sing only one thing. . . .

We rightly honor the saints when we recognize that they are held up before us as a mirror of the grace and mercy of God. . . . Honoring the saints, also, consists in exercising ourselves and increasing in faith and good works in a manner similar to what we see and hear they have done. . . .

MARRIAGE

. . . Discipline is to be maintained in marriage, and patience and love are to be shown and practiced by the one to the other, as enjoined in Ephesians 5[:22ff.]. And they should be taught that they may not be divorced or desert each other, as Christ himself commands in Matthew 19[:6, 9]. . . .

FREE WILL

Many talk improperly about the freedom of the will, wherefore we have composed here this brief statement.

Man has in his own power a freedom of the will to do or not to do external works, regulated by law and punishment. There are good works he can do and there is a secular goodness he can achieve through a power of his own that he has and receives from God for this purpose. . . .

But this freedom is hindered by the devil. For if man is not protected and ruled by God, the devil drives him to sin so that he has not even this external goodness. It is important that the people be taught and learn how weak and miserable man is when he does not seek help from God. . . .

CHRISTIAN FREEDOM

Others talk equally improperly about Christian freedom. Consequently some people think they are free in the sense that they need no government and even that they need pay no taxes. Others interpret Christian freedom to mean that they can eat meat, refrain from confession, and fasting, and the like.

Such wild illusions of the people the preachers should condemn and their teaching should lead to improvement and not to wickedness. . . .

THE TURKS

Some preachers clamor recklessly about the Turks, saying we should not oppose the Turks since Christians may not avenge themselves. This is seditious talk that should not be permitted or tolerated. For the government is given the power of the sword and commanded to punish all murder and pillage. Therefore it is obligated to wage war against those who start an unjust war and are responsible for pillage and murder. . . .

But the Christian is forbidden to avenge what is not undertaken by the government or authorized by it. Scripture forbids Christians to exercise personal and individual vengeance, but commands government to execute it and calls it a service of God when done by the government. . . .

DAILY WORSHIP IN THE CHURCH

Since the old ceremonies have been discarded altogether in many places of the land and little is read or sung in the churches, we have made the following arrangements as to what the procedure in churches and schools should henceforth be, especially in cities and places where there are many people.

First, in the daily Matins in the churches three Latin or German psalms may be sung. On days when there is no sermon a lesson may be read by the preacher. . . . He who reads the lesson shall then exhort the people to pray the Lord's Prayer for some common need appropriate at the time, such as peace, the needful fruits of the earth, and especially for the grace of God, that he may protect and rule over us. Then the whole congregation may sing a German hymn and the preacher read a collect.

At Vespers it would be excellent to sing three evening hymns in Latin, not German, on account of the school youth, to accustom them to the Latin. Then follows the simple antiphons, hymns and responses, and a lesson in German. . . . After the lesson the Lord's Prayer should be said. . . .

In small communities where there are no students it is not necessary to sing the daily offices. But it would be well to sing something when there is preaching.

During the week there should be preaching on Wednesdays and Fridays. . . .

On festival days there should be preaching at Matins and Vespers, on the gospel at Matins. Since the servants and young people come to church in the afternoon we recommend that on Sunday afternoons there be constant repetition, through preaching and exposition, of the Ten Commandments, the articles of the Creed, and the Lord's Prayer. . . .

If on Sundays we preach on the Ten Commandments, the Lord's Prayer, and the Creed, one after the other, we should also diligently preach about marriage and the sacraments of Baptism and of the altar. . . .

We have heard reports of unseemly preaching about the six weeks that the women observe following childbirth, so that women have been forced to go to work, without consideration of their weakness, with the result that some have become ill and are supposed to have died.

Therefore we have deemed it necessary to advise the pastors to speak cautiously about these and similar customs, for the six weeks

are ordained in the law of Moses, Leviticus 12[:4-8]. Though that law is superseded, still those things that not only the law but nature itself teaches are not superseded, namely, the natural and ethical truths that belong to the realm of nature and ethics. . . .

THE TRUE CHRISTIAN BAN

It were well, too, if we did not entirely do away with the penalty of the ban in the true Christian sense described in Matthew 18[:17-18]. It consists in not admitting to the Lord's Table those who, unwilling to mend their ways, live in open sin, such as adultery, habitual drunkenness, and the like. However, before taking such action, they are to be warned several times to mend their ways. Then, if they refuse, the ban may be proclaimed. . . .

Many pastors quarrel with their people over unnecessary and childish things, as pealing of bells (*Pacem* ringing) and the like. In such matters the pastors may well show themselves as sensible and for the sake of peace yield to the people, instructing them wherein the bells have been improperly used and how they may henceforth be rightly used. Although in some places the custom of ringing the bells against bad weather is retained, undoubtedly the custom has its origin in a good intention, probably of arousing the people thereby to pray God that he would protect the fruits of the earth and us against other harm.

Since, however, the people afterwards became superstitious and it was believed that bad weather was driven away by the bells and especially by the consecration of the bells, which had become a custom of long standing, it would not be amiss if in summertime the preacher explained to the people when storms threaten and the bells were rung, that the reason for the custom was not that the sound of the bells or the consecration of the bells drove away the storm or the frost, as had been taught, and believed hitherto, but that thereby each one should be reminded to pray to God for his protection of the fruits of the earth. . . .

THE OFFICE OF SUPERINTENDENT

This pastor *(Pfarherr)* shall be superintendent *(Superattendent)* of all the other priests who have their parish or benefice in the region, whether they live in monasteries or foundations of nobles or of others. He shall make sure that in these parishes there is correct Christian teaching, that the Word of God and the holy gospel are truly and purely proclaimed, and that the holy sacraments according to the institution of Christ are provided to the blessing of the people. . . .

If one or more of the pastors or preachers is guilty of error in this or that respect, the superintendent shall call to himself those concerned and have them abstain from it, but also carefully instruct them wherein they are guilty and have erred either in commission or omission, either in doctrine or in life.

But if such a one will not then leave off or desist, especially if it leads to false teaching and sedition, then the superintendent shall report this immediately to the proper official, who will then bring it to the knowledge of our gracious lord, the Elector. His Electoral grace will then be able in good time to give this proper attention. . . .

SCHOOLS

The preachers are to exhort the people to send their children to school so that persons are educated for competent service both in church and state. For some suppose it is sufficient if the preacher can read German, but this is a dangerous delusion. . . .

At present many faults exist in the schools. We have set up the following syllabus of study so that the youth may be rightly instructed.

In the first place the schoolmasters are to be concerned about teaching the children Latin only, not German or Greek or Hebrew as some

have done hitherto and troubled the poor children with so many languages. This is not only useless but even injurious. It is evident that these teachers undertake so many languages not because they are thinking of their value to the children but of their own reputation.

Second, they are also not to burden the children with a great many books, but avoid multiplicity in every way possible.

Third, it is necessary to divide the children into groups. . . .

[Editor's note: Specific recommendations are then given about what each of the three divisions of students should read and be taught.]

SELECTIONS FROM LUTHERAN CHURCH ORDERS

75. Catechization: The Wittenberg Church Order (1533)

This was the first Church Order for the central city of the Lutheran Reformation, although many of the topics it covered were already mentioned in the instructions for the 1528 visitation to the churches of Saxony. This excerpt shows once again the importance attached to the catechism as a tool for teaching basic doctrine and morality. It also shows how church leaders communicated the contents of the catechism to adults as well as to students in the schools.

From Richter 1:221.

On all holy days after the high Mass, the fourth deacon who is especially delegated to catechize the peasants and peasant children shall ride to the villages [surrounding the city of Wittenberg] and preach to the people from the catechism. He shall also retell the plain and

The Town of Wittenberg

simple stories or the gospel for the holy day. After the sermon, the entire catechism including the instructions of Christ concerning Baptism and the sacrament [of the Lord's Supper] shall be recited to the people. Then one shall admonish them to pray. The deacon shall sing a German hymn with the peasants before and after the sermon so that the peasants with their children and the hired workers shall learn to sing diligently and rightly. The deacon can indeed exhort them concerning this at the opportune time. . . .

There should be special preaching [in Wittenberg] on the catechism four times a year, one time by the pastor and the other three times by the other three priests. On the preceding Sunday, the pastor shall warn the people that they are obliged to send their children and hired workers. This shall take place in the first two weeks of Advent, the first two weeks after Quadragesima, in Cross Week and the week following it, and in the two weeks just after the harvest, before one has taken in the hops, around the Sunday before St. Bartholomew's day and the following two weeks.[1] Each time preach eight days, namely, Mondays, Tuesdays, Thursdays, and Fridays in both weeks after midday at the proper hour for Vespers. . . .

76. Baptism

Luther: The Order of Baptism, Newly Revised (1526)

As in the case of the Mass liturgy, Luther was still cautious in 1523 about making major changes in the ritual of Baptism. He waited until 1526 to omit certain traditional external actions such as blowing under the eyes, putting salt into the mouth, putting spittle and clay in the ears and nose, anointing the breast and shoulders with oil, and marking the crown of the head with chrism. He retained the making of the sign of the cross, the exorcism of the devil, and the putting on of a christening robe.

From *LW* 53:107–9, trans. Paul Z. Strodach, rev. Ulrich Leupold. See also Emil Sehling, *Die evangelischen Kirchenordnung des XVI. Jahrhunderts* 1/1 (Leipzig: Reisland, 1902), 18–23.

The officiant shall say: Depart, unclean spirit, and give room to the Holy Spirit. Then he shall sign him with a cross on his forehead and breast and say: Receive the sign of the holy cross on both your forehead and your breast. [Followed by two prayers.] Then the priest shall lay his hand on the head of the child and pray the Our Father together with the sponsors kneeling. . . . Then the child shall be brought to the font, and the priest shall say: The Lord preserve your coming in and your going out now and for evermore. Then the priest shall have the child, through his sponsors, renounce the devil. . . . [The sponsors respond to several questions.] Then he shall take the child and immerse it in the font and say: I baptize you in the name of the Father and of the Son and of the Holy Spirit. Then the sponsors shall hold the little child in the font and the priest shall say, while he puts the christening robe on the child: The almighty God and Father of our Lord Jesus Christ, who has regenerated you through water and the Holy Spirit and has forgiven you all your sin, strengthen you with his grace to life everlasting. Amen. Peace be with you. Amen.

The Brandenburg-Nürnberg Church Order of 1533

In addition to specifying how a baptism should be conducted, Church Orders frequently addressed issues such as the responsibilities of baptismal godparents and midwives, as the following excerpt illustrates. This particular Church Order was prepared by Andreas Osiander (see also doc. #68) with the assistance of Johannes Brenz, the influential reformer of the imperial city of Schwäbisch-Hall. Nürnberg, a city of over 50,000, was the seat of the imperial court and an important commercial center in southern Germany. It was gradually won over to the Lutheran reform movement between 1523 and 1533. The Church Order also applied to the territory of Brandenburg-Ansbach in the north because it was ruled since 1417 by descendants of a former ruler of Nürnberg.

From Richter 1:198.

Since Baptism is a sign of our Christian covenant, like the circumcision of the Jews in the Old Testament, one should baptize the little child, according to the wishes of the parents, as speedily as possible. According to the instructions of God in Genesis 17[:12], the little child was circumcised promptly on the eighth day. Christ says, "Who is not born again from water and the spirit may not see the Kingdom of God [John 3:3]," and Paul calls Baptism a bath of rebirth [Titus 3:5]. Now, since the little child must be reborn as soon as it is born in order to come into the kingdom of God, we believe that the Apostles also baptized children because they baptized entire households [Acts 16:15], and it is certain that no one can prove anything otherwise or oppose this from the Holy Scriptures.

But the pastor and church workers should be diligent to ensure that knowledgeable sponsors are chosen for this necessary work of Christian Baptism, who know why they are there and who will treat the Baptism with proper devotion, respect, and esteem. They should also be examined to see that they are not thoughtlessly frivolous, peevish, or drunk, so that they earnestly and knowingly speak the Christian prayers and the words by which the baptism is particularly enacted. They must not arouse frivolity or annoyance among the surrounding listeners but should rather move them to devotion and good Christian thoughts. In the same way, the other people who are present, especially the one who holds the child, should shun all frivolity, disorderliness, and scandal and should devoutly request grace, salvation, faith, and blessing for the child being baptized. . . .

And since until now a praiseworthy and well-grounded custom has been maintained in the Christian community that all Christian people, but especially the midwives, may baptize the little child when its life is endangered, what one calls emergency Baptism *(Jachtauf)*, the pastors should diligently instruct and admonish the midwives so that they approach the Baptism earnestly and in the fear of God and especially that they rightly understand and know properly how to speak the words ("I baptize you in the name of the Father and of the Son and of the Holy Spirit"). . . .

The one who has been given emergency Baptism is truly baptized, and it is not necessary to baptize a second time. That was an unnecessary abuse in former times and is especially to be avoided so that one does not give occasion to the gross errors of the Anabaptists. . . .

77. Confession: The Church Order of Albertine Saxony (1539)

This Church Order was prepared by Justus Jonas for Albertine (or Ducal) Saxony, which had been separate since 1485 from Ernestine (or Electoral) Saxony where Luther was based. The Reformation had been resisted in this territory until the death of Duke Georg in 1539. This excerpt illustrates two reasons why the rite of confession was retained: to provide an opportunity to the conscience of the hard-hearted and to console those who were burdened with guilt.

From Richter 1:310–11.

There are two kinds of people who come to confession. Some understand nothing and have little sense of conscience but are still not entirely wicked. One finds some who were not instructed about anything under the pope and did not learn what sin is, what results from it,

or how one can get free of it and obtain grace. They grew up in such ignorance that although they want to do what is right, they are ashamed still to learn in old age and find it very difficult to go to confession. Therefore they oftentimes remain apart from confession and the sacrament as long as it can be delayed or put off.

When such people come, who want to do what is right but know nothing, one should first touch their consciences and teach them to know and feel that they are poor sinners and need grace, in a way something like this:

If one comes and says, "Most worthy and esteemed master, I come, wanting to manifest all that pertains to being a God-fearing and pious man, but I do not know how I should do that or bring that about. Therefore I ask you to instruct me in the best way."

The pastor should then say:

"Dear friend, do you know the Ten Commandments and what they say about God's expectations concerning what people should and should not do?"

The penitent answers:

"No, master, unfortunately I do not know them, for under the pope few priests spoke to the poor laypeople about the Ten Commandments."

The confessor should say further:

"Dear friend, because you do not know the Ten Commandments, it is certain that you have not kept them. This is the greatest sin that a person can commit, to ask nothing about God although you have made daily use for twenty or thirty or forty years of so many of God's gifts and benefits, and have been given body, soul, senses, understanding, food and drink, and all necessities. You allowed his dear son to serve you with his suffering and death for your salvation and blessedness, and allowed this to be preached to you all the time, but not one time did you think about this or ask what you might be obligated to do to praise, thank, and serve your dear merciful God for such great and manifold benefits. When it is this way, the devil can do what he wills and always drive or pull your heart, which wants to know nothing of God, from one sin to another. Just think that if you should die now, you would never be able to defend yourself against his strong judgment for such horrible scorn of God and his holy word. You would be desperate and would be eternally lost. But since our loving God prolongs your life, you should feel sorrow for such horrible sins and should ask God for forgiveness and grace and also diligently listen to and learn his holy word and the gospel with sincerity and devotion in order to live in accordance with it and be pious. . . ."

But if there are [other] people who are aware of their sins or come themselves without a special reminder from the confessor and confess themselves to be poor sinners and desire to be instructed and consoled by God's Word so that they might be freed from their sins, they should be instructed and consoled in a way like this:

"Dear friend, because you recognize yourself as a poor sinner, this is a good and certain sign that you still have a gracious God. For where one does not recognize sins and has no regret or sorrow over them, that is an evil sign and indicates that the devil has entirely possessed and hardened the heart. Therefore you should hold it for certain that your confession of your sins, your regret and sorrow, and your desire to free yourself from them is an especially great grace of God and work of the Holy Spirit for which you should be thankful before God.

"Even more you should thank the Lord God that he does not leave you to despair because of your sins, regret, and sorrow but is so gracious to you that he teaches you by his holy gospel to seek consolation and forgiveness.

"But so that such grace might be all the more certain and secure in you, I also want to impart to you the word of absolution through which the grace that is proclaimed in general to all the world through the public preaching of the gospel may be given as a particular promise to you at this time. And, my dear friend, you should regard the word of absolution that I impart to you as God's promise as if God were declaring his grace and the forgiveness of your sins through a voice from heaven and should heartily thank God that he has given such power to the church and to Christians on earth. . . ."

78. The Lord's Supper: The Württemberg Church Order (1536)

Württemberg, the largest principality in southwestern Germany, established its Lutheran territorial church in 1534. This first Church Order was also prepared with the assistance of Johannes Brenz. Lutherans insisted that the Lord's Supper should never be celebrated without communicants. The following passage notes the careful steps taken to determine who the communicants would be. It also indicates that although Luther advocated frequent communion, not all Lutheran churches celebrated it on a weekly basis.

From Richter 1:267–68.

We have for various reasons observed that the Supper of Christ shall be held approximately six times a year in all of our principality's parishes, that is, once every two months and as often in between those times as there are people present who desire the most worthy sacrament. If one wishes to celebrate the sacrament on a certain Sunday, one shall announce this from the pulpit the Sunday before or at a more favorable time if there be one.

Accordingly, on Saturday evening, after the singing of a German hymn, the pastor shall give a sermon concerning the institution and

Johannes Brenz

use of the most worthy sacrament of the body and blood of Christ. Then, at the end of the sermon, he shall admonish the people who wish to go to the gracious table of the Lord on the following Sunday or feast day to proceed to the choir after the sermon and present themselves to the pastor or his assistant so that they might be counted and recognized. . . .

Since one has a count on Saturday evening of the number of people who want to partake of the Supper of Christ, one shall also count out the bread to the approximate number of people. Similarly, one shall set out the wine in its appropriate measure and prepare it along with the cup so that at the end none of it remains left over, all is handled properly and respectfully, and no one will give offense. . . .

79. Acts of Devotion
The Braunschweig Church Order (1528)

The guild masters and the commercial leaders in Braunschweig, one of the north German Hanseatic League cities, persuaded the city council to support the Reformation. Johannes Bugenhagen was then called in from Wittenberg to help settle quarrels between various religious factions, and the Church Order he drafted

for the city became an important model for the structuring of other Lutheran churches.

From Richter 1:116.

Good books have been written about images, noting that it is not improper or unchristian to have images, especially when one portrays stories by them. [But] we freely confess that we have many false images and much unnecessary clutter in our churches. Still, since we cannot be iconoclasts [image-attackers] and other well-known and pious people would not take offense at this, we have, using regular power and authority, only done away with those images before which people prayed and toward which idolatry and special honor were directed by the setting up of candles and candlesticks. All the others that are not troublesome we have allowed to remain in the churches. But if the same kind of idolatry and supposed worship takes place again before some other images, we will also do away with these, using regular power and authority. They are not worthy of this honor, for one should pray and make invocations to God alone, as he says in Isaiah 42[:8], "I am the Lord, that is my name; my glory I give to no other, nor my praise to idols."

The Formula of Reform for Wittenberg (1545)

This document was prepared by Melanchthon.

From Richter 2:86.

Here we add an article concerning the invocation of the saints who have departed from this life. For it is manifest that the world is full of the worship of idols in the form of this

Johannes Bugenhagen

invocation. It is expressly written in Deuteronomy 6[:13] and Matthew 4[:10], "The Lord your God," who disclosed himself to you through his Word and certain testimony, "you will adore and he alone will you serve."

However, it is customary for a great multitude of people to have recourse to the saints, as if they gave benefits of the body or soul. Manifestly, this error is a worship of idols.

But some look for excuses and paint or dress up this rite with various colors. The saints are not being invoked, they say, as authors or producers of these gifts but as intercessors. This disguise is refuted by this clear reply.

In the church, that is, the people of God, no invocation should be taught, instituted, or established that does not have the support of a commandment or example from the Word of God.

Yet, it is manifest that there is absolutely no commandment or example of this invocation [of the saints] in the writing of the prophets and apostles. And it is said in Romans 14[:23], "Whatever does not proceed from faith is sin."

When, therefore, there is nothing in the Word of God concerning this invocation, it is doubtful that the custom of such invocation pleases God. Therefore it should in no way be established. . . .

80. Marriage Orders
Luther: The Order of Marriage (1529)

From *LW* 53:111–12, trans. Paul Z. Strodach, rev. Ulrich Leupold.

Many lands, many customs, says the proverb. Since marriage and the married estate are worldly matters, it behooves us pastors or ministers of the church not to attempt to order or govern anything connected with it, but to permit every city and land to continue its own use and custom in this connection. Some lead the bride to the church twice, both evening and morning, some only once. Some announce it formally and publish the banns from the pulpit two or three weeks in advance. All such things and the like I leave to the lords and the council to order and arrange as they see fit. It does not concern me.

But when we are requested to bless them before the church or in the church, to pray over them, or also to marry them, we are in duty bound to do this. . . .

The Church Order for the City of Hannover (1536)

Urbanus Rhegius (1489–1541) was an important Lutheran preacher in Augsburg who was invited by the Duke of Braunschweig-Lüneburg to move to north central Germany in 1530 to help consolidate the Lutheran Reformation in that region. This excerpt from his Church Order for the city of Hannover gives an example of the permanent tribunals that the Lutheran churches introduced as a substitute for the Catholic ecclesiastical courts that dealt with marriage cases.

From Richter 1:275–76.

In order to prevent disorder and impropriety in the enactment of Christian marriage, we have delegated three persons, a [city] councilor, our syndic, and the [church] superintendent, to judge impediments to marriage such as degrees of kinship by blood or marriage, according to imperial and divine law. The pope's law is too strict with prohibitions, and it is too easy to get dispensations from it by the payment of money, but since he is not an authority for us, we will leave his law to his own realm.

The emperor is our natural lord and a divinely ordained authority, but when some marriage case is reported that cannot be easily decided by imperial law and must still be settled so that greater harm does not grow from it, we also wish, within the capacity of our Christian freedom, to take the divine law of Moses as a guide to provide better advice for conscience and [to promote] the common peace. Now if Moses was given the right to make legal judgments but gave us no command in the law, then no prohibition concerning that matter applies to us. And no one can doubt that Moses as a great prophet who spoke and wrote as he was inspired by the Holy Spirit also knew what was honorable or dishonorable in the state of marriage. For he certainly did not speak in vain to the people of Israel in Deuteronomy 4[:8], "What other great nation has statutes and ordinances as just as this entire law that I am setting before you today?"

A secret marriage bond that takes place without the knowledge and will of the parents by evil and irregular means we will, simply by imperial and divine law, not recognize as a marriage, and whoever carries out such a secret and dishonor-able practice shall be punished according to the particular circumstances of the misdeed.

Such persons as cannot bear to be with each other and wish to separate should present themselves before the aforementioned judges to see whether or not they have just cause for their proposal.

And in order that the holy state of marriage might be understood better and undertaken with more sincerity and fear of God, the preachers should at all times teach and admonish the congregation so that the people might learn what the state of marriage is and how each Christian within this state ought to live both for the sake of themselves and their children.

81. Burials: Visitation Articles for Electoral Saxony (1533)

From Richter 1:230.

This is how one conducts burials in Wittenberg. They may be performed in other ways, as long as one holds to God's Word and conducts the ceremonies in a Christian manner.

First. If a common person dies, the church bells are not rung [to assemble people], but the nearest neighbors go with the body to the grave.

Second. If a middle-class citizen dies, friendship requires the schoolmaster and his students to participate by singing "Out of the Depths I Cry to You" [see doc. #59a] on the way to the grave, etc. Now, at the graveside, when the body is about to be buried, the schoolmaster or his associates together with those assembled there shall sing "We All Believe in One God" [the Creed, see doc. #59b], so that the article of the resurrection of the flesh may be comprehended. Still, the church bells are not rung for the burial and it will not be required to call the chaplain.

Third. If one of the distinguished people dies, the body is buried with a procession. All of the church workers are not obligated to be there, but are requested to do so out of friendship. The schoolmaster attends along with the students. The people may be called together by the ringing of the large bells; however, this seldom happens.

82. Confirmation: The Brandenburg Church Order of 1540

This Church Order applies to Electoral Brandenburg, which was brought into the Lutheran movement quite late by Joachim II in 1539. The Lutheran church in the northern Markish provinces retained many traditional elements of church life, such as the episcopal form of church government and the practice of confirmation. Many of the early Church Orders contain no article on confirmation.

From Richter 1:325–26.

We want confirmation according to the old use to be maintained. Namely, that if the baptized come to the years when they know what they believe and pray and also know the content of the catechism, what it is to live in a Christian manner and to conduct themselves honorably, they shall be called and examined during the visitation of the bishop, and where it is found that they have a good report of their faith and Christian conduct, the bishop shall, with the laying on of hands, ask God the Almighty to remain constant with them, to uphold and strengthen them, and thus they are confirmed.

But if some are also found who come to this age and are still not rightly or sufficiently instructed in their faith, the bishop shall repri-mand the pastors and godparents and demand that the pastor diligently instruct the congregation and the sponsors so that they henceforth know what they believe and how they should live. This can surely take place if the catechism is diligently preached and promoted. . . .

83. Ordination: The Ordination of Ministers of the Word (1539)

From *LW* 53:124–26, trans. Paul Z. Strodach, rev. Ulrich Leupold.

First. The candidates shall be examined either on the same or the preceding day. If they are worthy, the congregation after due admonition by the preacher shall pray for them and for the whole ministry, namely, that God would deign to send laborers into his harvest and preserve them faithful and constant in sound doctrine against the gates of hell, etc.

Second. The ordinator and the minister or presbyters of the church shall place the ordinand in the center before the ordinator and all shall kneel before the altar. And the choir shall sing *"Veni sancte spiritus."*

V. Create in me a clean heart, O God.

R. And renew a right spirit within me.

The customary collect of the Holy Spirit shall be read.

Third. After this the ordinator shall ascend the step of the predella and facing the ordinands shall recite with a clear voice 1 Timothy 3 . . . [and Acts 20:28-31].

Fourth. The ordinator addresses the ordinands in these or similar words: Herein you hear that we bishops—that is, presbyters and pastors—are called not to watch over geese or cows, but over the congregation God purchased with his own blood that we should feed them with the pure Word of God and also be on guard lest wolves and sects burst in among the poor sheep. This is why he calls it a good work. Also in our personal conduct we should live decently and honorably and rule our house, wife, children, and servants in a Christian way.

Are you now ready to do this?

Answer: Yes.

Fifth. Then while the whole presbytery impose their hands on the heads of the ordinands, the ordinator says the Lord's Prayer in a clear voice. Let us pray. Our Father, etc. . . .

Sixth. The ordinator shall address the ordinands with these words of St. Peter, 1 Peter 5[:2-4]. . . .

Seventh. The ordinator shall bless them with the sign of the cross and use these or other words: The Lord bless you that you may bring forth much fruit. After this each one shall return to his own place. And if it is desired, the congregation may sing "Now Let Us Pray to the Holy Ghost."

This ended, the presbyter chants: Our Father, etc. And first the ordinands shall commune with the congregation, then likewise the ordinator if he so desires.

84. Visitation Procedures: Hesse Church Order (1537)

Hesse was a margraviate on the western border of Saxony. Philip of Hesse (1504–67), who ruled this territory for almost fifty years, provided early and important support for Luther's reform efforts (see doc. #49). This excerpt illustrates the techniques commonly used by visitors to gain information about spiritual and moral life.

From Richter 1:282.

Each superintendent shall visit every parish in his district at least once every two years and should diligently ascertain first of all what each pastor is doing with regard to his teaching and his life.

First, with regard to teaching, the superintendent shall have a friendly conversation with each pastor to find out his views on each point and article about which many sects raise disputes in our time, such as the divine and human natures of Christ, what law, sin, Christian repentance, the gospel, and good works are, how sins are forgiven and eternal life is attained, what Baptism and the Lord's Supper are and who should and should not participate in them, and many more such matters that are all most necessary to know, teach, and proclaim.

Second, in order to gain further knowledge about how teaching is upheld and improved in each parish, the superintendent, in every parish that he visits, should call the congregation together in the morning and let the pastor of the place give a sermon, the topic of which the superintendent has specified the evening before. [He shall] also inspect the pastor's church book and how he sings, prays, reads, celebrates Baptism and the Lord's Supper, and other evident practices. And after the sermon, he shall privately and in a friendly manner instruct, teach, and earnestly admonish the pastor to improve anything that he considers blameworthy and in need of correction.

The superintendent shall also diligently gain information about the manner of life of the pastor. After the conclusion of the sermon he shall let the pastor retire and shall ask the congregation to observe whether their pastor teaches purely or impurely, whether or not he lives honorably, uprightly, and irreproachably, and also whether he visits or operates a place to drink beer or wine or a public tavern, or if he occupies himself with the management of such an indecent establishment. [The superintendent shall also inquire] how the pastor conducts himself with regard to the poor people in his parish, those who are in the hospital or infirmary, the sick and the like and also toward his wife, children, servants, and neighbors.

Likewise, the superintendent should also ascertain who the chaplains [assistant ministers] and other church workers are and whether they are rightly submissive to the pastor and have committed their lives to their services toward the parishioners. . . .

And when the superintendent has sufficiently investigated the teaching, life, and behavior of the pastor and the other church workers, and has judged and corrected whatever faults he found in them, he should ask the pastor, in the absence of the parishioners, how they are disposed toward God and his dear Word, whether they diligently go to preaching, and encourage their children and servants to fear God and respect his Word. He shall ask whether there are any among them who have dealings with the Anabaptists and their teachings, also how they conduct themselves with regard to the Lord's Supper, Baptism, and the princely orders concerning marriages, the Baptism of children, and the like. . . .

And after everything necessary has been reported to the superintendent by the pastor, he shall summon the parishioners before him in order to find out for himself their actual understanding of such things. He shall let some of them, both young and old, say their prayers, the Creed, and the Ten Commandments and after that shall select certain articles and ask what they have learned and understand about this or that, such as the Lord's Prayer, the Creed, the Ten Commandments, Baptism, and the sacrament of the body and blood of Christ. . . .

85. Church Workers
The Church Order for the City of Braunschweig (1528)

From Richter 1:113.

In every church there shall be no more than one sexton [*Küster* or *Coster*] who unlocks the doors, rings the bell, brings water for baptism, remains by the altar [during the service], prepares the bread and the wine, etc. He shall obey the preachers and not grumble, doing in the church what he is called upon to do and helping the pastors in cases of emergency when they must go out. One shall count out and give him every pfennig that he needs to compensate the bell-ringers, and one shall arrange for and promise him an honorable wage for the work that he is obliged to do in the church. The sexton should ring to assemble the people a quarter hour before all services, according to the orders of the preacher. If he grumbles, is unwilling, or finds such duties troublesome, let him go and find another sexton.

Because organ-playing is also not unchristian, as it states in the Psalter (if one plays not idle or worthless songs but hymns and spiritual songs), every church shall pay a wage to their organist so that he will be obligated to perform such service.

General Articles for the Visitation in Electoral Saxony (1557)

From Richter 2:186–87.

In the villages, the sextons shall be obligated on all Sunday afternoons and on a certain day during the week to diligently and clearly teach the children the catechism and Christian hymns in German. Afterwards they shall ask questions and examine the children about the articles of the catechism that have been recited or read aloud. And where one or more branches belong to the parish, the sacristan shall teach in all places, alternating between them according to the advice of the pastor, so that the youth in all of the villages are instructed as is necessary and will not be neglected.

The sacristans should especially take pains to read the prayers aloud to the children and their elders, very slowly and clearly, distinctly reciting word for word as it is printed in the Small Catechism. And they shall not be so wanton, bold, or careless as to change, increase, decrease, or mix up the words in any way other than as they are designated in the printed copy. For in so doing, the young people will be poorly instructed and will afterwards learn to pray incorrectly from one another. . . .

No sexton who has not been examined and ordained shall be allowed to preach. But those who have been examined, appointed, and carefully called to the office of deacon shall not only preach but also be permitted to perform other church duties such as hearing confession and administering the sacrament. . . .

Justus Jonas

86. Discipline: The Order for the Wittenberg Consistory (1542)

Consistories were set up in three locations in Electoral Saxony: Wittenberg, Zeitz, and Zwickau. In each case there were four commissioners with expertise in law and theology. These regulations were prepared by Justus Jonas.

From Richter 1:367–71.

What cases should be heard by the Consistory: [The Consistory] shall hear cases concerning marriage and these articles in particular:

Which marriage vows are legally binding and which are not.

Whether there are sufficient reasons to advise and offer help again to an innocent partner who has been unjustly abandoned by her husband.

How to punish spousal violence *(saevitia Maritorum)* when the visitors receive daily complaints that the devil is causing much loathing and arousing all kinds of vexation by it, to the hindrance of the holy gospel.

How to judge when married people live with each other in daily quarreling, cause all kinds of irritation, and do not want to be reconciled with each other.

Adultery.

Rape of a virgin.

Incest or violation of degrees of prohibited relationships.

Public usury.

When children scorn and hold their parents in disrespect.

Women who smother their children during sleep or when drunk.

All blasphemy against God.

Mocking and derisive talk against the gospel, Christian doctrine, and ceremonies.

Secret associating with Jews and Jewesses.

Mutiny by the sexton or others against the pastor. . . .

For what cases a person should be excommunicated:

First, they should be excommunicated who spread seditious and seductive doctrines and will not cease from doing so.

Still, no one should be banned without being informed ahead of time of the doctrine. In cases where one sadly persists in error, the punishment shall at all times be imposed with the proviso of an appeal to the princes and by a decree of the elector.

Second, they should be excommunicated who, after being warned, persist in adultery, fornication, usury, etc., and do not reform.

Third, they shall be punished with the ban who scorn their father and mother and cause harm by this deed. So also those who prey on, strike, or apply a strong hand to their priest, pastor, and preacher, deacon or church worker and when many outcries about this reach the visitors. Still they shall first be accused and convicted of the committed deed and then condemned through sentencing.

Fourth, all blasphemers. Those who are convicted of using mocking, disdainful, or scornful speech about Christian teachings should be punished by excommunication.

Fifth, those who behave in a wanton, insolent, or frivolous manner or insult the preacher during Holy Communion, the sermon, or the time for singing in church. So also, those who out of scorn will not go to any church or preaching house for some weeks, a month, or a year. Also those who sing shameful songs composed about the preacher.

Sixth, those are to be banned who are found and convicted of practicing magic, circulating suspicious spells, committing perjury, or scorning the obligations of an oath they have sworn.

87. Pastoral Care: The Wittenberg Church Order (1533)

In Wittenberg, there was a chief pastor who was also called the superintendent and three assisting priests who were also called deacons or chaplains. A fourth assistant, called a village chaplain, was specifically appointed to conduct services in the surrounding villages.

From Richter 1:222.

Once the priests have been requested to hear the confession of or administer the sacrament to a sick person, they shall visit the sick person often after that, namely, every day or every second or third day, whichever is convenient, and console him with the Word of God until he either dies or returns to the hope of life. However, if the sick person has others with or around him who can console him, then such visits are not necessary. They also need not visit those who have a chronic illness or are not in danger of death, unless they are especially requested to do so. But they shall go two times a week to the hospital, if they wish, and teach the catechism to the people who cannot go out and to the others who are with them.

For all preaching in the villages, the pastor shall, by himself or in some way from another citizen, secure a horse for the fourth deacon at a certain definite time. The peasants should also be content with this favor, which did not happen in former times, although those who can should also come now and then to the preaching in the city. . . . The pastor is entirely not responsible for securing a horse [to visit] the sick among the peasants because this also cannot be done. For it can happen that in the morning or afternoon priests are requested for the sick in three or four villages. Then one would need to get four horses or else the neglect would be reckoned to the pastor. Therefore, the pastor is not responsible for securing a horse [to visit] the sick among the peasants, but the peasants should fetch a priest themselves with their own wagon. Still the three priests should be ready if they are summoned in such emergencies with a wagon. The fourth deacon is only responsible to visit the sick who are in need when he comes to preach with the pastor's horse. If it so happens that the same sick need a priest at another time and fetch him with their wagon, one of the other three priests shall be ready and willing to console the sick. . . .

The fourth deacon may hear the confessions of sick peasants and administer the sacrament to them but he is not obligated to do so. That is the duty of the other three deacons, but if the need arises, he may wish to do this. However, if a pestilence comes to one or more villages, only the fourth deacon shall go to hear the confession of the sick or to administer the sacrament, so that the other three deacons do not bring the pestilence into the city. This is because one cannot do without their services in the city.

88. Poor Relief—The Common Chest: The Leisnig Agreement (1523)

The parish of Leisnig in Electoral Saxony set up one of the earliest Lutheran plans for the systematic care of the poor. Luther showed his approval by arranging for the publication of the proposal.

From *LW* 45:182–89, trans. Walther Brandt.

. . . The administration of the common chest shall be set up in the following manner: annually each year, on the Sunday following the octave of Epiphany, at about eleven o'clock, a general assembly of the parish shall convene here in the town hall. There, by the grace of God united in true Christian faith, they shall elect from the entire assembly ten trustees or directors for the common chest who shall be without exception the best-qualified individuals; namely, two from the nobility, two from the incumbent city council, three from among the common citizens of the town, and three from the rural peasantry. The ten thus duly elected shall immediately assume the burden and responsibility of administration and trusteeship of the common chest. . . .

Every Sunday in the year, from eleven o'clock until two hours before Vespers, the ten directors shall meet in the parsonage or in the town hall, there to care for and exercise diligently their trusteeship, making their decisions and acting in concert in order that deeds of honor to God and love to the fellow-Christian may be continued in an unbroken stream and be used for purposes of improvement. These decisions of theirs shall be kept in strictest confidence and not be divulged in unauthorized ways. . . .

The ten directors shall appoint from among their number two building supervisors. These two, with the advice and knowledge of the other eight, shall have charge of the church buildings, the bridge, the parsonage, the school, the sacristan's place, and the hospitals. . . .

To the pastor or priest called and elected by our congregation, and to a preacher similarly called by us and appointed to assist the pastor (though the pastor himself should be able and qualified to preach God's Word and perform the other duties of his pastoral office), and also to a chaplain if the need for one arises, the ten directors on the unified resolution of the entire assembly are to furnish annually each year a specified sum of money, together with certain consumable stores and lands and properties subject to usufruct, to support them, and adequately meet their needs, one-fourth to be paid each quarter at the Ember fast out of the common chest, in return for a proper receipt.

The sacristan or custodian, to whom the assembly entrusts the locking up of the church and the suitable care of it, shall be given by the ten directors out of the common chest in quarterly installments a specified annual salary and certain usable stores and usufructs. . . .

The ten designated directors, in the name of our general parish assembly, shall have the authority and duty, with the advice and approval of our elected pastor and preacher and others learned in the divine Scriptures, to call, appoint, and dismiss a schoolmaster for young boys, whereby a pious, irreproachable, and learned man may be made responsible for the honorable and upright Christian training and instruction of the youth, a most essential function. . . . In accordance with a determination of the general assembly, the ten directors shall give a schoolmaster as compensation for his services a specified annual salary plus certain stores in quarterly installments out of the common chest. . . .

Likewise, the ten directors shall grant to an upright, fully seasoned, irreproachable woman an annual stipend and certain stores out of our common chest for instructing young girls

under twelve in true Christian discipline, honor, and virtue and, in accordance with the ordinance for our pastoral office, teaching them to read and write German, this teaching to be done during certain specified hours by the clear light of day and in a respectable place that is above suspicion. . . .

Those individuals in our parish and assembly who are impoverished by force of circumstances and left without assistance by their relatives, if they have any capable of helping, and those who are unable to work because of illness or old age and are so poor as to suffer real need, shall receive each week on Sunday, and at other times as occasion demands, maintenance and support from our common chest through the ten directors. This is to be done out of Christian love, to the honor and praise of God, so that their lives and health may be preserved from further deterioration, enfeeblement, and foreshortening through lack of shelter, clothing, nourishment, and care, and so that no impoverished person in our assembly need ever publicly cry out, lament, or beg for such items of daily necessity. For this reason the ten directors shall constantly make diligent inquiry and investigation in order to have complete and reliable knowledge of all these poor—as above—in the city and villages within our entire parish, and they shall confer on this matter every Sunday. . . .

✠ ✠ ✠

89. Schools: To the Councilmen . . . That They Establish and Maintain Christian Schools (1524)

From *LW* 45:350–71, trans. Albert Steinhaeuser, rev. Walther Brandt.

. . . Every citizen should be influenced by the following consideration. Formerly he was obliged to waste a great deal of money and property on indulgences, masses, vigils, endowments, bequests, anniversaries, mendicant friars, brotherhoods, pilgrimages, and similar nonsense. Now that he is, by the grace of God, rid of such pillage and compulsory giving, he ought henceforth out of gratitude to God and for his glory, to contribute part of that amount toward schools for the training of the poor children. That would be an excellent investment. . . .

When I was a lad they had this maxim in school: *"Non minus est negligere scholarem quam corrumpere virginem"*—"It is just as bad to neglect a pupil as to despoil a virgin." The purpose of this maxim was to keep the schoolmasters on their toes, for in those days no greater sin was known than that of despoiling a virgin. But, dear Lord God, how light a sin it is to despoil virgins or wives (which, being a bodily and recognized sin, may be atoned for) in comparison with this sin of neglecting and despoiling precious souls, for the latter sin is not even recognized or acknowledged and is never atoned for. O woe unto the world for ever and ever! Children are born every day and grow up in our midst, but, alas! there is no one to take charge of the youngsters and direct them. We just let matters take their own course. . . .

Since a city should and must have [educated] people, and since there is a universal dearth of them and complaint that they are nowhere to be found, we dare not wait until they grow up of themselves; neither can we carve them out of stone or hew them out of wood. Nor will God perform miracles as long as men can solve their problems by means of the other gifts he has already granted them. Therefore, we must do our part and spare no labor or expense to produce and train such people ourselves. . . .

Although the gospel came and still comes to us through the Holy Spirit alone, we cannot deny that it came through the medium of languages, was spread abroad by that means, and must be preserved by the same means. . . .

In proportion then as we value the gospel, let us zealously hold to the languages. . . .

A simple preacher (it is true) has so many clear passages and texts available through translations that he can know and teach Christ, lead a holy life, and preach to others. But when it comes to interpreting Scripture, and working with it on your own, and disputing with those who cite it incorrectly, he is unequal to the task; that cannot be done without languages. A saintly life and right doctrine are not enough. Hence, languages are absolutely and altogether necessary in the Christian church. . . .

To this point we have been speaking of the necessity and value of languages and Christian schools for the spiritual realm and the salvation of souls. Now let us consider also the body. Let us suppose that there were no soul, no heaven or hell, and that we were to consider solely the temporal government from the standpoint of its worldly functions. Does it not need good schools and educated persons even more than the spiritual realm? . . .

Now if (as we have assumed) there were no soul, and there were no need at all of schools and languages for the sake of the Scriptures and of God, this one consideration alone would be sufficient to justify the establishment everywhere of the very best schools for both boys and girls, namely, that in order to maintain its temporal estate outwardly the world must have good and capable men and women, men able to rule well over land and people, women able to manage the household and train children and servants aright. Therefore, it is a matter of properly educating and training our boys and girls to that end. . . .

If children were instructed and trained in schools, or wherever learned and well-trained schoolmasters and schoolmistresses were available to teach the languages, the other arts, and history, they would then hear of the doings and sayings of the entire world, and how things went with various cities, kingdoms, princes, men, and women. Thus, they could in a short time set before themselves as in a mirror that character, life, counsels, and purposes—successful and unsuccessful—of the whole world from the beginning; on the basis of which they could then gain from history the knowledge and understanding of what to seek and what to avoid in this outward life, and be able to advise and direct others accordingly. . . .

It is highly necessary, therefore, that we take some positive action in this matter before it is too late; not only on account of the young people, but also in order to preserve both our spiritual and temporal estates. . . .

Chapter Four

The Church's Struggle for Survival (1546–1648)

Duringthe twenty-five years between Luther's excommunication and his death, the reform movement he instigated had evolved into a new church noticeably different from Roman Catholicism in its doctrinal beliefs, modes of worship, and administrative structures. By the 1540s Lutheranism had become well established in many German territories and imperial cities. It was continuing to expand its influence in the adjoining regions of Scandinavia and eastern Europe. Most of the rulers who supported Luther were cooperating together as members of the Schmalkald League, and the leaders of the territorial churches in Germany were making progress in educating and transforming the religious outlook of the common people.

Nevertheless, there was considerable apprehension about what the future held for the Evangelical Lutheran churches. The meetings of theologians at several colloquies designed to promote doctrinal agreement and better relations between Catholics and Protestants resulted in no lasting progress. Negotiations between the emperor and the princes at various diets repeatedly ended in failure. Luther's polemical outbursts in his final years against the pope and the Jews and various other opponents reveal how convinced he was that the devil was at work preparing a final assault against everything for which he had labored. Yet even he could not have fully realized the extent to which internal divisions within the Lutheran movement and a new assertiveness on the part of its perennial enemies would set off a series of developments that, within a few months after his own death on February 18, 1546, almost brought an end to the movement he started.

The emperor, Charles V, had not been able to devote much attention to religious developments in Germany because of the wars he was conducting against France and the Turks. However, in 1544 he finally managed to get France to agree to a peace treaty. Shortly thereafter he paid tribute to the Turks in order to conclude an armistice with them. Freed from these distractions, he now proposed to assemble the German princes at an imperial diet and to address all of the religious and political issues that alienated him from the Lutherans. Fearing that the emperor might make undesirable concessions to the dissenting princes in order to reestablish peaceful coexistence, Pope Paul III intensified his efforts to assemble a general council to deal with the religious questions.

The Imperial Diet met at Worms in March 1545, and in the following December the first meeting of the general church council took place at Trent. The Lutherans did not feel that they could participate in the council under the terms the conveners had established and attempted instead to have the religious issues addressed at an Imperial Diet or another special council in Germany. However, when the Lutheran princes and their religious advisers met with Charles V once again at a Diet in Regensburg in June 1546, they could not ignore the signs that the emperor had secretly been preparing to reassert his authority over them by force. The emperor and the pope had, in fact, reached an agreement to work together to assemble the army for this purpose (doc. #90). The emperor had also worked out clandestine arrangements with several German princes either to gain their support or to ensure their neutrality when the war against the Protestants finally began. Most significant, Charles V secured the cooperation of a politically ambitious Lutheran ruler, Moritz (Maurice), Duke of Albertine Saxony (1521–53), by promising him control of the bishoprics of Magdeburg and Halberstadt and the territory of Electoral (Ernestine) Saxony governed at that time by his cousin, Duke Johann Friedrich.

The Schmalkald League quickly organized its own forces in order to prevent the imperial troops from entering Germany, and in July 1546, the Schmalkald War began. The inability of the Protestant princes to act decisively and in a cooperative manner, combined with a shortage of financial resources, severely limited their effectiveness. When the army of Duke Moritz linked up with the forces of the emperor at the critical battle of Mühlberg in April 1547, the Protestants suffered a crushing defeat. Duke Johann Friedrich, the leader of the Lutheran princes, was captured, and shortly thereafter, Philip of Hesse, the other major defender of the Protestant cause, surrendered after being promised that he would not be put to death for his resistance. In keeping with the promise he had made before the war began, Charles V turned over the lands of Duke Johann Friedrich to Duke Moritz and also gave him the title of Elector.

At this point, the emperor became angry with the pope for moving the council from Trent to Bologna. So, in September 1547, at the Diet of Augsburg, Charles V decided to deal with the religious divisions in Germany by himself. He formed a commission to work out a temporary settlement. The resulting proposal, the Augsburg Interim (doc. #91), published in May 1548, called for the reintroduction of some Catholic beliefs and practices but also realistically permitted the continuation of some important Protestant innovations, such as clerical marriage and the celebration of the Eucharist with both bread and wine, until these issues could be discussed more fully at a general church council. The emperor may have thought that he was making a significant conciliatory gesture to the Protestants by including a few important concessions, but the response he got was overwhelmingly hostile. The imprisoned Duke Johann Friedrich was told he could escape his death sentence if he supported the Interim proposal, but he refused to abandon his religious convictions. Even Duke Moritz, whom the emperor expected to provide an example of compliance, hesitated to do so because of the strength of the popular reaction to the Augsburg Interim.

The Lutherans were in almost total agreement that the Augsburg Interim was an unacceptable reimposition of Catholicism, but the church leaders and princes were not all of one mind about what step they should take next in order to ensure the survival of the Lutheran movement. Duke Moritz tried to balance his loyalties by suggesting that the Lutherans should propose a compromise to the emperor in the form of an alternative interim settlement. He persuaded Philip Melanchthon, the church leader whom many regarded as Luther's successor, and several other theologians from Wittenberg and Leipzig to draft such a proposal at a series of meetings in Pegau, Celle, and Leipzig. The resulting document, called the Leipzig Interim (doc. #92), was adopted in December 1548 and implemented by Duke Moritz as the standard for church belief and practice in Electoral Saxony.

Melanchthon and his associates replaced some statements in the Augsburg Interim that they thought could not be reconciled with essential Lutheran beliefs, but for the most part they went along with the restoration of many Catholic church practices. Conciliatory by nature, Melanchthon was especially convinced at this moment that the Evangelical churches could only escape fatal persecution if they gave the emperor some sign that they were willing to meet him partway. Melanchthon argued that many rites and ceremonies associated with the way Catholics celebrated the sacraments were not incompatible with Lutheran beliefs and could therefore be accepted without causing any harm.

Almost immediately after the adoption of the Leipzig Interim, a number of other Lutheran church leaders spoke out vehemently against any compromise with the emperor. The most notable of these critics were Matthias Flacius Illyricus (1520–75), professor of Hebrew at the University of Wittenberg, and Nikolaus von Amsdorf (1483–1565), bishop of Naumburg-Zeitz. They called Duke Moritz the "Judas of Meissen" for betraying his fellow Lutherans and suggested that the strategy he and Melanchthon endorsed would destroy Lutheranism by opening the door to a full-scale reintroduction of Catholicism (docs. #93 and 94). Forced to flee from Saxony, they found refuge in Magdeburg, which became the center of a determined resistance movement. Lutheranism was split between those who endorsed the strategy of Melanchthon and those who sympathized with Flacius and Amsdorf.

As Lutheran opposition to the emperor intensified, Duke Moritz began to reassess his commitments (doc. #95). Dissatisfied with what he had gained from his cooperation with Charles V and fearful of a new coalition of Lutheran princes in the far north of Germany, he signed a treaty with the king of France and proposed working with the other princes in a new campaign against the emperor. In 1552 Moritz swept back across the territories he had once conquered for the emperor and met with such success that he was able to persuade his Catholic opponents to meet at Passau to negotiate a peace treaty. Since neither side was satisfied with the results of these negotiations, warfare resumed in the following year. Duke Moritz died of wounds received in a battle in 1553, but the other Lutheran princes continued the fight until a more enduring settlement was concluded after negotiations with King Ferdinand, the emperor's brother, at the Diet of Augsburg in 1555. The Catholic allies agreed to recognize Lutheranism as a legitimate expression of Christianity and left it up to each prince to decide whether Catholicism or Lutheranism would become the required religion of his lands (doc. #96). The one exception to this policy pertained to the territories governed by ecclesiastical officials in Germany. King Ferdinand insisted that if any ruling Catholic bishops converted to Lutheranism they could not secularize their domains. He expected them to resign and relinquish jurisdiction to Catholic successors.

The Peace of Augsburg seemed to ensure the survival of Lutheranism, but it did little to relieve the resentment that different religious groups felt toward each other. Lutheran church leaders who had supported or rejected the Leipzig Interim traded accusations and attempted to exclude each other from leadership roles in the churches. The Interim crisis also revealed that there was no consensus among the Lutheran theologians about many issues of belief and church practice. The theological stance of Melanchthon and his associates provoked a series of doctrinal controversies that occupied the attention of church leaders for the next three decades (see chapter six).

The Peace of Augsburg stopped the war between the Protestants and the Catholics, but continuing fluctuations in the confessional allegiances of various German rulers raised new questions about the adequacy of the provisions it proposed to promote peaceful coexistence. Protestant church leaders grew fearful of the reviving strength of the Catholic church, particularly in southern Germany. Catholic rulers were equally upset when the Lutherans continued to extend their influence in several ecclesiastical territories in the north. The religious situation was complicated even further by the fact that the Peace of Augsburg had excluded Calvinism as a confessional option in Germany. To the dismay of both Lutherans and Catholics, Calvinist influence began to grow in Germany after it acquired the support of the Elector of the Palatinate in 1563. The territorial rulers who switched from Lutheranism to Calvinism were often more willing than the Lutherans to resist the Catholic princes, and they played an important role in a series of local conflicts in the final decades of the sixteenth century, bringing the religious parties even closer to a major confrontation.

In 1582, when the archbishop of Cologne converted to Protestantism and continued to claim the right to rule this important electoral territory, the Duke of Bavaria, the most assertive of the Catholic princes, sent troops to the city and expelled the Protestants. In 1607, when a Protestant mob attacked an illegal Catholic religious procession in the imperial city of Donauwörth, the Duke of Bavaria occupied the city and imposed allegiance to Catholicism. The Protestant princes protested at an Imperial Diet in Regensburg in 1608 and requested modifications in the terms of the Peace of Augsburg that would legitimate the territorial gains they had made since 1555. When the Catholic princes rejected their demands, the Protestant princes resorted to the formation of a Protestant Union in order to cooperate in the defense of their territories (doc. #97). This, in turn, prompted the Catholic princes to join together as a rival league.

War finally resulted in 1618 when the Protestant nobles of Bohemia resisted the efforts of their king to rescind the guarantee of religious toleration that had previously been given to them by the emperor. The Protestant Union, led by the Calvinist Elector of the Palatinate, came to their defense, and the Thirty Years War began. Not all of the Lutheran princes of Germany gave their support to the Protestant Union. Most notably, Duke Johann Georg of Electoral Saxony stayed out of the early stages of the struggle because of his hesitance to cooperate with Calvinists and his hope to gain some territory by siding with the emperor. Facing a divided opposition, the forces of the emperor and the Catholic League crushed the revolt in Bohemia and extended their campaign of reconquest into Austria and Germany. When the war spread into northern Germany by 1625, the Lutheran princes of Lower Saxony were drawn more fully into the conflict. Despite the assistance given to them by King Christian IV of Denmark, they were still defeated, and in 1629 Emperor Ferdinand II issued the Edict of Restitution, which required the Protestants to relinquish any territorial gains they had made since 1552 (doc. #98).

This was the low point in the war from the point of view of the Protestant princes, but their prospects for survival increased greatly in 1630 when King Gustavus Adolphus of Sweden decided to intervene. Although he presented himself as a defender of Lutheranism against Catholicism, his interests in the war were also clearly motivated by his desire to extend his own political influence over all of the territories bordering on the Baltic Sea (doc. #99). It took some persuading for him to gain the support of the Lutheran princes of Germany, since they did not wish to trade one overlord for another. Nevertheless, his successes in battle ultimately did much to restore confidence and encourage cooperation among the Protestant forces (doc. #100). After Gustavus Adolphus died in the battle of Lützen in November 1632, the Protestant forces once again suffered some setbacks. The Lutheran Elector of Saxony continued to keep his distance from the other Protestant princes and finally signed a separate treaty with the emperor in Prague in 1635. Those other princes who had not yet given up the fight were bolstered in the final stage of the war by support from both Lutheran Sweden and Catholic France. This coalition, now held together by political interests more than religious affinity, inflicted heavy losses on the troops of the Catholic League. At last, when it became clear that neither side could eliminate the other, the emperor, the German princes, and their foreign allies all agreed to a peace treaty, which was signed on October 24, 1648 (doc. #101). This Peace of Westphalia reaffirmed the ruling that princes would be free to determine the religion of their territories. When enforced again at this point, however, it meant that the Catholics regained control of some territories that had become Protestant during the sixteenth century, and Calvinism was recognized as an option that a prince could elect. Lutheran gains were mostly confined to some of the ecclesiastical territories of the north, which they were finally allowed to secularize.

It would take Germany a long time to recover from the destructive results of the Thirty Years War. The style of warfare used by the combatants contributed both directly and indirectly to the decimation of the population. The soldiers, many of whom were mercenaries, were not paid adequately, so their willingness to risk their lives was purchased by allowing them to plunder at will. Some towns were besieged more than ten times during the war. Those who escaped a violent death at the hands of the soldiers still faced a risk of starving to death or dying of plague. In some cases, the people became so desperate that they resorted to cannibalism (doc. #102). It is commonly estimated that one-third of the population of the cities perished during the war and as much as two-fifths of the rural population was wiped out between 1618 and 1648.

As society disintegrated, many Lutherans were deprived of adequate pastoral care due to the shortage of ministers and the deterioration of church institutions. Consequently, the communal aspects of religious life were often weakened. As is often the case in times of war, people were frequently willing to compromise their moral values or religious commitments in order to increase their chances of survival. This deterioration in religious life convinced some Lutherans, after the war, that a general reformation of spiritual life was desperately needed (see chapter eight). It was not uncommon for such reformers to view the destructiveness of the war as a divine punishment for the sinfulness of the German people (doc. #103). Deep pessimism about the possibilities of renewal encouraged others to seek refuge in an introspective, individualistic piety that looked for consolation in the ecstasy of religious experiences or the prospect of bliss in the life to come. Still others sought to promote recovery from the age of religious wars by clarifying and defending the doctrinal beliefs that defined the identity of Lutheranism in contrast to Catholicism and Calvinism. These responses to the situation in Germany in the late sixteenth and early seventeenth centuries will be examined more carefully in later chapters.

THE SCHMALKALD WAR AND INTERIM CRISIS

Pope Paul III (1534–49) and Emperor Charles V often interacted as rivals instead of allies. Although both of them favored the convening of a church council and the suppression of Protestant dissent, they disagreed about how to accomplish these goals. Four months after Luther's death, however, they overcame their mutual distrust, at least temporarily, and signed the following alliance. The pope offered financial support and twelve thousand Italian soldiers to help the emperor defeat the Schmalkald League.

90. The Alliance between Emperor Charles V and Pope Paul III (June 26, 1546)

From Walch 17:1453.

... Whereas Germany has been disturbed for many years by gross error and false belief, and some now continue to act in such a way that great harm, corruption, and destruction may occur in Germany; and whereas now for some time there have been those who have wanted to take some action with respect to such false belief in order to avoid divisions and errors and to maintain the unity of Germany; so an open and general council has been convoked and assembled at Trent. The Protestants, however, together with the Schmalkald League said that they did not want to submit to or attend the council that began to meet on the third Sunday in Advent just past and has since then, by the grace of God, been able to make some progress.

2. Therefore, his Holiness, the Pope, and his Majesty, the Emperor, have considered it advisable and productive that they should put

A Soldier in 1524

together and accept the articles described below, agreeing to comply with them faithfully, to the honor and praise of Almighty God and for the sake of the unity of all people, especially in Germany.

3. First, that his Imperial Majesty in the name of God and with the help and assistance of his Holiness, the Pope, should, in the upcoming month of June, supply himself with soldiers and military equipment to prepare for war against those who have protested against the council, against the Schmalkald League, and also against all those in Germany who persist in false belief and error. With all his power and might, he should bring them back again into the ancient, true, and undoubted faith and into obedience to the Holy See. At the same time, his Imperial Majesty should endeavor with all his zeal and perseverance to see whether he can bring the rebels back to the old Faith and to obedience to the Holy See in an amicable manner, without war. In any case, he should prepare himself so that if they cannot be persuaded peaceably within the announced time, his Imperial Majesty will still be armed and ready for war. ...

4. Furthermore, that his Imperial Majesty should not propose or accept any agreement with

the above-mentioned parties, which might be detrimental to this war effort or the faith of the Holy Christian Church, unless he has obtained the permission and consent of his Holiness, the Pope, or the Legate of the Holy See. . . .

91. The Augsburg Interim (May 1548)

The Augsburg Interim consisted of twenty-six articles, the first eight of which discussed theological issues related to sin and salvation. The excerpts below focus on the changes in church practice that it recommended.

From J. Mehlhausen, ed. *Das Augsburger Interim von 1548* (Neukirchen: Neukirchener Verlag des Erziehungsvereins, 1970), 66–142.

11. Of the Power and Authority of the Church

Although "Scripture," Christ says, "cannot be broken" [John 10:35], and for that reason is unshakable and greater than all human authority, nevertheless, it has always been in the power of the church to discern between true and counterfeit scripture. From this source came the canon of Scripture, which was introduced in the name of the apostles and disciples of the Lord to distinguish between genuine and false writings.

And just as the church has always had power and authority in this matter, so also it has the power to interpret the Scriptures and especially to extract and explain doctrines from them, since the Holy Spirit is present with it and leads it into all truth as Christ promised. . . .

Furthermore, it is certain that the church has the power to punish and to excommunicate and also the power to bind, as Christ has ordained. . . .

12. Of Ecclesiastical Ministers

The church also has teachings, given to it by God, which one should explain to the people. It has outward worship that one should treat and teach as holy and salubrious to the use of Christians. No less, the church has ministers who suitably administer such duties; neither can nor should the church lack such people. Not all Christians are called to these duties, for God himself has from the beginning given some to be apostles, some prophets, some evangelists, some pastors and teachers for the perfecting of the saints, in the work of ministry and to the upbuilding of the body of Christ [Eph. 4:11-12]. . . .

Therefore one should take care lest one mix together the spiritual priesthood, which all who are anointed by the Holy Spirit and are Christians have in common, with the external ministry, which does not belong to all but only to those who are called and ordained. For that cannot take place without causing grave and harmful disorder and ruin in the church.

13. The Pope and Other Bishops

Just as the church, which is the body of Christ, has one head so that it can more easily be maintained in unity, so also it has many bishops to rule the people whom Christ has purchased with his precious blood. Furthermore, by divine law, it has one highest bishop who presides over the others with a fullness of power, to guard against schism and division, through the prerogatives awarded to Peter. . . .

All Christians should be especially obedient to this highest bishop and every one of his bishops, as the Apostle says, "Be obedient to your leaders who keep watch over your souls" [Heb. 13:17].

17. The Sacrament of Penance

Now since men who are reborn often fall into grave sin, Christ has instituted the sacrament of penance, which serves us, like a second plank in a shipwreck, after Baptism. . . . As with the other sacraments, this one also has the power to sanctify. But this sacrament consists particularly in the absolution of the priest, which is grounded in the institution and words of Christ, who has delegated this power to the priests, saying: "As my Father sent me, so send I you. Receive the Holy Spirit. Those whom you forgive, their sins are forgiven" [2 John 20:21]. . . .

And although the satisfaction that expiates the guilt and eternal penalty of sin should be attributed to Christ alone, nevertheless, that satisfaction that consists of the fruits of repentance, namely, fasting, almsgiving, and prayers, is willingly received by us and is imposed by the priest in connection with the dispensing of the sacrament. . . .

18. The Sacrament of the Altar

Now whoever has been restored to life in the Lord through the sacrament of penance must also be sustained by food and must grow in spiritual gifts. Therefore, Christ has instituted the sacrament of the altar, under the visible elements of bread and wine, which offers to us the true body and blood of Christ and through these spiritual foods unites us with him as the head and members of the body so that we are nourished to all good, renewed and received through love into communion with the saints. . . .

And if now we attribute as much to Christ and his words as we ought, it is no doubt that as soon as the word is added to the bread and wine, they become the true blood and body of Christ and the substance of the bread and wine is changed into the true body and blood of Christ. But whoever denies this calls the omnipotence of Christ into doubt and accuses him of being a liar. . . .

19. The Holy Oil

The sacraments that we have considered above bring many great benefits to man when they regenerate the old man from the weaknesses of the flesh or confirm the regenerate in grace when they are received or restore again those who have fallen from grace or unite those restored more strongly with Christ. . . . And although these sacraments are always useful while we are in this life, as often as they are used, so that a sick man in his illness would not lack a special help in his time of danger, which could come to the aid of his body or strengthen his soul against the fiery dart of Satan, the sacrament of unction was instituted to which are added the prayers of the church. This oil the apostles first used as was mandated by the Lord when he sent them out to preach, "to cast out demons, and anoint the sick so they will be healed" [Mark 6:13]. . . .

Therefore, whoever scorns this sacrament scorns Christ himself and his grace, which he extended to us through this holy oil. And, the greater such scorn is, the greater the danger faced by the sick person, not only in body but also in soul, and the more culpable is the rejection of the sacrament. . . .

23. The Invocation of the Saints

When we consider the immeasurable benefits of Christ in the sacrifice of the altar, in which he made a sacrifice of himself for his entire spiritual body and for the salvation and welfare of all believers, it is appropriate, following the Lord's example and the admonition of the apostle, that prayers for the well-being of the whole church should be addressed to God and expressions of thanks for all his benefits. So the church assembles all its members together and gives thanks for all those who, having departed from this world, live with the Lord. And the church especially gives thanks by the veneration of the saints beloved by God, who, although they were weak in nature, were strengthened through the power of his grace so that they overcame the frailties of the flesh and with many fights against sin, the devil, and death, not through their own strength but by the strength of God, gained a crown of righteousness before the just judge. . . .

But we not only honor the saints and thank God for them but also wish that through their prayers and merits we may be protected by their help in all things. And we rightly believe that they, as members of one communion and one body, are also bound with us by one spirit and a chain of love and that they desire our salvation and suffer with us in misfortune. . . .

But we do not say that the merits belonging to the saints are the same as the merits we find in Christ, for since he gave himself for us and shed his blood for us he merited and acquired the perfect reconciliation of the world with God. . . . But out of the mercy and liberality of God and from the grace of Christ the merits of the saints are not only conducive to their own salvation but also useful for our protection and the obtaining of divine grace. . . .

26. Of Ceremonies and the Use of Sacraments

The old ceremonies relating to the sacrament of Baptism should all remain, namely, exorcism, the renunciation of the devil, the profession of faith, the chrism, and others, for they serve to show and signify the power of this sacrament.

So also the old ceremonies that have been added to the Mass by the Catholic church should not be changed, for they are all appropriate to what is done in the Mass. . . .

The ceremonies of the other sacraments should be used according to the old Agendas. Still, where they give cause for superstitious use, they should be improved with timely counsel. The altars, priestly vestments, vessels, signs of the cross, likewise crosses, candles, images, and pictures, should be retained in the church. Nevertheless, they are remembrances, and no worship should be accorded to them nor should any superstitious practices be attached to pictures or holy objects. . . .

One should retain all the holy days accepted by the church, and if all are not retained, at least the most important: Sundays, the Birth of our Lord, the Circumcision of our Lord,

Epiphany, Palm Sunday, Easter and the two following days, the Ascension of our Lord, Pentecost and the two following days, Corpus Christi, the feast days of the Virgin Mary and the days of the holy apostles: John the Baptist, Mary Magdalene, Stephen, Lawrence, Martin, Michael, and All Saints. And also in every church the day of its patron saint so that we honor God through his saints and so that we may be excited to imitate them and might desire to be associated with their merits. . . .

And since one should hold with the Apostle that he who is without a wife is concerned for the things of the Lord, it is to be wished that clergy will be found who are celibate and maintain true chastity. Nevertheless, since there are many performing ministerial functions who have taken wives, they should not be dismissed from their duties but should await the discussion of their situation and a judgment from the general council, for a change in these things cannot take place at this time without causing grave disorder. . . .

Likewise, the administration of the Eucharist under both kinds to which many have now become accustomed cannot be changed at this time without serious commotion. And because a general council to which all subjects of the Holy Roman Empire must submit will without doubt consider this issue with pious and zealous care so that in any case the consciences of people and the peace of the church will be taken into consideration, those who have received both kinds before this time need not give this up but should wait for the discussion and decision of the general council. . . .

92. The Leipzig Interim (December 1548)

The Leipzig Interim proposal followed the basic format of the Augsburg Interim but was a briefer document. To facilitate comparison, the selections included here roughly parallel the excerpts given above. Several other articles that provoked later doctrinal disputes are included in chapter six.

From CR 7:259–64.

+

It is our judgment that one should render obedience to His Majesty, the Holy Roman Emperor, our most gracious sovereign, and behave in such a way that His Imperial Majesty and everyone may note that we are all inclined to quiet, peace, and unity. This advice we faithfully admonish others to follow and will, as much as possible, also observe ourselves. . . .

Accordingly, we judge first that all that the ancient teachers have affirmed with regard to adiaphora, that is, matters of indifference that may be observed without violating the divine Scriptures and that, on the other hand, still remain in use, should also be maintained henceforth, and that therein no burden or augmentation should be sought or applied, since this cannot occur without offending a good conscience. . . .

Of Ecclesiastical Power and Authority

What the true Christian church, gathered in the Holy Spirit, acknowledges, determines, and teaches in regard to matters of faith should be taught and preached, since nothing it determines should or can be contrary to the Holy Scriptures.

Of Ecclesiastical Ministers

. . . Learned pastors and ministers should be ordained who are competent and fit to teach the Word of God and to preside over the people in a Christian manner. . . . All ministers should be subject and obedient to the supreme bishop and other bishops who administer their episcopal office according to God's command, and use the same for edification and not for destruction. These other ministers should be also ordained by such bishops upon presentation by their patrons. . . .

Of Baptism

Infant baptism, along with exorcism, the assistance and confession of sponsors, and other ancient Christian ceremonies, should be taught and retained.

Of Repentance

Repentance, confession, and absolution, and what pertains thereto, should be diligently taught and preached, so that the people confess to the priests, and receive absolution in God's stead from them. They should also be diligently admonished and urged to pray, fast, and give alms. No one should be admitted to the highly venerated sacrament of the body and blood of Christ unless he has first confessed to the priest and received absolution from him. Furthermore, the people should be diligently taught and instructed that in this sacrament we are united with Jesus Christ our Savior as the head with the members of his body, so that by it we are raised up and nourished to all good. . . .

Of Extreme Unction

Although in this land anointing with oil has not been in use for many years, it is written in Mark and James how the apostles used it. James says, "If anyone is sick among you let him call for the priests of the church so that they may pray over him and anoint him with oil in the name of the Lord, and the prayer of faith will make the sick man well, and the Lord shall raise him up" [James 5:14-15]. Therefore, such unction may be observed, according to the use of the apostle, and Christian prayer and words of consolation from the Holy Scriptures may be spoken over the sick. The people should be instructed concerning this in such way that they understand it rightly and all superstition and misunderstanding will be removed and avoided.

Of the Mass

Mass should be observed henceforth in this land with ringing of bells, with lights and vessels, with chants, vestments, and ceremonies. In places where there are sufficient persons, the priests and ministrants should go in a becoming way before the altar in their regular church vestments and robes, speak in the beginning the *Confiteor,* and the introit, the *Kyrie eleison,* the *Gloria in Excelsis Deo,* and the *Dominus vobiscum,* the collects, the epistle, and all that now current in Latin should be sung. . . . The Gospel to be sung in Latin and read to the people in German. . . .

Of Images

The images and pictures of the sufferings of Christ and of the saints may be also retained in the churches, and the people should be taught that they are only remembrances, and no things to which divine honors should be attached. To the images and pictures of the saints, however, no superstitious resort should occur or be encouraged.

Of Holidays

Sunday; the Birthday of our Lord, St. Stephen's Day, St. John the Evangelist's Day, the Circumcision of the Lord, Epiphany, Easter and the two following days, the Ascension of the Lord, Pentecost with the two days following, Corpus Christi, the Festivals of the Holy Virgin Mary, the days of the Holy Apostles, of St. John the Baptist, of St. Mary Magdalene, of St. Michael and some others, on which there should be only church services with preaching and Mass and communion, as of the Conversion of Paul; of the beheading of John, Thursday, Friday, and Saturday in Passion Week.

Of the Eating of Meat

One should abstain from the eating of meat on Fridays and Saturdays, also in fasts, and this should be observed as an external ordinance at the command of his Imperial Majesty. Still, those whom necessity excuses, such as hard laborers, travelers, pregnant women and those in childbed, old weak persons, and children, should not be bound hereby.

Of the Deportment of Ministers

And we consider it honorable and good that pastors and ministers in their vestments as well as otherwise should deport themselves in a priestly and creditable manner, and that with the cooperation and advice of the bishops or consistories they should make an arrangement with one another, and observe it, so that by their apparel a distinction may be observed between the ministers and worldly persons, and proper reverence may be shown toward the priestly state. . . .

93. Amsdorf: Warning against the Godless Duke Moritz (1549)

Born in the same year as Luther, Nikolaus von Amsdorf was involved in the earliest struggles of the Lutheran movement and continued to be a forceful presence for almost twenty years after Luther's death. Always noted for his uncompromising defense of Luther's teachings, he was quick to conclude that the churches needed to take a firm stand against both the political maneuvering of Duke Moritz and the theological manipulations of Melanchthon.

From the text cited in Theodor Pressel, *Nicolaus von Amsdorf nach gleichzeitigen Quellen* **(Elbersfeld: Friderichs, 1862), 57–59.**

. . . God has said that he neither can nor will endure scorning or blaspheming of the gospel

Duke Moritz of Saxony

and will in no way allow it to go unpunished, as the Jews and Romans who sinned unknowingly have truly experienced. But since Duke Moritz knowingly and with a well-considered mind has begun and undertaken this unheard of, horribly evil deed against God and his Word to exterminate the legitimate bloodline of the ruling family of Saxony out of pure envy and hate, he will get away with it even less than the Jews or Romans did. Therefore we poor Saxons under the Elector should neither lose heart nor be terrified by the coarse tyrant from Meissen, for he will not succeed, that I know for sure. God cannot suffer or endure such cruel and shocking disloyal ingratitude and will not help or support such a wanton fool but will much more strike out and exterminate him entirely as not only the Holy Scriptures but all of history also attests and proves. For Duke Moritz's departure from the gospel and God's Word as well as his disloyalty and ingratitude toward the Elector of Saxony is such a haughty claim of superiority that God can have no patience with it. His partners, those hypocrites, the forces of Meissen, may cover it up as much as they want, but his and their venomous evil, their deceit, lies, avarice, and false heart are known to everyone, and it is evident that the Lord Duke Moritz, himself the false

and disloyal claimant, has bound himself with their will, knowledge, and counsel to King Ferdinand against the Elector, the rightful heir and lineage of Saxony, in order to drive him out and exterminate him, as the secretly conducted conference at the castle in Prague will clearly point out, when it comes to light. . . .

Therefore, guard yourself against the disloyal Duke Moritz, who has begun such cruel, disloyal, and evil deeds to please the emperor and the pope, lest we forsake the hidden and unseen God and his Word and come again under the papacy, accepting its abominations and abuses. For it is certainly true that if Duke Moritz wants to stay in the good graces of the emperor he must allow the Mass to be prepared again and held everywhere in his land. Wait and see if he is not eventually chased out of the land. This will certainly happen if he does not improve, convert, and become pious, for God cannot suffer such disloyalty and falsehood. Therefore let everyone be warned sufficiently that they must protect themselves against Duke Moritz and his talk, guile, deceit, and wickedness. For whoever gives himself to Duke Moritz without necessity puts himself under the pope and the emperor, scorns God and his Word, and perjures himself against the Elector. . . .

94. Amsdorf: Letter against the Leipzig Interim (February 15, 1549)

From Theodor Pressel, *Nicolaus von Amsdorf nach gleichzeitigen Quellen* (Elbersfeld: Friderichs, 1862), 70.

1) What Christ our Lord is against no Christian can or should willingly accept. The Leipzig Articles are against and opposed to Christ for they do not teach or gather to Christ

but disperse from and oppose Christ. It is written: "Whoever is not with me is against me." Therefore all who accept and agree with these articles are Christ's enemies and persecutors.

2) It is certain that God cannot be served with human tradition. Now the Leipzig Articles are merely human and papist traditions; therefore one cannot honor or serve God with them. And although the heart knows that such traditions are not a divine service, still the emperor and pope have commanded them as if they were divine service and want them to be held and considered as divine service. Therefore, a word to anyone who accepts and holds the Leipzig Articles, who accepts them against his own heart and conscience and consents by that action to the pope's abominations and idolatry and gives others an example and justification for serving and honoring the true God with such human traditions: "You should not do what you think is good but what I command you." God and his dear Son, Jesus Christ, have not commanded the Leipzig Articles, and therefore the Christian cannot and should not accept the same articles in any way.

3) Christians cannot and should not accept any teaching of the devil, for all the devil's teachings are against the truth of the gospel and Christian freedom. Both of these cannot stand and remain alongside the devil's teachings because truth and lies do not rhyme together. Where the devil's teachings get the upper hand and rule, both Christian freedom and the truth of the gospel perish. Now rules in the Leipzig Articles related to the eating of meat and the like are merely teachings of the devil, since they are commands or prohibitions made by the emperor that erect the religion of the pope again. It is laughable that they should so impudently be called a civil law, since the pope formerly forbid them under the guise of piety and the emperor now has renewed the papal laws and decrees and ratified them with

great earnest. Therefore no Christian can or should accept the Leipzig Articles without violating the gospel and his conscience. For in so doing, he would be accepting the mandate of Antiochus, who set up his abomination and idol (the Interim) in the holy city (that is, holy Christendom) [1 Maccabees 1]. . . .

95. Manifesto of Duke Moritz against the Emperor (1552)

When it became disadvantageous to Duke Moritz to continue his alliance with Charles V, he claimed that during the Schmalkald War he had not understood the emperor's true political intentions. In this manifesto, he prepares to assume a new role as defender of the German people against a deceitful tyrant.

From *Quellenbuch zur Geschichte der Neuzeit*, ed. Max Schilling (Berlin: Gaertners, 1903), 103–6.

By God's grace, we (Moritz, Duke of Saxony; Johann Albrecht, Duke of Mecklenburg; Wilhelm, Count of Hesse), along with the other princes and nobles associated with us, offer our friendly service, favorable greetings, and wish for grace and all good things to all the electors and princes, princely houses, counts, lords, nobles, as well as the honorable cities and estates of the Holy Empire of the German nation. We want you to know that we have always and at this time still desire nothing more highly than a general peace in the holy realm of the German nation and seek to find and conclude a confirmation of the same in a true and Christian agreement concerning the strife and separation of the Christian religion, in accordance with the prophetic and apostolic word and divine doctrine. The emperor has many times given us fair words, written promises, pledges, and imperial decrees concerning such an agreement, yet, as you know, not only has it not materialized, but the reverse has happened when he has found the opportunity to reinterpret, call back, or abolish all such decrees, letters, promises, and fair words. . . .

It has not stopped at that, but he has furthermore now and again under the guise of religion embittered some evidently Christian rulers against us or our other associates, slandered and aroused hatred against us, incited us against each other, and given others an impression of our religion that is different from what it evidently is. The issue of religion appears to be of utmost concern to him, but the opposite is actually the case. Under the guise of attempting to resolve a religious schism, he would like to force through and achieve his own domination. . . .

We, the above-mentioned Elector and princes together and especially in common, have considered the present miserable state of the German nation, our very beloved fatherland, how it has gone into decline, and the extent to which we Germans have been overrun with troops from foreign nations. For many years, the poor subjects of the emperor from the nobility, cities, and villages have been neglected or run into the ground, and their women and children violated. Some of the same have been abused against all nature; one thing of value after another has been forced from them under false pretenses. Especially, in many ways our old praiseworthy freedom has been weakened, diminished, reduced, and smothered, and all our goods and possessions, our sweat and blood have been sucked out of us. . . . Thus, we have finally been brought by this and other means into such an unbearable, beastly, hereditary servitude, yoke, and bondage that our descendants and children's

Emperor Charles V

children cry to heaven and curse us under the ground for having watched this come about.

So we, therefore, have confidentially acted together and have revealed our intentions to other Christian rulers, such as the praiseworthy crown of France and other lords and friends of ours. We have united in the name of Almighty God, his beloved Son, Jesus Christ, and the Holy Spirit (which leads us and rules us) and, with a powerful hand, seek the acquittal of Count Philip of Hesse and the imprisoned Duke Johann Friedrich of Saxony. We, Duke Moritz and the Elector of Brandenburg, consider it our high duty to do what we can to throw off the burdensome yoke of beastly servitude and bondage and to rescue and recover the old praiseworthy liberty and freedom of our beloved fatherland, the German nation. May the Holy Trinity bestow grace, favor, and salvation upon us. Amen.

96. The Religious Peace of Augsburg (1555)

It took seven months for the Diet of Augsburg to work out the details of the following peace treaty. The principle of *reservatio ecclesiastica* (see #18, below) was still very much in dispute at the end of the negotiations.

From *Select Documents Illustrating Medieval and Modern History*, **ed. Emil Reich (London: King & Son, 1905), 230–32.**

15. In order to bring peace into the Holy Empire of the Germanic Nation between the Roman Imperial Majesty and the Electors, Princes, and Estates: let neither His Imperial Majesty nor the Electors, Princes, etc., do any violence or harm to any estate of the empire on account of the Augsburg Confession, but let them enjoy their religious belief, liturgy, and ceremonies as well as their estates and other rights and privileges in peace; and complete religious peace shall be obtained only by Christian means of amity, or under threat of the punishment of the Imperial ban.

16. Likewise the Estates espousing the Augsburg Confession shall let all the Estates and Princes who cling to the old religion live in absolute peace and in the enjoyment of all their estates, rights, and privileges.

17. However, all such as do not belong to the two above named religions shall not be included in the present peace but be totally excluded from it.

18. And since it has proved to be a matter of great dispute what was to happen with the bishoprics, priories, and other ecclesiastical benefices of such Catholic priests who would in course of time abandon the old religion, we have in virtue of the powers of Roman Emperors ordained as follows: where an archbishop, bishop, or prelate or any other priest of our old religion shall abandon the same, his archbishopric, bishopric, prelacy, and other benefices together with all their income and revenues that he has so far possessed shall be abandoned by him without any further objection or delay.

The chapter and such as are entitled to it by common law or the custom of the place shall elect a person espousing the old religion who may enter on the possession and enjoyment of all the rights and incomes of the place without any further hindrance and without prejudging any ultimate amicable transaction of religion.

20. The ecclesiastical jurisdiction over the Augsburg Confession, dogma, appointment of ministers, church ordinances, and ministries hitherto practiced (but apart from all the rights of the Electors, Princes and Estates, colleges and monasteries to taxes in money or tithes) shall from now cease, and [those adhering to] the Augsburg Confession shall be left to the free and untrammeled enjoyment of their religion, ceremonies, appointment of ministers, as is stated in a subsequent separate article, until the final transaction of religion will take place.

23. No Estate shall try to persuade the subjects of other Estates to abandon their religion nor protect them against their own magistrates. Such as had from olden times the rights of patronage are not included in the present article.

24. In case our subjects, whether belonging to the old religion or the Augsburg Confession, should intend leaving their homes with their wives and children in order to settle in another place, they shall be hindered neither in the sale of their estates after due payment of the local taxes nor injured in their honor.

The Thirty Years War (1618–48)

When they formed the Protestant Union, a number of Lutheran and Calvinist princes, including the Electors of the Palatinate and Brandenburg, set aside their religious differences to face a common opponent. As this document indicates, however, the Lutheran Elector of Saxony was not one of the original signatories.

PROMPTE   ET SINCERE·

John Calvin

97. The Formation of the Protestant Union (1608)

From *Germany in the Thirty Years War*, ed. Gerhard Benecke (New York: St. Martin's, 1979), 9–10.

In view of the urgent necessity, we, the undersigned Electors and Estates of the Holy Empire, much less to damage but much more to strengthen and uphold peace and unity in the Holy Empire, as dedicated and obedient Estates of the Empire of the German Nation, our beloved fatherland, in order to advance the common well-being, our land, and people, and also those Estates who will in future join us to further peace, order, and protection in the name of God the Almighty, have one and all reached the present amicable and confidential agreement that we acknowledge by virtue of this letter, as follows:

1. That each member shall keep good faith with the other and their heirs, land, and people, and that no one shall enter any other alliance; also that no Estate, jurisdiction, territory, or subjects shall damage, fight, or in any way harm another Estate, nor break the laws of the Imperial constitution, nor give aid in any manner if such a break should occur. . . .

4. It is our wish that in matters concerning the liberties and high jurisdictions of the German Electors and Estates, as also of the Protestant (*Evangelische*) Estates' grievances as presented at the last Imperial assembly concerning infringements of those selfsame rights, freedoms, and laws of the Empire, these shall all be presented and pressed at subsequent Imperial and Imperial Circle assemblies, and not merely left to secret correspondence with each other. We also agree to try to influence other Protestant Estates (that is, Saxony) toward an understanding with us.

5. We also agree that this secret union shall not affect our disagreement on several points of religion, but that notwithstanding these, we have agreed to support each other. No member is to allow an attack on any other in books or through the pulpit, nor give cause for any breach of the peace, while at the same time leaving untouched the theologian's right of disputation to affirm the Word of God.

6. If one or the other of us is attacked . . . the remaining members of the Union shall immediately come to his aid with all the resources of the Union, as necessity may demand, and as set out in the detailed agreement. . . .

98. The Edict of Restitution (1629)

The Edict of Restitution was issued after the King of Denmark had withdrawn in defeat from the Thirty Years War. Although the Protestants were now in a very vulnerable position, the emperor did not attempt to force their return to Catholicism. Realistically, he only attempted to reverse any gains made by the Protestants since the Peace of Augsburg.

From *Select Documents Illustrating Medieval and Modern History*, ed. Emil Reich (London: King & Son, 1905), 234.

We, Ferdinand, by the grace of God, Holy Roman Emperor . . . are determined for the realization both of the religious and profane peace to dispatch our Imperial commissioners into the Empire; to reclaim all the archbishoprics, bishoprics, prelacies, monasteries, hospitals, and endowments that the Catholics had possessed at the time of the Treaty of Passau (1552) and of which they have been illegally deprived; and to put into all these Catholic foundations duly qualified persons so that each may get his proper due. We herewith declare that the Religious Peace (of 1555) refers only to the Augsburg Confession as it was submitted to our ancestor Emperor Charles V on 25 June 1530; and that all other doctrines and sects, whatever names they may have, not included in the Peace are forbidden and cannot be tolerated. . . .

99. King Gustavus Adolphus: Farewell to the Swedish Estates (May 1630)

Although Gustavus Adolphus also had political motivations for getting involved in the war in Germany, this document shows that he described the cause to the Swedish people as a campaign to protect his fellow Lutherans from the advance of Catholic tyranny.

From *Readings in European History*, vol. 2, ed. James H. Robinson (Boston: Ginn & Co., 1906), 207.

I call on the all-powerful God, by whose providence we are here assembled, to witness that it is not by my own wish, or from any love of war, that I undertake this campaign. On the contrary, I have been now for several years goaded into it by the imperial party, not only through the reception accorded to our emissary to Lübeck, but also by the action of their general in aiding with his army our enemies, the Poles, to our great detriment. We have been urged, moreover, by our harassed brother-in-law [the Elector of Brandenburg] to undertake this war, the chief object of which is to free our oppressed brothers in the faith from the clutches of the pope, which, God helping us, we hope to do.

100. King Gustavus Adolphus: Reply to the Ambassador from Brandenburg (July 1630)

The Protestant princes needed the assistance offered by the King of Sweden in order to defeat the emperor, but some of them hesitated to let him get involved in Germany for fear that they would only exchange one foreign overlord for another. In this letter, Gustavus Adolphus attempts to assuage the concerns of the princes and offers an ultimatum to his brother-in-law, the Elector of Brandenburg.

From *Readings in European History*, vol. 2, ed. James H. Robinson (Boston: Ginn & Co., 1906), 210

. . . I have come into this land for no other purpose than to free it from the thieves and robbers who have so plagued it, and first and foremost, to help his Excellency out of his difficulties. Does his Excellency then not know that the emperor and his followers do not mean to rest till the Evangelical religion is wholly rooted out of the empire, and that his Excellency has nothing else to expect than being forced either to deny his religion or to leave his country? Does he think by prayers and beseechings and such like means to obtain something different? . . .

King Gustavus Adolphus

I seek not my own advantage in this war nor any gain, save the security of my kingdom; I can look for nothing but expense, hard work, trouble, and danger to life and limb. . . .

I tell you plainly that I will know nor hear nothing of "neutrality"; his Excellency must be either friend or foe. When I reach his frontier he must declare himself either hot or cold. The fight is between God and the devil. If his Excellency is on God's side, let him stand by me; if he holds rather with the devil, then he must fight with me; there is no third course—that is certain. . . .

101. The Treaty of Osnabrück, Westphalia (1648)

The Peace of Westphalia was concluded after months of negotiations at Osnabrück and Münster among France, Sweden, and the German Catholics and Protestants.

From *Renaissance and Reformation, 1300–1648,* ed. G. R. Elton (New York: Macmillan, 1968), 249.

ARTICLE 5: FROM PARAGRAPHS 1 AND 30

The Religion Peace of 1555, as it was later confirmed . . . by various Imperial diets, shall, in all its articles entered into and concluded by the unanimous consent of the Emperor, Electors, Princes and Estates of both religions, be confirmed and observed fully and without infringement. . . . In all matters there shall be an exact and mutual equality between all the Electors, Princes and states of either religion, as far as agrees with the constitution of the realm, the Imperial decrees, and the present treaty; so that what is right for one side shall also be right for the other; all violence and other contrary proceedings being herewith between the two sides for ever prohibited. . . .

Whereas all immediate states enjoy, together with their territorial rights and sovereignty as hitherto used throughout the Empire, also the right of reforming the practice of religion; and whereas in the Religion Peace the privilege of emigration was conceded to the subjects of such states if they dissented from the religion of their territorial lord; and whereas later, for the better preserving of greater concord among the states, it was agreed that no one should seduce another's subjects to his religion, or for that reason make any undertaking of defense or protection, or come to their aid for any reason; it is now agreed that all these be fully observed by the states of either religion, and that no state shall be hindered in the rights in matters of religion, which belong to it by reason of its territorial independence and sovereignty.

ARTICLE 7: FROM PARAGRAPHS 1 AND 2

It is agreed by the unanimous consent of His Imperial Majesty and all the Estates of the Empire that whatever rights and benefits are conferred upon the states and subjects attached to the Catholic and Augsburg faiths, either by the constitutions of the Empire or by the Religious Peace and this public treaty . . . shall also apply to those who are called reformed (Calvinists). . . . Beyond the religions mentioned above, none shall be received or tolerated in the Holy Empire.

THE EFFECTS OF WAR ON THE LUTHERAN PEOPLE OF GERMANY

102. The Diary of Hans Heberle (1618–49)

The following recollections, written by a Lutheran cobbler from a village near Ulm, provide a glimpse of the experiences and attitudes of a devout layperson who lived through the entire Thirty Years War. In addition to recording his own memories, Hans Heberle also included material from printed reports that described notable events in other parts of Germany (for example, the effects of the siege of Breisach).

From "Hans Heberles 'Zeytregister' 1618–72," in *Der Dreissigjährigen Krieg in zeitgenössischer Darstellung*, ed. G. Zillhardt (Ulm: Kohlhammer, 1975), 92–109.

. . . In the year 1617 a Lutheran festival was held on account of Dr. Martin Luther, the highly esteemed and dear prophet of Germany, the shining light that brought forth again the Word of God. To commemorate this [the start of the Reformation], a joyous festival was held in all of the Evangelical churches, and all the children in the territory of Ulm were given a special half *batzen,* called a jubilee coin, as a remembrance of the occasion. Special sermons and prayers were composed and delivered in the churches. Much was written about them and some of them I remember, but I cannot describe them here on account of their length. The celebration was held on St. Martin's Day, the eleventh day of November in the year 17. The anniversary festival was the beginning of the war, for one can read frequently in Catholic records about how the sight of this celebration stuck painfully in their eyes.

In the year 1618 a great comet appeared in the shape of a great and terrifying rod, which was a severe threat from God on account of our sinful lives for which we formerly and still deserve punishment; it was seen from fall until spring. In the 1620s and 1630s we would unfortunately experience what it signified about what was to follow, and we have lamented the same with hot tears. It is not enough to describe what happened but this little book will attempt diligently to do so. It was also during this year that the great and well-known market town of Plurß was destroyed by an earthquake.

In the year 1619 Ferdinand II became the Holy Roman Emperor, and under him a great persecution arose, with war, rebellion, and the shedding of much Christian blood, as a few examples will demonstrate. First, a great war began in Bohemia, which he attempted to restore by force to his religion. After that, war spread in the following years to the territories of Braunschweig, Mecklenburg, Lüneburg, Friesland, Brandenburg, Pomerania, Gottland, Austria, Moravia, Silesia, Heidelberg, indeed, to almost all of Germany, about which I cannot tell or describe everything. . . .

The year 1628, the twelfth day of May: On account of the events of the war, hours of prayer were appointed and established in city and country so that we might ask God Almighty to avert the current punishment and act beneficently toward us again.

In this same year the emperor extended his war and brought it as far as the moors and the city of Stralsund, which he vigorously attacked and besieged. But because the city lay on the moor and was exposed to the moor, it had strong help from the king of Sweden, whom it received as a protector and to whom it surrendered. He helped it considerably and rescued it from the enemy and drove off the imperial troops so that they had to withdraw with great injury and damage. This marked the beginning of the Swedish king's intervention in Germany. . . .

Now [1629: the year of the Edict of Restitution], since the Augsburg Confession was abolished in all places by the emperor, and Catholic properties had to be given back to the Catholics, the Evangelical estates were shocked and the Catholics were very glad. Then there was a true uproar, and no one had any security. Everyone feared that their things would be taken away.

Then some writings came from the king of Sweden to the Evangelical estates saying that he wanted to come and help the threatened religion. This brought great joy to the Evangelicals. They took heart in the fact that they would be helped and also became more resolute. Since the imperial forces were for the most part out of Germany and had gone to Italy, the Evangelicals became somewhat bolder. They got up the courage to complain publicly that what had taken place was a great injustice because it affected those who had never fought against the emperor as well as those who took up weapons again.

But because the emperor had issued a mandate or edict in which he ordered that all things that had been previously taken, contrary to the terms of the Peace of Religion, should be given up and returned to the Catholics, there was more than a little hesitation among the Evangelicals. There was not one among them who did not have some such goods in his possession. And because the negotiations went better than anyone could have thought, the protesters were overcome by the emperor. . . .

In this year [1630] the situation was very bad for the Evangelical religion in all places, and if the king of Sweden had not stood up against the emperor in war, the German princes would have been lost. They were all too weak and could not overcome the cunning horde. But God, who can complete and turn all things around, caused the one who dug the grave to fall into it.

It is appropriate to observe at the end of the year in this difficult, troubled, and tragic time that we could not easily forget what God has done for us up to the present, according to his holy Word, which has so clearly guided us. On the twenty-fourth of June, the feast day of St. John, we Evangelicals held a festival of thanksgiving in all churches, for it was a hundred years to the day that the Evangelical confession was delivered at Augsburg through some princes and the estates of the Holy Empire to the great emperor, Charles V. We held this celebration with beautiful worship services and prayer and song and communion. In the morning and afternoon sermons, the Augsburg Confession was read publicly from the pulpit by the pastor so that everyone would know what the confession contained. . . .

In the summer [of 1632] as the king of Sweden moved out of Bavaria to come to the help of the Saxons, whose land had fallen under the control of imperial troops, the imperial and Swedish armies fought at Lützen in Saxony and the Swedes held the field, but lost their king, who perished in the battle from a shot. . . .

On the thirtieth day of July [1638], the battle and strike against Breisach took place. The Bavarian and imperial troops fought badly with the troops from Weimar and France, so that the imperial and Bavarian side lost several thousand men along with many wagons and provisions that the city of Breisach had supplied. In this battle almost all the commanders were taken captive except for [General Franz Egon von] Fürstenberg, who escaped in a small boat down the Rhine. . . .

On the eighteenth of August, Breisach was besieged by Duke Bernhard of Weimar. . . . On the ninth day of December, Breisach reached an accord with Duke Bernhard because of the great starvation. The city surrendered due to the great hunger and besieging after having held out and bravely resisted from August 18 to December 9. To see how it was, a description follows:

The description of the hunger in Breisach during the siege. . . .

A horse's foot cost five shillings and a pound of dog's flesh 5 *batzen*. Many mice and rats were sold for a high price. . . . Almost all the dogs and cats in the city were eaten. Several thousand horses, cows, oxen, calves, and sheep were eaten up and devoured.

On November 24 a soldier under arrest in the prison died, and before the warden in charge could order his burial the other prisoners had cut up the body and eaten it. The prisoners even picked holes into the walls of their prison with their fingers and ate what they found. Two dead men who had already been buried were cut open, and their innards were taken out and eaten. In one day, three children were consumed.

The soldiers promised a pastry-cook's boy a piece of bread if he followed them into their camp. But when he got there, they butchered him up and ate him. On December 10 eight well-known burgher's children disappeared in the fishers' district alone, and were presumed to be eaten, since no one knew where they had gone. This is not to mention all the children of beggars and strangers whom no one knew anyway. In the town square alone ten corpses were found, not counting all those found in the alleys and on the dung-heap. . . .

Is this not a great calamity above all calamities that one should go through this and partly watch similar happenings every year, month, week, day, and hour?

No wonder that we are dying,
through such shocking and difficult events
to which God has subjected all of Germany.
I have myself unfortunately experienced this
from my youth onward
and especially during my married years,

as is clearly manifest
in what I have endured.
Yet God shall never forsake me.
He helps me through this difficult time,
through many fights and great conflicts,
in the distress of war and plague,
on the open field and on the frontier.
I thank you, Lord Jesus Christ,
you are always my helper,
who has saved me from many perils,
and helped me through hard times
with loose scoundrels, who are so many
and cause so much pain for pious folk.
With their godless living
they strive against God's order.
Oh true God, see what they do;
protect us and defend us against this false band,
who persecute you and your Holy Word
now in many places.
Stay with us, O Lord above,
and we will always praise you;
on your heavenly throne
hear me, Lord, through your Son.
I wish for nothing more at this hour,
I say 'amen' with all my heart.
My name is Hans Heberle,
Now God give me my eternal reward. . . .

This year [16]49 is a fortunate, exceptional jubilee and year of joy. Although peace was made in the year 48, the provisions of the treaty were not fully concluded. But glory be to God in the highest; now there is peace on earth in our Germany and in the entire Holy Roman Empire, among the emperor, the Swedes, the French, and all kings, princes, counts, and cities, and also villages, towns, hamlets, farms, and isolated places. Rich and poor, young and old, women and men, wives and children, even all the dear cattle and horses will all take delight and enjoy peace. Yes, also the dear acres and fields that lay deserted and desolate for a long time will be properly plowed and cultivated once more, and from them we poor human children will sustain ourselves again so that we may heal the great injury that we have experienced and overcome our grief. We may also carry on our trades in order to pay the cost assigned to us for horsemen along with the peace tax and finally bring an end to this great burden. . . .

Our lords reached an agreement with each other about how and when every regiment should be disbanded so that no mutiny might arise in the Empire accompanied by the soldiers' robbing, plundering, and other troubles. (This was necessary since the greater part of them were completely evil and daring scoundrels, as almost all soldiers are.) Still there were delays, and in the meantime we had to continue to pay the demobilization taxes every month and even every week and day. But praise and thanks be to God, our regiment was disbanded and withdrawn from the land, peaceably and without causing any harm, on the eleventh day of October, the same week as the blessing of the Holzchurch. . . .

103. The Autobiographical Writings of Johann Valentin Andreae (1634–35)

Johann Valentin Andreae (1586–1654), the grandson of Jakob Andreae, was an important theologian and church leader in southwest Germany. Early in his life he attempted to promote social and religious reform through a number of imaginative writings, which included a utopian work titled "Christianopolis" and several anonymous treatises that initiated the myth of a secret scholarly fraternity known as the Rosicrucians. From 1620 to 1639 he served as superintendent of the Lutheran churches in Calw. Subsequently he became court preacher in Stuttgart and general superintendent of the territorial church of Würt-

temberg. The following excerpts from his writings describe the hardships he faced as a minister serving during the Thirty Years War. His concerns about the degeneration of moral and spiritual life echo the preoccupations of the devotional writer Johann Arndt (see chapter seven), who was a strong influence on the development of his thought.

From *Ein Schwäbischer Pfarrer im Dreissigjährigen Krieg*, ed. P Antony and H. Christmann (Heidenheim: Heidenheimer Verlaganstalt, 1970), 90–94, and Johann Valentin Andreae, *Vita ab ipso conscripta* (Berlin: Schultz, 1849), 161–63.

The Destruction of the City of Calw (1634) from a letter to a friend

Through murder, plunder, scorching, and burning, the seizing of people and other destructive activities, the size of our population has diminished by two-thirds. We were 3,832, but 2,304 have departed, so now we are only 1,528. Those of us who remain would consider ourselves fortunate if only, as other places have been allowed to do, we were left alone to assess our own losses, which did not exceed a ton of gold, and were not furthered burdened by the other circumstances related to our poverty that have completely forced us to the ground and exhausted us. The number of destitute people is so large that they run to five hundred or six hundred head, and in our town treasury there is not one penny left. From among the citizens alone there are 125 persons in the hospital and still more, here and there in their houses, who have to be supplied regularly. It is not possible to say how much this service of love costs us, since even the richest can hardly provide for their own families.

Yet we would perhaps have been able to bear these costs, since Christian love always finds a way with charity, if only the fierce war tax had not, for a third time, sucked all the blood out of us. Our poor town had to pay eight hundred gulden weekly over and above the fixed rate others were assessed, and it was collected with extreme severity. How do you think we must feel when we see ourselves at the edge of an abyss that devours us, especially since plague and hunger wipes out 100 to 150 of us monthly, so that those who remain alive also have to pay the tax assessments of the dead. . . .

I am not so hardened that I do not also remember with horror the destruction of so many honorable married women, so many men and women citizens of whom on one day alone we buried eighty-three, and about whom we will keep a record, if we can. One should also include violated women and ravished virgins, and the young men, the bloom of the town who were led away to certain ruin in body and soul. . . .

Still, the war-tax collectors are threatening us anew with burnings and laying waste, with torture and forced labor. If they are allowed to carry on like this, we will all soon be dead. At least in this way we would escape their violence, but then my heart would still be troubled by thoughts of the heap of remaining orphans who would suffer all manner of injustice.

You would hardly believe what I say, that among those who have starved and frozen to death, there were some people who had over one thousand gulden a year in income. I saw the orphans of a former merchant who had an inheritance of fifteen thousand gulden wandering aimlessly through the alleys. They were finally taken into the homes of their relatives by command of the authorities. You can hardly imagine the liberties that are taken with the poor as they lie dying in their own filth and even now breathe their last breaths despite all our foresight and provisions. Corpses are often found in front of the gravedigger's home, stripped of their shrouds and the linen in

which they were wrapped, lying quite naked there, since people are so covetous of the rags that covered them. It is not worth speaking of medicines or painkillers since there are no doctors, chemists, or barbers left. Only the hangman remains in their place.

The few of us who remain alive do so more as a miracle of God than through nature or skill. We live and freely celebrate our church services. We publicly rebuke sins, which occur all the more readily in this anarchy time because they go unpunished more than is usually the case. Undaunted, we console depressed souls, and as far as we are able, we faithfully treat those who have suffered misfortune with real aid. . . .

From Andreae's Autobiography

The second half of the year [1635] was almost entirely dedicated to funerals, when the plague raged so severely in Württemberg and the neighboring areas that one can assume that it snatched away the greater part of the inhabitants. At least from those remaining among us it snatched 173 in August, 193 in September, 119 in October, 44 in November; overall in the whole year approximately 772 people. To be sure, at an outwardly inconvenient time, my colleague, Greins, went elsewhere, and on account of the needy circumstances no successor could be found, so for four long months the burden lay almost entirely on me, who myself struggled with indisposition. Still, I buried 430 bodies and gave 85 funeral sermons, one after another. . . .

The year 1636 was a more tolerable year with regard to public calamities and the almost unprecedented famine—as long as you disregard the difficulty of correcting outwardly corrupted morals and the mangling of flesh by local vultures. . . . Since now nothing more noteworthy about this year comes to mind, I will here give space to my sorrow about the preceding failings, for it is to be confessed publicly that God, irritated by our unrighteousness, has decreed our downfall. Our theology has surely been debased by the regurgitation of scholastic opinions and quarreling as well as by the irritation of mystics among the secular people, and by the infection spread by openly godless people. . . . Consciences have been lulled to sleep, and all types of evil have gained entrance: simony, church robbing, the destruction of spiritual seminaries, equivocation in preaching, the plundering of old learning, the banishment of what remains of a good spirit by useless prattle; in a word, all that fosters evil and entirely stifles what is good.

To speak of political defects, it does not seem right to me when it is judged that the foremost houses of Germany have gone under through the imprudence of counselors and the troublesome obtrusiveness of such helpers. Rather, I lament that religion has no more harmful enemy than most heads of states, through whose example and orders all blasphemies are incited, all piety exterminated, whatever is against Christ is led in and, to be sure, with such force that it is as if a law had been given about that. And we still wonder that all supports for the honoring of God as well as the establishment of the state collapse? They were long ago gnawed away as by a worm or sawed through to the bark. Although they have the appearance of durability, they cannot endure a jolt. . . .

So passed the fiftieth year of my sorrow-filled life. Should I consider myself unfortunate when I freely remember that I alone remain from my father's entire line, not only me but also my sister, Margaret, an afflicted widow, and how I am plagued with bodily weakness, twists of fate, and the persecution of envy? I have had to watch forty-three members of the second generation be reduced to eighteen heads. I have had to endure being a witness of the body of my fatherland and of its murderer, once my friend but now wilder than a tiger, and I must look at the decline of religion, the chaos

of politics, the destruction of learning, the ethical corruption of the youth under the yoke of slavery. Yes, I must almost convey, what can my life be other than its punishments and its length other than a roasting over a slow fire? But God has concluded that I, despite the errors of my life and so many shapes of death that no one can number or grasp them all, should live on and learn to have hope for better times as much as the power from above and our own weakness makes possible. Let it be so, so goes the will of the Lord, and amidst tears and sighs I will shout for joy to him.

104. Battle Hymn from the Thirty Years War

Hymns were written during the Thirty Years War to encourage soldiers and civilians alike in the times of great distress. The most famous of such "battle hymns" was written by Johann Michael Altenburg (1584–1640), a Lutheran pastor who throughout his career served various parishes in the vicinity of Erfurt. The text below was written after the victory of Gustavus Adolphus at Leipzig in 1631. It became a favorite of the Swedish king, who had it used at a service of prayer before the decisive battle of Lützen in 1632, during which he lost his life. Later, the Pietist leader Philip Jacob Spener used it in his family devotions every Sunday afternoon. (The original German version has five verses.)

From *Lyra Germanica*, trans. Catherine Winkworth (New York: Stanford, 1856), 15.

Verzage nicht du Häuflein klein
Fear not, O little flock, the foe
Who madly seeks your overflow,

Dread not his rage and power:
What though your courage sometimes faints,
His seeming triumph o'er God's saints
Lasts but a little hour.

Be of good cheer; your cause belongs
To him who can avenge your wrongs,
Leave it to him our Lord.
Though hidden yet from all our eyes,
He sees the Gideon who shall rise
To save us, and his word.

As true as God's own word is true,
Nor earth nor hell with all their crew
Against us shall prevail.
A jest and by-word are they grown;
God is with us, we are his own,
Our victory cannot fail.

Chapter Five

Factionalism in the Late Reformation
(1546–80)

When Philip Melanchthon participated in the process of formulating the Leipzig Interim, he was convinced that the compromises it contained only concerned nonessential matters of church practice (see chapter four). He believed that what he said in this document about justification, good works, and other doctrinal issues did not conflict in any significant way with the theological stance endorsed by the Lutheran churches in the Augsburg Confession (doc. #105). Other Lutheran church leaders, however, offered a very different interpretation of what Melanchthon was doing. They attacked him because they thought not only that his conciliatory actions were a blatant manifestation of cowardice and a strategy based on a tragic miscalculation of the intentions of the emperor, but also that he was actually demonstrating a willingness to alter some of the fundamental doctrinal teachings of the Lutheran churches. For several decades after the end of the Schmalkald War, the defenders and opponents of the Leipzig Interim continued to argue with each other about which group could rightly claim to be providing constructive leadership of the reform movement that Luther had inaugurated.

Most of the theologians of Electoral Saxony, especially the humanistically educated professors at the Universities of Wittenberg and Leipzig, were sympathetic toward the interpretation of Christian doctrine elaborated by Philip Melanchthon. Consequently, they came to be called Philippists. The critics of the Philippists, forcefully led by Matthias Flacius Illyricus, clustered in Magdeburg and later at the new University of Jena, which was founded in 1547. They called themselves the Gnesio-Lutherans, the genuine Lutherans, thereby signaling their belief that the Lutheran churches were endangered by the infiltration of false teachers, whose influence they intended to oppose. These factions faced off against each other in several extended doctrinal disputes that were only resolved by the emergence to prominence of another group of theologians who did not fully endorse the positions of either the Philippists or the Gnesio-Lutherans. Through patient negotiating, this mediating party managed to check the tendency of the opposing factions to drive each other into increasingly extreme positions. They were also successful in moving the churches toward a new consensus that was articulated in the most elaborate of the traditional Lutheran confessional documents, the Formula of Concord.

The doctrinal dispute that developed most directly out of the Interim crisis was the Adiaphorist Controversy. Both the Gnesio-Lutherans and the Philippists agreed that some church practices were neither commanded nor forbidden in the Scriptures and could therefore be observed or ignored without coming into conflict with the doctrinal teachings of the church. They reached different conclusions, however, about which ceremonies fell within this category of adiaphora. Even more importantly, they disagreed about whether these ceremonies continued to be matters of indifference when the churches were forced by some hostile power to accept them or face adverse consequences. The Gnesio-Lutherans argued that, in periods of persecution, yielding to the demands of the enemies of the church, even on seemingly nonessential matters, would be dangerous for several reasons. Simple believers would be confused by such compliance with the demands of their persecutors, and the absence of any resistance to the persecutors would encourage them to intensify their efforts to destroy the churches (doc. #106). To the Gnesio-Lutherans, coerced acceptance of nonessential customs and church practices was more than dangerous; it was also sinful because any failure to confess the true faith in a decisive way was tantamount to idolatry.

At first, Melanchthon answered the Gnesio-Lutherans by insisting that their unqualified resistance to any compromise with the emperor actually posed the greatest threat to the churches (doc. #105). Eventually, however, the polemical writings of Flacius and other Gnesio-Lutherans turned so many people against Melanchthon that he grew weary of defending himself and expressed regret over his decision to participate in the development of the Leipzig Interim proposal (docs. #106 and 107). Despite this shift in Melanchthon's position, some of his associates continued to argue against the Gnesio-Lutheran's views about adiaphora and about what should have been done during the Interim crisis. Over two decades after the debate had begun, the Philippist theologians of the Universities of Wittenberg and Leipzig still insisted that the Gnesio-Lutherans misunderstood Christian freedom if they taught that adiaphora change their status in times of persecution (doc. #108). Both sides claimed to find support for their positions in the Bible and the writings of Martin Luther.

In scrutinizing the Leipzig Interim proposal, the Gnesio-Lutherans also found several doctrinal statements that they considered just as problematic as the reintroduction of Catholic church practices. In particular, they took issue with language about the necessity of good works (doc. #110). Nikolaus von Amsdorf, a valued coworker of Luther in the early days of the Reformation who had been a fellow exile with Flacius in Magdeburg during the Schmalkald War, was most outspoken about this issue. As early as 1536 he had complained to Luther about passages in the writings of Melanchthon that suggested that justification cannot occur without the presence of good works. In 1551 he began again to publish critical treatises about this issue, naming Johannes Bugenhagen, another early coworker of Luther, and Georg Major, a colleague of Melanchthon at the University of Wittenberg, as the chief perpetuators of Melanchthon's viewpoint (doc. #112). Major responded at length to Amsdorf's charges, and, consequently, the prolonged debate about this issue that ensued has come to be called the Majorist Controversy.

As in the Adiaphorist Controversy, Melanchthon once again sought to distance himself from a position he had taken in the past. Recognizing that it was easy to confuse what his writings and the Leipzig Interim said about good works with the Catholic belief that good works earned merit, he proposed that Lutherans should be more cautious about using the language of necessity (doc. #115). Major, however, stood his ground.

Fearful of Antinomian tendencies in Lutheranism (that is, the belief that the Christian has been freed from the need to fulfill or seek guidance from the Law of God), he tried to emphasize the connection between justification and the life of new obedience to God that grace makes possible. He denied that true faith exists where there is no evidence of its fruits, namely, good works (docs. #111 and 114).

Other prominent Gnesio-Lutherans such as Flacius joined Amsdorf in raising questions about the implications of Major's arguments (doc. #113), but in the later stages of the dispute many of them felt the necessity to distance themselves from some of the intemperate pronouncements that Amsdorf began to make. Exasperated by Major's persistent defense of the necessity of good works, Amsdorf was driven to affirm the very opposite, that good works were actually detrimental to salvation (docs. #116 and 117). In saying this, he meant to point out the danger of trusting in good works as a way to gain salvation, but since this qualifying thought was not explicitly articulated in the slogan that Amsdorf circulated, he only contributed to the further polarization of the Gnesio-Lutherans and Philippists.

The Majorist Controversy was not the only doctrinal dispute in which the two parties tended to provoke each other into increasingly extravagant doctrinal assertions. The same phenomenon took place in the interrelated Synergist and Flacian Controversies about free will and original sin. Another disputed aspect of the Leipzig Interim was its assertion that a person cooperates with God in the process of salvation. This brief declaration reflected Melanchthon's discomfort with the position Luther had taken in his debate with Erasmus about free will (doc. #119). Unlike his mentor, Melanchthon felt that the will must contribute in some modest way to the salvation of an individual. If this were not the case, it seemed that the only way to explain why all people are not saved would be to conclude that God arbitrarily chooses to give grace only to certain individuals. Melanchthon believed that such an affirmation contradicted what the Bible taught (doc. #120).

The issue of the role of the will in salvation became a focus of intense discussion between the Philippists and the Gnesio-Lutherans in 1555, when Johann Pfeffinger, a professor at Leipzig who had assisted Melanchthon in the composition of the Leipzig Interim, published a short collection of theses on this topic (doc. #121). Pfeffinger argued that the will was not like a stone or a block in the process of salvation; rather it was drawn willingly to God. He emphasized this point in order to make it clear that humans alone are to blame if they are not saved. Like Melanchthon, Pfeffinger and his Philippist sympathizers admitted that original sin had weakened the power of the will, but, by their reckoning, this inherited deprivation did not entirely destroy the capacity of the will to accept or reject the gift of grace given through the Holy Spirit.

The Gnesio-Lutherans stood much closer to Luther in their emphasis on the bondage of the will. Writers such as Tilmann Heshus attempted to refute Pfeffinger's arguments by quoting biblical passages that use the language of slavery and death to describe the human predicament. In discussing the issue of predestination, they asserted that it was important to distinguish between God's general desire to be gracious to all creatures and the special election by which God chose those who would believe in Christ (doc. #122).

When the Philippists spoke of the will as a cause of salvation along with the Word of God and the Holy Spirit, the Gnesio-Lutherans responded that this could not be so because the impact of original sin was to make the will naturally resistant to God.

In 1559 the controversy became even more complicated when Victorin Strigel, a prominent theologian at the University of Jena, acknowledged his sympathy for the viewpoint of the Synergists and refused to ascribe to the anti-Philippist Book of Confutation, which the Duke of Saxony sought to implement as the doctrinal norm for his territory. Strigel was briefly imprisoned for his act of resistance, but the Duke eventually decided to let Strigel defend his views in a public debate against Matthias Flacius. This Weimar Disputation, held in 1560, had the unexpected result of provoking another controversy. As they discussed the impact of the Fall on human nature, Strigel began to employ Aristotelian metaphysical terminology in his assessment of original sin. He argued that original sin was only an accidental property of the substance of a person. Although the Fall had diminished and distorted the power of the intellect and will, this did not alter the fact that humans were still created in the image of God (doc. #124). When asked to address this philosophical question, Flacius totally contradicted Strigel's assertions. He asserted that the effect of the Fall was to make original sin the very substance of human nature. The image of God was actually transformed into the image of Satan (doc. #125).

The Synergist Controversy lingered on for more than a decade. The Philippists attempted to refute Flacius with both biblical and philosophical arguments and also raised pastoral questions about how simple believers would be affected by the declaration that human nature is imprinted by the image of Satan (doc. #126). Once again, as had happened in the Majorist Controversy, the Gnesio-Lutherans became divided among themselves. Many of the close associates of Flacius charged him with introducing new doctrinal error in the process of responding to the Philippists. This development significantly tarnished the reputation of the person who had been unsurpassed in his influence on the outlook of the Gnesio-Lutheran party since the early days of the Interim crisis.

Although the rest of the controversies that created unsettled conditions in the Lutheran churches involved some of the same disputants, they were not directly stimulated by the Leipzig Interim. The Osiandrist Controversy about essential righteousness takes its name from Andreas Osiander, the distinguished coworker of Luther who had played an important role in the formation of the Lutheran church in Nürnberg. During the Interim crisis, he had taken refuge in Prussia, where he was offered a position as professor of theology at the University of Königsberg. The other theologians in Königsberg resented this appointment because Osiander had never acquired an advanced academic degree in theological studies. They were even more disturbed by the interpretation of the doctrine of justification, which he began to defend in various writings and public disputations. Osiander taught that justification consists of more than the forgiveness of sins based on the imputation of the alien righteousness of Christ. In addition to being declared righteous by God, the sinner is infused with the righteousness of Christ. By the operation of the Holy Spirit, Christ enters the justified sinner and gradually causes the sinner to become righteous (docs. #128 and 129).

Joachim Mörlin, preacher at the cathedral in Königsberg, offered the most extensive critique of Osiander's viewpoint. In particular he objected to the description of justification as a gradual process and the subjective emphasis on the indwelling of Christ (doc. #130). This controversy was unique in that many Philippists and Gnesio-Lutherans, for once, united in condemning Osiander. Both Melanchthon and Flacius agreed that Osiander's ideas about justification by the infusion of righteousness were closer to the traditional emphasis of Catholic theology than to the forensic conception of justification that had been taught by Luther (doc. #131).

While the Osiandrist Controversy preoccupied the attention of theologians in Prussia, the Crypto-Calvinist Controversy began to develop in Saxony. This final dispute started in 1552, when Joachim Westphal, a Gnesio-Lutheran pastor in Hamburg, published an extensive critique of Calvin's view of the Lord's Supper. In 1549 the Reformed churches of Switzerland had worked out a common statement of their beliefs about the Lord's Supper called the Consensus of Zurich *(Consensus Tigurinus)* (doc. #133). This agreement convinced Westphal that there was no significant difference between the sacramental theology of the Calvinists and the ideas of Zwingli, which Luther had condemned in 1529 at the Marburg Colloquy. Westphal wanted to alert the Lutheran churches to this fact because he was disturbed by the growing influence of Calvinism in Germany.

Although the controversy specifically concerned the nature of Christ's presence in the Lord's Supper, it also prompted an extensive discussion of other christological matters. In response to Westphal, Calvin argued that after the resurrection, the body of Christ was in heaven. It was not possible for his body to be in many places at the same time. Therefore, although a believer is spiritually nourished by the body and blood of Christ in the Lord's Supper, the body and blood are not locally present in, with, and under the elements of bread and wine (doc. #134). Westphal, on the other hand, emphatically reasserted Luther's view that the divine attribute of omnipresence had been communicated to the body of the resurrected Christ. This made possible the local presence of Christ wherever the Lord's Supper was celebrated. Furthermore, it meant, contrary to the claims of the Calvinists, that all participants, the godly as well as the wicked, orally receive the body of Christ when they commune.

Although Melanchthon had originally shared Luther's views about the Lord's Supper, his personal discussions and correspondence with Calvin and Martin Bucer, the reformer of Strasbourg, had diminished his certainty about the reality of a sacramental union between the body of Christ and the bread. He tried to stay out of the controversy, but other Philippists, including his son-in-law Kaspar Peucer, became more active proponents of Calvin's sacramental theology in Electoral Saxony. By 1571 they had persuaded the Elector to accept the Dresden Consensus, a summary of teachings about the Lord's Supper that rejected the idea of the ubiquity of Christ's human nature (doc. #135). Two years later, an anonymous Philippist treatise on the controversy titled *Exegesis Perspicua* was even more explicit in calling for toleration of the Calvinist viewpoint (doc. #136). This development set off a major outcry on the part of the Gnesio-Lutherans, who in a short time managed to convince the Elector that he had been the victim of a Philippist conspiracy to replace Lutheranism by Calvinism in Saxony. To prevent this occurrence, he imprisoned or banished the most influential Crypto-Calvinists.

As this last episode indicates, the proliferation of doctrinal disputes became a matter of great concern to the Lutheran princes as well as the theologians. They were particularly worried that the emperor and the Catholic princes in Germany might take advantage of the disunity between the Gnesio-Lutherans and the Philippists and attempt once again to suppress Lutheranism altogether. Consequently, the Lutheran princes took various initiatives over several decades to promote reconciliation between the two major factions. They organized large-scale consultations between political and religious leaders, but these produced little progress. By 1570, however, they began to meet with some success on the regional level primarily because of the assistance they received from two able theologians who were not closely identified with either the Philippists or the Gnesio-Lutherans, Jakob Andreae and Martin Chemnitz. Andreae was the author of an important set of published sermons intended to evaluate the disputed issues in language that even simple believers could understand. These sermons became an important starting point for discussions with small groups of theologians in southwestern Germany that culminated in an agreement called the Swabian Concord. Chemnitz encouraged support for this proposal in northern Germany and helped draft a revised version of it known as the Swabian-Saxon Concord. After the suppression of the Crypto-Calvinist movement in 1574, the Elector of Saxony also supported the deliberations of Andreae and Chemnitz and sponsored the important consultations they held with several other theologians at Torgau and Cloister Bergen. At last, in May 1577, the theologians reached agreement on the Formula of Concord, which they submitted for approval by the Lutheran churches in two versions, a short form known as the Epitome and a longer form known as the Solid Declaration.

In general, the Formula of Concord evaluated the theology of the Gnesio-Lutheran party more favorably than the positions taken by the Philippists. This is particularly true with regard to the issues under discussion in the Adiaphorist, Synergist, and Crypto-Calvinist controversies. However, it also rejected the extreme view of original sin defended by Flacius in reaction to the Synergist tendencies of Strigel and the misleading language that Amsdorf had adopted in response to the view of good works defended by Georg Major.

For a variety of reasons, some doctrinal and some political, a number of Lutheran territorial churches never endorsed the Formula of Concord. Nevertheless, its preparation had the effect of reversing the trend toward factionalism that had gone on for several decades. By 1580, support for the Formula was clearly extensive enough to warrant its inclusion in the Book of Concord, the official collection of important documents summarizing Lutheran doctrinal beliefs that was published in Dresden to mark the fiftieth anniversary of the Augsburg Confession. As part of this collection it would exercise an important influence on the further development of systematic theology in the Age of Orthodoxy.

THE ADIAPHORIST CONTROVERSY

105. Melanchthon: Letter on the Leipzig Interim (1548)

This letter of December 18, 1548, was written to one of Melanchthon's friends in Weimar on behalf of Duke Georg of Anhalt.

From *CR* 7:251–53.

You indeed weep over the damage done to the churches, which are disturbed in various ways by the proclamation of a new form of doctrine. This sadness is common to many pious people. We see shadows covering the truth; many good and learned pastors expelled from their churches; exiles wandering with their families, who waste away from the hardships of exile and poverty; the kindling of new discords; the breaking up of the meetings of dissenters, where the voice of true doctrine has resounded. All these things are most sad in themselves, and they will bring about a limitless scattering among foreign peoples in the future unless the Son of God sitting at the right hand of the eternal Father, the guardian of his church, moves his work among us, for which I indeed pray with my whole heart along with you and all pious people, calling upon him to preserve his churches and their hospitality. . . .

In order, therefore, to retain necessary things, we are less rigid about those things that are not necessary, particularly since some of the rites [that they want to require] have, to a great extent, continued in use in the churches of these regions. . . . We know that much is said against this moderation, but the devastation of the churches such as is occurring in Swabia would be a greater scandal. If it is possible by this moderation it can be brought about that neither doctrine or liturgy are changed and pastors are not expelled, then we are being criticized unjustly. . . .

I am also not moved by the outcries that when a weakening of front has been made, the adversaries will afterwards seek a change of other matters. Our confession concerning necessary things is heard. In this, with God's aid, we will hereafter show constancy more eagerly, since they will not be able to accuse us of being stubborn about small and unnecessary matters. The affair will show that we are contending for great causes. Perhaps also the delay while these things are being discussed will be beneficial to the churches. But even if a delay will be of no advantage, still the consolation is not useless that we have so long spared the weak, and that we have not right away, in the very beginning, desolated the churches, which would occur if we gave up nothing to the powerful. Besides this very arrangement of rites, which many complain about too passionately as an infringement of liberty, is not in itself vicious. . . .

106. Response of Flacius and Gallus to Some Preachers of Meissen (1549)

Both the Augsburg and Leipzig Interim documents called for the use of all the traditional Catholic vestments. In 1549, when some pastors in Meissen asked for guidance in deciding whether to comply with this demand, Matthias Flacius and his coworker, Nikolaus Gallus (1516–70), based their advice on considerations of the effect compliance would have in a time of persecution.

From Friedrich Bente, *Historical Introductions to the Book of Concord in Concordia Triglotta* (St. Louis: Concordia, 1921), 110.

. . . We do not believe that the robber will let the traveler keep his money, although first he

Philip Melanchthon

only asks for his coat or similar things, at the same time, however, not obscurely hinting that, after having taken these, he will also demand the rest. We certainly do not doubt that you yourselves, as well as all men endowed with a sound mind, believe that, since the beginning is always hardest, these small beginnings of change are at present demanded only that a door may be opened for all the other impieties that are to follow. . . .

107. Melanchthon: Letter to Flacius Expressing Regrets (September 5, 1556)

A year after the conclusion of the Peace of Augsburg, Melanchthon still seemed unable to erase the memory of the Interim crisis. In this letter, he expresses some regret for his past actions but still criticizes Flacius for continuing to disparage his leadership abilities and doctrinal beliefs.

From *CR* 8:841–42.

I knew that even the most trivial changes [in church practices] would be unwelcome to the people. Nevertheless, since our doctrine was retained untainted, I thought it was better for our people to submit to this servitude than give up the ministry of the gospel. . . . Afterwards you began to contradict me. I yielded; I did not fight. According to Homer, Ajax fighting with Hector is satisfied when Hector gives up and admits that he is the victor. But you never put an end to your accusations. What sort of enemy is this that continues to strike at those who give up and cast their arms aside? You win! I retreat. I do not fight anymore concerning these rites, and I wish very much that there would be sweet concord in the churches. I also acknowledge that I have sinned in this matter and ask for God's pardon for not having fled far away from those insidious deliberations. But I will refute those false accusations that are hurled at me by you and Gallus. . . .

108. Final Report of the Theologians of Wittenberg and Leipzig (1570)

Until the end of the Crypto-Calvinist Controversy, most of the theologians at the Universities of Wittenberg and Leipzig were Philippists. In this Final Report they provide a comprehensive defense of their shared views about a variety of disputed matters, beginning with the adiaphora issue.

From *Endlicher Bericht der Theologen beider Universiteten Leipzig und Wittenberg* (Wittenberg: Hans Lufft, 1570), 137–38, 140–41.

First of all, their theses posit this definition: adiaphora or matters of indifference signify outward customs or practices one is in the habit of observing and using in the community of God that are neither expressly commanded nor forbidden in the Word of God.

But soon after, they made this definition: that some adiaphora are themselves free and unforbidden, but others are forbidden and not free. This nonsensical distinction and separation is obviously contradictory speech for it is entirely opposed to the description of adiaphora that they previously set up. For if adiaphora are ceremonies that are neither commanded or forbidden in God's Word, how can one truthfully say that some are forbidden and not free? For if some are forbidden and not free, how can they be adiaphora? . . .

It takes us by surprise that our opponents after so much public instruction should cite the invalid rule and so often repeat as a special argument that in times of persecution, the adiaphora or matters of indifference are no longer free but necessary things; namely, that a necessary confession of faith involves taking a stand upon such things. They cite the example of Daniel [Daniel 6], Eleazar, the seven Maccabees [2 Maccabees 6], and some words of our Lord Christ and Paul.

But they should reasonably concede that this fabricated rule is false and groundless, on account of the judgment that a necessary confession (at the time of persecution or otherwise) is based on those things that the church of God is commanded or ordered to believe, hold, and do in God's Word. For "to confess" signifies to speak, write, and publicly proclaim, according to one's station and calling, the necessary teachings revealed by God and all necessary articles contained in the same, seeking to give an account of the faith, freely and without show, also regardless of any danger to body and possessions, before all the world and everyone. But the adiaphora are not commanded in God's Word, or else they would be neither human traditions nor matters of indifference that are only instituted for the good order of people in the church. Therefore the confession cannot be based on the accepting or omitting of adiaphora, be it in the time of persecution or any other time. . . .

This belongs to a right confession, that one clearly and decisively confess every part of Christian doctrine according to the type and features of each part in particular. No danger, great or small, should come about to change the necessary confession nor any features of any part of the confession. Now everyone knows that there is a great difference between the faith having to do with the articles of necessary doctrine and outward practices that are not commanded in God's Word but are free and matters of indifference. Therefore, where pure doctrine is not displaced one should and must at all times in and out of danger maintain the correct understanding and use of adiaphora and let Christian freedom be seen so that everyone may understand that adiaphora do not necessarily bind the conscience and that they who do not maintain a ceremony or church practice are not judged or condemned to be cast out and separated from the church. . . .

This has continuously been the church's teaching about adiaphora as Luther himself clarified many times in his writings and thoughts. For when he was dealing with the papists, he himself was prepared to concede and put up with outward customs, so long as they would not extend into forbidden misuse or get forced on the conscience but would be observed for the retention of peace, good order, and discipline. And this was especially his opinion in the judgment that he wrote with his own hand about Augsburg 1530 when a confession was also demanded of our church and the danger was as imminent as it would ever be afterwards.

"So they should not think," he says, "that we are stiff or obstinate about the main point,

I for myself am willing and ready to accept all such outer customs and wish for peace as long as my conscience is not thereby burdened, as I have almost always requested in all my books. And in the Apology of the Augsburg Confession, in the chapter on human traditions in the church [article 15] it ends with these explicit words: 'At this Augsburg Reichstag we have let ourselves be examined and have been found willing, out of love, to observe some adiaphora with others. For we have among us considered general unity and peace, so long as it can be maintained without burdening consciences, to be preferred above all other things.'"[1]

But the Flacians cite the example of Daniel as a proof that outward matters of indifference should be considered necessary in the time of persecution, because Daniel, after the king of the Medes gave the order that anyone who for thirty days asked for something from any God or man except the king should be thrown to the lions, nevertheless knelt daily in his summer house, when the window was open toward Jerusalem, and petitioned, praised, and thanked his God as he was accustomed to do. This did not fall under the category of adiaphora, for since the royal command tried to omit and abolish the worship of God, which Daniel showed to the true God of Israel according to the law of the Lord and that was even expressly sought by the enemy, Daniel either had to put himself in outward danger or forsake his divine worship. And if he were to persist continually in the invocation of his God, he could not demonstrate this at that time other than by the outward gestures. So he was not free, and it was not an adiaphora, for in this case to refrain from his prayer and invocation entirely and in an open place was to neglect his confession. But it is a far different thing if one maintains pure doctrine and all Christian worship undefiled and witnesses enough about this and still yields something with good discretion in outward matters of indifference without

scorning the truth, wishing for peace, and maintaining necessary doctrine. Rather, one will thereby show the right understanding and use of free matters of indifference.

The example of Eleazar and the seven Maccabees who would rather have died than eat swine's flesh also does not belong here, since the Jewish polity was still in effect and the eating of pork was earnestly forbidden for the Jews in the law of God. The tyrannical Antiochus publicly ignored that which the Bible said and subjected the people to all abominations so that they would forget the law of God and would accept other ways. So, it was truly not an adiaphora or a free matter of indifference for the Jewish people. . . .

109. Epitome of the Formula of Concord: Article 10 (1577)

From *BC* 515–16.

X. Concerning Ecclesiastical Practices Which Are Called Adiaphora or Indifferent Matters

Affirmative Theses

The Proper, True Teaching and Confession concerning This Article

1. To settle this dispute, we unanimously believe, teach, and confess that ceremonies or ecclesiastical practices that are neither commanded nor forbidden in God's Word, but have been established only for good order and decorum, are in and of themselves neither worship ordained by God nor a part of such worship. "In vain do they worship me" with human precepts (Matt. 15[:9]).

2. We believe, teach, and confess that the community of God in every place and at every time has the authority to alter such ceremonies according to its own situation, as may be most

useful and edifying for the community of God. . . .

4. We believe, teach, and confess that in a time of persecution, when an unequivocal confession of the faith is demanded of us, we dare not yield to the opponents in such indifferent matters. As the Apostle wrote, "Stand firm in the freedom for which Christ has set us free, and do not submit again to a yoke of slavery" [Gal. 5:1]. And: "Do not put on the yoke of the others; what partnership is there between light and darkness?" [2 Cor. 6:14]. "So that the truth of the gospel might always remain with you, we did not submit to them even for a moment" [Gal. 2:5]. For in such a situation it is no longer indifferent matters that are at stake. The truth of the gospel and Christian freedom are at stake. The confirmation of open idolatry, as well as the protection of the weak in faith from offense, is at stake. In such matters we can make no concessions but must offer an unequivocal confession and suffer whatever God sends and permits the enemies of his Word to inflict on us.

The Majorist Controversy

110. The Leipzig Interim of 1548

Articles 4 through 7 of the Augsburg Interim presented a Catholic interpretation of the doctrine of justification and stressed the importance of love and good works. Melanchthon drafted completely new statements on these topics for the Leipzig Interim, but the Gnesio-Lutherans still thought that what he said retained the spirit of the original Catholic document.

From *The Book of Concord or the Symbolical Books of the Evangelical Lutheran Church*, ed. Henry Jacobs (Philadelphia: General Council Publication Board, 1908), 265–67.

How a Person Is Justified before God

. . . In those thus reconciled, virtues and good works should be called righteousness, yet not in the sense that the person on this account has forgiveness of sins or that the person is, in God's judgment, without sin, but that for his Son's sake God regards this weak, inchoate obedience of the believers in this miserable, infirm, impure nature with pleasure; and of these works as righteousness John speaks when he says: "He that does right is righteous" [1 John 3:7]. And it is true that where the works are contrary to God, there is contempt of God, and no conversion to God has occurred in the heart. As is the tree, so also are the fruits. . . .

Of Good Works

. . . He who perseveres in sins contrary to conscience is not converted to God and is still God's enemy, and God's wrath abides upon him if he be not converted. This is precisely in accord with Gal. 5:21: "I tell you, as I have told you before, that they who do such things shall not inherit the kingdom of God." . . .

Further, if anyone who has been in God's grace acts against God's command or his conscience, he grieves the Holy Ghost, loses grace and righteousness and falls beneath God's wrath; and if he be not again converted he falls into eternal punishment as Saul and others. . . .

For this reason, to speak briefly, it is readily understood that good works are necessary, for God has commanded them; and if the course of life be in opposition thereto, God's grace and Holy Ghost are rejected, and such sins merit eternal condemnation. But virtues and good works please God thus, as we have said, in the reconciled, because they believe that God receives their person for Christ's sake and will be pleased with this imperfect obedience; and it is true that eternal life is given for the sake of the Lord Christ out of grace, and at the same time that all are heirs of eternal salvation who are converted to God and by faith receive forgiveness of sins and the Holy Ghost. Nevertheless, the new virtues and good works are so highly necessary that if they are not quickened in the heart, there would be no reception of divine grace. . . .

Thus regeneration and eternal life are in themselves a new light, fear of God, love, joy in God and other virtues; as the passage says: "This is life eternal, to know you the only true God, and me, Jesus Christ." As, now, this true knowledge must shine in us, it is certainly true that these virtues, faith, love, hope, and others, must be in us, and are necessary to salvation. All this is easy for the godly to understand who seek to experience consolation from God.

And since the virtues and good works please God, as has been said, they merit also a reward in this life, both spiritual and temporal, according to God's counsel and still more reward in eternal life, because of the divine promise. . . .

111. Major: Answer to Amsdorf (November 1552)

Georg Major (1502–74) was rector of the University of Wittenberg during the Schmalkald War and was about to become superintendent of the churches of Eisleben when Nikolaus von Amsdorf published a book attacking him for his association with the drafters of the Leipzig Interim. After this critical evaluation of his candidate, Count Albrecht of Mansfeld withdrew the appointment. In reply to Amsdorf, in 1552, Major tried to disclaim any responsibility for the composition of the Leipzig Interim but continued to support some of what it said about good works. The boldness of Major's defense prompted a flood of Gnesio-Lutheran

polemics. Amsdorf published a brief rebuttal, and his associate, Flacius, alerted others to some problematic implications of Major's position. Major then attempted to clarify his position in great detail in his book on the conversion of Paul. His mentor, Melanchthon, retreated from the controversy, but Major continued to find support elsewhere, especially from Justus Menius (1499–1558) in Leipzig.

From Johann Gieseler, *Church History*, vol. 4, 1517–1648, trans. Henry Smith (New York: Harper & Brothers, 1868), 438.

I do confess that I have previously taught and still teach, and furthermore will continue to teach all my days that good works are necessary to salvation. And I say publicly with clear words that no one is saved through evil works and also that no one is saved without good works. In addition, I say, let whoever teaches otherwise, even if it is an angel from heaven, be accursed. . . .

Although we teach that works are necessary to the salvation of the soul, nevertheless, such good works cannot or may not effect or merit the forgiveness of our sins, be reckoned as righteousness, or give the Holy Spirit and eternal life. Such precious heavenly benefits are acquired for us only through the death of our one mediator and savior, Jesus Christ, and must be received only through faith. However, good works must be present, not as merits but as required obedience to God. . . .

112. Amsdorf: Brief Instruction concerning Major's Answer (1552)

From Gottlieb Planck, *Geschichte der protestantischen Theologie* (Leipzig: Siegfried Lebrecht Crusius, 1796), 482.

We know well, praise God, and confess that a Christian should and must do good works. Nobody disputes and speaks concerning that; nor has anybody doubted this. On the contrary, we speak and dispute concerning this, whether a Christian earns salvation by the good works that he should and must do. . . . For we all say and confess that after his renewal and new birth a Christian should love and fear God and do all manner of good works, but not that he may be saved, for he is saved already by faith. This is the true prophetic and apostolic doctrine, and whoever teaches otherwise is already accursed and damned. I, Nikolaus von Amsdorf, therefore declare that whoever teaches and preaches these words as they stand, "Good works are necessary to salvation," is the same as a Pelagian, a mameluke, a denier of Christ, and a duplicitous papist. For the papists, Cochlaeus, Witzel,[2] and others use these words in the same form and manner as Major reintroduces them to us. Therefore, Major is also entirely possessed with the spirit of the papists because he here, without any need, with such defiance and offense asserts and defends the words of the papists. And although he afterwards maneuvers about and offers clarifications of his position, that is only a dissembling by which he sets himself outside of the suspicion that he accepted and went along with the Leipzig Interim.

113. Flacius: Against the Evangelist of the Holy Gown, Dr. Miser Major (1552)

From Wilhelm Preger, *Matthias Flacius Illyricus und seine Zeit*, Bd. 1 (Erlangen: Theodor Bläsing, 1859), 363.

Now if good works are necessary to salvation, and if it is not possible for anyone to be saved without them, then tell us, Dr. Major, how will a man be saved if all his life until his last breath he has lived sinfully, but now, just as he is about to die, he desires to lay hold of Christ, as is the case with many on their deathbed or on the gallows? How will Major comfort such a poor sinner?

It is certainly true that one says to the sinner after absolution: "Go and sin no more," or "Do the righteous fruits of repentance," or "Let your good works shine forth," but how will he produce the fruit or good work that is supposedly necessary for salvation if he is about to die? The poor sinner will declare: "Major, the great theologian, writes and teaches as most certain that no one can be saved without good works, and that good works are absolutely necessary to salvation; therefore I am damned, for until now I have never done any good works." Here, Major will say: "Do them from now on." Then the poor man will answer, as those who teach works-righteousness do: "If I had any longer to live I could do such works are necessary for salvation, but now I am dying."

Furthermore, the devil will also charge his poor conscience with the words of Isaiah who said: "All our good works are as a filthy raiment," or the words of Luther who said, "No good work is without sin. Where then are your good works that are necessary for salvation?" Dr. Luther, as one who experienced many difficult temptations, often said that the devil can easily make our good works dissolve away. But Major speaks, as Dr. Martin used to say it, like an inexperienced theologian and tongue-thrasher.

Major will also have to state and determine the least number of ounces or pounds of good works one must have to be saved. He will also have to determine the exact hour at which a sinner began to do good works so he can be certain that he has some good works. And so we come back again to the old attack of conscience.

114. Major: Sermon on the Conversion of Paul (1553)

From Wilhelm Preger, *Matthias Flacius Illyricus und seine Zeit*, Bd. 1 (Erlangen: Theodor Bläsing, 1859), 370, and Gottlieb Planck, *Geschichte der protestantischen Theologie*, Bd. 4 (Leipzig: Siegfried Lebrecht Crusius, 1796), 481.

When I say the new obedience or good works that follow faith are necessary for salvation, this does not mean that one must earn salvation by good works, or that they can make up, effect, or impart the righteousness by which a person may stand before the judgment seat of God, but that good works are effects and fruits of true faith, which should follow it and which Christ effects in the believers. For whoever believes and is justified is now bound and obligated to begin to be obedient to God the Father, to do good and avoid evil, or else that person risks losing his or her righteousness and salvation. . . .

If now you are justified by faith alone and had become a child and heir of God and if Christ and the Holy Spirit now dwell in you through this faith, then your good works are not done in order to attain salvation (which you already have by grace alone without any works), but in order to retain salvation and not lose it again, good works are necessary to such an extent that, if you do not do them, it is a certain sign that your faith is dead and false, a painted faith, and only an imagined.

115. Melanchthon: Judgment concerning Good Works (1553)

This public position statement by Melanchthon appeared in December 1553.

From *CR* 8:194.

New obedience is necessary. It consists of renewal of life, spirit, light, contemplating and knowing God, joyfully submitting to God, invoking God, submitting ourselves to God, being set on fire by the hearing of the gospel through Word and spirit.

Yet when it is said: New obedience is necessary to salvation, the papists understand that good works merit salvation. This proposition is false; therefore I give up using this way of speaking. Nevertheless, it is customary to say: New obedience is necessary, not as merit but by the necessity of formal cause such as when I say: a white wall is necessarily white. . . .

116. Amsdorf: Preface to Luther's Sermons on John 18–20 (1557)

According to Amsdorf, it was not enough to stop asserting that good works are necessary for salvation. The Lutheran emphasis on grace and faith could only be preserved by a firm rejection of the worth and significance of any human achievement. Amsdorf contradicted Major by stating that good works are detrimental to salvation and supported this position by an appeal to the writings of Luther.

From Walch 8:846.

Everyone can see and observe from what Dr. Martin Luther professed that he showed no favor to any sects, rabble, or Enthusiasts. Rather, he condemned and rejected them all, as he also would have condemned those of this sort who appeared after his death, such as the Interimists, Adiaphorists, or Majorists. Therefore, it is unfair and shameless of them to associate themselves with D. M. L., crying, writing, and boasting that Doctor Martin taught and wrote as they write and teach, even though the very opposite is obviously found in his books. I shall point out a single, most wicked and dangerous example of this: All who teach that good works are necessary for salvation blatantly teach and write contrary to Luther, yes, against Luther himself. For Luther, of blessed and holy memory, writes many places and especially in Galatians, that good works are not only not necessary, they are also harmful to salvation.[3]

117. Amsdorf: Good Works Are Injurious to Salvation (1559)

From Theodor Pressel, *Nicolaus von Amsdorf nach gleichzeitigen Quellen* (Elberfeld: Friderichs, 1862), 123.

The proposition "Good works are injurious to salvation" is unfairly condemned, for these words can be understood only with reference to the type and nature of works by which one claims to merit grace and salvation. Therefore such a proposition is aggravating to human understanding, wisdom, and holiness and to monks, nuns, and the highly learned; therefore they think it can be fairly condemned. Worldly people also have such a high regard for human understanding and wisdom that they cannot understand how the good works by which they think they acquire salvation can be injurious. But this is not surprising since it is not possible to hear the Word of God without God's Spirit and grace. All those who believe and teach about religious matters according to the measure of the understanding and busy themselves with philosophy are heretics who have always taught and written that one can grasp and understand with the intellect. Therefore they also judge contrary to God's Word, glossing and interpreting it according to the meaning that is congenial to the intellect and philosophy. In accordance with the human wisdom known to everyone, even the heathen, they all teach in their churches and schools that good works are necessary and good for salvation; in no way will they suffer in the school of the Holy Spirit in which one praises and honors that which the Word of God believes and proclaims. In the schools of the jurists and sophists, the proposition "Good works are injurious to salvation" is condemned. But divine and heavenly wisdom teaches that all men, however pious or holy they may be, even believers, are unrighteous sinners before God and also that all their works are sins that, except for the grace that makes believers and their works pleasing to God, they would be damned as much as the others and their works would be sins, detrimental to their salvation. If they do all that God has commanded and serve God day and night with all good works, they would still be damned with all their works if God went to them in judgment. But that their works are not harmful or damnable is due merely to Christ in whom they believe. . . .

118. Epitome of the Formula of Concord: Article 4 (1577)

From *BC* 498–99.

Affirmative Theses . . .

2. We also believe, teach, and confess that at the same time, good works must be completely excluded from any questions of salvation as well as from the article on our justification before God, as the apostle testifies in clear terms, "So also David declares that salvation pertains to that person alone to whom God reckons righteousness apart from works, saying, 'Blessed are those whose iniquities are forgiven, and whose sins are covered'" (Rom. 4[:6-8]), and also, "For by grace you have been saved through faith, and this is not your own doing; it is the gift of God—not the result of works, so that no one may boast" (Eph. 2[:8-9]).

3. We also believe, teach, and confess that all people, particularly those who have been reborn and renewed through the Holy Spirit, are obligated to do good works.

4. In this sense the words "necessary," "should," and "must" are used correctly, in Christian fashion, also in regard to the reborn; in no way is such use contrary to the pattern of sound words and speech.

5. Of course, the words *necessitas, necessarium* ("necessity" and "necessary") are not to be understood as a compulsion when they are applied to the reborn, but only as the required obedience, which they perform out of a spontaneous spirit—not because of the compulsion or coercion of the law—because they are "no longer under the law, but under grace" [Rom. 6:14].

THE SYNERGIST CONTROVERSY

119. Melanchthon: Letter to Spalatin concerning the Luther-Erasmus Debate (1524)

During the debate between Luther and Erasmus about free will, Melanchthon was in touch with both disputants, trying to get them to moderate what they said to each other. On this particular issue, his humanistic background predisposed him to sympathize with Erasmus more than Luther.

From *CR* 1:673.

Erasmus has written a book on free will. We are sending this book to you. It seems that he has not treated us with contempt. A short while ago I also received letters from him, which you will see. They will also be brought to you by this young man. I desperately desire that this subject, which is the most important in the Christian religion, should be carefully examined, and for this reason I rejoice that Erasmus has taken up the struggle. For a long time I have wished that some prudent person should oppose Luther on this matter. If Erasmus is not this man, I am greatly deceived.

120. Melanchthon: *Loci Communes* of 1548

Melanchthon continuously revised his basic summary of Christian theology. In the edition of 1548, written in the year of the Interim crisis, it became more evident to the public that Melanchthon did not totally agree with Luther about the effect of sin upon the power of the will.

From *CR* 21:658–59.

I have seen many who, when troubled by their sins, have asked: "How can we hope to be accepted by God when we perceive no new light and no new virtue in us? Free will does nothing, so we must live in mistrust and doubt until we become conscious of rebirth in us." This impression that the will is not active is a dangerous delusion from which one must free the mind. Pharoah and Saul opposed God freely and without compulsion, although he had given them frequent and convincing proofs of his presence. On the other hand, the conversion of David did not occur in such a manner as when a stone is turned into a fig. Free will cooperated in him; for when he heard the threats and the promises of God, he willingly and freely confessed his faults. . . . God has ordered the preaching of his Word in such a way that when someone considers and accepts the promise, while still struggling with doubt, the Holy Spirit begins to work within. Therefore, when people excuse their idleness because they think that free will does nothing, I answer: "It is an eternal and unchanging commandment of God that you should obey the voice of the gospel, hear the Son of God, and acknowledge the Mediator." You may say, "I cannot." But in a manner you certainly can, and when you have consoled yourself with the gospel, then ask God to assist you, and know that the Holy Spirit is efficacious in such consolation. Convince yourself that God intends to convert us in this manner, when we, moved by the promise, wrestle with ourselves, pray for help, and resist our lack of trust, our disbelief, and other evil inclinations. For this reason some in former times have said that free will has the capability of turning toward grace; that means hearing the promise, endeavoring to assent to it, and struggling against sin. . . . Since the promise is universal, and there are no

contradictory wills in God, the reason for the acceptance of some and the rejection of others must necessarily be within ourselves. The right use of this doctrine in the practice of faith and in the consolation of the soul will confirm the truth that these three causes concur: the Word of God, the Holy Spirit, and the Will.

121. Pfeffinger: Five Questions on the Freedom of the Human Will (1555)

The Leipzig Interim had asserted that God "does not work with man as with a block, but draws him so that his will also cooperates." Johannes Pfeffinger (1493–1573), who had assisted Melanchthon in composing this statement, defended it more fully in the following theses.

From Friedrich Bente, *Historical Introductions to the Book of Concord in Concordia Triglotta* (St. Louis: Concordia, 1921), 131.

#14. . . . Some assent or apprehension on our part must occur when the Holy Spirit has aroused the mind, the will, and the heart. Hence Basil says: Only will, and God anticipates; and Chrysostom: He who draws, draws him who is willing; and Augustine: He assists those who have received the gift of the call with becoming piety, and preserves the gifts of God as far as man is able. Again: when grace preceded, the will follows. . . .

#17. If the will were idle or purely passive, there would be no difference between the pious and the wicked, or between the elect and the damned, as between Saul and David, between Judas and Peter. God would also become a respecter of persons and the author of contumacy in the wicked and damned; and to God would be ascribed contradictory wills, which conflicts with the entire Scripture. Hence it follows that there is in us a cause why some assent while others do not. . . .

#30. For since the promise of grace is universal, and since we must obey this promise, some difference between the elect and the rejected must be inferred from our will, namely, that those who resist the promise are rejected, while those who embrace the promise are received. . . . All this clearly shows that our will is not idle in conversion or like a stone or block in its conduct. . . .

#34. Some persons, however, shout that the assistance of the Holy Spirit is extenuated and diminished if even the least particle be attributed to the human will. Though this argument may appear specious and plausible, yet pious minds understand that by our doctrine—according to which we ascribe some cooperation to our will, namely, some assent and apprehension—absolutely nothing is taken away from the assistance rendered by the Holy Spirit. For we affirm that the first acts must be assigned and attributed to him who first and primarily, through the Word or the voice of the gospel, moves our hearts to believe, to which thereupon we, too, ought to assent as much as we are able, and not resist the Holy Spirit, but submit to the Word, ponder, learn, and hear it, as Christ says: "Whosoever has heard of the Father and learned comes to me." . . .

#36. And although original sin has brought upon our nature a ruin so sad and horrible that we can hardly imagine it, yet we must not think that absolutely all the knowledge that was found in the minds of our first parents before the Fall has on that account been destroyed and extinguished after the Fall, or that the human will does not in any way differ from a stone or a block; for we are, as St. Paul has said most seriously, coworkers with God, whose coworking, indeed, is assisted and strengthened by the Holy Spirit.

122. Heshus: On So-called Free Will—Against the Synergists (1562)

Although Tilmann Heshus (1527–88) is best known for his involvement in the Crypto-Calvinist Controversy, he was actively involved in many of the doctrinal debates of his age. This intense Gnesio-Lutheran lost several positions during his career as a pastor and professor because of the offense caused by his polemics.

From Tilmann Heshus, *Vom Vermeinten Freyen Willen: Wider die Synergisten* (Magdeburg: Kirchener, 1562), 2:2; 4.

Part 2:2

That the human will cannot cooperate or do anything in its conversion, justification, or rebirth is demonstrable from the entire Scriptures, which testify that man is not free by nature and does not have his heart, will, or thought in his power, but affirm to the contrary that his best powers, related to his understanding and will, are ensnared and imprisoned and locked up under the power and tyranny of sin and are the enslaved servant of the devil—thus that he by himself can wish, desire, or choose nothing other than what is opposed to righteousness, pleasing to the devil, and worthy of hellfire. . . .

Origen[4] imagined that the will of man is its own lord who sits on a stool like a judge with virtue and sin, life and damnation before him, and it is up to him to give himself to righteousness or sin as he so chooses. The intellect dreams this and philosophy supports this lie, but God's Word speaks otherwise of this matter, declaring that the natural understanding and will are as if a man lies bound in stocks and cannot move himself. Yes, sin is so much his own that he wants or can do nothing but sin and pervert himself in his lusts.

Many passages in the Scripture testify to this. John 8:34: Everyone who commits sin is a slave to sin. When the Son makes you free, you will die to your sins. Romans 6:20: When you were slaves to sin, you were free from righteousness. Romans 7:14: I am carnal, sold into slavery under sin. Isaiah 50:1: Because of your sins, you were sold. Isaiah 52:3: You were sold for nothing and redeemed without money. How do you reconcile such servitude or slavery with the freedom by which a man can do something for himself? They are as opposed as day and night. . . .

Part 4

Since we have now, with God's help, clarified the pure and scripturally based doctrine of the unfree will and the conversion of man through God's grace and have also pointed out the errors and falsifications of which we must beware, we will, at last, consider some of the objections of the Synergists. From this everyone may see how our opponents have no ground for their errors in God's Word and will, therefore, hold more firmly to the truth. . . .

The primary false argument of the Synergists is this: If there is no cooperation by a person in conversion, and it is only the work of God, then God must not be of one mind toward all people. Yet Scripture testifies that God is good toward everyone and does not want anyone to be lost (2 Pet. 3:8; 1 Tim. 2:4). Therefore, there must be a free will in a person, which is the cause why some receive the Word and others reject it.

Answer: This is without a doubt the most difficult argument related to this matter, and the foremost writers of all times have given much consideration to it. . . . It is rightly and truly believed of God that he wants all men to be saved, but it in no way follows that one may

conclude from this that there is some power of free will remaining in man and some cooperation in conversion. Rather, it only follows that God is not the cause of the damnation of men and also does not hinder the salvation of anyone. . . .

It is like a pious father who always wants it to go well with his children. If a child does evil, he orders that one to be flogged. Nevertheless, he continues to wish that it should go well with the child. So, the promise of the gospel demands that one believe in the name of Jesus Christ. God wants all people to be saved insofar as they believe in Christ. But he also wills that the others who do not believe should be damned.

Therefore, it is one thing to speak about the general will of God and quite another to speak about the election and plan of God. For God's election and eternal plan has no condition, but as God has concluded from eternity, so it happens. It is a matter not only of his will, counsel, and pleasure, but also of his work and plan, which no one can understand. If God makes a Christian believe, he does not only give his Word and does not only proclaim his will, but grasps him effectively and renews the man, directs him to faith and the new life without any conditions or cooperation.

123. Epitome of the Formula of Concord: Articles 2 and 11 (1577)

From *BC* 491–94, 552–55, 517–18.

Epitome of the Formula of Concord:
Article 2
Affirmative Theses . . .

1. On this article it is our teaching, faith, and confession that human reason and understanding

are blind in spiritual matters and understand nothing on the basis of their own powers, as it is written, "Those who are natural do not receive the gifts of God's Spirit, for they are foolishness to them and they are unable to understand them" [1 Cor. 2:14] when they are asked about spiritual matters.

2. Likewise, we believe, teach, and confess that the unregenerated human will is not only turned away from God but has also become God's enemy, that it has only the desire and will to do evil and whatever is opposed to God, as it is written, "The inclination of the human heart is evil from youth" [Gen. 8:21]. Likewise, "The mind that is set on the flesh is hostile to God; it does not submit to God's law—indeed, it cannot" [Rom. 8:7]. As little as a corpse can make itself alive for bodily, earthly life, so little can people who through sin are spiritually dead raise themselves up to a spiritual life, as it is written, "When we were dead through our trespasses, God made us alive together with Christ" [Eph. 2:5]. Therefore, we are not "competent of ourselves to claim anything [good] as coming from us; our competence is from God" (2 Cor. 3[:5]). . . .

Negative Theses . . .

4. [We reject and condemn] that, although human beings are too weak to initiate conversion with their free will before rebirth, and thus convert themselves to God on the basis of their own natural powers and be obedient to God's law with their whole hearts, nonetheless, once the Holy Spirit has made a beginning through the preaching of the Word and in it has offered his grace, the human will is able out of its own natural powers to a certain degree, even though small and feeble, to do something, to help and cooperate, to dispose and prepare itself for grace, to grasp this grace, to accept it, and to believe the gospel. . . .

8. . . . Some ancient and modern teachers of the church have used expressions such as, "*Deus trahit, sed volentem trahit*," that is, "God

draws, but he draws those who are willing"; and "*Hominis voluntas in conversione non est otiosa, sed agit aliquid,*" that is, "The human will is not idle in conversion but also is doing something." Because such expressions have been introduced as confirmation of the natural free will in conversion contrary to the teaching of God's grace, we hold that these expressions do not correspond to the form of sound teaching, and therefore it is proper to avoid them when speaking of conversion to God.

On the other hand, it is correct to say that in conversion God changes recalcitrant, unwilling people into willing people through the drawing power of the Holy Spirit, and that after this conversion the reborn human will is not idle in the daily exercise of repentance, but cooperates in all the works of the Holy Spirit which he performs through us.

9. . . . Therefore, before the conversion of the human being there are only two efficient causes, the Holy Spirit and God's Word as the instrument of the Holy Spirit, through which he effects conversion; the human creature must hear this Word, but cannot believe and accept it on the basis of its own powers but only through the grace and action of God the Holy Spirit.

SOLID DECLARATION OF THE FORMULA OF CONCORD
II. Concerning the Free Will or Human Powers . . .

It is indeed true that both the Enthusiasts and the Epicureans misuse in unchristian fashion the teaching regarding the impotence and wickedness of our natural free will and the teaching that our conversion and rebirth are the work of God alone and not of our powers. Because of such talk, many people become dissolute and disorderly as well as indolent and sluggish in all Christian activities, such as prayer, reading, and Christian meditation. They say that because they cannot possibly convert to

God on the basis of their own natural powers, they want to continue to rebel against God or to wait until God converts them against their will with his brute power. . . .

Other timid hearts may fall into troubling thoughts and doubts, whether God has chosen them and wants to make His gifts effective in them through the Holy Spirit, because they do not have a strong, burning faith and heartfelt obedience. Instead, they perceive in themselves only weakness, worry, and wretchedness.

Therefore, on the basis of God's Word we now want to give a further account of how the human being is converted to God; how and through which means (namely, through the oral Word and the holy sacraments) the Holy Spirit desires to be active in us and to give and effect true repentance, faith, and the new spiritual power and capability to do the good in our hearts; and how we should respond to such means and use them. . . .

A person who has not yet been converted to God and been reborn can hear and read this Word externally, for in such external matters, as stated above, people have a free will to a certain extent even after the fall, so that they may go to church and listen or not listen to the sermon.

Through these means (the preaching and hearing of His Word), God goes about His work and breaks our hearts and draws people, so that they recognize their sins and God's wrath through the preaching of the law and feel real terror, regret, and sorrow in their hearts. Through the preaching of the holy gospel of the gracious forgiveness of sins in Christ and through meditating upon it, a spark of faith is ignited in them, and they accept the forgiveness of sins for Christ's sake and receive the comfort of the promise of the gospel. In this way the Holy Spirit, who effects all of this, is sent into their hearts. . . .

However, if people do not want to hear or read the proclamation of God's Word, but disdain it and the congregation of God's people

and then die and perish in their sins, they can neither find comfort in God's eternal election nor obtain mercy. For Christ, in whom we are chosen, offers his grace to all people in the Word and in the holy sacraments, and he earnestly desires that people should hear it. He has promised that where "two or three are gathered" in his name and are occupied with his holy Word, he will be "there among them" [Matt. 18:20].

If such people disdain the tools of the Holy Spirit and do not want to hear, no injustice is done to them if the Holy Spirit does not enlighten them but lets them remain and perish in the darkness of unbelief. . . .

Although God does not force human beings in such a way that they must become godly (for those who persistently resist the Holy Spirit and stubbornly struggle against what is recognized truth, as Stephen said of the obdurate Jews in Acts 7[:51], will not be converted), nonetheless God the Lord draws those people whom he wants to convert and does so in such a way that an enlightened understanding is fashioned out of a darkened understanding and an obedient will is fashioned out of a rebellious will. Scripture calls this creating a new heart [Ps. 51:12].

Epitome of the Formula of Concord
XI. Concerning the Eternal Predestination and Election of God . . .
The Pure, True Teaching concerning This Article . . .

4. *Praedestinatio,* however, or God's eternal election, extends only to the righteous, God-pleasing children of God. It is a cause of their salvation, which God brings about. He has arranged everything that belongs to it. Our salvation is so firmly grounded on it [cf. John 10:26-29] that "the gates of hell will not prevail against it" [Matt. 16:18]. . . .

7. This Christ calls all sinners to himself and promises them refreshment. He is utterly

serious in his desire that all people should come to him and seek help for themselves [cf. Matt. 11:28; 1 Tim. 2:4]. He offers himself to them in the Word. He desires them to hear the Word and not to plug their ears or despise his Word. To this end he promises the power and activity of the Holy Spirit, divine assistance in remaining faithful and attaining eternal salvation.

11. That "many are called and few are chosen" [Matt. 20:16] does not mean that God does not want to save everyone. Instead, the reason for condemnation lies in their not hearing God's Word at all or arrogantly despising it, plugging their ears and their hearts, and thus blocking the Holy Spirit's ordinary path, so that he cannot carry out his work in them; or if they have given it a hearing, they cast it to the wind and pay no attention to it. Then the fault lies not with God and his election but with their own wickedness [cf. 2 Pet. 2:9-15; Luke 11:47-52; Heb. 12:15-17, 25].

The Flacian Controversy

124. The Weimar Disputation between Valentin Strigel and Matthias Flacius (1560)

The Weimar Disputation was arranged by Duke Johann Friedrich of Saxony and took place August 2–8, 1560. In discussing the impact of original sin on free will, during the second session of this debate, Strigel, the Philippist, raised the issue that provoked the Flacian controversy.

From Simon Musaeus, *Disputatio de Originali Peccato et Libero Arbitrio inter M. Flacius et V. Strigelium* (1563), 22–26.

STRIGEL: Original sin is a defect and deprivation in all of the powers and faculties of man

and chiefly in these three: first in the mind, second in the will, and third in the heart. In the mind, it is a loss of divine light, that is, of the knowledge of God's nature and will. This darkness appears as terrible and dismal doubts about all divine things, about providence, and the promises and threats of God. These evils, I believe I have made clear, are both privative and positive. Furthermore, in the will, it is not only an aversion to God as the proper object to which it ought to be directed, but also a conversion, that is, an appetite for things that are illicit and prohibited by God such as seeking security in secondary things, contempt for God, and murmuring against God. Third, in the heart, it is an ataxia, that is, a manifold confusion of appetites or desires, wrongful love of ourselves, lust for vengeance, and the proliferation of inordinate passions. On account of this defect and deprivation, God has become angry with the whole human race for, indeed, this poison or evil is propagated to all the posterity of Adam. . . .

Original sin [however] is not a substance or a certain substantial quantity. Rather, it is a quality of a secondary sort, that is, a loss of strength or power: It has a liability attached to it, that is, an assignment to eternal punishment by the judgment of the most just God. From this, it is possible to discern what it really is, namely, not a substance or a property that differentiates one species from another but an accident, a privation that comprises both a deficiency and a disordered movement or impulse. . . .

FLACIUS: I have cited testimonies where the Word of God says that original sin is the very composition of the old man. They all understand it to be the same mass. Ezekiel 11 and 36 say that the heart is like a stone, that a new heart must be created, and many other things that distinctly indicate that original sin is a substance.

STRIGEL: Then you deny that original sin is an accident?

FLACIUS: Luther distinctly denies that it is an accident. But, second, it should be noted that you are continuing to dispute from philosophy concerning substance and accident, which ought not to be the way of thinking of theologians in matters concerning religion and truth. Third, you say that the will cannot be deprived of its own free action without the annihilation of man. Scripture testifies to the contrary that what pertains to the divine in the intellect has not only been killed, put to death, and destroyed, but man also has been transformed into the image of Satan. Look at Colossians 2[:11-13], which speaks of the circumcision of a corpse, etc. Here Paul is speaking of inherent evil, or the annihilation of the good powers. To this he adds that the will is the possession of Satan. See 2 Timothy 2[:26]. Just as a Christian captured by a Turk is not free but is restricted to doing what his master wills or commands, so Satan effectually holds the hearts of his captives like an ox by the nose. . . . You digress from the aim of our deliberation and deviate into plausibilities. You do not refute my arguments from the Word of God. Luther speaks of original sin as a corruption of nature like the flesh or total mass of a man changed by leprosy. I say, Scripture does not allow us to speak of original sin as if it were a trivial accident, but just as yeast leavens a total mass, so the total nature of man is subjected to corruption. I say that man is poisoned, is entirely prone or inclined to evil and entirely unable to do good. Scripture testifies to this. . . .

STRIGEL: I am not saying that man can grasp the grace of God of his own powers, but that the Holy Spirit stretches out our hands. And so that no ambiguity will remain, I will clarify this through an example. Only a mother or wet nurse can nourish a child, for a child is too weak to seek its nourishment by its own exertions. If the mother or wet nurse does not nourish it, it will die of hunger. Now the question is how the poor child draws the milk from its mother's breast. I say that the child sucks and draws in the milk, but only if the mother has directed the mouth of the child to her breast. If this does not happen, the child would not know what to do. . . .

FLACIUS: The mother not only offers her breast, but the child also feels hunger in itself and possesses the power in its body to receive food. Yes, it moves its mouth and lips and is prepared to suck.

Strigel, then, would have it that there is a power in us to desire and receive the food, that is, the benefits of God. In fact, you thereby attribute to corrupt man a very great power with respect to spiritual things. Now, then, deny that this opinion is Pelagian. . . .

I explain my entire view as follows: Man is purely passive. If you consider the innate faculty of the will, its willing, and its powers, then he is purely passive when he receives. But if that divinely bestowed willing or spark of faith kindled by the Spirit is considered, then this imparted willing and this spark are not purely passive. But the Adamic will not only does not operate or cooperate but, according to the innate malice of the heart, even operates contrarily.

125. Flacius: Treatise on Original Sin from *Clavis Scripturae* (1567)

Flacius resisted the introduction of Aristotelian metaphysical categories into the discussion of theology. In his 1567 guide to the study of the Bible, he emphasized this fact. Nevertheless, in the treatise on original sin appended to this volume, he persisted in speaking of original sin as part of the substance of human nature.

From *Clavis Scripturae* (Leipzig: Ery-thropilius, 1695), 771–72, 787.

I believe and assert that original sin is a substance, because the rational soul (as united with God) and especially its noblest substantial powers, namely, the intellect and will, which before had been formed so gloriously that they were the true image of God and the fountain of all justice, uprightness, and piety, and altogether essentially like unto gold and gems, are now, by deceit of Satan, so utterly perverted that they are the true and living image of Satan, and, as it were, filthy or rather consisting of an infernal flame, not otherwise than when the sweetest and purest mass, infected with the most venomous ferment, is altogether and substantially changed and transformed into a lump of the same ferment. . . .

Some object that I introduce new opinions into the church when I affirm that original sin, or rather a certain part of original sin, is a substance. I respond: there is no good reason to say this opinion is new since it is taught in so many works not only by Luther and the writings of others as I will afterwards show, but also most wisely in sacred Scripture itself, where truly this sin is many times described in essential words. . . .

Luther in a sermon for the feast of the circumcision says:[5] the disease that should be cut out adheres not in any works but in nature itself. The substance of man is totally corrupted so that sin is the origin of man and whatever is in him. Furthermore, this sin is original, or rather the whole nature of man is sin, even if no actual sin, as it is called, is committed. This sin is not committed as all other sins are but exists in itself, lives, and produces all sin. It is a substantial sin that is not sinned at a certain hour or time, but as long as a man lives that sinning endures. . . .

Flacius Illyricus

In sum, original evil is that same fount of all evil, of all guilt and penalty in man. Scripture therefore says the heart is depraved, perverted, and distorted, that it rushes headlong to evil or ranges even from infancy. Genesis 6:5; 8:21; Jer. 17:9—the heart is blind and hardened, stony and adamantine (Deut. 29:4; Ezek. 11:19; 31:26; Rom. 1:21; Eph. 4:18).

126. Final Report of the Theologians of Wittenberg and Leipzig (1570)

For once, the Philippists found Flacius in a vulnerable position. He had raised questions about the pastoral implications of speaking of the necessity of good works. Now they questioned the impact of speaking of original sin as part of human substance.

From *Endlicher Bericht* (Wittenberg: Hans Lufft, 1570), 164.

Let every rational, God-fearing man consider what an immeasurable and unholy misery, cross, and grief it would be for the poor female sex if a pregnant woman should think and conclude that the fruit that she bore is not, in essence, a special gift of God but of the devil who formed it essentially according to his image, who dwells in it and powerfully—yes, essentially—impressed and implanted his devilish larva in its flesh and blood. Yes, what will one in this case say to the poor female sex? All Christian fathers and mothers to whom God gives children search their own hearts and think what a joy or pleasure they will have in their children, if this great consolation should be received that children are a work, gift, present from God as Psalms 127, 128 testify. But how would a Christian father or mother view the shape of the child if we must say: This fruit of your body is the flesh and blood of Satan dwelling in you and your wife, formed and created in an essential way according to his image and likeness, that it is from Satan that your child received and obtained, through you, a so highly corrupted, evil nature, substance, and essence, such a gruesome, horrible larva. If, we ask, a pious, God-fearing father and mother viewed their children with this thought, what kind of joy, comfort, and pleasure would they have in marriage? . . .

In opposition to this horrible, abhorrent blasphemy, which is basically nothing other than the old, damned Manichaean abomination, except that it is advanced and excused with more crafty and poisonous words, we differentiate the substance and essence and the entire life of man, which God alone gives and sustains, from original sin, that dung and poison clinging to the essence that comes from and is derived from the devil. And we continually say that the devil takes no part along with God in forming the substance and essence, the entire life and all that is essential in man, and that this human nature, although it is sinful and corrupted (and though this sin is inherited in birth along with and next to the nature and

essence of man and is originally from the devil), still it is not from the devil but is a work and creation of God alone, as can be shown from countless passages in the Word of God. The entire 139th Psalm (139:13-16) is a splendid and comforting testimony that our life and essence is formed, given, and sustained by God alone. "You, O Lord," this psalm says, "were with me in my mother's body and I thank you that I am so wonderfully made. Marvelous are your works, that my soul confesses. My bones were not hidden from you when I was made in secret, when I was formed within the earth. Your eyes saw me when I was still not ready to be born. All my days were written in your book and still shall be and it could not be otherwise."

127. Epitome of the Formula of Concord: Article 1 (1577)

From *BC* 488–91.

Affirmative Theses . . .

1. We believe, teach, and confess that there is a difference between original sin and human nature—not only as God originally created it pure, holy, and without sin, but also as we have it now after the fall. Even after the fall this nature still is and remains a creature of God. This difference is as great as the difference between the work of God and the work of the devil. . . .

3. On the other hand, we believe, teach, and confess that original sin is not a slight corruption of human nature, but rather a corruption so deep that there is nothing sound or uncorrupted left in the human body or soul, in its internal or external powers. Instead, as the church sings, "Through Adam's

fall human nature and our essence are completely corrupted." . . .

Negative Theses . . .

[13.] Concerning the Latin words *substantia* and *accidens,* since they are not biblical terms and are words unfamiliar to common people, they should not be used in sermons delivered to the common people, who do not understand them; the simple folk should be spared such words.

But in the schools and among the learned these terms are familiar and can be used without any misunderstanding to differentiate the essence of a thing from that which in an "accidental" way adheres to the thing. Therefore, these words are properly retained in scholarly discussion of original sin.

For the difference between God's work and the devil's work can be made most clear through these words because the devil cannot create a substance but can only corrupt the substance, which God has created, in an "accidental" way, with God's permission.

The Osiandrist Controversy

128. Osiander: Concerning the Only Mediator (1551)

This treatise contained the fullest development of Andreas Osiander's thought about human righteousness and the nature of justification.

From *Von dem Einigen Mitler Jesu Christo und Rechtfertigung des Glaubens, Bekantnus* (Königsberg, 1551) in H. R. Frank, *Die Theologie der Concordienformel*, Bd. 2 (Erlangen: Theodor Bläsing, 1861), 99–100; and Gottlieb Planck, *Geschichte der protestantischen Theologie*, Bd. 4 (Leipzig: Siegfried Lebrecht Crusius, 1796), 268–69.

Since we are in Christ through faith and he is in us, we also become the righteousness of God in him, just as he became sin for us [2 Cor. 5:21]. That is, he showered us and filled us with his divine righteousness, as we showered him with our sins, so that God himself and all the angels see only righteousness in us on account of the highest, eternal, and infinite righteousness of Christ, which is His Godhead itself dwelling in us. And although sin still dwells in our flesh and clings to it, this sin is just like an impure little drop in comparison with an immense pure ocean, and God does not want to see it on account of the righteousness of Christ that is in us. . . .

By the fulfillment of the law and by his suffering and death, Christ merited and acquired from God, his heavenly Father, this great and exalted grace: He has not only forgiven our sin and taken the unbearable burden of the law away from us, but also wishes to justify us through faith in Christ, to infuse justification or righteousness, and, through the working of His Holy Spirit and the death of Christ into which we are incorporated by Baptism, to kill, wipe out, and entirely exterminate the sin that, though already forgiven, still dwells in our flesh and clings to us.

Therefore the second part of the office of our dear and faithful Lord and Mediator Jesus Christ consists of his turning toward us and dealing with us poor sinners, as with a guilty party, in such a way that we acknowledge this great grace and receive it by faith with thanksgiving. In so doing, he can make us alive from the death of sin by faith, and completely mortify and exterminate that sin, which, though already forgiven, still dwells in our flesh and clings to us. This, above all else, is the act of our justification.

Andreas Osiander

129. Osiander: Disputation on Righteousness (October 24, 1550)

The following text reveals the biblical texts with which Osiander supported his arguments about the righteousness that comes from Christ's indwelling in the Christian.

From Gottlieb Planck, *Geschichte der protestantischen Theologie*, Bd. 4 (Leipzig: Siegfried Lebrecht Crusius, 1796), 271–73.

The entire fullness of deity dwells in Christ bodily and consequently also in those in whom Christ dwells. . . .

And he promised us that this would take place when he said: "Whoever eats my flesh and drinks my blood abides in me and I in him." John 6:56. And again: "Whoever loves me will keep my word and my Father will love him, and we will come and dwell with him." John 14:21. . . .

He also diligently admonishes us to abide in him and says: "You have already been purified by the word that I have spoken to you. Abide in me as I abide in you." John 15:3-4. . . .

Therefore St. Paul boasts and audaciously says: "I live, yet it is no longer I, but Christ, who lives in me." Galatians 2:20. . . .

Thus we are justified with his essential righteousness: One will call him "The Lord is our righteousness." Jeremiah 23:6 and 33:16. . . .

Therefore we live with his essential righteousness and will also henceforth live, as he says, "Just as the living Father has sent me, and I live because of my Father's will, so whoever eats of me will also live because of my will." John 6:57. . . .

But to eat the flesh of Christ and to drink his blood means in this passage nothing other than to believe that he has offered his body for our sins—but thus that through this faith we become one flesh with him and are purified with his blood from our sins. . . .

Whoever does not hold to this manner of our justification, no matter what he may confess with his mouth, is certainly a Zwinglian at heart, for it is impossible for one to believe that the true body of Christ is in the bread and his true blood is in the cup without believing that Christ truly dwells in the Christian. . . .

They also teach things colder than ice who hold that we are simply regarded as righteous on account of the forgiveness of sins, and not on account of the essential righteousness of Christ, who dwells in us through faith. . . .

130. Mörlin: Apology concerning the Osiandrist Enthusiasts (1557)

Joachim Mörlin wrote several important treatises against Osiander's position. The following excerpt concisely shows the counter-arguments that he drew from biblical texts.

From *Apologia auff die vermeinte widerlegung des Osiandricher Schwermers in Preussen M. Vogels* (Magdeburg: Lotter, 1557), Dii–Diii.

The Opposition between the Teachings of Paul and Osiander

For Paul, "to impute" means that God reckons an alien innocence to us and on account of this receives us as righteous and pious, although we are still not so in ourselves. Romans 2 and 4.

To the contrary, for Osiander, it means that righteousness is present and at hand in us.

For Paul, "justification" means that the godless one who has no good work or good reputation can easily be accounted or accepted as righteous on account of the obedience of Christ to eternal life. Romans 4.

To the contrary, for Osiander, it means that righteousness pours out, flows, and evidently bubbles up through a little funnel.

For Paul, "righteousness" means the gracious forgiveness of our sins, which we experience without the law and any works, through faith in the obedience of Christ and his merits, by which we are eternally accepted and saved by God. Romans 3 and 4.

To the contrary, for Osiander, righteousness means the piety with all virtues that moves us to do good.

In summary, Paul credits it all to the grace of God, the merits of Christ, and because of that the forgiveness of sins. He cannot allow the law or works to be used or praised along with renewal as righteousness before God, but modestly excludes them with words such as: by faith alone, grace, not of ourselves, without the law, without works, and so forth. This is powerfully declared in Romans 3 and 4, 1 Corinthians 4, Ephesians 2. He also considers renewal a result or fruit of the righteousness of faith and repentance.

To the contrary, Osiander teaches in one summary that the grace of God, the merits of Christ, the forgiveness of sins in his blood are not and cannot be righteousness, and, in rebuttal, states that when one teaches this, it is a horrible idolatry and blasphemy.

For Osiander, our righteousness before God to eternal life is the renewal and entirely new life that comes from God dwelling and working in us.

131. Melanchthon: Confutation of Osiander (September 1555)

For once, Melanchthon basically agreed with a theological judgment made by his Gnesio-Lutheran opponents.

From *CR* 8:582–83.

We clearly affirm the presence or indwelling of God in the reborn. We do not say that God is present in them like the power of the sun at work upon the veins of the earth, but that the Father and the Son are actually present, breathing the Holy Spirit into the heart of the believer. This presence or indwelling is what is called spiritual renewal. This personal union, however, is not the same as the union of the divine and human natures in Christ but is an indwelling like someone living in a separable domicile in this life.

We should say in addition that although this indwelling or renewal is necessarily present in the reborn, it does not endure unless that faith first shines that justifies a person before God, that is, the faith by which one has the remission of sins, and is reconciled and accepted by God to eternal life on account of the obedience of the mediator, as it says in Daniel [Dan. 9:18] and many other places: We are heard by the Lord not on account of our own righteousness but on account of his mercy. Although God dwelt in Moses, Elijah, David, Isaiah, Daniel, Peter, and Paul, nevertheless none of them claimed to be righteous before God on account of this indwelling or the effecting of their renewal but on account of the obedience of the Mediator and his gracious intercession, since, in this life, the remnants of sin were still in them. Therefore, although this renewal is pleasing to God, infinitely greater preference should be given to the obedience and intercession of the Mediator, since, as Paul says, we are chosen in love [Eph. 1:4]. And Ephesians 3: through whom we have access in confidence through faith in him.

Osiander especially makes an issue of this article and contends that man is righteous on account of the indwelling of God, or on account of the indwelling God, not on account of the obedience of the Mediator, and not by the imputed righteousness of the Mediator through grace. He corrupts the proposition "By faith we are justified" into "By faith we are prepared that we may become just by something else," that is, the indwelling God. Thus in reality he is saying what the papists say: "We are righteous by our renewal," except that he mentions the cause where the papists mention the effect. We are just when God renews us. He therefore diminishes the honor due to the Mediator, obscures the greatness of sin, destroys the chief consolation of the pious, and leads them into perpetual doubt. For faith cannot exist unless it contemplates the promise of mercy concerning the Mediator. Nor is there an inhabitation unless consolation is received by this faith. It is preposterous to teach that first one is to believe in the indwelling and afterward in forgiveness of sins. Therefore, since this dogma of Osiander is both false and pernicious to consciences, it should be shunned and condemned.

132. Epitome of the Formula of Concord: Article 3 (1577)

From *BC* 494–96.

CONCERNING THE RIGHTEOUSNESS OF FAITH BEFORE GOD . . .
Affirmative Theses . . .

2. Accordingly, we believe, teach, and confess that our righteousness before God consists in this, that God forgives us our sins by sheer grace, without any works, merit, or worthiness of our own, in the past, at present, or in the future, that he gives us and reckons to us the righteousness of Christ's obedience and that, because of this righteousness, we are accepted by God into grace and regarded as righteous. . . .

5. We believe, teach, and confess that according to the usage of Holy Scripture the word "to justify" in this article means "to absolve," that is, "to pronounce free from sin": "One who justifies the wicked and one who condemns the righteous are both alike an abomination to the Lord" (Prov. 17[:15]); "Who will bring any charge against God's elect? It is God who justifies" (Rom. 8[:33]). When in place of this the words *regeneratio* and *vivificatio,* that is "new birth" and "making alive," are used as synonyms of justification, as happens in the Apology, then they are to be understood in this same sense. Otherwise, they should be understood as the renewal of the human being and should be differentiated from "justification by faith."

THE CRYPTO-CALVINIST CONTROVERSY

133. The Consensus of the Churches of Zurich and Geneva (1549)

Although the Zurich Consensus (also called the *Consensus Tigurinus*) never gained the status of a formal confession for the Reformed tradition, it was important as the first successful effort to reconcile the eucharistic theology of the churches influenced by Zwingli and Calvin.

From *Consensus Tigurinus,* trans. Henry Beveridge (rev. ed.; Edinburgh: Calvin Translation Society, 1849), 218–20.

16. ALL WHO PARTAKE OF THE SACRAMENTS DO NOT PARTAKE OF THE REALITY

We carefully teach that God does not exert his power indiscriminately in all who receive the sacraments, but only in the elect. For as he enlightens unto faith none but those whom he has foreordained to life, so by the secret agency of his Spirit he makes the elect receive what the sacraments offer.

21. NO LOCAL PRESENCE MUST BE IMAGINED

We must guard particularly against the idea of any local presence [of the body and blood of Christ with the bread and wine of the Lord's Supper]. For while the signs are present in this world, are seen by the eyes, and handled by the hands, Christ, regarded as man, must be sought nowhere else than in heaven, and not otherwise than with the mind and eye of faith. Therefore it is a perverse and impious superstition to enclose him under the elements of this world.

22. EXPLANATION OF THE WORDS "THIS IS MY BODY"

Those who insist that the formal words of the Supper—"This is my body; this is my blood," are to be taken in what they call the precisely literal sense, we repudiate as preposterous interpreters. For we hold it out of controversy that they are to be taken figuratively—the bread and wine receiving the name of that which they signify. . . .

25. THE BODY OF CHRIST LOCALLY IN HEAVEN

And that no ambiguity may remain when we say that Christ is to be sought in heaven, the expression implies and is understood by us to intimate distance of place. For though philosophically speaking there is no place above the skies, yet as the body of Christ, bearing the nature and mode of a human body, is finite and is contained in heaven as its place, it is necessarily as distant from us in point of space as heaven is from earth.

134. Calvin to all Ministers of Christ in the Churches of Saxony and Lower Germany (1556)

This personal defense and appeal from John Calvin to the Lutherans of Germany appeared as a preface to his "Second Defense of the Sacraments in Answer to Westphal."

From *CR* (1870) 37:46–50.

Because the dispute concerning the sacraments that was unhappily carried on among the learned for more than twenty years has now with some effort been calmed for a short while, and people's minds are disposed to moderation, it seemed especially fitting to facilitate a full settlement by giving a public statement in few and simple terms of the doctrine that the churches of Switzerland follow. . . . Most of you are acquainted with the short description that we published five years ago with the title *Consensus Tigurinus,* in which, without attacking anyone and without any bitter words, we not only compiled a summary of the whole controversy under distinct headings, but also endeavored, insofar as a frank confession of truth allowed, to heal all offenses completely. . . .

About two years later, a certain Joachim Westphal arose who, rather than being softened to concord by the temperate simplicity of that doctrinal summary, seized upon the name of *Consensus* as a kind of Furie's torch to rekindle the flame. . . . He writes that my books were highly prized and esteemed by the people of his sect during the time when they thought I differed from the teachers of the church of Zurich. Then why this sudden alienation now? Is it because I have deviated from my former opinion? . . . How can it be that the doctrine that formerly pleased him in my writings now repulses him so strongly when it is professed by the people of Zurich? . . . I was forced to refute the perverse attack of this man in a short treatise. He, as if an inexpiable crime had been committed, has flamed forth much more intemperately. It has now become necessary for me to repress his insolence. . . .

The dispute with him concerns three articles: First, he insists that the bread of the Supper is substantially the body of Christ. Second, to explain how Christ may exhibit his presence to believers in the Supper, he maintains that the body is boundless and exists everywhere without locality. Thirdly, he does not want to allow for any figure of speech in the words of Christ, however much agreement there may be as to this matter. He considers it so important to take a stand on these words that he would prefer to see the whole world convulsed than admit any interpretation. We defend the view that the flesh and blood of Christ are truly offered to us in the Supper such that they vivify our souls, and we unambiguously specify that our souls are invigorated by this spiritual food that is offered us in the Supper, just as our bodies are nourished by earthly bread. Therefore we maintain that in the Supper there is a true participation in the flesh and blood of Christ. If anyone is moved to dispute about the word "substance," we assert that Christ breathes life into our souls from the substance of his flesh; indeed, he infuses his own life into us, although it should in no way be imagined that there is a transfusion of substance.

This is the cause of the implacable wrath of Westphal: when we confess that the flesh of Christ gives life and that we are truly partakers of it in the Supper, he is not satisfied with this simplicity but urges and contends that the bread is substantially the body. From this another dogma emerges, namely, that the body and blood of Jesus Christ are taken into the mouth of an impious person in the very same way as bread and wine. For how can it be that he affirms so obstinately that the body of Christ was taken by Judas no less than by Peter, unless it is because the substance of the sign is not changed by a person's unbelief? Furthermore, he imagines a substance that is not at all consistent with the Word of God, namely, that Christ fastens his own flesh substantially to the bread. . . .

The second question arises from no other source than the mode of communion that Westphal considers to be necessarily connected up with the boundless nature of Christ's body. According to him, if the body of Christ be not actually placed before us, there is no real communion. We hold the contrary view that no distance of space hinders the boundless energy of the Spirit, which transfuses life into us from the flesh of Christ. And here we detect the depravity of those who odiously scatter the idea among the people that we take away the presence of Christ from the Supper because we estimate the power of God according to our own sense. As if the sublimity of this mystery did not transcend the reach of human intellect, the mystery that Christ, though remaining in heaven with regard to the placement of his body, still descends to us by the secret grace of his Spirit, so that, having united us to himself, he makes us partakers of his life. The power of God is less magnificently extolled by one who teaches that life flows into us from the flesh of Christ, than by another who draws his flesh out of heaven so that it may give us life. . . .

In order not to delay your reading of my book any longer, I will now touch on the last issue in this dispute. He thinks it sinful to inquire into what Jesus Christ meant when he said that the bread is his body because, in his mind, the clarity of the words precludes the need for any interpretation. We again appeal to the familiar and common usage of Scripture, which, whenever it deals with the sacraments, transfers the name of the thing signified to the sign. Examples of this occur not only once or twice, but so frequently that those who are practiced in the interpretation of Scripture consider it to be the common rule. . . . Therefore, those who deny that the body of Christ is represented to us under the symbol of bread pervert not only the whole order of Christ but the Spirit of God of its customary mode of speech. Westphal attributes the name of body to the bread. But where is his modesty when he is so puffed up as to cry out that any interpretation of the words must be considered the greatest sacrilege?

It is appropriate to point, as with the finger, to the sources of the whole controversy in order to expose the fact that a disagreement that ought to have been extinct is again kindled, more from the haughty disdain of the opposing party than from any just cause. If you fear a deadly and lamentable result, as one certainly ought to fear (and there is certainly ground to fear it), I entreat you, by the sacred name of Christ and the bond of our unity in him, to endeavor earnestly to find a remedy. Whatever be the method of conciliation offered, I declare that I will be not only favorably disposed but also eager to embrace it. . . .

135. The Dresden Consensus of 1571

In 1570 the Philippist theologians of Saxony published a new catechism that contained hints that they were sympathetic to Calvin's view of the Lord's Supper. When asked to clarify their views, they produced this document.

From Johann Gieseler, *Church History*, vol. 4 (New York: Harper, 1868), 466–67.

Although the human nature of Christ was transfigured after the resurrection and ascension and purified of all weaknesses to which it was previously subject, and although it was endowed with higher properties than those belonging to angels and men, nevertheless it remained a truly human nature and had the essential attributes that pertain to such a nature. It was not deified or endowed with eternity, or infinitude of being or with other similar divine attributes, but truly and certainly remained flesh of our flesh and bone of our bone. . . .

We interpret the description and story of the ascension of Christ to heaven literally, maintaining that the ascension was not a mere appearance and not only a visible spectacle and that our Lord Jesus Christ has retained his true body from earth in heaven. He penetrated the visible heavens and occupied his heavenly dwelling where, in glory and majesty, he retains the essence, attributes, form, and shape of his true body and from where he will visibly come again in the last days to judge with great majesty. . . .

We believe and maintain that in the dispensation of the Lord's Supper, our Lord Jesus is truly and certainly present and that with the bread and wine he gives us his true body sacrificed for us on the cross and his true blood that he shed for us, and thereby testifies that he receives us, makes us members of his body, purifies us with his blood, gives us forgiveness of sins, and truly wishes to dwell and be efficacious in us. . . .

We shun all the alien disputes pertaining to the institution of this Supper, conflicts that

Luther himself zealously tried to avoid. He often said that there should not be disputes about omnipresence or ubiquity. But in recent times restless people have begun to inflict them upon us again, just as we have also experienced much grief concerning other issues since the German war, so that everything that had formerly been considered right and undisputed has now been mischievously interpreted wrongly and falsified. These restless people bring charges against the churches and schools of this land, which always maintained one form of teaching. They do not seek either the truth or peace but provoke very dangerous and vexing disputations not only about the article concerning the true presence of the body and blood of Christ in the Lord's Supper but also about other articles. And what is most dreadful, they corrupt simple and certain teachings with unfounded and alien opinions.

136. *Exegesis Perspicua* (of the Saxon Crypto-Calvinists) (1573)

This document appeared anonymously in 1573. Later it was attributed to Joachim Curaeus, a Silesian physician with Philippist sympathies. In addition to calling for toleration of a range of views about the Lord's Supper, it restated Philippist reservations about the Lutheran doctrines that had been contested by Calvin and criticized in the *Consensus Tigurinus*.

From Joachim Curaeus, *Exegesis Perspicua et ferme integra controversiae de sacro coena* (Heidelberg: Maier, 1575), 190–92.

All purified churches should be in harmony with one another, and this harmony should not be disturbed on account of disagreements about the Lord's Supper. Let us be brothers; let us be one in Christ. Omitting this dangerous talk about ubiquity, about the eating of the true body by the impious and similar things, the teachers in our churches should agree upon a certain formula that can provoke no offense. With Paul, they should say that the bread is the communion of the body of Christ [1 Cor. 10:16]. The way of speaking that has been handed down in the writings of Melanchthon should be used and much should be said of the benefits that result when this is the foundation in this case. . . .

It would be advantageous to put to rest all public disputations concerning this matter, and if contentious persons stir up quarrels and unrest among the people, the proper thing to do, as Philip advised, is to remove such persons from either party and substitute more modest people in their places. . . . Teachers ought to serve with a spirit of harmony, recommend the churches and teachers of the opposing party, and publicly denounce the wrongful beliefs that people have devised concerning them.

137. Epitome of the Formula of Concord: Articles 7 and 8 (1577)

From *BC* 503–11.

VII. CONCERNING THE HOLY SUPPER OF CHRIST . . .

To explain this controversy, it must first of all be noted that there are two kinds of sacramentarians. There are the crude sacramentarians, who state in plain language what they believe in their hearts: that in the Holy Supper there is nothing more than bread and wine present, nothing more distributed and received with the mouth. Then there are the cunning sacramentarians, the most dangerous kind, who in part appear to use our language and who pretend that they also believe in a true presence of the true, essential, living body and blood of Christ in the Holy Supper, but that this takes place spiritually, through faith. Yet, under the guise of such plausible words, they retain the former, crude opinion, that nothing more than bread and wine is present in the Holy Supper and received there by mouth.

For "spiritually" means to them nothing other than "the spirit of Christ" that is present, or "the power of the absent body of Christ and his merit." The body of Christ, according to this opinion, is, however, in no way or form present, but it is only up there in the highest heaven; to this body we lift ourselves into heaven through the thoughts of our faith. There we should seek his body and blood, but never in the bread and wine of the Supper.

Affirmative Theses

The Confession of Pure Teaching concerning the Holy Supper, against the Sacramentarians

1. We believe, teach, and confess that in the Holy Supper the body and blood of Christ are truly and essentially present, truly distributed and received with the bread and wine.

2. We believe, teach, and confess that the words of the testament of Christ are not to be understood in any other way than the way they literally sound, that is, not that the bread symbolizes the absent body and the wine the absent blood of Christ, but that they are truly the true body and blood of Christ because of the sacramental union. . . .

6. We believe, teach, and confess that the body and blood of Christ are received not only spiritually through faith but also orally with the bread and wine, though not in Capernaitic fashion but rather in a supernatural, heavenly way because of the sacramental union of the elements. The words of Christ clearly demonstrate this, when Christ said, "take, eat, and

drink," and the apostles did this. For it is written, "and they all drank from it" (Mark 14[:23]). Likewise, St. Paul says, "The bread, which we break, is a Communion with the body of Christ" [1 Cor. 10:16], that is, who eats this bread eats the body of Christ. The leading teachers of the ancient church—Chrysostom, Cyprian, Leo I, Gregory, Ambrose, Augustine, and others—unanimously testify to this.

7. We believe, teach, and confess that not only those who truly believe and are worthy, but also the unworthy and unbelievers receive the true body and blood of Christ, though they do not receive life and comfort, but rather judgment and damnation, if they do not turn and repent. . . .

Negative Theses . . .

[We unanimously reject and condemn . . .]

5. That the body of Christ in the holy sacrament is not received orally with the bread, but only bread and wine are received by mouth; the body of Christ, however, is received only spiritually, through faith.

11. That the body of Christ is enclosed in heaven, so that it can in no way be present at the same time in many or all places on earth where his Holy Supper is being conducted.

21. We also hereby completely condemn the Capernaitic eating of the body of Christ. It suggests that his flesh is chewed up with the teeth and digested like other food. The sacramentarians maliciously attribute this view to us against the witness of their own conscience, despite our many protests. In this way they make our teaching detestable among their hearers. . . .

VIII. CONCERNING THE PERSON OF CHRIST

Out of the controversy regarding the Holy Supper there arose a disagreement between the theologians of the Augsburg Confession who teach purely and the Calvinists (who also led some other theologians astray) over the person of Christ, the two natures in Christ, and their characteristics.

Status controversiae

Chief Issues of Disagreement in This Dispute
The chief question was whether on the basis of the personal union the divine and human natures—and likewise the characteristics of each—are intimately linked with each other within the person of Christ, in reality (that is, in fact and in truth), and to what extent they are intimately linked.

Affirmative Theses . . .

11. According to the personal union he always possessed this majesty, and yet dispensed with it in the state of his humiliation. For this reason he grew in stature, wisdom, and grace before God and other people [Luke 2:52]. Therefore, he did not reveal his majesty at all times but only when it pleased him, until he completely laid aside the form of a servant [Phil. 2:7] (but not his human nature) after his resurrection. Then he was again invested with the full use, revelation, and demonstration of his divine majesty and entered into his glory, in such a way that he knows everything, is able to do everything, is present for all his creatures, and has under his feet and in his hands all that is in heaven, on earth, and under the earth, not only as God but also as human creature, as he himself testifies, "All authority in heaven and on earth has been given to me" [Matt. 28:18], and St. Paul writes: He ascended "above all the heavens, so that he might fill all things" [Eph. 4:10]. As present everywhere he can exercise this power of his, he can do everything, and he knows all things.

12. Therefore, he is able—it is very easy for him—to share his true body and blood, present in the Holy Supper, not according to the manner or characteristic of the human nature, but according to the manner and characteristic of God's right hand, as Dr. Luther says in [his explanation of] our Christian creed. This presence is not an earthly nor a Capernaitic presence, but at the same time it is a true and essential presence, as the words of his testament say, "This is, is, my body," etc.

Chapter Six

Theology in the Age of Orthodoxy
(1580–1700)

✛

The writings of Martin Luther are full of references to the importance of correct doctrine. In an early confrontation with a Catholic opponent, Luther boldly stated: "Bad doctrine is a thousand times more harmful than a bad life" (WA 6:581). In a 1530 sermon he clarified the basis for this conviction: "Where doctrine is not right, it is impossible for life to be right and good; for life must be prepared by doctrine and must follow it" (WA 32:408). For this reason, Luther would repeatedly call for vigilant attendance to the task of defending true doctrine and refuting false teachings. In response to another Catholic opponent, he wrote, "Whether you are pious or evil does not concern me. But I will attack your poisonous and lying teaching that contradicts God's Word; and with God's help I will oppose it vigorously" (WA 7:279). Luther reformulated this sentiment as a general principle in his commentary on Galatians: "In matters concerning faith we must be invincible, inflexible, and exceedingly obstinate; indeed, if possible, harder than steel" (WA 40/1:188).

In the post-Reformation era that from the perspective of church history is usually called the Age of Orthodoxy, most Lutheran theologians were preoccupied with this concern. Indeed, they rivaled Luther in their zeal for the clarification and defense of correct doctrine. The adoption of the Book of Concord as the fullest measure of the Lutheran confessional position can, for the sake of convenience, be considered the starting point of this new period. By 1580 the original leaders of the Lutheran reform movement had all passed from the scene. The Lutheran church had also successfully disposed of a recent, internal threat to its unity by agreeing upon the Formula of Concord, a more elaborate statement of confessional beliefs addressing the disputed issues that had divided church leaders into several competing factions in the decades immediately after Luther's death. The initial, formative stages in the development of the Lutheran tradition were over. In the next phase of Lutheran history, extending throughout the seventeenth century, theologians tended to see themselves as conservators of the achievements that had been gained by the first two generations of reformers and as defenders of a distinctive doctrinal viewpoint that defined their identity over against other rival religious movements.

Martin Chemnitz (1522–86) was the most important transitional figure between the late Reformation and the Age of Orthodoxy. Along with Jakob Andreae, he had been the driving force behind the composition of the Formula of Concord. While attending to the problem of disunity within the Lutheran movement, he had also devoted considerable energy to refuting the doctrinal positions of other religious groups. In his *Examination of the Council of Trent*, Chemnitz produced the definitive Lutheran evaluation of the dogmatic decrees that had been formulated by the Roman Catholic Church in response to the Protestant Reformation (doc. #146). Chemnitz also wrote more focused books on Christology and the Lord's Supper that were inspired, to a large extent, by his desire to clarify and defend Lutheran doctrine in response to the criticisms of Calvinist Protestants (docs. #143 and 144). While serving as a pastor and church administrator in northern Germany, he also prepared an explanation of the *Loci Communes* of his teacher, Philip Melanchthon. When this book was posthumously published in 1591 as the *Loci Theologici*, it was widely honored as a valuable corrective to the more controversial aspects of Melanchthon's interpretation of Lutheran doctrine.

After the death of Chemnitz, theological leadership was generally exercised by clergy who taught at several prominent German universities. In the early part of the seventeenth century, the greatest representative of Lutheran Orthodoxy was Johann Gerhard (1582–1637), a professor at the University of Jena. In his multivolume (approximately 2,800 pages) systematic theology, also titled *Loci Theologici*, Gerhard broke new ground in the development of theological method. To clarify the nature and sources of theological knowledge, he discussed the objectives of theological investigation and the authority of the Bible before he began his analysis of specific Christian doctrinal beliefs (docs. #138–142). Gerhard also introduced more extensive use of Aristotelian metaphysical categories in his analysis of the articles of faith. This initiative began a trend among Lutheran theologians who, in subsequent generations, would continue to reappropriate the philosophical resources that had been commonly used in Catholic theology and would increasingly write in a style reminiscent of medieval scholasticism (docs. #143–146).

Many prominent Lutheran theologians taught at other universities in Tübingen, Strassburg, Giessen, Leipzig, and Helmstedt, but the institution that had the most sustained effect on the development of Lutheran Orthodoxy was the University of Wittenberg, where Luther had taught. At the beginning of the seventeenth century, its theological faculty was noted for the contributions of Aegidius Hunnius (1563–1616), who wrote extensive biblical commentaries, and Leonard Hutter (1563–1616), whose *Compend of Lutheran Theology*, in simple question-and-answer format, would be used for generations as a concise textbook for the training of pastors and teachers. By the middle of the century, Wittenberg had developed a widespread reputation as the chief bastion of strict Lutheran Orthodoxy. Nikolaus Hunnius (1585–1643), son of Aegidius Hunnius, was especially noted for clarifying the distinction between fundamental and non-fundamental articles of faith, a topic of great significance in the ongoing debates about how Lutherans should relate to Catholics and Calvinists (doc. #142). Abraham Calov (1612–86) produced the most influential Lutheran biblical commentary of the century, his *Biblia Illustrata*, and was renowned for his skill as a polemicist. He wrote extensively and passionately against other religious groups, such as the Roman Catholics, Calvinists, Arminians, and Socinians, but devoted his greatest energy to combating the Syncretists, advocates of reconciliation between different church groups who supported the liberal viewpoint about fundamental articles introduced by Georg Calixtus of the University of Helmstedt (doc. #147).

In the latter half of the seventeenth century, Johann Quenstedt (1617–88), another Wittenberg theologian, became the dominant voice among Lutheran dogmaticians. His *Didactico-Polemical Theology* ranks with the major works of Chemnitz and Gerhard as one of the outstanding theological systems written during the Age of Orthodoxy (docs. #138–141). Quenstedt's popularity in his own age and his influence upon theologians in subsequent centuries were due not so much to his creativity as to his ability to produce an effectively organized and thorough summary of a century of Lutheran theological reflection since the adoption of the Formula of Concord. This is also true of the last notable dogmatician of the Age of Orthodoxy, David Hollaz (1648–1713), who had studied under Calov and Quenstedt at Wittenberg. His meticulously categorized *Examination of Acroamatic Theology* marked the culmination of the scholastic tendencies that had developed in Lutheran dogmatics (docs. #138–141). In other respects, however, Hollaz was untypical of the Orthodox theologians. First of all, he spent his whole life as a pastor in northern Germany and never taught at a university. Secondly, his extensive attention to the issue of how doctrinal belief relates to the practical matter of living a Christian life reveals the influence of the Pietist reform movement that would make this concern the preeminent issue in the next period of Lutheran history.

Although all of these dogmatic theologians were especially interested in demonstrating continuity among the Formula of Concord, the earlier Lutheran confessions, the theology of Luther, the early creeds of the church, and the Scriptures, it would be a mistake to portray them merely as systematizers of earlier thought. They extended the analysis of certain issues that had been treated quite briefly during the Reformation and, in some cases, developed convictions about the method and content of theology that diverged from the viewpoints of Luther and his associates. Theologians in the first half of the seventeenth century mostly followed the *Locus* method pioneered by Philip Melanchthon. They treated Christian theology as a collection of articles of faith that could be separated into discrete topics or *loci*, arranged synthetically in a cause-to-effect sequence, and verified by evidence derived from the teachings of the Bible. Starting with consideration of the nature and creative work of God, they proceeded to describe human nature before and after the Fall, the problem of human sin, the way to salvation offered through Christ, and finally, the doctrine of the Church and the Last Things. Within this common framework, they nevertheless displayed much variety in the way they divided up the subject matter of theology. At times, they created new subcategories to distinguish between various facets of key topics, and some of these distinctions eventually became standard elements of systematic theology. For example, whereas earlier Lutheran systematicians presented the doctrine of salvation quite simply in a single *locus* on justification, Orthodox theologians from the time of Nikolaus Hunnius onward laid out a detailed order of salvation *(ordo salutis)*, which differentiated between six or seven aspects of the application of grace, beginning with the divine call to the sinner and reaching a completion in mystical union with God (doc. #148).

In the second half of the seventeenth century, some theologians began to depart more extensively from the arrangements introduced by Melanchthon. Instead of favoring the synthetic method, they developed an analytic method that first considered the goal of the divine plan for humanity and then proceeded to show how attainment of this goal has been made possible. For example, Johann Dannhauer (1603–66), the most noted theologian at the University of Tübingen, began his innovative systematic theology, *Hodosophia Christiana*, by describing God as the *summum bonum* toward which all of life was intended to point and depicting humans as pilgrims traveling the sacred way toward this goal. He described sin as an obstacle along the way, Christ as the savior who leads humans back to God, and Scripture as the light that illuminates the path of their journey.

From the time of Gerhard onward, the theologians continued to work out their thoughts about the nature of theological investigation and greatly expanded the prolegomena with which they introduced their systematic theologies. The issue of the role of reason and philosophy in the work of the theologian attracted renewed attention. Like Luther, the Orthodox dogmaticians always emphasized the limits of reason and the need for the revelation recorded in the Scriptures, yet they were also concerned to show how reason and philosophy could be valuable as secondary resources to help explicate and defend the conclusions derived from revelation (doc. #139). Luther had strongly criticized the scholastic theology of the Roman Catholic tradition for its use of Aristotle, but the Orthodox theologians once again argued for a selective use of the terminology and categories that this type of theology and philosophy provided.

As they probed the nature of revelation and responded to Catholic criticisms of the Lutheran understanding of Scripture, the Orthodox theologians also greatly expanded their analysis of the normative authority of the Bible. In their efforts to establish the dependability of the Scriptures as a source of divine truth, they went beyond Luther in their insistence upon the divine inspiration of the specific words of the biblical books, the inerrancy of the texts with regards to all aspects of truth, and the complete reliability of every part of the traditional biblical canon (doc. #141).

In addition to affirming the reliability of the Scriptures and showing how the articles of faith of the Lutheran confessions were true and consistent with this source of revelation, the theologians also attempted to point out the weaknesses of antithetical viewpoints defended by other religious groups (docs. #143–146). The systematic theologies of this period were almost always both didactic and polemical. The doctrinal debates of the Reformation era were not forgotten, and the task of confronting and refuting the beliefs of Roman Catholics and Calvinists seemed all the more urgent because political trends in this period convinced the theologians that these groups in particular continued to pose a serious threat to the very survival of Lutheranism. In 1555 the Peace of Augsburg had awarded a degree of toleration to the Lutherans in parts of the Holy Roman Empire, but by 1618 Catholics and Protestants were once again clashing on the battlefield. Decades of bitter confrontation with Catholics in the Thirty Years War sharpened the resistance of most secular and religious leaders to the thought of toleration or coexistence. At times, however, the Lutheran dogmaticians seemed to be even more concerned about the threats posed by the Calvinists. Again, political factors helped to intensify this consciousness. Even before the start of the Thirty Years War, the Lutherans had lost control of several German territories when rulers switched their support to the Calvinist tradition. This happened in the Palatinate in 1561, in Hesse and Bremen in 1581, in Anhalt in 1595, and finally in Brandenburg in 1613.

There were exceptions, however, to this intense feeling of rivalry between religious groups. While the other theologians engaged in their polemics, Georg Calixtus (1586–1656) of the University of Helmstedt called for the establishment of closer fellowship between Lutherans and other Christian groups on the basis of their shared acceptance of the Apostles' Creed. In addition, he argued that the points of differences between the groups were not over matters that would affect the salvation or damnation of individual believers (doc. #147). To most Lutheran theologians, the irenic perspective of Calixtus and his fellow Syncretists looked dangerous and based on faulty assumptions, but the chorus of voices lamenting the excesses to which polemics were taken would grow steadily as the seventeenth century progressed. This issue would also be taken up in the writings of several of the major Lutheran devotional writers of the Age of Orthodoxy and would surface again as a concern of the Pietists.

THEOLOGICAL PROLEGOMENA

In Philip Melanchthon's *Loci Communes*, the first Lutheran systematic theology, published in 1521, there was no preliminary discussion of the nature and character of theology. This topic was only addressed elsewhere in Melanchthon's writings about the use of dialectics. In the later half of the sixteenth century, Andreas Hyperius (1511–64) and David Chytraeus (1531–1600) devoted whole books to the topic of how theology should be studied, concentrating particularly on issues related to the interpretation of the Bible. In the seventeenth century, these topics became a standard focus of attention in the introductory sections or prolegomena of any systematic theology. In their fullest development, the formal prolegomena to dogmatics discussed the definition of theology, its subject matter, the purpose and proper method of theological study, and the sources of religious knowledge. This involved analysis of the role of reason and natural theology as well as divine revelation and its relation to the canon of the Bible.

The following excerpts give some representative samples of what major dogmaticians had to say about these topics. Johann Gerhard was the first dogmatician to construct a formal prolegomenon. Quenstedt and Hollaz summarized the consensus of belief as it had developed in the later stages of the Age of Orthodoxy.

The following selections have been translated from: Johann Gerhard, *Loci Theologici* (Frankfurt/Hamburg: Hertelius, 1657) (first published 1610–25); Johann Quenstedt, *Theologia Didactico-Polemica* (Leipzig: Fritsch, 1715) (first published 1685); and David Hollaz, *Examen Theologicum Acroamaticum* (Leipzig: Kiesewetter, 1735). [first published 1707]

138. The Discipline of Theology

GERHARD: *Loci Theologici*
Bk. 1, Prooemium 31
Theology, considered systematically and abstractly, is doctrine drawn from the Word of God by which men are instructed in true faith and pious living to eternal life. Theology, considered in the way of practice and concretely, is a divinely given disposition conferred upon a man by the Holy Spirit through the Word, whereby he is not only instructed in the knowledge of divine mysteries, by the illumination of the mind, so that what he understands leads to a salutary effect upon the feelings of his heart and the actions of his life, but also rendered fitted and ready to inform others concerning these divine mysteries and the way of salvation, and to vindicate heavenly truth against the corruptions of its disparagers; so that men, radiant with true faith and good works, are brought into the kingdom of heaven.

QUENSTEDT: *Theologia Didactico-Polemica*
Pt. 1, ch. 1, sect. 2, q. 3
A distinction is made between theoretical sciences, which consist wholly in the mere contemplation of the truth, and practical sciences, which, indeed, require a knowledge of whatever is to be done, but which do not end in this, nor have it as their aim, but which lead to practice and action. We think that theology is to be numbered, not with the theoretical, but with the practical sciences.

Pt. 1, ch. 1, sect. 1, theses 15–24
Revealed theology, drawn from the revealed word of Scripture, is knowledge of God and divine things that God communicates in verbal

revelations to men in this life, to the praise of his glorious grace and for the salvation of man.

Catechetical theology, which extracts only the preeminent parts of Christian doctrine, educates the uncultured common people. It is also called elementary or initial theology because it first deals with the elements and rudiments of the Christian religion and occupies itself especially with laying the foundation of the doctrine of faith.

Acroamatic theology, which teaches the mysteries of the faith more accurately and extensively, confirms sound doctrine and confutes errors that are contrary to the truth. It informs bishops and presbyters of the church and primarily those in the academies who are not only Christians but will become teachers of Christians. Note: Catechetical and acroamatic theology do not differ in what they consider but in the manner and object of their considerations.

Acroamatic theology, as to the manner of its treatment, is either exegetical, or didactic strictly so-called, or polemical, or homiletical, or casuistic, or historical.

Exegetical or biblical theology, which is also called prophetic by some, is concerned with the paraphrasing or richer explication of sacred Scripture and with the comparing of commentaries. It investigates the true and genuine meaning of the whole or particular books or texts.

Didactic theology, strictly so-called, which is also called systematic or thetic or positive theology, presents the commonplaces (loci communes) of theology in order, states them clearly, exactly defines the dogmas of the faith, and, having separated them into parts, deduces and demonstrates them from the foundation of faith, which they have in sacred Scripture.

Polemical theology, both controversial and elenctic, which some call scholastic or, more often, academic, treats past and recent theological controversies, rightly delineates the state of a question, confirms the celestial truth of argu-

ments sought from sacred Scripture, vindicates what has been confirmed against exceptions, asserts what has been vindicated against objections, and occupies itself in building up truth and destroying falsehood.

Homiletical theology, which they also call ecclesiastical theology, informs those who will become ministers of the church about the method of public speaking and the practice of preachers.

Casuistic theology, which some also call consistorial, reflects on matters of conscience, or contributes to the formation of conscience in doubtful cases, so that it may be strengthened if weak, emended and corrected if in error, and firmly established if troubled or in doubt.

Historical theology explains the history of the ancient, primitive church and how the doctrine of the gospel was propagated in it by the orthodox, attacked by the heretics, defended by councils, and then proclaimed by teachers orally and in writings.

HOLLAZ: *Examen*
ch. 1, Prolegomena, q. 18

A theologian, in the general sense of the term, is a man well instructed in the discipline of theology, whereby he is rendered prompt in explicating and defending heavenly truth. The theologian, in a special and more excellent sense, is said to be a reborn man, offering unshakable assent to the truths that reveal the mystery of the faith and relying on the same by trust, who is adept in teaching others and confuting opponents.

ch. 1, q. 30

The study of theological controversies is especially necessary for those aspiring toward the higher offices in the church. Knowledge of controversies is likewise necessary for those preparing themselves for lower positions. . . .

Controversies that are useless and thorny and arise from the domination of perverse states of mind are unworthy of theological inquiry or discussion.

139. The Sources of Theology: Reason and Revelation

GERHARD: *Loci*

Bk. 1, *Locus* 21: *De Scriptura Sacra,* 474

Divine revelation, not human reason, is the starting point of faith, nor are we to judge concerning the articles of faith according to the dictates of reason, otherwise we would not have articles of faith, but only opinions of reason. The thoughts and pronouncements of reason are to be restrained and restricted within the sphere of those things that are subject to the decision of reason, and not to be extended to the sphere of those things that are placed entirely beyond the grasp of reason. . . .

Sound reason is not opposed to faith, if it is understood to be that which is truly and properly called reason, namely, that which does not transcend the limits of its sphere, and does not arrogate to itself decisions concerning the mysteries of faith, or that which, illumined by the Word, and rectified by the Holy Spirit, does not follow its own principles in the investigation of the mysteries of the faith, but is led by the light of the Word and the guidance of the Holy Spirit. . . .

QUENSTEDT: *Theologia Didactico-Polemica*

ch. 3: *De Theologia Principio,* sect. 2

A distinction should be made between human reason before the Fall and after the Fall. Formerly, it was never opposed to revelation, but now, vitiated by corruption, it is very often an adversary. . . .

A distinction must be made between [1] the organic or instrumental use of reason and its

Johann Gerhard

principles, when they are employed as instruments for the interpretation and exposition of the sacred Scriptures, in refuting the arguments of adversaries drawn from nature and reason, in discussing the signification and construction of words, and rhetorical figures and modes of speech; and [2] the normal use of philosophical principles, when they are regarded as principles by which supernatural doctrines are to be tested. The former we admit, the latter we repudiate. . . .

A distinction should be made between pure theological questions and mixed ones (in which both philosophy and theology are used). We concede that in the mixed questions, principles particular to philosophy may be employed, not for the purpose of decision or demonstration, but merely for illustration or as a sort of secondary proof where the matter has already been decided from Scripture.

HOLLAZ: *Examen*

ch. 3, q. 4

Without the use of reason, we cannot comprehend and confirm dogmatic theology, nor vindicate it from the artifices of adversaries. Certainly, God revealed the wisdom of eternal salvation in his Word not to irrational brutes but to men possessing sound reason, and bestowed on them the grave mandate that they should read, hear, and study his Word (Deut. 6:6; John 5:39). And so intellect is required for receiving this subject and apprehending its methods. For just as we cannot see without eyes, or hear without ears, so we can understand nothing without reason. However, human reason is not the source or primordial element from which the proper and most immediately related principles of faith are derived.

140. Natural and Revealed Theology

GERHARD: *Loci*

Bk. 1, *Locus* 2: *De Natura Dei*, ch. 4, 59

It is possible to demonstrate the existence of God either from nature or from Scripture. For that reason, Augustine in book eight of *The City of God* distinguishes between natural and revealed knowledge of God. . . .

The Book of Nature can teach in two ways, internally and externally; consequently natural knowledge [of God] is divided into two types, εμθυτον (innate) and επικτητον (acquired). Innate knowledge has its origin in certain common notions (κοινοις εννοιαις), which are the obscure rubble of the lost divine image or vestiges of the light that enlightened the human mind before the Fall, certain sparks through which that common notion that there is a God is naturally engraved in the minds of all men. Therefore, we also refer those things to the internal book of nature that pertain to the internal testimony of conscience that the Scholastics call *synteresis* (συνιηρησιν). . . .

Acquired knowledge from the Book of Nature is collected by the human mind from contemplation of the works and effects of God and the investigation of nature. . . .

The Book of Scripture supplies a more certain foundation for the proof of the existence

of God; hence revealed knowledge yields more perfect and reliable results.

QUENSTEDT: *Theologia Didactico-Polemica* ch. 4: *De Deo*, sect. 2, q. 1

We must distinguish between natural knowledge of God, viewed in its original integrity, and the same in its crude remains; the former is a perfect θεογνωσια (knowledge of God), constituting a part of the mental aptitude of our first parents, as it was graciously imparted; the latter, on the other hand, is a partial and imperfect knowledge of God, still left behind in our corrupt nature after the Fall. It is, as it were, a little spark of primeval light, a tiny drop from a vast ocean, or a small particle of a splendid house that has burned down. . . .

Natural knowledge of God is not sufficient to secure salvation or even to prevent condemnation, nor has any mortal ever been redeemed, nor can any one ever be redeemed, by it alone.

sect. 2, q. 2

There were many scholastics who taught that it was possible to attain eternal salvation without knowledge of Christ . . . [and] certain Calvinists, such as Zwingli[1] (in his "Exposition of Faith to the King of France") number Hercules, Numa, Aristeides, Socrates, Cato, Scipio, and others among the heavenly blessed and ascribe eternal salvation to them. . . .

We should distinguish between the pedagogical and didactic utility of natural knowledge of God and its utility for generating faith and procuring salvation. We concede the former and deny the latter. . . .

We should distinguish between the full salvation of the Gentiles and a certain mitigation of their punishments in eternal damnation. Our adversaries challenge us based on the authority of Luther, who in chapter twenty-two of the Table Talk said, "Cicero was a wise man, so was Seneca; I hope God will be gracious to them." But he is speaking here not of full salvation but of the mitigation of punishments in eternal damnation. For there are grades of glory in heaven and grades of punishment in hell.

141. Sacred Scripture as Divine Revelation

GERHARD: *Loci*
Bk. 1, *Locus* 1: *De Scriptura Sacra,* ch. 2

The efficient cause of Scripture is either principal or instrumental. The principal cause is the true God, three persons in one essence, Father, Son, and Holy Spirit. . . . The instrumental causes of sacred Scripture are holy men of God (2 Pet. 1:21), that is men, such as the prophets in the Old Testament and the Apostles in the New Testament, who were peculiarly and immediately called and elected by God to record divine revelation in writing. For that reason, we call them the *amanuenses* of God, the hands of Christ, the scriveners or notaries of the Holy Spirit, who did not speak or write according to their own human will but were led, impelled, inspired, and governed by the Holy Spirit.

QUENSTEDT: *Theologia Didactico-Polemica*
ch. 4: *De Sacra Scriptura,* sect. 2, q. 4

The Holy Spirit did not simply inspire the meaning or sense of the words contained in Scripture, which the prophets and apostles then set forth, expressed and embellished with their own words by their own will. The Holy Spirit supplied, inspired, and dictated the very words and each and every utterance to the writers.
sect. 2, q. 5
The original canon of sacred Scripture is infallibly true and free from all error. The canon of sacred Scripture contains no lie, no falsehood, not the least error in word or sense, but all of it

is most true, whatever matter it treats, be it dogmatic, moral, historical, chronological, topographical, or onomastic, for the Holy Spirit must not and could not allow any ignorance, thoughtlessness, forgetfulness, or lapse of memory on the part of the recorders in the consigning of the sacred letters.

HOLLAZ: *Examen*
Prolegomenon 3, *De Scriptura,* q. 17

Erasmus, Suarez, Beza,[2] and others deny that the individual words of the prophets and apostles are divinely inspired. They argue that if each and every word of sacred Scripture were inspired by one Spirit of God, the manner of speaking of all the sacred *amanuenses* would be one and the same style. But their styles are very different.

Our response: It happens among men that a secular author distinguished for his eloquence and talent will display various styles of speaking. Certainly Cicero expressed and cultivated grand, mediocre, and humble styles of speaking and writing. The same practice is found in divine writers: St. John wove together diverse types of writing in his Gospel, his Letters, and the book of Revelation, influenced by the diversity of arguments to which a particular style was appropriate. The Gospel of John sets forth the divinity of Christ by the gravity of its words; the Letters stir up love by the sweetness of their diction; and Revelation explains the fate of the church, in a manner familiar to the prophets. The Holy Spirit gives to each to speak as the circumstance warrants (Acts 2:4).

142. Fundamental Articles of Faith

Efforts to classify doctrines according to their importance first appeared in the writings of Johann Gerhard. This topic attracted further attention when certain Calvinists suggested that the differences between themselves and the Lutherans were not very important. In 1626 Nikolaus Hunnius argued against this viewpoint in his "Careful Examination of the Fundamental Doctrinal Differences between the Lutherans and Calvinists" and thereby stimulated much further debate about the differences between fundamental and non-fundamental articles.

From Διασκεψις *Theologica de Fundamentali Dissensu Doctrinae Evangelicae-Lutheranae et Calvinianae seu Reformate* (**Wittenberg: Fincelius, 1663**), **36, 37, 42.**

ARTICLES OF FAITH: FUNDAMENTAL AND NON-FUNDAMENTAL

HUNNIUS: Διασκεψις

ch. 2, sect. 6:116

The true foundation of faith is one. . . . It is a chain consisting of several loops or articles, which are mutually connected and make up a complete unity. . . . So the foundation of faith contains many particular dogmas, but all are mutually coordinated to make up one whole.

ch. 1, q. 1, sect. 12:51, 54

An article of faith is a part of Christian doctrine through which we are led to eternal salvation.

I distinguish the historical word from the dogmatic word, and the moral teachings, which give rules for how to live, from the dogmas of faith, which teach what one should and should not believe. These latter are actually and properly dogmas. . . . Since now I am not concerned with the foundation of piety but with the foundation of faith, not with what should be done

but with what should be believed, the historical and moral, which at no time deserve to be called articles of faith, should be wholly withdrawn from consideration.

ch. 1, q. 1, sect. 12:56, 57

An article of faith is either fundamental or not fundamental. . . .

Furthermore, fundamental articles are of diverse types: Some are called primary, and others secondary, according to the cause to which they are assigned. The distinction between them consists in this: To be unacquainted with some articles prevents faith and salvation, while it is possible to lack knowledge of certain other articles and still be saved. Nevertheless, to deny the latter jeopardizes salvation. The diversity to which this distinction points can be understood by an example. . . .

Whoever does not know that God wills to be merciful to men living in a state of original sin cannot rest in the firm trust that God wants to be merciful to him. For can he who does not know that God wills to be merciful to anyone conclude that God wants to be merciful to him in particular? Whence it follows that this dogma is a primary fundamental article. . . .

On the other hand, it is clearly possible not to know that God, who made his will known in the writings of the prophets and apostles, is infinite, boundless, and immutable without losing salvation, because trust in God can be preserved inviolate without knowing this. Many simple and good Christians never consider this and many similar doctrines throughout their whole lives without losing faith and salvation on this account. . . .

ch. 1, q. 1, sect. 14:65

It is clear and plain . . . that they who are ignorant of or deny what has been taught in the church concerning the fall and perpetual rejection of certain angels, the confirmation of the good angels, the immortality of man before the Fall, the unforgivable sin against the Holy Spirit . . . and a good many other doctrines of this type are not per se damned, although these matters are nonetheless correct in their substance.

Articles of Faith in Scripture and the Symbolic Books
Hollaz: *Examen*
ch. 2, q. 25, 26

A summary of religion and of the articles of faith is contained in the ancient and more recent symbols. The ancient symbols that are ecumenical or universal are the Apostles' Creed, the Nicene, the Constantinopolitan, the Ephesian, the Chalcedonian, and the Athanasian Creeds. . . .

The more recent symbols of our church are the unaltered Augsburg Confession, the Apology of the Augsburg Confession, the Schmalkald Articles, Luther's Small and Large Catechisms, and the Epitome of Twelve Articles as well as the Solid Declaration, which is called the Formula of Concord. . . . The sacred canonical Scriptures carry the weight of divine authority so that they are the infallible norm by which true dogmas of the faith are distinguished from false ones. The symbolic books have the authority of the church, and they are said to be the respective norm, certainly in respect to the external profession of faith by which we testify to the unanimous consensus of the church as regards the doctrine of the faith. . . .

Sacred Scripture adequately contains all that should be believed and done. No symbolic book perfectly comprehends each and every dogma of faith and precept of morality. . . .

The symbolic books are not absolutely necessary, but hypothetically, the removal of the symbols would have the most grave effect on the state of the church.

Disputed Issues in Didactic and Polemical Theology
Christology and the Lord's Supper

In their disputes with other Protestants about the sacrament of the Lord's Supper, the Lutheran theologians defended the view that Christ could be present with his body and blood in more than one place at the same time. This issue stimulated extensive discussion of how humanity and divinity were united in the person of Christ. In his 1578 book on the two natures of Christ, Martin Chemnitz addressed the latter issue and attempted to show that what Lutheranism taught about the implications of the hypostatic union was supported by the testimony of the Scriptures and consistent with the beliefs of the most venerable theologians of early Christianity. Later, in 1590, in his book on the Lord's Supper, he proceeded to show how the communication of attributes between the two natures of Christ made possible the kind of presence of Christ in the sacrament that the Lutheran confessions affirmed. The following excerpts are interesting for what they reveal about the concerns of this influential theologian and the mode of argumentation he used to defend Lutheran doctrine.

143. Chemnitz: The Two Natures of Christ (1578)

From Martin Chemnitz, *The Two Natures in Christ*, trans. J. A. O. Preus (St. Louis: Concordia, 1971), 15, 19, 20, 22, 261–63.

Dedicatory Epistle

The knowledge of the person of Christ is described in the Word of God as knowing that he is the true God and equal with God

(John 5:18; Phil. 2:6; 1 John 5:20), and that he is made a partaker of flesh and blood as we are, except for sin (Heb. 4:15). That is, there are two natures, the divine and the human, in the incarnate Christ. . . . Scripture also shows that in the works of Christ as Mediator and Savior, because of the hypostatic union, each nature performs in communion with the other that which is proper to it, so that, as in Heb. 2:14, "Through death he destroyed him who had the power of death," and Acts 20:28, "God has redeemed the church with his own blood." On this basis Scripture then leads us to the communication of the majesty *(genus maiestaticum).*[3] For although cleansing from sin and vivification are essentially properties of the majesty of the divine nature of Christ, yet Scripture also predicates vivification, or making alive, to the flesh of Christ (John 6:54). It is written in 1 John 1:7: "The blood of the Son of God cleanses us from sins." Moreover, this communication of majesty does not take place through commingling *(confusio),* conversion, or equating of natures, but through the plan *(oikonomia)* of the hypostatic union, as the ancients used to say. These are the headings under which we customarily divide the explanation of the doctrine of the person of Christ, namely, the two natures, their hypostatic union, and the communication of attributes *(communicatio idiomatum).* . . .

In our own time on the occasion of the controversy over the Sacrament [of the Lord's Supper] I saw that a dispute concerning the hypostatic union of the two natures in Christ, the communication of his attributes, and related matters was raging with heavy debate in the church. Danger signals were becoming evident on both sides, and since I was much concerned with this dispute, I decided that the safest way to educate and remedy my own simplicity would be to consult the fathers of the church, who, in the times of the pristine purity

and learning directly after the apostles, were active in expounding this subject publicly and with characteristic diligence, and to hear them as they conferred among themselves and shared their well-considered and pious opinions on the basis of God's Word. For in this way, like Gregory's pigmies sitting on the shoulders of giants, we can more easily and correctly form a judgment on the basis of God's Word concerning this difficult question, we can acquiesce with more conviction to sound and simple teaching, and we can more safely escape the danger of falling. . . .

To this end I have with considerable zeal and effort collected from approved teachers of the ancient church whose writings have come down to us certain notable citations that seem to serve a useful purpose in elucidating this discussion. I have subjoined them to the testimonies of Scripture, added a brief and simple interpretation, and so distributed them that one can note with what diligence and with what rationale the ancient church constructed the form of true doctrine and sound words concerning this mystery on the foundation of the Word of God, and from what notions and errors it preserved its faith and confession in the midst of this controversy.

I have also cited certain things from the Scholastic writers, wherein they have followed in the footsteps of the ancients; for, as in the case of other doctrines, here also they have often departed from the norm of Scripture and from the paths of the true ancient church. Their disputatious methods, however, ought not produce any prejudice against the truth. . . .

The true and real reason for our faith and confession that Christ wills to be present with his body and blood in the celebration of the Lord's Supper is his own words of institution in which, by a testamentary decree, he reveals his will. For the Son of God says about those elements that are exhibited in the celebration of the Lord's Supper and received in the mouths of the communicants: "This is my body, which is given for you. This is my blood of the New Testament, which is shed for many." But since the essential and natural properties and conditions of a physical body do not permit or allow such a body to be present in different places at the same time, and since the adversaries complain that this kind of presence conflicts with the reality of Christ's human nature, it must surely be demonstrated that, because of the hypostatic union of the divine Logos with the assumed human nature, the Son of God can manifest the presence of his body and blood, which he has promised to the church by his testamentary institution, and that this does not conflict with the actuality of his human nature. . . .

CH. 21: THE COMMUNION OF CHRIST'S HUMAN NATURE WITH THE DIVINE

In Col. 2:9 Paul says: "In Christ dwells the whole fullness of the Godhead bodily." Now it is certain that this whole fullness of the Deity is not some created quality or a finite gift, nor can we say that the whole fullness of the Deity dwells in the divine nature of Christ. Therefore, this passage correctly applies to the body and to his human nature. The adverb "bodily" is so interpreted by Augustine, *Epistola* 57, and also by other fathers.

Origen in his *De Principiis,* Bk. 2, ch. 6, says: "We are sure that some warmth of the Logos must be reckoned to have come to all the saints, but we must also believe that the divine fire itself dwells substantially in the soul of Christ, and from this some warmth comes to others." . . .

Athanasius, *De Ariana et Catholica Confessione:* "God is not changed into human flesh or substance, but in himself he glorified the nature that he assumed, so that human nature with its weak and mortal flesh was exalted into divine glory, whereby it possessed all power in

heaven and on earth, which it did not possess before it was assumed by the Logos." . . .

[Editor's note: Chemnitz cites several passages from other church fathers.]

From these few statements of Scripture and antiquity it becomes clear that as a result of the hypostatic union with the Logos, not only created or finite qualities but also many other things, which cannot be understood as created gifts or qualities but of necessity must be understood as attributes that are proper to the divine nature, have been given to the human nature in Christ above and beyond its essential or natural properties. It is certainly manifest from these quotations that these qualities are predicated as given to Christ in time, not simply according to his divine nature but because of and with respect to the assumed human nature, or according to the human nature, not only to the person in general through concrete terms that designate the person, but expressly to the flesh or to the human nature of Christ; so that I do not understand how anyone can deny it, unless in these matters the god of this world has blinded the minds of those who do not believe.

Therefore the correct understanding of Scripture compels us to hold that above and beyond these divine gifts that were produced or created and are inherent formally in Christ's human nature because of the hypostatic union, there is another and the highest category of gifts given or communicated to Christ according to his humanity, namely the attributes of the divine nature of the Logos themselves, with which the assumed nature of Christ by reason of its union has the kind of communion that fire has when it communicates its essence and power to shine and burn to heated iron, through the union without commingling, so that the heated iron by this union and through the communing shines and burns, as we shall explain more fully later. Therefore, Christ, according to his human nature and insofar as this nature is personally united with the Logos, differs from the other saints not only by reason of his gifts, which by comparison excel the others in number and degree, but also by reason of the union he differs totally from the saints. For in no other nature does the divine glory of the Only-Begotten so shine forth, through no other does it so manifest itself, as in the assumed human nature. . . .

Ch. 23: The True Mode of the Communication of the Majesty

Now let us turn our attention to the true mode of the communication. For no matter how often we reject and deny the commingling, conversion, abolition, and equating, yet the adversaries always vociferously raise the object that we are guilty of an implied contradiction in application and are protesting our innocence contrary to the facts, if by our words we deny the commingling or equating and yet assert that the attributes of the divine nature are actually and truly communicated to the assumed nature because of the personal union. For they cry that this is impossible without commingling and equating. Yet nature itself in the physical world, or rather God in nature, furnishes us clear examples in which we are able not only to understand but also to see and even feel before our very eyes, as it were, how this can take place in the union of two substances, and that there actually is a true and genuine communication of the characteristics of one substance to those of another, without any commingling or equating of the two. In the case of heated iron (this example has been used by the entire ancient church to describe the personal union of the two natures in the person of Christ) the intimate union of the two natures of the fire and the iron takes place through interpenetration (περιχωρησις).

The fire, to be sure, does not take on the properties of the iron, so that it becomes black and cold. Nor is there an abolition of the properties of the iron, for it remains a solid body, and in this union or communion the iron retains essentially also its natural blackness and coldness (although under the heating they do not appear); and when the fire is separated from the hot iron, we see that it has not lost them by abolition. For the blackness and coldness are not added again to the iron from without, but the iron, when it is separated from the fire, then shows that it has retained its own natural properties even under the heating, and it has retained them unimpaired. Nor does the fire produce a different kind of heat and transfer it outside itself to the heated iron, as in the case of boiling water or when the fire is carried in an iron vessel. For through the union the fire communicates to the heated iron its own essence and its essential qualities, such as its glow and the power of giving light and heat; and because of the union the method of communication is that the fire does not glow or give heat of itself or wholly in an absolute sense, as if without burning (πυρωσις), but rather in, with, and through the hot iron. . . .

Since in the case of the union of fire and iron we are able to see and understand that this kind of communication of properties of the iron takes place without commingling or equating, how does the conscience or the godly mind dare to say in the presence of God that this cannot take place in the case of that high and ineffable personal union of the divine and human natures in Christ without commingling or equating, since we have the Scripture as our authority and all antiquity as our witness that such attributes are neither created gifts nor finite qualities but attributes and characteristics of the divine nature itself were given to Christ in time according to his assumed human nature, as we have said before and will show more fully in succeeding chapters? . . .

. . . With my whole mind and body I rebel against the notion which has come from Peter the Martyr[4] that "God with all his omnipotence could not cause a true human body, not even the body of the Son of God, although it is united with the deity and exalted above every name, to be at one and the same time in more than one place with its true essence unimpaired." I also rebel at Beza's statement that "Christ could not have instituted the kind of presence of his body in the Supper that the words indicate." Augustine says that he dared to make no limitations concerning the grace, the activity, and the state of glorified bodies, and that he was unable to form any opinion about them, that it was wholly brash to pontificate about this glory, because the eye has not seen it, nor the ear heard it, and it has not entered into the heart of man. Therefore, how can we venture to say with good conscience that the body of Christ—which is above every name, not only that which is named on earth but also in the world to come and is exalted to the throne of the majesty and power of the eternal Father—that this body is hemmed in and restricted by the normal limits of its nature and the obviously narrow limits of our reason, so that the Son of God in union with his body, with his true nature intact, cannot be present in the Supper, although the words of his will and testament in their simple, proper, and natural sense do teach and promise his presence?

144. Chemnitz: The Lord's Supper (1590)

Martin Chemnitz, *The Lord's Supper,* trans. J. A. O. Preus (St. Louis: Concordia, 1979), 198, 204–5.

CH. 12: CONCERNING THE ARGUMENTS OF THE ADVERSARIES

. . . Human reason understands and our senses themselves grasp that a true human body by reason of its proportions and size cannot be extended and diffused into infinity, but rather has a certain symmetry of its proportions and a certain position of its parts and members, and is circumscribed to one particular place in such a way that by its own natural power it cannot at one and the same time be truly and substantially present in many difference places. Now Scripture certainly affirms that the Son of God according to his human nature has been made like unto his brethren in all respects except for sin.

Therefore, although the proper and natural meaning of the works of institution asserts the true and substantial presence of the body and blood of the Lord in all those places in which the Lord's Supper is celebrated, yet because the human mind cannot comprehend how this can take place while the true integrity of the human nature remains intact, it seeks various pretexts on the basis of other Scripture passages in order that it can under some appearance of being biblical depart from the proper and natural meaning of the testament of the Son of God. . . .

If the major proposition of this argument is stated thus: The human body according to the common and usual condition of its nature is circumscribed to one certain place in such a way that by its own physical nature and power it cannot be in many different places at the same time, then the proposition is true, but it draws no conclusions that are in opposition to the substantial presence of the body of Christ in the Supper. For this does not come about by the common and usual mode of nature, nor by natural power and human reason, but by divine power and heavenly reason. . . .

They object that the essential or natural properties of a body are finite and circumscribed, which we freely grant; but Christ in his Supper is not acting according to the natural properties of a body. For because Scripture predicates them, we accept and believe many other things concerning the flesh of Christ because of the hypostatic union with the divine nature, things that far exceed the natural and essential properties of our bodies, far above every name, as has been indicated. Similarly, because we have an express word regarding the substantial presence of the body and blood of the Lord in the Supper, just why should we depart from the natural meaning of the words of Christ's testament? It is not a sufficiently great or compelling reason, on which conscience could rightly or safely rely, that it does not coincide with our notions of the essential or natural properties of a true body. For it is absolutely certain that the human nature of Christ has received from the hypostatic union with the divine nature countless other gifts that are not only far above the essential properties of a true body but above every name. . . .

Justification, Faith, and Good Works

The Jesuit Order was a major source of revitalization within the Roman Catholic Church during the Age of Orthodoxy, and a number of Jesuit theologians were involved in prolonged polemical exchanges with the Lutheran dogmaticians. The following texts show the strategies used by the two most important Lutheran theologians in response to Catholic critics. Martin Chemnitz's *Examination of the Council of Trent*, published in several volumes between 1566 and 1573, was stimulated by a defense of Catholicism written by a Portuguese Jesuit named Jacob Payva de Andrada. Johann Gerhard's *Catholic Confession*, published in 1626, was a direct response to the "Disputations on the Controversies over the Christian Faith against the Heretics of This Time," written by Cardinal Robert Bellarmine (1542–1621), the most formidable Jesuit theologian of the Counter-Reformation.

Cardinal Robert Bellarmine

145. Chemnitz: Examination of the Council of Trent (1566–73)

Martin Chemnitz, *Examination of the Council of Trent: Part 1*, trans. Fred Kramer (St. Louis: Concordia, 1971), 538–44.

PART 1, TOPIC 8: JUSTIFICATION; SECT. 5: CONCERNING THE GROWTH OF JUSTIFICATION AFTER IT HAS BEEN RECEIVED
Council of Trent: Canon 24

"If anyone says that the justice received is not preserved and is also not increased before God through good works, but that the works are only the fruit and the signs of the justification received, not also a cause of its increase, let him be anathema."

Examination

The testimonies of Scripture are clear, that the renewal of the new man, as also the mortification of the old, is not perfect and complete in this life but that it grows and is increased day by day until it is perfected in the next life, when this corruptible will have put on incorruption. Profitable also and necessary in the church are exhortations that the regenerate should not neglect, extinguish, or cast away the gifts of the Spirit which they have received but that they stir them up with true and earnest exercises, calling on the help of the Holy Spirit, that he may give an increase of faith, hope, life, and of the other spiritual gifts; for what the punishment of spiritual negligence is the parable of the talents shows. . . .

If it were these chief points of the doctrine that are dealt with in this chapter of the Tridentine decree, there would be no controversy, for the matters are true. But let the reader again note the insidious cunning of the synod. They take the teaching and the testimonies of Scripture on how the renewal ought to grow from day to day, how the inherent gifts of the Spirit must increase through prayerful exercises, but behind this facade they are after something far different. For the title speaks of the growth of the justification that has been received, and the chapter says that those who have once been freely justified are afterwards justified more through the keeping of the commandments of God and of the church, so that afterwards a man is justified by works, and not by faith alone. . . .

[The Tridentine fathers] want to confirm and obtrude on the church the papalist distinction of a first and a second justification. For they call that the first justification when an unregenerate man is first permeated with the inherent righteousness, when the first quality, or infused characteristic, of love has been received. And of this first infusion of love they say that no works merit it as a deserved reward. But they call that the second justification when the infused love exercises its operations, bringing forth good works. And this second justification, they say, can and should be obtained through good works. And these works, they think, merit a greater righteousness than the one that is infused freely, for Christ's sake, in the first justification. Yes, they add that those works in which their second

justification consists finally merit eternal life, which, they say, must be bestowed as a deserved reward upon our works performed in love. So say the Jesuits. . . .

It is not hard to see that this opinion conflicts diametrically with the teaching of Scripture. For the Scripture is not speaking only of the beginning of conversion when it says that we are justified before God to life eternal by grace, for Christ's sake, without works, so that justification occurs in a moment but that afterwards, in order that we may obtain salvation, we are throughout our whole life justified through and on account of our good works. For in Romans 4 Paul proves that Abraham was justified by faith, freely, for Christ's sake, without works not only in the beginning of his conversion but that also when, a new man, he had obeyed God with good works through many years, there was imputed to him righteousness without works, not as to one who worked but as to one who believed. . . .

In Romans 5 there is found a glorious division. The first is concerning the beginning: "Through Christ we have access by faith to this grace that, being justified by faith, we may have peace with God." The second is concerning the middle: "In that same grace we stand by faith." The third is concerning the end: "Through the same grace we glory by faith in hope of the glory of God," that is, as we by faith have access to grace, so also we hope that we shall by the same faith and grace arrive at glorification. As, therefore, we have peace with God in the beginning of our justification by faith, freely, for Christ's sake, without works, so we have it also in the middle and the end. . . .

TOPIC 9: FAITH; SECT. 1: CONCERNING PREPARATION FOR JUSTIFICATION

Canon 9: "If anyone says that the ungodly is justified by faith alone in such a way that he understands that nothing else is required that cooperates toward obtaining the grace of justification and that it is in no way necessary for him to be prepared and disposed by the movement of his own will, let him be anathema."

Since it was their purpose to establish the entire form of Scholastic doctrine for their own churches and to foist it on ours again, they had to think out such trickery, lest this fraud should be noticed by everybody at first glance. For this reason they studiously flee and avoid in most things the terms, or modes of speech, that originated without Scripture in the philosophical workshops of the Scholastic writers, but the matters themselves, as they are taught by the masters of the sentences, they simply retain, except that they add a smoke screen by means of certain terms borrowed from Scripture in order that the reader who is not versed in the useless disputations of the Scholastic writers but only accustomed to the language of the Holy Spirit may think at first glance that the council gave serious thought to some degree of reformation of the Scholastic doctrine according to the norm of Scripture when he hears that here they do not so frequently use only the terminology of the Scholastics but bring in also, in some places, the words and phrases of Scripture. But later, as he progresses, he finds out, both from the matters and from the words, something far different, yes, the very opposite. . . .

What defect then, you ask, is found in that decree? I reply: 1) They want to have faith understood as historical knowledge and bare assent, so that they deny that it is trust in the divine mercy that forgives sins for Christ's sake. 2) They imagine that divine grace only moves and excites free will, which thereafter is able, from its own natural powers, to begin and render those preparations. 3) In those preparations they set up some merit and some worthiness, in view of which we are justified. For they say that faith should hold that when a man does what is in him, then God must of necessity

infuse grace. 4) That which is the true function of faith, namely, to lay hold of Christ for righteousness and salvation, that they ascribe to love. And they simply invert the order shown in Scripture. For they imagine that the love toward God in us must precede reconciliation with God, although it is impossible that true love toward God should be begun, unless there is previously heard and apprehended by faith the voice of the gospel concerning the reconciliation through the mercy of God for the sake of the Son and Mediator. These things certainly do not agree with Augustine (to say nothing of the Scripture), who constantly inculcates this rule: "Good works do not precede him who is to be justified, but follow him who is justified."

146. Gerhard: *Confessio Catholica* (1633–37)

The full title of this treatise is: "Catholic Confession in Which Catholic and Evangelical Doctrine Professed by the Church of the Augsburg Confession Is Confirmed by Support from Roman Catholic Writers." It was first published in 1626.

From *Confessio Catholica* (Leipzig: Genschius, 1679), 1513–17.

Bk. 2, Part 3, art. 23, ch. 6: The Necessity of Good Works

First Thesis: In the Evangelical church, the necessity of good works is not denied, much less are good works prohibited. . . .

Second Thesis: Although we say that works are necessary, nevertheless we deny that they are necessary for the attainment of salvation.

Subthesis: 1. The necessity of good works can be asserted in two ways: The necessity of presence *[necessitas praesentiae]*, of course, and the necessity of efficient causation *[necessitas efficientiae]*. The first signifies no more than that it is necessary for one who would be saved to labor with great care. The other, however, signifies something more, namely, the cause of that necessity, truly that good works are necessary to the effecting of salvation. We defend the prior sort of necessity, as a species or mode. The papists, however, defend the other.

2. A distinction should be made between external and internal works. We deny that external works are necessary in those who immediately after laying hold of baptism depart from this life. Nevertheless, we teach the necessity of internal works, that is, interior renewal, since baptism is a "washing of regeneration and renewal" (Titus 3:5). The Apostle teaches, moreover, that internal renewal is classifiable as a work when he pronounces man to be "justified by faith without works of the law" (Rom. 3:27). . . .

[Editor's note: Further technical distinctions about connotations of necessity are made.]

4. Chemnitz in the chapter on good works in part three of his *Loci* extends this point a little more. "Scripture especially uses the designation of necessity in four ways, which indeed relates to this question.

"First, for that which is necessary for justification and salvation (Acts 15:5; Gal. 2:4; 6:12).

"Second, the mention of necessity in certain places in Scripture signifies something either forced or involuntary as when external work is forced out against one's will or involuntarily, contrary to the intention of the mind (2 Cor. 9:7; Philem. 14).

"Third, Scripture uses the designation of necessity for when something is not arbitrary or a matter of indifference but an obligation by reason of a divine will and command (Acts 14:46; 15:21; Rom. 13:5; 1 Cor. 9:16).

"Fourth, more frequently the word is used generally for the necessity of consequence *(pro necessitate consequentiae)* or immutability *(immutabilitatis)* (Heb. 7:12). This usage applies to when there is a definite and important reason why something should not be omitted but should be done (Phil. 1:24).

"Although good works are not necessary in accordance with the first and second mode, nevertheless, they are necessary in the sense of the third and fourth modes."

5. We say good works are necessary not only by internal necessity, because true and living faith is not without good works (which basis for necessity Bellarmine claims is the only one handed down by us), but also on account of external necessity, which is due to the divine command that bids us to apply ourselves to good works.

Antithesis: Bellarmine in Book 4 on justification states: "Our adversaries agree in this that good works are not necessary to salvation, except by necessity of presence. The sense of this proposition is that there ought to be good works, since faith, otherwise, is not alive or true unless it produces good fruits in the same manner that fire is not fire unless it glows with heat. Nevertheless, good works do not have any relation to salvation as merits, causes, or conditions of it. To the contrary we [Roman Catholics] say that good works are not necessary to salvation only by reason of presence, but also by reason of efficient causation, since they effect salvation and without the same, faith alone does not bring about salvation."

We now demonstrate our judgment [against this antithesis]:

1. From apostolic disputation: Romans 3 and 4; Galatians 2; Ephesians 2. The Apostle, conjoining justification and salvation in the scriptural texts that constitute the proper foundation *(sedes doctrinae)* of the doctrine of justification, proclaims from the judgment of Moses and David, that is from the law and all the prophets, that "we are justified and saved

by grace through faith without works. Blessed are those whom God accepts without works. Blessed is the one to whom God does not impute sin but saves by grace through faith. This is not of ourselves; this is a gift of God, not of works lest someone should glory in it." The Apostle by this pronouncement directly opposes those who place works in a position to be necessary for the attainment of salvation.

2. From the distinction of law and gospel: Justification and salvation are not from the law but from the gospel (Gal. 3:11, 21; 5:4). Now indeed the gospel predicates justification and salvation on believing in Christ by grace without the condition of works (Rom. 4:5, 6).

3. From a reckoning of what is sufficient: If good works are necessary to effect salvation they must be reckoned either as merit or cause in the matter of salvation. Yet they are not the merits of our salvation as has been demonstrated earlier, neither are they the efficient cause or instrumental cause of our salvation because by the grace of God the remission of our sins, justification, and eternal life is put forth in Christ alone, our mediator (John 3:36; 1 John 5:1). Nor are they the conserving cause of salvation because the conservation of our salvation is not attributed in Scripture to our works, but to the power of God and faith (1 Pet. 1:5, 9; Rom. 11:20; Mark 16:16).

4. From the consequence of absurdities: If good works are placed in a position of necessity for the attainment of salvation, the promises of the gospel are no longer left to grace but are said to include the condition of works. The promise of salvation is rendered unsure when consciences timid and terrified by a sense of divine wrath are constantly disposed to doubt whether they have enough good works with which to effect their salvation (Acts 15:24). Other causes of justification and salvation are set forth, or at least more things are required for justification even though these very causes

of justification and salvation, namely, the grace of God and the merit of Christ, are established in the proper authoritative passage (Acts 4:12; 15:11—faith; 1 Pet. 1:5—not works; Eph. 2:8; 2 Tim. 1:9; Titus 3:5).

Support for our assertions:

1. That some of them recognize that faith alone justifies. For if faith alone justifies, at least works are not necessary to the attaining of salvation. [Even though] the connecting of faith and works is approved by the very words of Bellarmine in Book 4, "We," that is, the Roman Catholics, "say good works are necessary to the salvation of a man, not only by reason of presence but also by reason of efficient causation, since they effect salvation and, without the same, faith alone does not effect salvation."

2. That the papists themselves recognize that good works are not absolutely and simply necessary to the salvation of all. (If works are necessary by reason of causation, they are necessary for the salvation of everyone, inasmuch as the effect is absent where the necessary cause producing it is not present.)

Thomas de Vio, Cardinal Cajetan, writing on James, chapter 2, says: "It is established that one is justified through faith also without works as is evident for one who, baptized as a child or as an adult, straightaway dies." (They indeed are not only justified but also are saved without works.)

Jacobus Faber [Lefèvre d'Étaples] on James, chapter 2, says: "Faith alone suffices where there is no time for works; faith alone suffices for little ones for their justification." . . .

Bellarmine in Book 1 states: "Origen teaches that man is able to be justified occasionally even if he does no external works. For he posits the example of the sinful women and the robber, who were not observed to have fasted or given alms before they were justified [Luke 23:39-43?]. So, . . . Origen excludes the external necessity of works when evidently the power or occasion of the doing of works is lacking in a similar manner."

In the same book and chapter: "Chrysostom teaches that faith alone without external works occasionally suffices but external works without faith never suffice. And the reason is rendered: Faith brings forth works; works do not bring forth faith."

In Book 4 on justification: "We understand good works to be necessary to men having the use of reason and as long as they live after obtaining the grace of remission whenever the occasion of fulfilling the law occurs. Indeed we do not deny that infants and also adults recently baptized are saved if immediately thereafter they depart from this life. They are judged to fulfill the whole law who living on after justification do not violate the precepts of the law and who at least display love, which is the fulfillment of the law in the heart." (Perfect love is also perfect fulfillment of the law and effects salvation. Yet truly, perfect love occurs in no man in this life. Therefore it is inefficacious to the attaining of salvation.)

Book 5: "Even though little ones who die soon after baptism are given eternal life only by the law of heredity, nevertheless God wants his sons who have use of reason to acquire that by their own labors and merits so that eternal life is owed to them by two claims, clearly by the claim of heredity and by the law of recompense of wages." (If baptized little ones do not acquire eternal life by their own labors and merits but only are given eternal life by the law of heredity, it follows that good works are simply not necessary to the attainment of salvation.) . . .

[Editor's note: Gerhard goes on to analyze and reply to quotes from several other Roman Catholic theologians.]

147. The Syncretist Controversy: Calixtus and Calov

Georg Calixtus was the most controversial Lutheran theologian during the Age of Orthodoxy. Educated at the University of Helmstedt, which was a center of Humanism more noted for its philosophers than for its theologians, he developed an intense aversion to the theological controversies of his day. Throughout his forty-year career as a professor at Helmstedt, he committed himself to the promotion of cooperation between opposing religious groups. He was in contact with other irenicists throughout Europe and participated in the Convention at Thorn in 1645 assembled by the King of Poland to promote the unification of different church traditions. Calixtus asserted that few of the articles of faith about which the theologians argued were fundamental beliefs necessary for the attainment of salvation. He suggested that common acceptance of the earliest and simplest ecumenical creed could and should be the basis for the unification of the churches.

Abraham Calov of Wittenberg questioned the presuppositions of this specific proposal and charged Calixtus with promoting Syncretism. He argued that the similarities that Calixtus saw between the different churches were very superficial and that any willingness to mix truth and error was a sign of an indifference to doctrine that endangered the salvation of individuals and the integrity of the Lutheran church. Not all of Calixtus's antagonists were as hostile as Calov, but few were truly sympathetic to his irenic efforts.

The selections from Georg Calixtus are in Heinrich Schmid, *Geschichte der synkretistischen Streitigkeiten* (Erlangen: Heyder,

1846), and are from the following of Calixtus's works: *Responsum maledicis theologorum Moguntinorum I* (1644); *Epicrisis et consideratio, scriptis ad colloquium Thoruniense* (1645); *Verantwortung an den Churfürsten von Brandenburg* (1649); and *Dissertatio de desiderio et studio concordiae ecclesiasticae* (1650). The selections from Abraham Calov are in Heinrich Schmid, *Calov: Digressio de nova theologia Hemstadio-Regiomontanae* (1648) and *Syncretismus calixtinus* (1653).

CALIXTUS

Verantwortung §27 (Schmid, 170–71)

I must confess, and confess willingly and gladly, that it has pained my heart as long as I have been able to consider it and more than I can express in words that those who are separated from each other by almost irreconcilable hatred and enmity and who anathematize and condemn each other were [all] baptized in the name of the Father, the Son, and the Holy Spirit and believe in one, Almighty God, Creator of Heaven and Earth. . . . [Consider those who] believe that the only-begotten Son of the Father willed to rescue us from sin, death, and damnation, assumed human nature, suffered and died, was resurrected from the dead, ascended into heaven, is seated at the right hand of the God and will come again to judge the living and the dead; who meanwhile believe and preach the gospel as Christ commanded and gather a church and fellowship that is well-pleasing to God through which forgiveness of sins is obtained; who believe that the dead will rise again bodily, that those who have lived well will enter eternal life while those who have done evil will go into the eternal fire; who firmly believe these things and live, not according to the flesh, but chastely, uprightly, and piously in this world, doing nothing contrary to their conscience, neither affirming nor denying any controversial position that does not seem right, and who make use of the Lord's Supper as they can and as it seems right to them. I cannot believe and state anything other than that they are Christians and therefore worthy of being met with Christian love and kindness.

If a single error should cast a man out of Christendom and cause his damnation, few if any Christians would remain and escape damnation. Besides, it is said that all who believe in the only-begotten Son of God will not perish but will have eternal life. St. Paul said [1 Cor. 3:11-15]: No other foundation can anyone lay than that which is laid, Jesus Christ. Now if anyone builds on this foundation with wood, hay, stubble (that is unnecessary, unuseful, impertinent, superstitious, or erroneous things that would better be left off), he will suffer loss (his work will be lost, he will not get the reward that those who built with gold and silver on the foundation will receive), but he will [still] be saved (which reveals that not all errors deprive men of salvation). He will be saved, but only as through a fire. . . . From what I quote one learns that what has just been mentioned pertains to salvation and those who believe and live accordingly are not to be excluded from the number of Christians.

Desiderium #6 (Schmid, 172)

Whoever is convinced in his mind that there is no papal infallibility, no papal primacy administering divine law, no purgatory, or no transubstantiation, cannot confess with good conscience that he believes that. . . . Whoever is convinced that he is bound by a divine command to receive both elements of the Eucharist cannot be content with one element without violating his conscience. Whoever is convinced that the presence of the body and blood of the Lord in the holy Eucharist is confirmed by the Word of God cannot deny this without immeasurable guilt. . . . But there is an enormous difference between the sentences: "I do not believe that this opinion is true," and "I maintain that this opinion is heretical and that all who hold it are cut off from divine grace and the heavenly kingdom." The former can be said of many things without the danger of initiating or establishing schisms, but not the latter.

Epicrisis, thesis 32 (Schmid, 164)

I point out again and again that our theology is practical, and, consequently, I must say, questions that do nothing for the carrying out and exercising of [religious] practice should be considered indifferent and should not be disputed odiously or to the detriment of mutual Christian love. Our concern should be to do and accomplish, with as much industry as we can, what God demands and wants us to do.

ad Moguntinos, thesis 62 (Schmid, 146)

The slow-minded and uneducated are not served by one faith and the clever and erudite by another, but all are Christians through one and the same faith, whether one is uncultured and a learner or refined by literary pursuits and a teacher, particularly for adults and those endowed with the use of reason.

Epicrisis, thesis 2 (Schmid, 153)

It suffices to believe that there is one God, Father, Son, and Holy Spirit, that the Son was incarnated and became man, that the world was created by God and the dead will be raised. Furthermore, we need not probe in what way three persons are in one nature, or how two natures subsist in one person, nor need we comprehend how divine power produces something from nothing or how God reintegrates what dissipates in thin air. None of this is prejudicial to us or our salvation.

ad Moguntinos, thesis 42 (Schmid, 143)

The Apostolic Symbol [the Apostles' Creed] contains the chief doctrines, the knowledge of which is necessary for the making of a true and faithful Christian and for the attainment of salvation. . . . [In the past], when catechumens had confessed the Creed, they were admitted to Baptism and were called and considered believers. Any artisans and farmers, any of the uncultured and simple people, be they men or women, are believers and stand in the state of grace, although all or many of them know and understand nothing more than the chief summary of the faith simply expressed in the Creed. And yet that is enough for their salvation.

Desiderium, thesis 4 (Schmid, 169)

Whoever is outside the body or is not a member of the body under the headship of Christ cannot be saved. Yet those who are members of the body under the head of Christ are brothers and sisters. Therefore, as far as relates to the papists and the reformed, either it is fitting to deny that any of them are members of Christ and to affirm that all of them, however many they are or were, have been placed beyond hope of salvation and destined for eternal death, although they never acted contrary to their conscience and were afflicted by an ignorance that they were unable to overcome, or [to affirm that] if they can be or were able to become participants in eternal life with us, then they are sons of the same father, coheirs, brothers and sisters, who ought to be loved.

Desiderium, thesis 5 (Schmid, 178)

Although actual and external communion through the sacrament is prohibited on account of unfortunate controversies concerning the same, there may persist, nevertheless, a virtual and internal communion, consisting of mutual benevolence and love of the kind that a Christian owes to another Christian and in the desire and zeal for the removing of impediments that block actual and external, perfect communion.

Calov

Syncretismus, 10 (Schmid, 247)

It is not a matter of seeking to know in whatever manner all things that should be believed can be traced back to the Apostolic Symbol, or whether they are at least implicitly or virtually contained in it. Rather, it is a matter of investigating whether all articles of faith that should be believed are explicitly and expressly included in the Symbol as it is used today.

Digressio, 910 (Schmid, 252)

It was not within the scope of the ecumenical councils to express all the fundamental articles of faith in the symbols, but to define those matters that came up for debate at that time, leaving out other articles about which there was little controversy even though they were no less fundamental than the ones they had labored with great care to define in the symbols.

Syncretismus, 167 (Schmid, 262)

If the only true heretics who should be subjected to anathema for doctrinal errors are those who directly deny articles expressed in the symbol, then the whole catholic church erred in the [later] ecumenical creeds in anathematizing certain dogmas that are not expressly contrary to the symbol. . . . Then the church erred in condemning those heretics who accepted the symbol or did not unquestionably contradict any of its articles. . . .

Digressio, 923 (Schmid, 263)

If Calixtus's definition is admitted, then neither the Pelagians, nor the Anabaptists, nor the Arminians, nor the Calvinists, nor the Catholics have been heretics, for the articles that Calixtus asserts as necessary to believe for salvation have scarcely been corrupted by them. And where does it stand with the Arians and the Socinians? Surely they should not be called heretics for they do not deny any of the articles of the symbol that Calixtus thinks are the only necessary beliefs, but they claim to allow all of them! And therefore, those also who are ignorant of necessary articles of faith because of a defect of institution should be considered wholly Christian, as Calixtus affirms. In any case, ignorance of the articles of faith that must be believed for salvation could not be damnable or pernicious for salvation, and they

who do not believe certain necessary articles but simply do not know about them would be able to become participants in salvation.

Digressio, 1105 (Schmid, 282)

Is it not absurd that some want to regard Calvinists and papists as catholic Christians, provided only that they are not so devoted to their own sect that they completely curse us but embrace whatever in our tradition [they think] is right and in agreement with catholic faith and observance? This is ironwood (ειδηροξυλον) or opposites in opposition: for he who embraces our confession is not a Calvinist or papist but a genuine (γνησιως) Lutheran; thus he who is and remains a Calvinist or papist will, as such, embrace least of all whatever is right and in agreement with true faith and observance; to the contrary, the papist curses our doctrine and is understood to curse it as such.

QUENSTEDT

Theologia Didactico-Polemica, ch. 5: De Articuli Fidei, sect. 1, q. 5

Truly, we constantly assert that Calvinists and Lutherans differ not only in fundamentals but in many other articles of faith.

Whence it should be observed: It is not enough that some fundamental article or some part of it is explicitly embraced while the rest are called into doubt, denied, or impugned, but it is necessary to hold to the total and complete fundamental article and not to mix in something false either directly or indirectly nor consider the remaining dogmas to be unnecessary for the foundation of faith. . . .

To us, it is certain that the controversial questions with the Calvinists remain absolutely irreconcilable as long as they remain in their errors. . . .

THE ORDO SALUTIS

148. Hunnius: *Epitome* (1625)

The *Epitome Credendorum* published by Nikolaus Hunnius in 1625 was a brief summary of doctrine that became very popular among the laity as well as the clergy. One of its most important features was the description of the doctrine of salvation as a series of acts by which the Holy Spirit bestows the gift of grace. Later dogmaticians continued to use this pattern, although they did not always exactly follow the order presented by Hunnius. For example, Quenstedt spoke of the call *(vocatio)*, rebirth *(regeneratio)*, conversion *(conversio)*, justification *(justificatio)*, repentance *(poenitentia)*, and mystical union *(unio mystica)*. The idea of a spiritual union between God and the individual believer also became a topic of great interest to the devotional writers of the seventeenth century, whose writings are examined in the next chapter.

From *Epitome Credendorum*, trans. Paul Edward Gottheil (Nürnberg: Sebald, 1847), 124–25, 127, 129–30, 137–38, 144–45, 155, 165–67, 171, 174. Revised by Eric Lund.

CHAPTER 17: OF GOD'S MERCIFUL CALLING

439. The Lord Jesus Christ has brought about a reconciliation between God and sinful men, so that now nothing is hindering them from acknowledging and accepting this benefit with grateful hearts. In which latter act the Lord Jesus again faithfully assists them, in order to lead them to their heavenly Father. But for the better understanding of the same, we have to inquire:

I. In which manner the Lord Jesus proceeds in this act, and

II. Which means he employs to bring about the desired effect.

440. Christ is brought near to the sinner:

a. by the calling,

b. by repentance,

c. by justification,

d. by conversion,

e. by renewing,

f. by the new birth,

g. by the union with Christ.

441. The calling is the first act, by which men are requested to become partakers of the benefits of Christ; this calling we stand in great need of. Suppose a prison being filled with prisoners who had all been ransomed; but as long as this their redemption is not communicated to them, and they requested to leave the prison, their redemption would be of no avail to them. Exactly so this great work of mercy, by which Christ has delivered us from the pains of hell by his blood, would be of no avail, if we had it not announced to us, and if we were not requested to become partakers of the benefits connected therewith.

449. a. The Lord Jesus calls all men to come to him, Matt. 11:28: "Come unto me all you that labor and are heavy laden, and I will give you rest." Now as all men must be said to labor and to be heavy laden, it follows that Christ has called them all unto him. . . .

CHAPTER 18: OF REPENTANCE

455. To insure us of our eternal salvation in his presence, God has made ample preparations, in all the proceedings that have been already treated of. It is true that the Lord Jesus has delivered us from our sins, reconciled us to God, opened unto us heaven and eternal salvation, even so that God has called upon us to partake of his grace and of the merit of the Lord Jesus Christ. But in to the enjoyment of these benefits, we have only then success, if we are aided by divine power. This aid God bestows upon us, thus raising again and upholding sinful men.

456. But this restoration of man is not accomplished at once, but only partly, so that only

the beginning of it is made in this life. In this respect three different points are to be attended to, namely:

1. man, who requires help, and whose restoration is called repentance;

2. God the Lord, who is either bringing sinful men before the judgment seat, or forgiving them their sins, which latter is called justification, or forgiveness of sins; men, who are induced to turn away from their evil and sinful life, giving themselves with all their might to the service of God—this is called conversion, new birth, and renewing; and

3. Christ, and the fact that men become united with him, which is called the engrafting in Christ. But the complete restoration is only brought about after the death of this body, in eternal life and in the kingdom of glory.

457. The first of these works of mercy is repentance. Concerning which we have to inquire:

a. its nature,

b. its necessity,

c. of how many parts it consists,

d. its source,

e. whom among men it might concern, and

f. its fruits and consequences.

458. What is repentance? Repentance means a real acknowledgement and sincere repentance of the sins of which we feel ourselves guilty, along with the firm assurance that God is willing to forgive them for the sake and the merits of his beloved Son.

461. Of how many parts repentance consists? We answer: of two parts, namely, the act of repentance and of faith.

The act of repentance consists of

a. man's conviction of being a sinner,

b. the conviction that God is zealous against sin and that he is determined to punish the same with hellfire in all eternity;

c. the conviction that man is by no means able to help himself in this emergency, and

that he has to expect this help from no creature whatsoever;

d. of a deep-felt repentance and sorrow with which the sinner feels himself sorely afflicted on account of his sin; and finally

e. of a heartfelt desire, if possible, not to have sinned at all, together with an intense hatred against sin.

Chapter 19: Of Justification

478. We have been considering man in his sinful state, in consequence of which state (if God would deal with him according to justice), he would be brought before the judgment of God, there to be convicted of sin, and condemned to eternal death. We have now to look for the means by which he might be saved from this emergency, delivered from his transgressions, and the punishment consequent to it. As such means are to be considered justification and forgiveness of sins. . . .

485. . . . In the act of our justification two different things are accomplished; namely, in the first place, the righteousness of Christ and his fulfilling the law are imputed unto man, as if he had done these things himself, and second, the sins that he had committed are not imputed to him, as if he had never committed the same. By the first act he is delivered from a debt, which he never possibly could have paid; whilst by the second he is freed from the burden of sin, which he never could have atoned for, and the punishment for which he could never have sustained. By these two acts he is delivered from the judgment of God in such a manner that henceforward he has not any more to fear either guilt or transgression, nor the evils that are the consequence of them.

500. The manner in which our justification is proceeded with is as follows. The righteousness is

1. offered by God unto man, and

2. received and accepted by man.

Thus God offers his righteousness unto man by means of his Gospel and by the Holy Sacraments, of which we propose to treat subsequently. From the last mentioned springs the faith by which the justification is accepted, as we intend to prove immediately. If man has offered unto him the justification, then he accepts of it by faith, which is, as it were, the spiritual hand, by which the grace of God, the merits of Christ, the forgiveness of sins, righteousness, life, and salvation are laid hold of.

502. I. the nature of faith. Three things are necessary for our belief, namely:

a. A knowledge of all that which God has revealed concerning our salvation, of which St. Paul writes, Rom. 10:14: "How shall they believe in him of whom they have not heard?"

b. An undoubted assent and conviction, as to the truth and inspiration of the divine work. If there is one, who has occasion to hear and to perceive that which God teaches, but considers it as a fable, contradicting it within his heart, such a one cannot have faith. For he has no faith in God; he grieves the Holy Spirit, putting away the word of God from him, and judges himself unworthy of everlasting life, Acts 13:46.

c. An unflinching confidence in God, whereby man has the firm assurance that God is able and willing to bring to pass all his kind promised for his benefit and for that of all mankind.

507. II. The source of this faith is to be found in the Word of God and in the holy sacraments.

a. In the Word of God for "faith comes by hearing, and hearing by the word of God," Rom. 10:17.

b. In the holy sacraments; for Baptism "is the washing of regeneration," Titus 3:5. But regeneration cannot take place where there is no faith; hence faith comes by Baptism.

The Holy Supper appropriates the merits of Christ to the communicants in such a manner that, thereby, the Lord Jesus testifies to have given his body as well as shed his blood for them. This every man is requested to apply to himself individually, as if the Lord Jesus did say to everyone especially: this is my body, which is given for you for the forgiveness of sins, and this is my blood, which is shed for you for the forgiveness of sins.

CHAPTER 20: OF CONVERSION

537. With reference to conversion, the following points are to be considered:

a. the nature of conversion,

b. God, who works the conversion,

c. man, who becomes converted, and

d. the fruit of conversion.

538. a. The nature of conversion; this change is described to take place, when men are pricked in their hearts, Acts 2:37; when their hearts are smitten, 2 Sam. 24:10; when their hearts are opened, so that they attend unto the word of God, Acts 16:14; when the stony heart is taken out of them and a new and pure heart given them, when a new and a free spirit is put within them, and they thus become the people of God and walk in his statutes, Ezek. 11:19; 36:26; Ps. 51:12. . . .

559. The question as to how it is, that, in the whole, but a few men are converted, every one will easily answer himself when attending to that which has been stated already. For although it is true, that man can know nothing for the furtherance of his conversion, yet he may do a great deal to hinder it. It is true that he cannot work out his own conversion, but it is as true that he can hinder his being converted. Suppose a man is falling ill, then he cannot cure himself; but he can easily put an obstacle in the way of his recovery, in that he does not obey the injunctions of his medical adviser, and, casting from him his medicines, does everything to augment his sickness. . . .

Chapter 22: Of Regeneration

567. Regeneration has been compared to the natural birth. As man is born from his parents, so he is, as it were, spiritually born anew, or a second time, by God. For which reason the latter act is not called simply a birth, but a new birth, or regeneration. . . .

574. . . . b. The nature of regeneration and what it consists of. In this respect we have to observe

1. mortification of the sinful nature. This does not mean to say that the members of the body were to be subjected to mortification, but that they are to be made captive to the obedience of Christ, 1 Cor. 10:5; that sin should have no more dominion in our members, but that they should be henceforth members of righteousness, Rom. 6:12, 13; that they who are Christ's should crucify the flesh with the affections and lusts, Gal. 5:24. . . .

575. . . . b. The second part consists in the awakening of the soul and all of its powers to an activity with which God is well pleased. Every one who is not performing some sort of work is like a dead body, and accordingly as we are by nature unfit for any thing that is good, the Holy Ghost designates us as "dead," Eph. 2:1; Col. 2:13: "when ye were dead in trespasses and sins." Now if God imparts unto us the ability to do whatever is good and spiritual, then he makes us alive, and by becoming alive, we are able to perform good works. . . .

Chapter 23: The Believer's Union with Christ

590. That the Lord Jesus stands in a close union with the believer, we find stated in Scripture partly in express terms, partly in figures and parables.

Express terms we met with: John 6:56, "He that eats my flesh, and drinks my blood, dwells in me, and I in him"; John 14:20, "At that day you shall know that I am in my Father, and you in me, and I in you"; 1 Cor. 6:17, "He that is joined unto the Lord is one spirit"; Gal. 2:20, "I live, yet not I but Christ lives in me"; Eph. 5:30, "We are members of his body, of his flesh, and of his bones"; 1 John 3:24, "If that which you have heard from the beginning shall remain in you, you also shall continue in the Son and in the Father"; 1 John 4:13, "Hereby know that we dwell in him and he in us, because he has given us of his Spirit"; 2 Pet. 1:4, "Whereby are given unto us exceeding great and precious promises: that by these you might be partakers of the divine nature."

597. This circumstance is beautifully explained in Scripture by the figure of marriage: Gen. 2:24, "They shall be one flesh"; 1 Cor. 6:16, 17, "Know you not that he who joined himself to a harlot is one body with her? For two, he says, shall become one flesh. But he that is joined unto the Lord is one spirit"; Hosea 2:19, 20, "I will betroth you unto me for ever, yea I will betroth you unto me, in righteousness, and in judgment, and in lovingkindness, and in mercies; I will even betroth you unto me in faithfulness." A promise by which God in his part rests the spiritual union upon righteousness that he alone can give, and upon grace and mercy that he bestowed upon man. While on the part of man, God rests this union upon nothing but faith, by which they might trust in him that he is seeking their best, and that he is willing to be gracious unto them. All that causes a spiritual union, but not a bodily union.

Chapter Seven

Seventeenth-Century Devotional Literature and Hymnody

The common practice of describing the post-Reformation era as the Age of Orthodoxy emphasizes the strict confessional consciousness of the period and the important developments that took place in systematic theology. Seventeenth-century Lutheranism, however, should not be characterized only in terms of the outlook and achievements of the influential dogmaticians. It was also a period in which many of the best-loved hymns and most widely read devotional books of the Lutheran tradition were written. These texts reveal to us another set of concerns and attitudes that were also common in the Age of Orthodoxy and equally significant in shaping the future development of Lutheranism.

In the Reformation period, Lutheran reformers produced a variety of writings that were intended to edify ordinary believers. Simple catechisms summarized the most important beliefs and gave practical instruction about how people should live. Published collections of sermons provided easily understandable interpretations of the Bible, and small prayer books or hymnbooks gave families guidance for the observance of devotional practices in their homes. Toward the end of the sixteenth century, however, many Lutheran pastors felt that much more needed to be done to improve the state of religious life among the common folk. Convinced that the laity were often indifferent to moral and spiritual values, the writers of devotional literature attempted to show more clearly how Christian belief should affect the way people live.

Stephen Praetorius (1536–1604), Martin Moller (1547–1606), and Philip Nicolai (1556–1608) were three of the most notable early devotional writers in the Age of Orthodoxy (doc. #168). Each of them in different ways stressed the importance of holy living as a product of faith and described the transformative effect of the indwelling of Christ in the believer. They all used mystical language in their description of Christian experience, and Moller in particular was explicitly indebted to medieval spiritual writers for what he had to say about this topic. The practice of reappropriating selected resources from the medieval spiritual tradition soon became commonplace. This constituted one of the most distinctive but controversial features of the work of the seventeenth-century devotional writers.

As important as these early writers were, they are minor figures compared to Johann Arndt (1555–1621), a north German pastor who served in later life as general superintendent of the churches in the Duchy of Braunschweig-Wolfenbüttel. His *Four Books of True Christianity*, first published in 1605 and later expanded into six books, became the single most influential devotional text in Lutheran history. Arndt also wrote a very popular prayer book called *The Little Garden of Paradise* and republished medieval spiritual writings, such as *The Imitation of Christ*, by Thomas à Kempis, and the *Theologia Deutsch*. Simple people who could read were more likely to own a book by Arndt than any of the writings of Luther. Over 140 editions of Arndt's writings were published during the next century, and *True Christianity* was also translated into Latin, Dutch, English, French, Russian, and several other languages.

Arndt was convinced that Germany in his day was in a state of moral and spiritual decay and suggested that the misguided preoccupations of many of the clergy were partially to blame for this development (docs. #149 and 150). Through his writings he attempted to reorient attention to the practical matter of encouraging repentance and spiritual renewal. Arndt stressed the importance of both active and contemplative aspects of piety (docs. #150 and 152). He insisted that true, living faith becomes active in love toward other people, but he also encouraged believers to set aside time for careful introspection and solitary meditation.

The famous dogmatician Johann Gerhard (1582–1637) had been directed to the study of theology by Arndt, who was his pastor while he was growing up in the city of Quedlinburg. The personal influence of Arndt on Gerhard's life is evident in his lifelong interest in providing practical spiritual guidance for all believers as well as the sophisticated theological analysis that only the most educated could understand. Even before he became well known for his systematic theology, Gerhard was influencing people through his *Sacred Meditations*, first published in Latin in 1606 and circulated five years later in a German translation (docs. #155–157). The ponderous style of his later devotional writings limited their appeal, but the amount of devotional literature he produced is significant evidence that the dogmaticians were concerned with how people lived as well as what they believed.

The tremendous devastation resulting from military battles, plague, and famine during the Thirty Years War (1618–48) created new challenges for those who were committed to the revitalization of popular piety. Many Lutheran pastors believed that widespread suffering and uncertainty about the future had dulled the moral and spiritual sensitivity of many people. This tragic situation stimulated the production of a vast quantity of new devotional books and inspired the writing of some of the best-known Lutheran hymns of the seventeenth century.

Many of the great hymnwriters of the Age of Orthodoxy such as Johann Heerman, Martin Rinkart, and Paul Gerhardt had firsthand experience of the suffering caused by the war, yet out of their profound faith in Christ they composed lyrical poetry that conveyed messages of consolation and hope (docs. #168, 169, and 171). Their meditations on the sufferings of Christ on the cross helped people put some perspective on their own hardships and remember to be thankful for the gift of salvation (docs. #167, 170, and 171). When earthly life seemed so bleak, the hymnwriters called attention to the peace and joy that could be found now in an experience of the presence of Christ and more fully in the future after passing through death into eternal life with God.

After the Thirty Years War the city of Rostock became a notable gathering place for reform-minded clergy who were deeply influenced by the writings of Arndt. While some of these reformers, such as Theophilus Grossgebauer (1628–61), campaigned for reform of the institutions of the church, others attempted to promote the transformation of individual lives through their preaching and the publication of edifying literature. Joachim Lütkemann (1608–55), a pastor who taught at the University of Rostock, promoted practical piety in a number of devotional books that rivaled Arndt's in popularity. The Arndtian orientation at Rostock continued through the often controversial reform efforts of Heinrich Müller (1631–75), who taught Greek and theology at the university. In a number of books, including *Spiritual Hours of Refreshment* (1664), Müller criticized both clergy and laity for their worldliness and, like Arndt, asserted that the work of divine grace in a person should bring about a clearly evident conversion or rebirth (docs. #158–160). The last of the great disciples of Arndt connected to Rostock was Christian Scriver (1629–93), who, after receiving his education there at the university, went on to pastorates in Magdeburg and Quedlinburg. Much of what he wrote repeated the themes found in the writings of Arndt and Müller, but he was especially creative in the way he depicted the process of spiritual growth and the spiritual problems people faced in daily life. This is most evident in his emblematic book *Gotthold's Occasional Devotions* (1663–69) (docs. #161–166).

Since most of these writers dealt extensively with ordinary people in their church work, they differed from the dogmaticians in the vocabulary they used to convey the Christian message and developed a different sense of what were the most pressing problems facing the Lutheran church. They wrote in German, the language of daily life, instead of Latin, the language of scholars. In their books they attempted to touch the hearts and stimulate the wills of people, while the arguments of the dogmaticians appealed primarily to the intellect. Both dogmaticians and devotional writers offered instruction about true faith and pious living, but the latter group offered a fuller explication of how people's lives should be practically affected by the doctrines that the dogmaticians had shown to be true.

The devotional writers of the seventeenth century were very conscious of their Lutheran identity, but their outlook differed from Luther's in several respects. They were generally more optimistic than Luther about the potential for spiritual growth in this life and were more inclined to measure the effect of divine grace by external signs of changed behavior (docs. #149 and 161). The devotional writers were also less suspicious of claims to an immediate experience of God. Luther had strictly disassociated himself from the Enthusiasts of his day, who believed themselves to be guided by the inward testimony of the Spirit of God. He had also criticized some of the doctrinal assumptions and ascetic practices that the medieval mystics had defended in their pursuit of mystical union with God. Most of the seventeenth-century devotional writers, however, were as interested in cultivating the subjective experience of the indwelling of Christ as they were in proclaiming the objective work of Christ for the salvation of humanity (docs. #151, 155, and 158). In some people, this inwardly oriented piety, influenced by medieval ascetic and mystical literature, seemed to lead to a world-negating outlook, which was also in tension with Luther's concern to bring religious life back into association with the secular world. On the other hand, the devotional writers frequently emphasized that true faith becomes active in love, a theme that was central to Luther's theology (doc. #160). The subjective experience of conversion usually brought about a new commitment to holy living, which included concern for the welfare of other people.

The dogmaticians and devotional writers of the Age of Orthodoxy generally maintained respectful relations, but at times, their different orientations led to tensions between them. Johann Arndt was not alone in criticizing the adverse consequences of the polemical preoccupations of the dogmaticians. Nor was he alone in suspecting that the faith of some dogmaticians was only a matter of intellectual assent *(assensus)* and not the saving faith *(fiducia)* that affects the whole orientation of a person. In turn, the most zealous guardians of doctrinal orthodoxy went so far as to charge that writers such as Arndt and Müller were heretics because of what they had written about the sacraments, good works, and the experience of mystical union with Christ. Conflicts of this sort increased within Lutheranism toward the end of the seventeenth century, when the Pietist reform movement extended the discussion of the issues first introduced by the devotional writers.

JOHANN ARNDT

Six Books of True Christianity (1605–10)

Johann Arndt (1555–1621) studied medicine and theology at Helmstedt, Strassburg, and Basel. During his early pastorates in Anhalt, Quedlinburg, and Braunschweig, he lived through several disturbing disruptions of communal life caused by conflicts between opposing religious or political factions. Seeking to make religion a more influential force in people's daily lives, he began to write a comprehensive guidebook describing an ideal of spiritual growth. In 1605 he published the first book of *True Christianity*, which interpreted what the Bible had to say about the loss and recovery of the image of God in human nature. This "Book of Scripture" was soon after supplemented by "The Book of the Life of Christ," which portrayed Christ as the doctor who heals the disease of sin and as a model of the godly life. The third book, called the "Book of Conscience," described the indwelling of Christ and how the Christian could come to experience it. The fourth book, the "Book of Nature," presented meditations on the six days of creation in order to show the knowledge of God that could be derived from nature.

In all but the first book, Arndt extensively paraphrased medieval writers such as Angela of Foligno, Thomas à Kempis, Johann Tauler, and Raymond of Sabunde. He also borrowed selectively from controversial sixteenth-century Spiritualists, such as Valentin Weigel and Paracelsus. Some Lutheran pastors and theologians recognized this fact and raised questions about his orthodoxy. Toward the end of his life, the criticisms of Arndt's theology became so public that he had to write an

Johann Arndt

extensive defense of his writings, which was circulated along with some of his shorter treatises as books five and six of *True Christianity*. Arndt salvaged his reputation and became an extremely popular author. Nevertheless, some later theologians would continue to blame Arndt for introducing alien elements into the Lutheran understanding of Christianity.

Selections are taken from Arndt WC, 14–16, 31, 118–21, 333–36, 339–42, and 566–75.

149. Foreword to Book One

Dear Christian reader, the godless and impenitent behavior of those who praise Christ and his word with their mouths and still lead entirely unchristian lives as if they lived in heathendom instead of Christendom, attests clearly to the great and shameful misuse of the holy gospel in these last days. Such ungodly conduct has prompted me to write this book so that simple people might see what true Christianity is, namely, the demonstration of a true, living, active faith through sincere godliness and the fruits of righteousness. I also want to show that we bear the name of Christ not only because we believe in Christ, but also because we ought to live in Christ and Christ in us. True repentance must proceed from the innermost ground of the heart; heart, mind, and spirit must be changed, so that we become conformed to Christ and his holy gospel; we must be renewed daily, made new creatures through the Word of God. (For just as every seed produces fruit of its own kind, so the Word of God must daily produce new spiritual fruits in us. If we are to become new creatures by faith, we must live according to the new birth.) In summary: Adam must die in us, and Christ must live in us. It is not enough to know God's Word; one must also put it into effect in a living, active practice. . . .

150. Book One, Chapter Five: What True Faith Is

He who believes that Jesus is the Christ is born of God (1 John 5:1).

Faith is a heartfelt confidence and undoubting trust in the grace of God promised in Christ and in the forgiveness of sins and eternal life. It is kindled by the Word of God and the Holy Spirit. Through this faith we obtain forgiveness of sins, completely freely, out of sheer grace (Eph. 2:8), not by our own merit but by the merit of Christ. Therefore, our faith has a certain foundation and does not waver. This forgiveness of sins is our righteousness, which is true, perpetual, and eternal before God. For it is not the righteousness of an angel but of the obedience, merit, and blood of Christ and becomes our own through faith. Even if it is weak and we are still burdened with many remaining sins, these are covered over out of grace, as Christ wills it (Ps. 32:2).

By this heartfelt confidence and heartfelt trust, a man gives his heart entirely and absolutely to God, rests in God alone, gives himself over to God, clings to God alone, unites himself with God, becomes a partaker of all that which is of God and Christ, becomes one spirit with God, receives new power from him, new life, new consolation, peace and joy, rest of soul, righteousness and holiness: and also, from God through faith, a man is born anew. For where true faith is, there Christ is with all his righteousness, holiness, redemption, merit, grace, forgiveness of sins, kinship of God, inheritance of eternal life. This is the new birth that comes from faith in Christ. Therefore, the Epistle to the Hebrews in chapter 11:1 calls faith a substance or an undoubting, true assurance of things for which man hopes and a conviction concerning things that one does not see. The consolation of living faith becomes powerful in the heart to such an extent that it convinces the heart, in that one feels heavenly blessing in one's soul, rest and peace in God, so certain and true that one could die then and there with a happy heart. This is strength in the Spirit in the inner man and the joyfulness of faith, or *parrhesia* (Eph. 3:12; Phil. 1:4; 1 John 2:28; 3:21), that is, joyfulness in God (1 Thess. 2:2), and *plerophoria,* a completely undoubting certainty (1 Thess. 1:5).

Now when I die, this faith must strengthen me in my soul and assure me within by the Holy Spirit. It must be an inner, living, eternal consolation; it must also hold me and strengthen me as a supernatural, divine, heavenly power to conquer death and the world in me, and there must be such an assurance and union with Christ that neither death nor life can separate me from it (2 Tim. 1:12; Rom. 8:38). Therefore, St. John (1 John 5:4) says: "Whatever is born of God conquers the world."

Everything that is born of God is truly no shadow work, but a true life work. God will not give birth to a dead fruit, a lifeless and powerless work, but a living, new man must be born from the living God. Our faith is the victory that conquers the world [1 John 5:4].

Now that which conquers must be a mighty power. If faith is to be victorious over the world, it must be a living, victorious, active, real, divine power; indeed, Christ must do everything through faith. Through this power of God we are once again drawn into God, inclined toward God, transplanted and implanted in God, taken out of Adam as from a cursed vine and placed in Christ the blessed and living vine (John 15:4). Thus, in Christ we possess all his benefits and are made righteous in him.

Just as a shoot grafted into a good stem becomes green, blossoms, and brings forth fruit in it, but dies apart from the stem, so a man outside of Christ is nothing other than a cursed vine and all his works are sins (Deut. 32:32-33). "Their clusters are like gall, they have bitter grapes, their wine is the poison of serpents." In Christ, however, he is righteous and holy. Therefore, Paul in 2 Cor. 5:21 says: "God made him who knew no sin to be sin for our sake, so that in him we might become the righteousness that is worthy before God."

From this you now see that works cannot make you righteous. You must first of all be transplanted into Christ through faith and be righteous in him before you can do any good work. See indeed that your righteousness is the grace and gift of God that comes before all your merit. How can a dead man move, stand, or do anything good if someone does not first make him living? Thus, since you are dead in sins and dead to God, you can do no work pleasing to God unless you are first made living in Christ. Righteousness comes only from Christ through faith, for faith is in man as a newborn, small, naked, and simple child that stands bare and unclothed before his Redeemer and Sanctifier, and receives all from him who

brought it forth, namely, righteousness, piety, holiness, grace, and the Holy Spirit.

Thus, if this naked, bare child is to be clothed with God's mercy, it must lift both its hands up and receive everything from God, grace together with all holiness and piety. This reception makes him pious, holy, and blessed.

Therefore, righteousness comes only from faith and not from works. Indeed, faith receives Christ entirely and makes him entirely its own with all those things that he is and has. Then, sin, death, the devil, and hell must give way. If you had all the sin of the whole world upon you, it could not harm you, for Christ with his merit is so strong, mighty, and living in you through faith.

Since Christ now dwells and lives in you through faith (Eph. 3:17), his indwelling is not a dead work but a living work. As a result, the renewal comes from Christ through faith. Faith brings about two things in you: first, it plants Christ in you and makes you his possession; second, it renews you in Christ so that you grow, blossom, and live in him. What is the use of a graft in a stem if it does not grow green and bring forth fruit? Just as formerly through Adam's fall, through the seduction and deception of the devil, the seed of the serpent was sowed in man—that is, the evil, satanic kind, out of which an evil, poisonous fruit grew—so through the Word of God and the Holy Spirit faith was sowed in man as a seed of God in which all divine virtues, qualities, and characteristics were contained, in a hidden manner, and grew out to a beautiful, new image of God, to a beautiful, new tree on which the fruits are love, patience, humility, meekness, peace, chastity, righteousness, the new man, and the whole kingdom of God. The true sanctifying faith renews the whole man, purifies the heart, unites with God, makes the heart free from earthly things, hungers and thirsts after righteousness, works love, gives peace, joy, patience, consolation in all suffer-ing, conquers the world, makes children of God and heirs of all heavenly eternal benefits and coheirs of Christ. If you find someone who does not have the joy of faith but is weak of faith and lacking in consolation, do not reject him because of this but console him with the promised grace in Christ, for it always remains firm, certain, and eternal. Likewise, if we fall out of weakness and stumble, God's grace does not fall away if we rise up again through true repentance. Christ always remains Christ and a Sanctifier who can be grasped with weak or strong faith. Weak faith belongs as much to Christ as strong, because whether a man is weak or strong of faith, he is Christ's own. The promised grace is common to all Christians and is eternal. Faith must rest on this, whether it be weak or strong. God will, in his due time, allow you to come again to refreshing, joyous consolation, even if he hides in your heart for a long time (Pss. 37:24; 77:8-11). For more on this, see Book Two.

151. Book One, Chapter Thirty-Nine: The Purity of Teaching and of the Divine Word Is Upheld Not Only with Disputations and Many Books But Also with True Repentance and Holy Life

"Follow the pattern of the sound words that you have heard from me, in the faith and love that are in Christ Jesus. Guard the truth that has been entrusted to you by the Holy Spirit who dwells within us" (2 Tim. 1:13-14).

The pure teaching and truth of the holy Christian faith must necessarily answer the rabble and heretics and be defended according to the example of the holy prophets, who preached firmly against the false and idolatrous prophets in the Old Testament. It must also follow the example of the Son of God, who earnestly disputed against the Pharisees and scribes in Jerusalem. Again, it must follow the example of John the Evangelist, who wrote his Gospel against the heretics Ebion and Cerinthus and who wrote his Revelation against the false church of the Nicolites and others.

We also see how St. Paul, against the false apostles, defended the article of justification by faith (Rom. 3:21ff.; 4:1ff.), of good works (2 Corinthians 9–8ff.), of the resurrection of the dead (1 Cor. 15:1ff.), and of Christian freedom (Gal. 5:1ff.) and other doctrines. The holy bish-ops and fathers of the early church followed and continued his example, writing many well-grounded polemical books against the pagan idolatrous religion and other heretics who arose out of it. To this end the chief councils were set up by the praiseworthy Christian emperors against the arch-heretics Arius, Macedonius, Nestorius, and Eutyches. Also, in our own time, the whole world knows that the false practices of the papists and other sects have been demolished by the polemical writ-ings of that dear man, Dr. Martin Luther.

It is reasonable, then, that one should write, preach, and dispute against heretics and the rabble, for the upholding of pure doctrine and true religion. For the apostle Paul commanded that one should dispute with and overcome those who contradict sound doctrine (Titus 1:9). Still, these activities have deteriorated into such misuse in our time that with so many heavy disputations, polemical sermons, writ-ings, and rebuttals, Christian life, true repen-tance, godliness, and Christian love are being entirely forgotten. It is as if Christianity con-sists only in disputations and the multiplica-tion of polemical books, and not far more in seeing to it that the holy gospel and the teach-ing of Christ are applied in a holy life.

1. Look then at the examples of the holy prophets and apostles, even the Son of God himself. They not only strove firmly against false prophets, false apostles, and idolaters, but they also insisted on repentance and a Christian life. With powerful preaching, they proclaimed that religion and worship would be destroyed by impenitence and godless living, that the church would be laid waste and the land and people punished with hunger, war, and pestilence, as experience has shown to happen. What else did the prophet Isaiah preach (Isa. 5:6)? "If no grapes can be found in the vineyard of the Lord but only wild grapes, the Lord God will lay waste to the vineyard." This is indeed an earnest warning that godlessness is the reason why God withdraws his Word from us. What else did the Lord Christ preach in John 12:35? "Walk in the light while you have it so that the darkness may not overtake you." What is it to walk in the light other than to follow Christ in life? What is it to be overtaken by darkness other than to lose the pure doctrine of the gospel? From this it is thus clear that no one without true repentance and a holy life can be enlightened with the light of truth. For the Holy Spirit, which enlightens the heart, curses the godless and continually gives itself to holy souls and makes prophets and friends of God (Wis. 7:27). "The fear of the Lord is the beginning of wisdom," says Ps. 111:10 and therefore godlessness is the beginning of foolishness and blindness.

2. Thus, true knowledge and confession of Christ and pure teaching does not consist in words only but in action and in a holy life, as St. Paul says in Titus 1:16: "They say they know God but they deny him by their works; hence, they are an abomination, disobedient and unfit for all good works." In this passage we hear that Christ and his word are denied as much by a godless life as by words, 2 Tim. 3:5: "They have an appearance of godliness but deny the power of it." What kind of true knowledge of Christ can that be that one does not demonstrate in action? He who has not felt and tasted the humility, meekness, patience, and love of Christ in his heart cannot truly know Christ. How should one confess Christ when in distress? Whoever confesses Christ's teaching and not his life confesses only half of Christ, and whoever preaches Christ's teaching and not his life preaches only half of Christ. Much is written and disputed concerning teaching but little concerning life. We may be well served with polemical books on doctrine, but pure repentance and Christian life are served little by them. For what is teaching without life? A tree without fruit. Truly, he who does not follow Christ in his life also does not follow him in his teaching, for the chief article of the teaching of Christ is: Love from a pure heart, a good conscience, and a sincere faith (1 Tim. 1:5). As a result, many a man learns to speak and argue much concerning disputed articles of belief so that he might look good, but in his heart he is an evil man, full of pride, envy, and avarice, worse than any basilisk. St. Paul, not without cause, ties faith and love together (2 Tim. 1:13), and this is to point out that teaching and life are to agree together.

3. We do not of course mean to say that through our power and piety blessedness is achieved, for we are preserved for blessedness through the power of God (1 Pet. 1:5). It is clear that through a godless life the Holy Spirit is expelled with all his gifts among which the gifts of faith, knowledge, understanding, and wisdom are not the least. How can the truth of pure doctrine be upheld without a holy life? Clearly, the godless who do not follow Christ cannot be enlightened with the true light. On the other hand, whoever walks in the light, that is, who follows Christ in life, is enlightened by the true light (John 1:9), which is

Christ, and is preserved from all error. Concerning this, the holy and spiritual teacher [Johann] Tauler said: "If a man gives himself and resigns himself to God and denies his will and flesh, then the Holy Spirit is able to enlighten him and to teach him properly since God keeps the pure Sabbath and rest-day in his heart and frees it from all evil lusts, wishes, and works." Now this should be understood to concern the state after conversion and of daily enlightenment and increase of new gifts after conversion.

4. It is not without cause that the Lord says in John 14:6, "I am the way, the truth, and the life." He calls himself first "the way" because he has shown us the way. But how? Not only through his holy teaching but also through his innocent life. His life is nothing other for us than true repentance and conversion to God, which leads us to truth and life, in which the whole of Christianity consists, in which all the books and the commandments are contained. We have this Book of the Life of Christ to study throughout our life, namely, in true repentance, in living, active faith, in love, hope, meekness, patience, humility, prayer, and the fear of God, the right path to truth and to life that is in all respects Christ himself. He is the narrow way and the small gate (Matt. 7:14), which few of you find, and the only Book of Life, which few of you study. Everything is contained in it that is necessary for a Christian; thus, we do not need any other book for our holiness. The Holy Scriptures are only composed of a few books so that we might know that Christianity does not consist in innumerable books but in living faith and the following of the Lord Christ. Thus, Solomon writes in Eccles. 12:12-13: "Of the writing of books, there is no end. The sum of all doctrine is: Fear God and keep his commandments." . . .

7. Finally, that faith is true that is active through love (Gal. 5:6), through which man

becomes a new creature, through which he is newborn, through which he is united with God, through which Christ dwells in us (Eph. 3:17), lives in us, and works in us, by which the kingdom of God is established in us, through which the Holy Spirit purifies and enlightens our hearts (Eph. 4:23). Many splendid passages bear witness to this: 1 Cor. 6:17, "He who is united to the Lord becomes one spirit with him." What does it mean "to become one spirit" with Christ other than to be of a like mind, heart, and spirit with Christ? This is indeed the new, holy, noble life of Christ in us. Again, 2 Cor. 5:17: "If anyone is in Christ, he is a new creature." What does "to be in Christ" mean? Not only to believe in him but also to live in him. Again, Hosea 2:19: "I will betroth myself with you for eternity; indeed, I will promise myself to you in faith." What is this other than that a man will become completely, spiritually united with Christ so that where faith is there is Christ. Where Christ is, a holy life exists in man. Where Christ's life is there is his love, and where his love is, there is God himself, for God is love. There also is the Holy Spirit. Everything necessary must be together there and cling together as a head with its members and as a cause from which an effect and fruits must follow. Such unity of Christian faith and life is described by St. Peter in his second epistle, 1:5ff: "Make every effort to supplement your faith with virtue and virtue with knowledge, and knowledge with temperance, and temperance with patience, and patience with godliness, and godliness with brotherly affections, and brotherly affection with love. If these things richly exist in you, you will not let yourself become rotten or unfruitful in the knowledge of our Lord Jesus Christ. But whoever does not have these is blind and gropes about with his hand and forgets his purification from former sins." Peter expressly says that whoever does not have such unity and

Christian faith does not know Christ, has lost faith, and walks in darkness. That is true faith that renews and makes the whole man alive in Christ so that he lives and remains in Christ and Christ in him.

152. Foreword to Book Three

Just as our natural life has its different steps—childhood, adulthood, old age—so it is also in our spiritual life. Our Christian life has its beginning in repentance, by which a man daily improves himself; next, like middle age, comes more enlightenment by meditation on divine things, prayer, and bearing the cross, through which all the gifts of God are increased. Last comes the completeness of old age that consists of full union through love. St. Paul names this the perfect maturity of Christ and mature manhood in Christ (Eph. 4:13).

I have taken this order into consideration, as much as possible, in the first three books, and reckon that all of Christianity is covered in them (along with my little prayer book), as much as is necessary, although all may not be perfect or more might be desired. I have added the fourth book to the rest in order to show how Scripture, Christ, human nature, and all of nature harmoniously agree and how all things lead toward and flow back to the one, eternal, living origin of all which is God.

So that you may rightly understand what I say in this third book, you should know that it points out how you may seek and find the kingdom of God within you (Luke 17:21). For this to happen, you must give your whole heart and soul to God, not only your understanding, but also your will and heartfelt love. Many think today that their Christianity is sufficient

or even more than satisfactory, if they grasp Christ with their understanding, through reading and disputation. This is the focus now of the common course of theological study, which consists of mere speculation and scholarly learning and does not consider that the other powers of the soul, namely, the will and affections must also be engaged. You must also consecrate both of them to God and Christ so that you have given your entire soul to him. There is a great difference between the understanding by which we know about Christ, and the will by which we love him. We know Christ as much as we can, but we love him as he really is.

To know Christ with our understanding and not to love him are worth nothing. It is a thousand times better to love him than to be able to dispute and discourse about him (Eph. 3:19). Therefore, we should learn so to seek Christ with our understanding that we may love him with our heartfelt will and pleasure. From true knowledge of Christ, true love of Christ also comes. If we do not do that, we may indeed find him but to our own great detriment. For this is what the Lord says in Matt. 7:21: "Not every one who says to me, Lord, Lord, shall enter into the kingdom of heaven." There are two ways of obtaining wisdom and knowledge. The first group does it through much reading and disputing; these are the learned. The other group seeks through prayer and love; we call them the saints. Between these two there is a great difference. Those who are only learned but not lovers of God are proud and puffed up, but the holy are lowly and humble. If you take the first way, you will never find your internal treasure; if you take the other way, you will find it within yourself. The entire third book seeks this second way. . . .

153. Book Three, Chapter Two: The Means by Which a Man Attains His Inward Treasure, Namely, through True, Living Faith and through Turning within Himself

"You transgressors, go into your heart" (Isa. 46:8).

The truest way to turn within to this inward treasure and highest blessing is by a true and living faith. Although we have already explained its power and character in the first and second books, how it clings to Christ alone and is grounded only in him, we must treat the topic [of faith] more sublimely here, showing now how it relates to the matter at hand. It is the property of a true and living faith to cling loyally to God, to put its whole confidence in him, to trust him with a whole heart, to give itself entirely to him, to leave itself to his mercy, to unite itself with God, to be and remain one with God, to rest alone in God, to hold his inner Sabbath, to let God alone be its highest desire, wish, longing, delight, and joy, shutting out all creatures, wishing and desiring nothing but God alone as the highest, eternal, unending, perfect Good, which is all Good, without which no true Good can be in heaven and earth, in time and eternity, and all this in and through Christ Jesus, our Lord, who is "the beginner and completer of our faith" (Heb. 12:2). . . .

Faith is the means of attaining our inward treasure, when God holds a still Sabbath and a man turns within himself. For just as the motion of the heavenly bodies is, therefore, the most noble and perfect, because it returns to the origin from which it began its course: so also the life journey of man may be accounted most noble and perfect, when it returns to its origin, which is God. But this cannot happen unless a man goes within himself with all his powers, withdraws his understanding, will, and memory from the world and all fleshly things, turns his soul with all its desires to God through the Holy Spirit, flees from the world and rests in the still Sabbath, which God can cause to take place within him. God waits for this Sabbath of the heart, and it is his highest joy when he can bring it to pass within us. For God is so ready to come to us and hastens so much that it seems as if he would rather that his divine essence would be broken up and rendered nothing if he could not reveal all the ground of his Godhead and the fullness of his essence and nature to us. God hastens to be our own just as he is his own. Man can do nothing better than be at rest and hold this Sabbath. All that God needs for his work is for one to give him a humble and resting heart; then he effects his work in the soul into which no man can come. The eternal wisdom of God is so delicate in its work that it cannot allow a creature to see it.

The more the soul rests in God, the more God rests in it. If you rest completely in God, then God will rest completely in you. But if you use your own will, understanding, memory, and desires according to your own pleasure, God cannot use them or do his work within you. If two are to become united, one must rest and be receptive while the other must act. God is an infinite, constant, active power, pure movement, never resting, acting in you as far as he can without your hindering him. This can be understood better by a comparison: If the eye would see and receive an impression, it must be empty of all other images and forms. For if it already has an image or form within it, it cannot see or contain another image. Likewise, the soul cannot contain God with its powers, understanding, will, memory, and desires if it is full of the world and worldly things. Just as the ear must be empty of all other tones if it is to hear a good piece of string music, so also the soul must be empty of the world to hear the sweetness of God. The more, therefore, you fight fleshly lusts, the more you will "partake of the divine nature." (2 Pet.1:4).

Nature cannot allow a vacuum to exist. It fills all things with itself. But before Nature can intrude, something must be empty and remain so. Through this principle and means, great arts have been contrived. Thus, if a man empties his heart of love of the world and self-will, of lusts and desires and keeps himself free from these, God will not allow him to remain empty. He must fill the vacuum with his divine grace, love, wisdom, and knowledge. But if you want to be full of this world, you will be empty of heavenly things. When Abraham, at the command of God, went out from his homeland and friends, then, he was enlightened by God (Gen. 12:1, 13:1). Our carnal affections, self-love, self-will, our own wisdom, honor, and desire, are our nearby friends. It pains the flesh to forsake these and to leave them. But to do that is the beginning of the search for the hidden treasure, "the costly pearl in the field" about which our Lord speaks in Matt. 13:46: "A man sold all his things so that he might find the pearl." Is it not this about which our Lord speaks in Mark 10:29? "Whoever will leave father, mother, brother, sister, houses, or lands for my sake, will receive a hundredfold and eternal life." Our fleshly affections, will, and desires are our brothers and sisters which we should leave. Just as the blessed Virgin Mary was a pure, undefiled virgin (and remained in eternity as she lovingly received Christ, Luke 1:27), so if our soul is as a pure, undefiled virgin, that is, unpolluted by love of the world, unspotted, free from all the pollutions of the world, it will spiritually conceive Christ. It has the highest treasure within it, "the king's daughter inwardly clothed" (Ps. 45:13), her treasure hidden within her. But if the soul is wedded to the world, how can it be wedded to Christ?

The Lord Christ says in Luke 12:49: "I am come to kindle a fire." Would to God that the fire of divine love would burn up all our affections, fleshly will, and lusts, so that only God's will and pleasure would be accomplished in us. He adds, "Do not think that I have come to bring peace, but war and a sword" (Luke 12:51). Would to God that all your fleshly senses and desires were strangled and killed so that God might live and be active in us. But if your office or calling hinders you from going into your heart, then you should look for a small place and choose a time in the day or night to turn inward to the ground of your heart in whatever way you can and say with St. Augustine: "O dear Lord, I want to make a pledge to you: I want truly to die to myself so that you might live in me. I myself want to be silent, so that you might speak within me. I want to be still within myself so that you might act within me."

154. Book Six: Defense of Book Three

The foundation and ground of all that I wrote in the third book of True Christianity is the saying of the Lord: "The kingdom of God is within you" (Luke 17:21). St. Paul also says in Eph. 1:13: "You who believed in him were sealed with the Holy Spirit." This happens in our heart and soul. Concerning this, Tauler said that we must be guided to the inner ground of our heart to seek our inner treasure. There we will find it; there the power of faith will reveal itself, the inner spiritual beauty, *decor internus*. . . . Every chapter is a little portion of the seal of the Holy Spirit and if the book is opened with prayer and meditation, many benefits of this treasure and the kingdom of God will come to pass. This is not

Enthusiasm, as some despicable men think; rather it is what St. Paul calls "αναζωπυρειν" [to light up again]. Out of a little spark a fire will flare up and out of a little seed a great tree will grow. It is also not Schwenkfeldianism, as you might think, for [I believe that] a Christian is already born anew, made a believer, and converted from God's Word and the most worthy sacrament of baptism. Some just lack the practice and exercising of active faith. It is also not Osiandrism, for it is the grace-rich righteousness of Christ not essential righteousness that works pure fruits of grace in us. Note well that it is not papism, for [the inner treasure] comes through grace, not our own merit. Furthermore, it is not Weigelianism, for [it is attained through] the power of the living Word of God.[1]

JOHANN GERHARD

Sacred Meditations (1606)

In *School of Piety*, a lengthy, practical manual published in 1622, Johann Gerhard stated that the devil fights against the Christian church in two ways: by encouraging false teaching and by planting the weeds of false security in the hearts of people.[2] Gerhard attempted to promote purity of teaching through his systematic theology and purity of life through his devotional writings. In *Sacred Meditations* he emphasized the need for true repentance, consoled the penitent sinner by reflecting on the salvific Incarnation and Passion of Christ, and then described the new life that should flow from true faith. Although Gerhard, like Arndt, used mystical language to describe the union of the believer with God and encouraged imitation of the life of Christ, the way he

presented these themes never provoked any controversy. *Sacred Meditations* was first published in 1606.

From *Meditationes sacrae ad veram pietatem excitandam* (Frankfurt: Hermsdorff, 1685), #13, 28, 30.

155. Spiritual Marriage of Christ and the Soul

JESUS IS THE BRIDEGROOM OF THE SOUL

"I will betroth you unto me forever," Christ says to the faithful soul [Hos. 2:19]. Christ wanted to take part in the wedding celebration in Cana of Galilee [John 2:2], in order to show us that he had come to earth to celebrate a spiritual wedding. "Rejoice gladly in the Lord and take delight, O faithful soul, in your God for he has clothed you with the garments of salvation, he has covered you with the robe of righteousness, as a bride adorns herself with necklaces" [Isa. 61:10]. Rejoice because of the honor of your bridegroom; rejoice because of the comeliness of your bridegroom; rejoice because of the bridegroom's love. His honor is the greatest: "for he is true God, blessed forever" [Rom. 9:5]. How great then is the dignity of this creature, this faithful soul, that the Creator himself wishes to take her as a spouse to himself! His beauty is the greatest: "For he is more handsome in form than the sons of man" [Ps. 45:2]; since "they beheld his glory, the glory as of the only-begotten of the Father" [John 1:14]; "his face shone like the sun" [Matt. 17:2] "and his garments were white as snow" [Mark 9:3]; "grace is also poured onto his lips" [Ps. 45:2]; "he is crowned with glory and honor" [Ps. 8:6]. How great then is his mercy, that, though he is the perfection of beauty, he does not disdain to choose for his bride the soul of the sinner deformed by the stain of sins. How great is the majesty of the

Bridegroom and the infirmity of the bride; the beauty of the Bridegroom and the deformity of the bride; and yet the Bridegroom's love toward the bride is greater still than the bride's toward her most esteemed and most beautiful Bridegroom.

Consider the immense love of your bridegroom, O faithful soul; a love that drew him down from heaven to earth, which bound him to the pillar to be scourged, that affixed him to the cross, that enclosed him in the sepulcher, that dragged him down to hell. What made him do all this, if not love for his bride? But our hearts must be harder than stone and lead that the bond of such love does not draw us upwards to God, from whom it first drew God down to us. "The bride was naked" [Ezek. 16:22]; nor could she be brought into the royal palace of the heavenly kingdom; but he "clothed her with the garments of salvation and righteousness" [Isa. 61:10]. When she lay wrapped in the dirty tunic of her sins and in the most foul rags of her iniquities, he gave her linen, bright and pure, so that she might cover herself; "the linen is the righteous deeds of the saints" [Rev. 19:8], the garment is the righteousness procured by the death and passion of the bridegroom. . . .

Acknowledge, O faithful soul, so many and such great signs of his infinite love; cherish, O faithful soul, the love of him, who out of love for you descended into the virgin's womb. We ought to love him as much as and more than we love ourselves, since he who gave himself up for us is greater than we are. All of our life should be given back to him, in conformity to him who out of love for us totally conformed himself to us. Whoever does not return love to Christ who first loved him, is deservedly considered most ungrateful. O how much we ought to love him who out of love of us disregarded his majesty. O happy the soul that is united to Christ by the bonds of this spiritual

marriage: She may securely and confidently apply all the benefits of Christ to herself, just as a wife, in other respects, radiates the reflected honor of her husband.

It is by faith alone that we are made participants in this blessed spiritual union, as it is written, "I will betroth you unto me in faith" (Hos. 2:19). Faith grafts us into Christ like branches into a spiritual vine (John 15:2), so that we draw all our life and strength from him; and as those who live together in marriage are no longer two but one flesh (Matt. 19:6), so "anyone who clings to the Lord through faith is one spirit with him" (1 Cor. 6:17), because "Christ dwells in our hearts through faith" (Eph. 3:7). Faith, if it is true, is efficacious through love (Gal. 5:6). Just as, in the Old Testament, the high priests were restricted to taking virgins as their wives (Lev. 21:7), so this heavenly High Priest spiritually unites himself with the virgin soul which keeps herself whole and unspotted from the embraces of the devil, the world, and the flesh. Make us worthy, O Christ, to be admitted someday to the marriage of the Lamb (Rev. 19:7). Amen.

156. General Rules for a Godly Life

"PIETY IS THE PERFECTION OF WISDOM"
Every day you are drawing nearer to death, to judgment, and to eternity. Consider, therefore, every day, how you will face death, withstand the severe test of the judgment, and live for all eternity. You should take great care respecting all your thoughts, words, and actions, because one day you must give a precise accounting of all your thoughts, words and actions [Matt. 12:36]. At evening time, consider that death could be at hand this very night; and in the

morning, keep in mind that death might approach you during the day. Do not put off conversion and the practice of good works until tomorrow, because it is not certain that there will be a tomorrow for you. It is certain, however, that death is impending. Nothing is more adverse to piety than procrastination [Sir. 18:22]. If you continue to disparage the inward call of the Holy Spirit, you will never be truly converted. Do not put off conversion and good works until old age; instead, offer to God the flower of your youth. Old age is not certain to come to the young, but it is certain that destruction is prepared for impenitent young people. No time of life is more suitable for the service of God than [the days of your] youth when you have a vigorous body and a lively mind. You should never commit an evil deed to gain the favor of any man, for God, not that man, will one day judge your life. Therefore, never set up the favor of any man in preference to the grace of God. We are either advancing or retreating in the way of the Lord; therefore, examine your life every single day to see whether you are going forward or backwards in your zeal for piety. To stand still in the way of the Lord is really to regress; therefore, do not choose to stand still in the journey of piety, but strive earnestly always to walk forward in the way of the Lord. In your conversation, be pleasant to all, harsh to none, and familiar with few. Live dutifully toward God, upright with regards to yourself, [and] justly toward your neighbor [Titus 2:12]. Act graciously toward your friends, patiently with your enemies, benevolently toward everyone, and also generously, as far as you are able. While you live, die daily to yourself and to your vices, so that when you die you may live unto God.

Show mercy always in the disposition of your mind, kindness in your countenance, humility in your manner, modesty in your dealings with others, and patience in tribula-

tion. Always reflect on three things about the past: the evil you have committed, the good you have omitted, and the time you have let slip away. Always consider three things about the present: the brevity of your present life, the difficulty of salvation, and the small number of those who will be saved. Always ponder these three future things: death, than which nothing is more horrible, the judgment, than which nothing is more terrible; and the punishments of hell, than which nothing can be more intolerable. Let your evening prayers emend the sins of the day which has gone by; let the last day of the week rectify the faults of the preceding days. Every evening, think about how many have fallen headlong into hell this day, and give thanks that God has granted you more time for repentance. There are three things above you of which you should never lose sight: the all-seeing eye of God, the all-hearing ear of God, and the books [of judgment] in which all things are recorded. God has totally shared himself with you; so give yourself totally to your neighbor. The best life on earth is that which is completely devoted to serving others. Show reverence and obedience toward your superiors, give counsel and aid to those who are your equals, watch over and discipline your inferiors. Let your body be subject to your mind, and your mind subject to God. Weep over your past misdeeds, give little weight to your present welfare, and with the total desire of your whole heart crave future blessings. Remember your sins, so that you may grieve over them; be mindful of death, so you may avoid sin; keep divine justice in mind, so you may fear to sin; yet remember the mercy of your God, so you do not give in to despair.

Pull yourself away from the world as much as you can, and devote yourself totally to the service of the Lord. Always bear in mind that your purity is endangered by the allurements of the world, your humility by its riches, and your piety by its business affairs. Seek to please no one but Christ; do not be afraid to displease anyone but Christ. Always pray to God that he might order [for you] what he wants and give [you] what he orders; that he might cover what you have done and might control what will unfold for you in the future. Let what you truly are correspond to what you want to appear to be, for God judges not according to appearance but according to truth. In speech, beware of talkativeness, for at the judgment you must supply a reason for every idle word [Matt. 12:36]. Your works, whatever they are, do not pass away, but are scattered abroad, as it were, like seeds sown for eternity. "For if you sow to your flesh, you will reap corruption from your flesh; but if you sow in the Spirit, you will reap the reward of eternal life from the Spirit" [Gal. 6:8]. The honors of this world will not follow you after death, neither will all your accumulated riches nor the pleasures and vanities of the world; but all the works which you have done will follow you after the end of this life [Rev. 14:13]. Therefore, you should appear in God's sight today as you want to appear at the judgment. Do not calculate the worth of what you are now, but estimate more how you fall short of what you ought to be; instead of feeling pride about what has been given to you, humble yourself because of what you have been denied. Learn to live rightly, while you are still permitted to live. Eternal life is either won or lost in this life; after death, the time for working is past and the time for weighing what you have done begins. Let holy meditation produce knowledge within you and from this knowledge a conviction of sin. May this conviction of sin lead to devotion, and this devotion to prayer.

Silence of the mouth is a great good for peace of heart. The more you are separated from the world, the more pleasing you will be to God. Whatever you desire to have, seek it from God; whatever you have already, credit it to God. You are not worthy of receiving more if you are not grateful for what you have already been given. Grace ceases to descend upon you when you cease to return gratitude to God. Convert whatever happens to you to good account: As often as favorable times come your way, consider what a reason they provide for blessing and praising [God]; if hard times overtake you, consider these as warnings to repent and convert. Display your physical powers in helping others, your wisdom in instructing others, and the quantity of your wealth in beneficence. Do not let adversity crush you, nor prosperity elate you. Let Christ be the aim of your life whom you will follow in this world so that you might reach the heavenly fatherland. In all things let your greatest care be to display profound humility and ardent love. Elevate your heart to God in love so you may cling to him; plant humility deep in your heart lest you become proud. See God as Father in his clemency, and as Lord in his discipline; as your Father when his power is manifested gently, as your Lord when it is displayed severely; love him reverently as a Father; fear him, of necessity, as a Lord and Master. Love him because he desires to be merciful; fear him because he takes no delight in sin. Fear the Lord, and put your trust in him [Ps. 37:5]; acknowledge your own wretchedness and proclaim his grace.

O God, who has enabled us to seek to do your will, give us also the power to do it [Phil. 2:13].

157. Imitation of the Holy Life of Christ

LET CHRIST BE THE RULE OF YOUR LIFE

The holy life of Christ is the most perfect model of virtue; indeed, every action of Christ is for our instruction. Many wish to attain to Christ, but draw back from following him;

they want to enjoy Christ, but not to imitate him. "Learn from me, for I am gentle and humble in heart," says our Savior [Matt. 6:29]. Unless you are willing to be a disciple of Christ, you will never be a true Christian. May the Passion of Christ be your merit, but also the actions of Christ a model for your own life. "Your beloved is dazzling white and ruddy" [Song of Sol. 5:10]; and so may you too be ruddy by the sprinkling of the blood of Christ, and dazzling white by the imitation of Christ's life.

How do you truly love Christ, if you do not love his holy life? "If you love Me," says the Savior, "keep My commandments" [John 14:15,23]. Therefore, he who does not keep his commandments also does not love him. The holy life of Christ is a perfect rule of conduct for our lives. The unique rule of the life of Christ should be preferred to all the rules of St. Francis and St. Benedict. If you want to be an adopted son of God, observe whatever is associated with the only-begotten Son of God. If you want be a co-heir with Christ, you should also be an imitator of Christ. He who chooses to live a vice-filled life, has given himself up to the service of the devil. Indeed, how can one who wants to be with the devil, also be in any way with Christ? To love vice is to love the devil; because all sins are of the devil [1 John 3:8]. And how can one be a true lover of Christ who is a lover of the devil? To love God is to love a holy life, because every holy life is from God; how then can one be a lover of God who is not a lover of a holy life? The proof of love is in the exhibition of works; it is characteristic of true love to obey the loved one, to think and will the same as the loved one. Therefore, if you truly love Christ, you will obey his commands, you will love a holy life with him, and, renewed in the spirit of your mind, you will meditate upon heavenly things [Eph. 4:23]. Life eternal consists in knowing Christ [John

17:3]: for he who does not love Christ does not even know him; he who does not love humility, purity, gentleness, temperance, charity, also does not love Christ, for the life of Christ is nothing other than humility, purity, gentleness, temperance, and love. Christ says that he does not know those who do not do the will of his Father [Matt. 7:21]; therefore those who do not do the will of the heavenly Father have no knowledge of Christ. What, in fact, is the will of the Father? "Our sanctification" [1 Thess. 4:3], says the apostle. "Whoever does not have the Spirit of Christ does not belong to Christ" [Rom 8:9]; but where the Holy Spirit is there his gifts and fruits will also appear. What are fruits of the Spirit? "Love, joy, peace, mildness, kindness, goodness, faith, gentleness, temperance" [Gal. 5:22]. Just as the Holy Spirit rested upon Christ [Isa. 11:2] so he rests also upon all those are in Christ by true faith, for the bride of Christ hastens toward the sweet smell of the ointments of Christ [Song of Sol. 1:3]. "Whoever is joined to the Lord is one spirit with him [1 Cor. 6:17]. Just as the union of the flesh of a man and wife joined makes one flesh out of two [Matt. 19:6] so the spiritual union of Christ and the faithful soul makes them one spirit. Truly, where there is one spirit, there is the same will; and where there is the same will, there are also the same actions. Therefore, if one's life does not conform to the life of Christ, it is proven that the person neither clings to Christ nor has the Spirit of Christ. Is it not right that all of our life should be conformed to Christ's, since he, out of love for us, has totally conformed himself to our life? "God manifesting himself in the flesh" [1 Tim. 3:16] has displayed for us a perfect example of a holy life, so that no one who departs from a holy life to the flesh can take refuge in an excuse. No life can be more pleasing and tranquil than the life of Christ, because Christ was true God; and what can be more pleasing and tranquil than the true God, the highest good? Life in this world bestows short-lived joys which carry eternal sorrow in their train. To whomever you conform yourself in this life you will also be conformed in the resurrection. If you begin to conform yourself to the life of Christ here, then in the resurrection you will be more fully conformed to him; but if you join yourself to the devil through shameful acts, then in the resurrection you will join him in torment. "if you wish to follow me, deny yourself and daily take up your cross," says our Savior [Matt. 16:24]. If in this life you deny yourself, then in the judgment Christ will acknowledge you as his own. If, for Christ's sake, you renounce your own honor, your own love, your own will in this life, then Christ will graciously make you share his own honor, his own love, his own will in the future life. If you join him in bearing the cross in this life, you will join him in his eternal light in the life to come. If you are a partner in tribulation with him now, you will share in his consolation in the future. If you suffer persecution with him in this life, you will partake of a plentiful recompense in the future life. "Whoever acknowledges Me in this generation," says Christ, "I will also acknowledge in the presence of My Heavenly Father" [Matt. 10:32]. Now indeed we ought to confess Christ not only by a profession of doctrine, but also by conformation of our lives to his; and so at last, he will recognize us as his own in the day of judgment. "Whoever will deny Me before men, I will also deny before My Heavenly Father" [Matt. 10:33]. Christ is not only denied by words, but also much more by ungodly living. Therefore, whoever denies Christ by actions in this world, Christ will also deny by his actions at the judgment. He is not a Christian who does not have true faith in Christ; moreover, true faith in Christ engrafts us as branches into his spiritual vine [John 15:4]. Every branch in Christ that does not

bear, the celestial farmer destroys, but "whoever abides in Christ and in whom Christ dwells by faith, bears much fruit" [Eph. 3:17]. That branch that does not draw its sap from the vine is not really in the vine; the soul that does not draw the spiritual sap of love from Christ through faith is not really united to Christ through faith.

Make us more conformed to your life in this world, O gracious Jesus, so that we may be fully conformed to you in the life to come!

HEINRICH MÜLLER

Spiritual Hours of Refreshment (1664)

Many of the devotional writers developed their books out of sermons they had preached. Thus, their writings retain some of the rhetorical features of lively preaching. This is particularly evident in several of Heinrich Müller's devotional books. His exhortations to holy living were often presented as if he were recording a conversation between himself and another person. He frequently used pithy phrases which were easily remembered because of his use of rhyme or wordplay. Some of his books were designed to console people beset by suffering. Others were highly affective meditations on the love of God. Occasionally, however, Müller could be bluntly critical and polemical. This is most evident in his well-known critique of superficial, sacramental religiosity, which offended some theologians to whom it sounded like a radical attack on the traditional focus of Lutheran worship. Like Arndt, Müller was forced to write a defense of himself to assuage the suspicions of those who thought his efforts to reform Lutheranism were really reshaping it in unacceptable ways. *Spiritual Hours of Refreshment* was first published in 1664.

From Heinrich Müller, *Geistliche Erquickstünden* (Berlin: Rüdiger, 1735), #31, 152, 262.

158. Spiritual Drunkenness

"The wine speaks through me."

That is what the drunk says. That is not good. You laugh, but I am shocked. The wine speaks through you; the devil speaks through the wine; the devil speaks through you. If the devil controls your tongue, he also possesses your heart. Nature has connected the heart and tongue closely together through a little vein. The heart is the well within which the Evil One brews his poison; the tongue is the gutter through which it pours out. "How can the devil come into the wine?" you ask. My dear one, how did he come into the snake? He knows how to coil himself nimbly into the creature and slink through the same into the heart. Truly I have nothing to do with you. If he could deceive Eve through the snake, why not you or me?

But let that be. You boast that the wine speaks through you, I myself can also boast. The wine speaks through me perhaps more often than through you. Do you not notice, when I preach, how the fullness of the Spirit often flows out to my mouth? Many times my heart stands in a thousand springs and each spring goes up to heaven. I become so courageous that I want to force my way with my Jesus through spear and sword, through fire and flame, through trouble and death. I don't know myself how I have this courage and, as it were, am captivated by the Spirit. The carnal man does not understand, but whoever has tasted the powers of heaven perceives that I am [spiritually] intoxicated. Hear then [what I say]. When my Jesus has bitterly afflicted me and wants to make it up to me, he leads me

Heinrich Müller

into his wine cellar [Song of Sol. 2:4] and lets me drink with delight as from a river [Ps. 36:8]. Then I become full of the Spirit and when the heart is full, the mouth overflows. I sing and say of my Jesus, how sweet he is. I shout for joy and invite the souls which are bound in the Spirit with me: "O, come then, taste and see how friendly the Lord is. Blessed is he who trusts in him" [Ps. 34:8]. Then, I am not speaking; the fullness of the Spirit, the heavenly joy-wine speaks through me. It is as Paul says: "Be filled with the Spirit and speak among each other with psalms and hymns and spiritual songs, sing and make melody to the Lord in your heart" [Eph. 5:19]. See then, the wine does not speak only through you but also through me. O Jesus, let me taste your sweetness in my heart and thirst instead after you.

159. The Idolatry of the Mouth Christians

"**Divine Worship, Idol Worship**"

O, whose heart does not break from sorrow and dismay. God is made to adorn idols. How much worship of idols *[Götzendienst]* the

Mouth Christians conduct under the appearance of and in the name of worship of God [*Gottesdienst*]. With tears, I wrote about this in my Apostolic Chain of Inferences and now, weeping, I write about it once more. Christianity today (I speak here of the hypocritical Christians as the surrounding text sufficiently shows) has four dumb church idols which it follows: the baptismal font, the pulpit, the confessional seat, and the altar. They console themselves with their outer Christianity, that they are baptized, hear God's Word, go to confession and receive the Lord's Supper, but they scorn the inner power of Christianity. They scorn the power of Baptism since they do not live in accordance with the new nature, but keep to their old nature, even though baptism is a bath of rebirth and renewal. They scorn the power of the Word of God, since they do not live as the Word intends, but refute the Word with their godless living and make a lie of it. They scorn the power of absolution, since afterwards they remain unchanged in their character, living today just as they did yesterday, even though the heart, if it is quickened with the consolation of divine absolution, will no longer love evil and hate the good. They deny the power of Holy Communion since they do not live in Christ with whom they are united, but live according to the lusts of their flesh and pour forth all kinds of sins. "What accord has Christ with Belial?" (2 Cor. 6:15). All this is idolatry. For God is a Spirit and desires that we should worship him in spirit and in truth (John 4:24).

How is this? Isn't it like the Anabaptists to call baptism, the Word, confession and the Lord's Supper dumb idols? Friend, is there, then, no difference according to you between baptism and the baptismal font, preaching and the pulpit, confession and the confessional bench, the Lord's Supper and the altar? The Anabaptists abolish the right use of the baptismal font, the pulpit, the confessional seat, and the altar; I endeavor to abolish the invalid reliance of the Mouth Christians who depend on and base themselves on these things. Is there no difference between use and abuse? I say then: It is idolatry if the heart attaches itself to something and trusts in something which is not actually God. Whatever the heart of a Mouth Christian relies on or trusts, other than God, that is its idol. For example, he relies on the altar and pulpit, trusting in them despite the fact that he does not believe in Christ and exercise his faith through love. He expects to become holy because he was carried to the baptismal font in his childhood, although now he does not demonstrate the power of baptism in his life, or because he sees and hears the preacher in the pulpit, although he does not receive the Word in faith nor bring it into his life, or because he comes quarterly to the confessional seat even though his heart neither means nor feels what his mouth confesses, or because he goes with other communicants to the altar, although there is neither devotion nor faith in his use of the Lord's Supper. Isn't that called idolatry when I base my salvation not on true faith in Christ but on a delusive faith in wood, lime, or stone?

I say it one more time: Whoever does not serve God as one should according to his Word, in Spirit and in Truth, but merely with outward pretenses and actions, is idolatrous. Semblance without the Word of God is as much an idol as a wooden or silver image. Tell me why our theologians call the papist worship service idolatry? Because it does not have the Word of God as its measure and rule. I call the service of the Mouth Christians idolatry precisely for this reason, because God in his Word expressly rejects the sacrifice without fat [Lev. 3:16], the work without faith [Rom. 3:28].

O, one should not make many disputations about this, but muster courage in the Lord to endeavor to struggle with Elijah against the Baalites [1 Kings 18], to purify the Temple of the Lord and tear down the self-made idols in the hearts of men. It does not help for one to say: "The Anabaptists can misuse such words and thereby excuse their lies." God put up with the devil ripping the word from his mouth and speaking falsely against Christ in the wilderness [Matt. 4, Luke 4]. When Paul consolingly taught that where sin is, there also the grace of God is mighty [Rom. 5:20, 1 Cor. 9:8?], he approached the insolent heap and concluded: so now we must trust to heap sin with sin that the grace of God can show its power to us. Who has gotten them to draw that conclusion? Not Paul and his well-intended words but the devil and their perverted thinking. Poison from the rose. Who can be against [what I say]? Now in the preface of my Apostolic Chain of Inferences, I wrote to the Christian reader: "Should a slanderer dare to sharpen his poisonous teeth on this book, I will not fret myself to death because of that; my dear Savior, his apostles and true servants in the world endured such misfortunes patiently. I have not desired a better fate for myself than my Lord and my brothers in the Lord had before me. Right must remain right and all pious hearts will cling to it. It is a bad habit of the world that it blasphemes the good because it is, itself, evil. What the fleshly man does not understand, he must malign." So it remains. Apply this to yourself, you Pharisee.

160. Faith and Love

"Up and Out"

The ascent of the angel on the ladder of heaven, which Jacob saw in his dream [Gen. 28:10-12], is a lovely image of Christ. He is true God and Man, became the mediator between God and Man, united in himself God and Man, Heaven and Earth, going down in his Incarnation and going up in his Ascension. It is also a marvelous image of the Christian. For what is our Christianity other than a steady going up and going out? Up to God, out to our neighbor; to God through faith, to the neighbor through love. Upwards, heart! Grasp the bountiful Jesus in the arms of faith and say: "You are mine and that which is yours, is all mine." O how rich you are in your Jesus; you can say *Jesum meum et omnia.* Let the world step up and display its riches; what does its treasure amount to? A little bit of poor earth. What you can show in comparison to that is more costly than heaven and earth. With a treasure in your sight, will you settle for a mite? Jesus above all and all in all. What the world gives is a bunch of scraps *[Stückwerck];* what Jesus gives is whole and complete *[Vollwerck].* The former brings thirst, the latter quenches it; the one agitates, the other gratifies. *Jesum meum et omnia.* Jesus is mine and in Jesus all is mine. He is my light in the darkness, so I cannot go astray, my righteousness against sins, my blessing against the curse, my life against death, my salvation against damnation, my protection against oppression, my joy in suffering, my fullness in need, my one and only, outside of him I desire nothing, my all, for in him I find all. The Lord is my shepherd, I shall not want [Ps. 23:1].

> In him alone is my delight,
> Far more than golden treasure,
> If I have him, then all is right
> My joy is without measure.

Outwards, heart! And grasp the poor Jesus in love's arms. O! how he goes there hungry, thirsty, sad, naked, and wretched before your eyes. Will you let him hunger, he who gives you daily bread and feeds your soul with the hidden manna [John 6:32, Rev. 2:17]? To thirst, who gives you to drink with delight as from a river [Ps. 36:8]? To go sad and weeping, who consoled you so bountifully in your need and wiped all tears from your eyes [Rev. 21:4]? To go naked, who clothed you with the robe of righteousness and adorned you with the garments of salvation [Isa. 61:10]? To wallow in wretchedness who stepped into your distress so that you might enter into his joy [Matt. 25:21]? No! my heart. Embrace him and say: I am yours and what is mine is all yours. Are you hungry, my Jesus? I will feed you. Are you thirsty? I will give you drink. Are you naked? I will clothe you. Do you weep? Here is a cloth of consolation with which I will wipe away your tears. He is entirely content with few and little. A morsel of bread is enough to him for his nourishment; a drop of cold water for his refreshment; an old rag to cover him; have you nothing else, [at least] give him a comforting word. You are completely accountable for all you have, and he will reward you from grace for all which you do to one of the least of his believers [Matt. 25:40].

I want to say to you in a few words what I think. In Christ, that faith is only worth something which is active in love [Galatians 5]. Faith makes the Christian; love reveals the Christian. The former leads to God, the latter to the neighbor. The one takes, the other gives. The one receives what God has given, the other lets the neighbor receive. The richer the inflow, the richer the outflow. Do you want to be a Christian? Then practice outwardly what you receive according to the inner man. I want to be a tree which is rooted in heaven but bears fruit on earth. God will give moisture and growth, so my neighbor may break off and eat [the fruit].

CHRISTIAN SCRIVER

Gotthold's Occasional Devotions (1663–69)

Christian Scriver is best known as the author of the widely-read *Treasure of the Soul*, which he first published in 1675 but continued to expand until 1692. This lengthy study of the process by which the soul escapes from sin and recovers its original innocence frequently used imagery or stories to illustrate its spiritual message. Scriver was clearly influenced by the genre of emblem literature, which first appeared in Italy during the sixteenth century and quickly spread throughout Europe. Emblem books presented a series of pictorial images that were then given an allegorical interpretation by an accompanying text. In *Gotthold's Occasional Devotions*, first published in 1663, Scriver devoted a whole book to short descriptions of natural objects or events from daily life, which he then used as symbols of the problems people faced in their pursuit of spiritual growth. The direct inspiration for this book appears to have been a similar book of meditations written by Joseph Hall, an English bishop.

From Christian Scriver, *Gottholds zufälliger Andachten* (Leipzig: Johann & Friedrich Lüderwald, 1686), #1:8, 2:11, 2:27, 2:89, 3:16, 3:70.

161. The Sailors

While walking alongside a river full of ships, Gotthold saw that some sailors were propelling a ship against the current with great effort. They either stepped out onto the shore, harnessed themselves to ropes, and towed the ship behind them, or attached a long rope to a tree or pole and (pulled on it in order to) convey the ship forward.

Here, said he, I have a representation of my own voyage to heaven. The world is the powerful current which pulls many along with it into the sea of perdition. I, with my little ship, must struggle against this current because I have been commanded not to be conformed to the world, nor to love either it or its lusts. (Rom. 12:2; 1 John 2:15.) This requires effort. My sighs and yearnings are my ropes, my resolution my pole, and my strength is in God and his Spirit. I strive and strain forward toward what lies before me (Phil. 3:13). Here there must be no pause or relaxation. For just as the ship will disappear downstream and take the sailors along with it if they should cease to struggle against the current, so it happens in our Christian life. If we cease to fight with ourselves and the world, or become lax in our prayer or other holy practices, we will soon become aware of our decline and the harm this causes.

My God! help me always to strive resolutely, and press forward through death and life.

Christian Scriver

162. The Rowers

Gotthold saw several sailors step into a boat to cross a river. Two took the oars, and, as usual, sat with their backs facing the shore toward which they intended to sail. A third remained standing at the helm and kept his eye unaverted on the place where they wished to land, and so they swiftly reached the shore. See here, Gotthold said, to those around him, we have a good reminder of our labor and vocation. Life is a swift and mighty river flowing through all of time into the ocean of eternity and never returning. On this river, each of us floats in the little ship of our vocation, which we must urge forward with the oars of our diligent labor. Now we should, like these sailors, turn our backs away from the future and, putting our trust in God who stands at the helm and skillfully steers the vessel toward what is profitable and blessed for us, we should diligently labor, unconcerned about anything else. We would laugh if we saw these men turn round and assert that they cannot row blindly but must see the place where they are going. Similarly, is it not foolishness for us, with our anxieties and thoughts, to insist on apprehending all things happening now and in the future? Let us row, and work, and pray and leave it to God to steer, and bless, and govern.

My God, stay with me in my little ship, and steer it according to your good pleasure. I will turn my face toward you, and in accordance with the ability you give me, I will diligently and faithfully labor, leaving it to you to provide all else.

163. The Plant in the Cellar

When Gotthold went into a cellar to look for something, he found a turnip which, having been left there by accident, had grown and sent forth long but weak and slender shoots which were more pale yellow than green and therefore unfit for use. Here, thought he, I have an exemplification of a human undertaking God has not blessed or allowed to prosper. This plant lacks sunshine and open air and therefore cannot thrive. It grows weakly for awhile and then withers. So it is with all our aspirations and endeavors which are not irradiated by the grace of God, nor nurtured by his blessing. As our Savior also said, "Every plant which My Father has not planted, will be uprooted" (Matt. 15:13).

After a while it further occurred to him that this plant could also be a very good illustration of an inexperienced and unpracticed man who places himself in some obscure corner and endeavors to teach himself about many things. Based on such learning, he considers himself a great person and thinks that he is qualified, with his self-taught wisdom, to govern and make prosperous not only a city and church, but even half of the world. However, when he sets about a task, he cannot find in his whole schoolsack skill enough to execute with success this or that trifling matter, and he learns that it is one thing to know something by yourself and quite another thing to bring it to bear among other people who also know something.

This can also happen in our Christianity. We may imagine that our faith, love, and patience have grown splendidly and still we often stand on very weak feet. Experience makes people capable, and bearing the cross produces good Christians. This plant was never shone on by the sun, nor moistened by the dew, nor watered by the rain, nor assailed by the wind, nor hardened by the cold; and, therefore, it is good for nothing. So also, a Christian who has not been tested by both prosperity and adversity, favor and affliction, cannot yet be considered fit or proficient.

Therefore, the dear and much-afflicted Apostle says: "Tribulation works patience; and patience, experience; and experience, hope; and hope makes not ashamed" (Rom. 5:3-5).

164. The Butterfly Catchers

Gotthold saw some boys in a garden, chasing butterflies, and was amused to observe what pains these simple fowlers took to catch the colorful insects. He said to a good friend: Do you know whom these children resemble? They are like those learned and clever scholars who demonstrate not so much their skill and understanding as their curiosity and pride in their excitement over many useless questions. What else are high-flying and useless thoughts and questions but insects such as these; and is the foolishness of these children any greater than that of the learned who imagine that they have hunted down something special when they come up with all sorts of strange, wonderful, and intricate questions and thoughts concerning spiritual and worldly things? Tell me, is any more benefit to be derived from one catch than from the other? And yet, unfortunately, it has almost come about in the world that whoever will not or cannot hunt and catch such flies and motley flying things is looked upon as an inept person. I, for my part, hold that there is a difference in worldly things between a learned and an intelligent person; as also in spiritual things there is a difference between a learned and a godly or pious person. When both are together, it is like the diamond glittering and sparkling in a setting of gold, or like golden apples in dishes of silver. If, however, I could have only one, I would prefer piety, and would rather grasp hold of heaven with the unlearned, than be damned while possessing great skill and aptitude. What is science without conscience? What help is it to learn all things and forget the most important? I have seen people who have many books only for the purpose that, if asked, they can say that they have them. I have known artisans who have many good tools, inherited from their elders or bought from others, but who still do not know how to use them. Do you think these serve any purpose? It is the same with learned people who do not use all of their skills as a tool for honor of God or for the improvement of themselves or their neighbors. I might have imagined that many more clever, learned people would get to heaven if the most learned of all the learned had not said that, on that day, he will say to many who prophesied in his name: I never knew you, go away from me you evildoers (Matt. 7:22, 23).

There are two kinds of people who do futile work and suffer in their hearts as a result: those who gather much money and possessions and do not make use of them, and those who learn and know many things but do not regulate their lives by them.

My God, I know that our knowledge is imperfect in this life and that the most noble and highest wisdom consists in the recognition of you and the Lord Jesus. Therefore, I will direct all my diligence toward believing in the crucified Lord Jesus, loving him, and following him in patience; and if I only comprehend a little, I will still not be deceived with the learned of this world.

165. The Vine

When Gotthold wanted to visit a man who was troubled and sorrowful, the family said that he was in the garden. Gotthold went to him and found him at work removing leaves from a vine. After a friendly greeting, he asked the man what he was doing. I find, said the man, that, on account of the abundant rain, this vine is overgrown with wood and leaves, which prevents the sun from getting to the grapes and ripening them. Therefore, I am pruning some of them so that the vine can produce mature, ripe fruit. Gotthold replied: Do you sense that the vine resists and opposes you when you do this work? If not, then why should you be displeased with a loving God who does to you what you do to the vine? You prune off the unnecessary leaves in order that the vine might bear better fruit; and God takes away your temporal blessings and earthly comforts, in order that faith along with its noble fruits, love, humility, patience, hope, and prayer might become greater, and finer, and sweeter in you. Whatever one might say, when a person has an overabundance of things, and knows nothing of the cross, the Sun of Righteousness, with its rays of grace, can scarcely reach the heart; and the Christian life is not as it should be. It bears only the tart and sour fruits of hypocrisy, pride, ill will, and harshness. Therefore, let God do with you as he wishes; he will not harm you. Now you strip off some leaves and, earlier, in spring, you hoed, made layers of the vines, pruned, and tied up the branches. My dear friend, you are also a branch on the spiritual vine which is the Lord Jesus. God is the vinedresser who knows well that without his grace and care he can expect nothing good from you. For this reason, he allows contempt to lay you in the earth and trials to prune you. He binds you up through affliction and strips you through poverty, all to the end that his grace may be made sweeter to you and your heart sweeter to him.

O my God! do not withdraw me from your care, or else I will grow wild and corrupt. Prune, bind, and strip me as you will; through it all, my comfort shall be that you cannot mean it for evil.

166. Tuning a Lute

Gotthold found one of his good friends busy with the tuning of his lute. Since this involved much effort, he said: The Christian may very appropriately be compared to such an instrument. The lute is made of plain and thin wood, and has not itself, but the hand of the artisan, to thank for fashioning it into such a beautiful instrument. Similarly, a Christian has no superiority over other people with regard to the weakness and corruptions of human nature, unless the hand of a merciful God has made of him an instrument of his grace. Now, just as a lute must be strung and skillfully tuned and touched, so also must the finger of God fill the heart of the Christian with good thoughts, and then tune and adjust them to the honor of his name and for the common good. Although a lute is a beautiful instrument, it very often gets out of tune, and therefore needs continual care. So it goes with our Christian life, which is often put out of tune by the devil, the wicked world, and our own will. It would sound badly unless the gracious hand of the Most High daily regulated and corrected it.

Having noted this, let us also remember our own duties. If we apply such effort to tune a lute so that its sound may not be disagreeable to human ears, why do we not also take the trouble to tune and regulate our thoughts, words, and works so that they may not offend the most holy and keen eyes and ears of God? We hear at once and declare our displeasure if but a single string is out of tune; and yet we often do not perceive or care if there is discord between our lives or conduct and the holy

commandments of God. People instantly tell us if a string is out of tune or misplayed. My friend, let us also remind each other when we perceive a flaw or discord in our Christianity. Self-love and false security can often keep us from noticing our own faults, so it is useful if another person feels free to give a good and suitable reminder to a pious and faithful heart. We should consider it good if someone shows us a better way. Friendship which is not grounded in holiness is not worth having and ends up as eternal enmity.

My Lord Jesus! tune, regulate, and shape my life, to make it consonant with your life. It is true that my weak strings cannot be stretched so tight that I might attain your perfection. I console myself, however, with the thought that as in this lute there are higher and lower pitches, so you have both strong and weak Christians and you are satisfied with both, provided only that they are not false.

SEVENTEENTH-CENTURY HYMNWRITERS

167. Nicolai: How Brightly Beams

Philip Nicolai (1556–1608) served as a Lutheran pastor in Westphalia, at several places in the principality of Waldeck, and finally in Hamburg. He was keenly interested in dogmatic theology and actively participated in a variety of doctrinal controversies with Catholics and Calvinists during his lifetime, but in 1599 he also published an influential devotional work called *Mirror of Joy of Eternal Life*, written to console Christians during a period when plague was working its destructive way through his region. Nicolai introduced the use of the distinction between "true" and "false" Christians, which became standard in much seventeenth-century devotional

Philip Nicolai

literature. He also talked frequently about spiritual "rebirth" and union with Christ. Two of the hymn texts that first appeared in his devotional book rank among the most enduringly important pieces to come out of seventeenth-century Lutheranism. "Wake, awake, for night is flying" *(Wachet auf)* is drawn primarily from the imagery of Matt. 25:1-13 and comforts believers with the vision of the return of Christ. The other hymn, recorded below, is based on Psalm 45 and gives expression to the ardent love for Christ, which Nicolai made a major theme of his devotional book. This hymn (the original German version has seven verses) was commonly used at weddings and to comfort people on their deathbed. Both hymns employ the bride–bridegroom imagery that so many authors used to describe union with Christ.

From Henry Harbaugh, *Christ in Song*, vol. 2, ed. Philip Schaff (New York: Randolph, 1895).

Wie schön leuchtet der Morgenstern
How lovely shines the Morning Star!
The nations see and hail afar
The light in Judah shining.
Thou David's Son of Jacob's race,
My Bridegroom, and my King of grace,
For Thee my heart is pining!
Lowly, holy,
Great and glorious, Thou victorious
Prince of graces,
Filling all the heavenly places!

O highest joy by mortals won!
Of Mary and of God, the Son!
Thou high-born king of ages,
Thou art my heart's best, sweetest flower,
And thy blest gospel's saving power
My raptured soul engages.
Thou mine, I thine;
Sing Hosanna! Heavenly manna
Tasting, eating,
Whilst thy love in songs repeating.

Now richly to my waiting heart,
O thou, my God, deign to impart
The grace of love undying.
In thy blest body let me be,
E'en as the branch is in the tree;
Thy life my life supplying.
Sighing, crying,
For the savor of thy favor;
Resting never,
Till I rest in thee for ever.

168. Heermann: O Holy Jesus

Another important hymnwriter of the period of the Thirty Years War was Johann Heermann (1585–1647), a pastor in Silesia who experienced lifelong suffering, from childhood poverty, physical illness, and the ravages of war. The town of Köben where he served for many years was sacked four times between 1629 and 1634 by Catholic troops. Among the many hymns that have earned Heermann the reputation of being second only to Paul Gerhardt among the many great hymnwriters of the seventeenth century was the following text, which first appeared in 1630 (the original German version has fifteen verses). Like several others of his hymns, it was inspired by a meditation, now attributed to St. Anselm of Canterbury, which appeared in a well-known medieval devotional handbook called the *Manual of St. Augustine*. The vivid description of the sufferings of Christ reflects the spirit of an earlier Lutheran devotional writer in Silesia named Valerius Herberger, with whom Heermann had lived while a schoolboy. His hymns are often seen as marking the transition from the objective focus of earlier Reformation era lyrics to the more subjective focus of later seventeenth-century texts.

From Catherine Winkworth, *Choral Book for England*, ed. William Bennett (London: Longman Green, 1865), #52.

Herzliebster Jesu

1. Alas, dear Lord, what law then hast thou broken,
   That such sharp sentence should on thee be spoken?
   Of what great crime hast thou to make confession,
   What dark transgression?

2. They crown his head with thorns, they smite, they scourge him,
   With cruel mockings to the cross they urge him,
   They give him gall to drink, they still decry him,
   They crucify him.

3. Whence come these sorrows, whence this mortal anguish?
   It is my sins for which my Lord must languish;
   Yes, all the wrath, the woe he doth inherit,
   'Tis I do merit! . . .

8. O mighty King! no time can dim thy glory!
   How shall I spread abroad thy wondrous story?
   How shall I find some worthy gift to proffer?
   What dare we offer? . . .

12. I'll think upon thy mercy hour by hour,
    I'll love thee so that earth must lose her power;
    To do thy will shall be my sole endeavour
    Henceforth for ever.

169. Rinkart: Now Thank We All Our God

Despite the war-related suffering that disrupted so many of their lives, Lutheran hymnwriters from the first half of the seventeenth century still produced some of the most enduringly popular hymns of thanksgiving to God. Perhaps best known of these is the following text by Martin Rinkart (1586–1649), a pastor in Saxony whose town was also sacked more than once (but in this case by Swedish troops). Written sometime around 1636, as a paraphrase of Eccles. 50:29-32, its frequent use for centuries at public festivals of thanksgiving has earned it the label of "Te Deum of Germany."

From Catherine Winkworth, *Lyra Germanica*, series 2 (New York: Randolph, 1863), 194.

Nun Danket Alle Gott
Now thank we all our God
With heart and hands and voices
Who wondrous things hath done
In whom his world rejoices;
Who, from our mother's arms,
Hath blessed us on our way
With countless gifts of love,
And still is ours today.

O may this bounteous God
Through all our life be near us,
With ever joyful hearts
And blessed peace to cheer us;
And guide us when perplexed,
And free us from all ills
In this world and the next.

All praise and thanks to God
The Father now be given,
The Son, and him who reigns
With them in highest heaven;
The one eternal God,
Whom earth and heaven adore;
For thus it was, is now,
And shall be evermore.

170. Rist: O Living Bread from Heaven

Some hymnwriters of the seventeenth
century were also noted for a wider range
of literary achievements. Johann Rist
(1607–67), a pastor who spent most of his
career in the vicinity of Hamburg, also
wrote plays and secular poems in addition
to his 680 hymns. In 1644 he was designated poet laureate of Germany by the
Emperor Ferdinand II. The following
hymn is one of the best known from this

period composed for use in the celebration
of the sacrament of Holy Communion; the
original German version has nine verses.

**From Catherine Winkworth, *Lyra German-
ica*, series 2 (New York: Randolph, 1863),
144.**

Wie wohl hast du gelabet
O living Bread from heaven,
How well you feed your guest!
The gifts that you have given
Have filled my heart with rest.
Oh, wondrous food of blessing,
Oh, cup that heals our woes!
My heart, this gift possessing,
With praises overflows!

My Lord, you here have led me
Within your holiest place,
And here yourself have fed me
With treasures of your grace;
For you have freely given
What earth could never buy,
The bread of life from heaven,
That now I shall not die.

Lord, grant me then, thus strengthened
With heav'nly food, while here
My course on earth is lengthened,
To serve with holy fear.
And when you call my spirit
To leave this world below,
I enter, through your merit,
Where joys unmingled flow.

171. Gerhardt: Two Hymns

The most famous and influential of all the
seventeenth-century Lutheran hymnwriters was Paul Gerhardt (1607–76). A Saxon

educated at Wittenberg, he spent most of
his life as a pastor in the region of Berlin
until a conflict with the Calvinist Elector
of Brandenburg forced his resignation in
1666. Gerhardt wrote 133 hymns, many of
which have continued in use down to the
present day. The two selections that follow
illustrate how some of his hymns are moving declarations of Orthodox doctrine,
while others are of a more subjective and
emotional nature. The first, "A Lamb
Goes Uncomplaining Forth," in the original German version has ten verses. The
second hymn, "Jesus, Thy Boundless Love
to Me" (sixteen verses in the original German version), is based on a prayer from
The Little Garden of Paradise, Johann
Arndt's widely used prayer book. One of
the best known of his other hymns is "O
Sacred Head Now Wounded" *(O Haupt
voll Blut)*, a free translation of a medieval
hymn by St. Bernard of Clairvaux.

**"A Lamb . . ." is from Elizabeth Charles,
Voices of Christian Life in Song (London:
Nelson, 1872). "Jesus . . ." is from John Wes-
ley, ed., *Hymns and Sacred Poems* (Bristol:
Farley, 1744).**

Ein Lämmlein geht und trägt die Schuld
A Lamb goes uncomplaining forth,
The guilt of all men bearing;
Laden with all the sin of earth,
None else the burden sharing!
Goes patient on, grows weak and faint,
To slaughter led without complaint,
That spotless life to offer;
Bears shame, and stripes, and wounds, and
    death,
Anguish and mockery, and saith,
"Willing all this I suffer."

Paul Gerhardt

That Lamb is Lord of death and life,
God over all forever;
The Father's Son, whom to that strife
Love doth for us deliver!
O mighty Love! what hast Thou done!
The Father offers up his Son—
O Love, O Love! how strong art Thou!
In shroud and grave thou lays him low
Whose word the mountains rendeth!

O Jesu Christ! mein schönstes Licht
Jesus, Thy boundless love to me
No thought can reach, no tongue declare;
O knit my thankful heart to Thee
And reign without a rival there.
Thine wholly, Thine alone, I am,
Be Thou alone my constant flame.

O grant that nothing in my soul
May dwell, but Thy pure love alone;
O may Thy love possess me whole,
My joy, my treasure, and my crown:
Strange fires far from my soul remove;
My every act, word, thought, be love.

172. Ludaemilla Elisabeth: Jesus, Only Jesus

Some of the most influential Lutheran women of the seventeenth century were daughters of territorial rulers. Although there was no place for them to contribute as dogmatic theologians, they offered their talents to the church as writers of hymns and devotional literature. One example of such a noble woman writer was Ludaemilla Elisabeth (1640–72), daughter of Count Ludwig of Schwarzburg-Rudolstadt. Her hymns were initially composed for her own private edification, but 206 of them were eventually published as a book in 1687. This hymn has five verses in the original German version.

From *Evangelical Lutheran Hymnal of the Evangelical Lutheran Joint Synod of Ohio*, trans. A. Crull (Columbus: Lutheran Book Concern, 1888), 282.

Jesus, Jesus, nichts als Jesus
Jesus, Jesus, only Jesus,
Can my heartfelt longing still;
See, I pledge myself to Jesus,
What he wills, alone to will.
For my heart, which he hath filled,
Ever cries: Lord, as thou wilt.

One there is for whom I'm living,
Whom I love most tenderly;
Jesus, unto whom I'm giving,
What in love he gave to me.
Jesus' blood hides all my guilt;
Lead me, Lord, then, as thou wilt.

Chapter Eight

Lutheran Pietism (1670–1750)

The term "Pietism" is used most broadly today to describe a particular kind of religious orientation that became influential within several branches of Protestantism during the seventeenth and eighteenth centuries. The most distinctive characteristics of Pietism were a belief in the importance of a personal spiritual transformation, usually associated with an experience of religious conversion, and an intense concern for the promotion of holy living within the church and all of society. In light of these concerns, Pietism may be seen as a forerunner of the type of religiosity that is more commonly known in modern Christianity as Evangelicalism.

The term "Pietist," however, was originally used more narrowly to refer to the people associated with a practical movement of spiritual renewal that began within German Lutheranism in the 1670s through the efforts of Philip Jacob Spener. It was first used derogatorily, but eventually these Lutherans accepted the designation and used it to differentiate themselves from two other groups: those committed believers who remained attached to certain assumptions and attitudes of Lutheran Orthodoxy that the Pietists considered problematic and a larger number of people who, though baptized and accustomed to considering themselves Lutheran, exhibited few signs of any deep religious commitment in their daily lives.

Philip Jacob Spener (1635–1705) was born into a devout Lutheran family in Alsace and received a solid training in philosophy and theology at the University of Strassburg. The professors who influenced him the most, Johann Schmidt and Johann Conrad Dannhauer, were noted for combining a fervent concern for the defense of Lutheran doctrine with an interest in the promotion of church reform and practical piety. Spener's religious outlook, however, was also shaped by contact with Reformed Protestantism. An avid reader of devotional literature, his spiritual development was deeply affected not only by the writings of Johann Arndt and other Lutheran authors but also by English Puritan writers such as Lewis Bayly. In addition, during two years of postgraduate travel outside of Germany, he came in contact with Jean de Labadie, a French Reformed minister whose ideas about spiritual rebirth and efforts to promote church reform left a lasting impression on him.

In 1666 Spener was appointed senior of the clergy in Frankfurt am Main, a position of considerable authority seldom given to someone as young as he was. He began almost immediately to speak out in his sermons against what he considered to be the moral decay of Germany and the lack of true Christian piety among those who professed allegiance to Lutheran doctrine. Most of the themes he emphasized were not novel. They had already been expressed frequently by many seventeenth-century Lutheran devotional

writers. (For this reason, the roots of the theology of the Lutheran Pietists have often
been traced as far back as Johann Arndt.) Spener, however, did not consider it enough to
preach and write about the importance of rebirth. He also began to explore new ways of
organizing church activities in order to facilitate the development of true faith and holy
living. He initiated measures to improve the quality of catechetical instruction for children and regularly preached catechetical sermons on Sunday afternoons in order to
reach adults as well. Spener also attempted to revive the ritual of public confirmation,
which had largely disappeared within the Lutheran territorial churches. He considered
this ceremony to be an important opportunity for young people to commit themselves
personally to the vows that had been made on their behalf by sponsors when they were
baptized as infants. In 1670 Spener initiated another practice which would become one
of the most common measures adopted by the Pietist movement to stimulate renewal. He
began to hold twice-weekly meetings in his home, during which he and a small group of
pious laypeople discussed a reading from the Bible or a devotional book and supported
each other in their efforts to grow spiritually (doc. #178). As these conventicles or *colle-
gia pietatis* began to proliferate and attract a diverse group of people, some of the clergy
criticized Spener for his innovative practices and his tendency to shift the focus of attention from purity of doctrine to purity of life.

Despite these criticisms Spener's influence within the Lutheran churches gained
strength after 1675 when he published *Pia Desideria*, a document that came to be seen as
a kind of manifesto for the Pietist movement. Spener expressed deep dissatisfaction with
the state of Lutheran church life and explicitly listed the moral weaknesses that were
most common in each social class. He intimated that the Lutheran church, which had set
out to reform the Roman Catholic tradition, was itself now in need of a full-scale reformation. Despite his somber assessment of the current state of religious life, Spener was
very optimistic about the possibility of achieving better conditions in the church. From
reading the book of Revelation, he had concluded that God was certain to bring about
spiritual renewal, after which two momentous events would take place: The Jews would
convert to Christianity, and the tyrannical power of the papacy would finally be overcome. Spener also made several concrete proposals that he hoped would turn the situation around (doc. #174). He emphasized the need to increase familiarity with the whole
Bible and to promote its use in church worship, conventicles, and private homes as a
practical guide for spiritual growth. He also called for an expansion of the ministry of
laypeople in the church, increased attention to the practice of Christian love, and a shift
in the focus of pastoral training away from the acquisition of disputational skills and
toward the nurturing of a Christian manner of life.

Without challenging the basic tenets of Lutheran theology, Spener argued that the
preoccupation of Orthodox church leaders with the task of maintaining pure doctrine
had degenerated into a focus on subtle controversies that were far less important than the
need to teach people about conversion and the practice of true piety. He also suggested
that the contrapositioning of faith and good works, which Luther had established as a
central feature of Lutheran theology, needed to be reexamined in a changed social setting
in which people seemed more inclined to be complacent about spiritual growth than

guilt-ridden by the inadequacy of their efforts to fulfill the commandments of God (doc. #174).

Spener continued to defend his dynamic conception of the life of faith and appeal for reform during his later ministry as a preacher and church administrator in Dresden and Berlin. Along the way he reoriented the lives of many people who carried on his work long after his death. One of the most significant of his younger associates was August Hermann Francke (1660–1727), who had participated in a conventicle while studying theology at the University of Leipzig and had become fully committed to Spener's understanding of Lutheranism after passing through a dramatic conversion experience in 1687 (doc. #175, cf. doc. #185). When he became pastor at Glaucha and professor at the newly established University of Halle in 1692, Francke began a period of intense activity that culminated in the establishment of Pietism as a powerful force all across northern Germany. At Halle he established an orphanage, numerous schools for different social classes, a publishing house, and institutions for the care of the indigent, all of which were designed to contribute to the spiritual reform of society through the transformation of individual lives (doc. #180). Francke managed to get a group of like-minded professors appointed to the faculty of the University of Halle and established this institution as the chief training ground for future Pietist leaders. He enjoyed a very positive reputation at the court of the King of Prussia and benefited greatly from the support given him by the Prussian nobility. Francke also contributed to the spread of Pietism within the Lutheran churches of Scandinavia. This in turn led to the first Lutheran efforts at foreign missions, for it was the King of Denmark who provided the financial support for Francke to send missionaries from Halle to Tranquebar on the southeast coast of India in 1706 (doc. #182).

Württemberg, in southwestern Germany, became the other major region in which Pietism established an enduring influence. Although it had ties to the work of Spener and Francke, Württemberg Pietism nevertheless developed a character quite distinct from the north German Pietist movement centered at Halle. Whereas Pietism in Prussia established a close relation with the state and gained a significant following among the upper classes, Pietism in Württemberg was predominantly a middle-class and peasant movement that tended to be less politically assertive. Although Pietism maintained a strong popular character in the southwest, it also gained intellectual respectability as a result of its extensive influence among teachers at the University of Tübingen and the nearby cloister school at Denkendorf. In contrast to the Pietist professors at the University of Halle, whose educational focus was mostly practical and experiential, these academic Pietists recognized the value of critical theological study. Their contributions to the field of biblical interpretation were particularly notable.

The most prominent figure in the history of Württemberg Pietism was Johann Albrecht Bengel (1687–1752), a dedicated pastor with a wide following among the common people who also gained an international reputation as a scholar for his work in the area of text criticism. Disturbed by the proliferation of new versions of the Bible that he considered unreliable, he devoted much of his life to the preparation of a critical edition of the New Testament. In the process, he developed an important set of principles for use in determining which of the variant readings in ancient manuscripts of the Bible was most trustworthy (doc. #183).

The Pietists were primarily interested in finding guidance in the Bible for their daily lives, but they also frequently manifested a strong interest in eschatological speculation. Spener's optimism about the future was based on his belief that Christ would reign on earth for a thousand years before the last judgment, and other more radical Pietists such as Eleonore von Merlau Petersen claimed to have divinely inspired insights into the meaning of the book of Revelation (doc. #186). Bengel shared these interests but used historical research and linguistic analysis in his efforts to discover the future workings of divine providence. The results of his exegesis were quite controversial, for he attempted to correlate the symbolism of the book of Revelation with a whole series of historical events, including the efforts at church reform carried out by Johann Arndt and Philip Jacob Spener (doc. #184). On the basis of some elaborate mathematical calculations, he also reached the conclusion that the second coming of Christ would take place in 1836.

Valentin Ernst Löscher

The Orthodox Lutherans generally abstained from such chiliastic predictions and pointed to them as evidence that the Pietists had an aberrant theology that could not be reconciled with traditional Lutheranism. Valentin Ernst Löscher (1673–1749), author of *Timotheus Verinus*, the best-known Orthodox critique of Pietism, described the movement as an illness that threatened the well-being of the churches. Among the most dangerous symptoms of this illness were chiliasm, perfectionism, indifferentism, and Enthusiasm. Löscher charged that the Pietists reintroduced good works as a condition for salvation and expected more of a change in people's lives than was realistically possible. In their criticisms of Orthodox polemics, he perceived an indifference to the fundamental articles of Lutheran belief and in their stress on religious experiences a tendency toward fanatical mysticism. Löscher concluded that Pietist theology and practice would lead to schisms within the Lutheran church or illegitimate alliances with other confessional groups.

Löscher's charges hold true for some Pietists more than others. Several of the original members of Spener's conventicles did, in fact, withdraw from the Lutheran church and form their own separatist sect, and some of those who separated from the church, such as Eleonore von Merlau Petersen, were preoccupied with their prophetic visions and private ecstasies (doc. #186). Radical Pietists such as Gottfried Arnold (1666–1714) were clearly more influenced by medieval mysticism and the theosophy of Jacob Böhme than they were by the theology of Luther. Arnold kept his distance from organized Lutheranism throughout most of his life because he considered it to be so corrupt, yet in his later years he moderated his judgments and became a Lutheran pastor. Another prominent Pietist, Count Nicholas von Zinzendorf (1700–1760), never explicitly rejected his Lutheran background but came to believe that each church tradition possessed some valuable insight that contributed to a fuller understanding of Christianity. Although he had been ordained as a Lutheran minister, Zinzendorf devoted his energies to the formation of a new religious community among Moravian refugees in Germany and used this Moravian church as a starting point for the promotion of fellowship between Christians of various confessional backgrounds.

In response to Orthodox critics, most Pietists within the Lutheran churches sought to disassociate themselves from the radicals. Spener took precautions to prevent the development of separatism and went to great lengths to prove his loyalty to the theology of Luther and the Lutheran confessions (doc. #173). Francke and his associates at the University of Halle responded point by point to the charges made by Löscher and suggested to the Orthodox that the Pietists posed far less of a threat to the church than the new currents of rationalist thought that were gaining ground in Germany. Bengel expressed respect for some of the accomplishments of Count Zinzendorf but also wrote a lengthy critical evaluation of his piety and theology that deepened the gulf between the Moravians and the Lutheran Pietists.

Despite the controversial nature of the Pietist movement, it was never repudiated so categorically as the Philippist party had been in the late sixteenth century. Pietism contributed much to the revitalization of religious life throughout Germany and Scandinavia and in some regions became more influential than the perspective associated with Lutheran Orthodoxy. The Orthodox and Pietist Lutherans coexisted in mutual suspicion until the second half of the eighteenth century, after which time they gradually discovered a greater degree of commonality in their shared opposition to the deism and atheism of the Enlightenment.

PHILIP JACOB SPENER

Toward the end of his life, Spener collected and published several volumes of letters and papers that had been written in response to inquiries from other people. In these *Theological Reflections*, he defended himself against his critics, evaluated the writings of others, and offered concrete advice to people who had questions about theology, piety, or morality. Two of the following selections show both his respect for Luther and his assessment of some of the reformer's limitations. They show his concern to relate the Pietist reform movement to traditional Lutheranism and his eagerness to lead the Lutheran church in new directions in response to new problems. The selections on conversion and questions of personal conduct show his insistence on a transformed life but also his concern to avoid simplistic judgments about what should be considered normative.

173. An Evaluation of Martin Luther

From Spener TB 266–67.

I continue to believe that Luther was a dear man of God for the sending of whom we cannot thank God enough as much on account of the blessed work of the Reformation, his struggle with the papacy, his many useful writings as on account of his incomparable German translation of the Bible. I am also certain that Luther never taught anything harmful in his articles of faith. All of this I confess and believe. On the other hand, it is not inconsistent that I consider Luther to be a man whose writings are to be regarded far differently than the inerrant writings of the prophets and apostles. For I find that in secondary matters that do not exactly touch on the foundation of faith, one cannot make acceptance of his opinions necessary; indeed, I do not always follow them myself. Although he had an excellent gift for translating the Scriptures such that few among the old fathers could match him in his spirit, it still remains certain that he also sometimes faltered in his explanations and sometimes did not see what others coming after him saw. I call his translation an incomparable work in comparison to which I do not consider any previous translation to be equal or preferable. It is not a contradiction, however, to admit that his interpretation of various passages can clearly be shown to be the wrong meaning and that others who came after him found more light in those texts. Still I gladly confess that the gift of Luther was greater that those who came after him and that they could not nor would not have come so far if Luther had not illuminated the way for them. A giant is always tall and a dwarf small, and no comparison can be made between the size of the two of them, but when the dwarf stands on the shoulders of the giant, he still sees farther than the giant because his stature is higher. It is no wonder, then, when a dwarf that is some teacher far from equal to Luther now many times sees something in Scripture that Luther himself had not seen. Still this would not have been seen if he had not already been raised so high by Luther. Luther remains the universal teacher, but sometimes the student observes one or another thing that the teacher has overlooked. . . .

The fact that our church unfortunately stands at this time in a troubled and miserable state lies clearly before our eyes, but I do not believe that the cause of this is that the teachings of Luther are not accorded their proper worth. May the Almighty be thanked that we still have the teachings of Luther at this hour in the church without the exception of a single article of faith; may God allow it to remain so in the future. Rather, the deficiency consists in this, that while the pure teachings of Luther have endured, the pure, true faith that he always praised in his writings has for the most part not remained, but the illusion has developed that where one possesses the true and pure teaching of Luther, one has salvation already from the same. This security and unbelief that unfortunately prevail so powerfully along with the true teaching is the reason why God's wrath holds us by the throat. If that is not changed, God may well also deprive us of the pure doctrine which we do not put to right use and may let the papacy in many places again gain the upper hand. May God give us here a right knowledge of this state of affairs in order to escape from future wrath.

174. Whether Luther Urged Works Enough (1688)

From Spener TB 258–60.

Now concerning our Luther: the dear man to be sure also had a great measure of grace in other respects, but his chief gift was this, that he was given to stress with excellent force the doctrine of the saving power of faith, which had been neglected since the time of the apostles, and to make known how we must be justified through faith and thus by divine grace without any mixing in of works. The reason for this emphasis was that God had called him to the reform of the church at a time when such teaching about grace had been almost entirely extinguished and when consciences had for some time been directed toward good works. Thus he did not face coarse, secure people such that he had to direct his chief aim to the subduing of security, but for the most part he found persons who were hungry for the conso-

Philip Jacob Spener

lation of the gospel, who had been made anxious long enough by the teaching of works and who had needed this gospel for a good long time because the teaching of works was so well known to them. On the other hand, especially because efforts had long been made to insert good works into the action of justification, he chiefly contested this error.

When Luther speaks at various times of faith and works, he appears to raise up the one only and entirely reject the other. Nevertheless, where all his writings are considered together at one time, it is clear that what he is really opposing is the delusion of their working together with faith for salvation. When all of his words are considered in light of this intention and when one passage is clarified by another, then all will be set right.

The dear man, however, also in many places (for proof one need only open to the sermon on the Wednesday after Easter in his Church Postil) earnestly stressed godly living as much as one can do: but not from the law and only as a duty to which we must be driven, but much more in the sense that it is a never-absent fruit of true faith. The divine faith by which a person grasps the grace of God thus also brings about a new birth in the same man and makes him into someone entirely different, so that henceforth he cannot help but do good, not due to the coercion of law but because of a new type of spirit that simply considers works to be pleasing to God but not those that are forced by law. Where such works do not follow, true faith is not there but only a human dream and thought in the heart that is never experienced in the ground of the heart, as Luther says in the golden forward to the Epistle to the Romans.

Our blessed Martin Statius[1] in his tract on Luther's Christianity notably points out from his words how devoutly the dear man also taught about the power of faith in life. If he speaks about works, then, sometimes more harshly than would seem appropriate, this should be understood to pertain to the abuse of works and the inserting of them into justification. [Similarly] we must remember how harshly dear Paul himself sometimes spoke about divine law, not rejecting the law as such but the misuse to which the false apostles put it. Luther may not have said much about the special testing of every virtue, as far as I recall, but we should take to heart what he said in general about the character of true works, how they must come forth from within, namely, from faith, from rebirth, and from the power of the Holy Spirit. The basis for all this is shown in the little book on nature and grace that I put together.

But the reason why holiness of life must be dealt with more now is because we live in a time when people, from misunderstanding, mostly misuse the gospel and the doctrine of faith. Therefore, we should not speak much now against works when hardly anyone thinks to join works to justification and when most consider them to be neither possible nor necessary, but we must much more earnestly struggle against this error, which is no less dangerous than the other. We should mostly extol the power of faith, which is active

through love and holy living, although we do not want to forget, on the other hand, that such holy living is not that which saves us but only faith itself. Although Luther emphasized the one aspect in his time, he did not forget the other. Divine teaching always remains the same at all times, but sometimes one aspect of it must be earnestly impressed upon some people and at other times some other aspect. When we read the writings of Paul and James and do not rightly see their intention, we might well think that they were truly opposed to each other, which is nevertheless not so. Where we consider all such matters rightly in the fear of God, we will much more take delight in our God's wisdom in the distribution of his gift than be disturbed if everyone does not speak in the same way about it at all times. May the Lord open our eyes more and more to know all aspects of his wise rule; may he stand powerfully by us in all our struggles; let us feel the witness of the Holy Spirit more and more, strengthen us in the inner man against all weaknesses of the outer man, and give us as much power as is necessary for the praise of God and service to our neighbor.

175. Whether Everyone Ought to Know the Hour of His or Her Conversion (1690)

From Spener TB 197–98.

. . . I come now especially to the other question, whether it is clearly necessary that a man should know the time and hour of his conversion. Some may have adopted this idea from some English authors, but I am not in agreement and simply cannot unite with them on this matter. For those who have persisted for a long time in public evil and blasphemous living, I willingly admit that it is almost impossible that they should not know the actual time of their repentance and conversion, because the change is so evident. At the same time, I also do not want to deny that for others who have lived an ethical life but still according to the world and outside of grace, it may happen that they are stirred through a sudden occasion and that God presently carries out his work in them such that again a strong change is noticeable enough in them. But I also maintain that it is possible that for such people who have lived for a long time in the past in an ordinary way and have thought themselves to be good Christians (discovering only subsequently that all was not right with them in that condition), our good Father may begin his work gently and advance it in such a way that first the literal being becomes alive and after that the new being increases little by little. When finally such a man becomes aware of being quite other than he had been and finds the difference to be entirely evident, he praises divine grace but cannot say at what time so to speak the breakthrough in his life happened. Since nothing can be brought against this from God's Word, believers should not make weak, but upright hearts have scruples about the genuineness of their repentance when it is not possible to determine the exact time of it. As for the actual experience to which Christian hearts might on the other hand appeal, I consider it weak to conclude that because one person has experienced the leading of God in a certain way, it follows that therefore also all others have been or must necessarily be led in the same way. In this and all other similar things God retains his free hand to deal with each one in whatever way seems appropriate to his goodness and wisdom. Therefore I consider the description of the conversion of one or another person according to all particulars to be useful, but the

misuse of the same can also be harmful. One person finds in every divine leading much evidence of divine goodness and wisdom to the praise of God and our own strengthening. But another, when some feel scruples because they have not found it to be the same in them, wants to place their rebirth in doubt or because God did not carry out the same process as with them, wants to hold them in suspicion because of this. On the other hand, I am at peace when the witnesses and proofs of true rebirth are encountered by me or another, even though I cannot reckon well the type and order of the divine work. It is enough for me to feel the wind blowing powerfully even though the first blast was not observed by me.

176. On Tobacco (1691)

From Spener TB 484–85.

We come now to special questions, the first of which concerns the cultivation of tobacco. I am not in agreement with the dear brother [who brought up this issue]. It is not merely a question of the plant itself, which is as much a creation of God as any other, but of its use by humans. And although it cannot be doubted that tobacco is mostly unnecessary and is used in a sinful manner, I still hear from doctors as well as other people (I do not know of this from my own experience nor have I used it) that moderate use is beneficial to the health of certain people and may almost be necessary for some; for example, those who serve on ships and likewise those in war who cannot get healthy food. Thus, tobacco has its benefits, but while one place and land are well suited to supplement its nourishment when a moderate quantity is cultivated and prepared, in another

Men Smoking Tobacco

place it is seductive when tobacco brings money into the land. Indeed, I know places that gain most of their income from tobacco—it is being mishandled this way in the Netherlands.

Since tobacco, then, is, as such, a useful plant, the abuse of the same, however much it has gained ground, does not make the cultivation or preparation of it sinful so long as this does not contribute in itself to the abuse. No less than with the preparing of wine, the brewing of beer, or the distilling of brandy, it may not be considered wrong, even though the number who misuse it is not much less than those who employ it rightly.

177. On Dancing (1680)

From Spener TB 487.

Where one speaks of dancing in the abstract and as an idea, one cannot say that it should be clearly forbidden. The movement of the body according to a certain melody or rhythm cannot be considered sinful in itself but remains a neutral matter. So it was not sinful when in 2 Sam.

6:24 David danced with all his power before the ark of the Lord and Solomon in Eccles. 3:4 accorded dancing its appropriate time. . . .

But since we must not base a judgment in every case merely on how it can be considered in the abstract but rather on how we find it in practice, I note that now in this case the issue is not the theory or idea of the matter but what we encounter and commonly see happening. We cannot simply expect that people will keep dancing within its proper bounds. So when we speak of the dancing that is common in our time, I do not see how it can be excused since much sinfulness creeps in along with it. . . .

We know that we Christians are obliged to give an account of all that we do or permit, of our speech, behavior, and work before a strict judge. We should not do anything that does not contribute to the honor of God or that is not useful to our neighbor in spirit or body or necessary to us and beneficial to our own apparent advantage. When something does not have such an inducement, it may not pass approval before God. Now, I do not see how dancing can be related to any one of these rubrics, for it is merely an idle thing, useful neither to body nor soul, that gives free play to the vanity of the senses and fleshly lusts.

178. *Pia Desideria* (1675)

Spener's *Pia Desideria*, the most famous of his many writings, first appeared in 1675 as a preface to a new edition of the postil sermons of Johann Arndt. Later it was published separately. The following brief excerpt concentrates on his proposals for church reform.

From Philip Jacob Spener, *Pia Desideria*, trans. Theodore G. Tappert (Philadelphia: Fortress, 1964), 31, 32, 37, 87–89, 92–97, 103, 107, 108, 115, 116.

FOREWORD

. . . Where one sees distress and sickness, it is natural to look about for remedies. The precious spiritual body of Christ is now afflicted with distress and sickness. Since in certain respects it is committed to the care of every individual and at the same time to all and sundry together, and since we must all be members of the body and hence should not regard affliction anywhere in the body as alien to us, it is therefore incumbent on us to see to it that medicine that is suited to its cure be found and applied. . . .

Let us begin by putting ourselves at the disposal especially of those who are still willing to accept what is done for their edification. If everybody in his own congregation makes provision for these above all others, they may little by little grow to such a measure of godliness that they will be shining examples to others. In time, then, by God's grace we may also gradually attract those who at present seem to be lost in order that they, too, may finally be won. . . .

[Editor's note: The first two sections of the treatise describe the corrupt conditions within
society and the reasons why Spener has hope for better times.]*

[PART III]
[Proposals to Correct Conditions in the Church]

I

Thought should be given to a more extensive use of the Word of God among us. . . . It may appear that the Word of God has sufficiently free course among us inasmuch as at various places (as in this city) there is daily or frequent preaching from the pulpit. When we reflect further on the matter, however, we shall find that with respect to this first proposal, more is needed. . . . If we put together all the passages of the Bible that in the course of many years are read to a congregation in one place, they will comprise only a very small part of the Scriptures that have been given to us. The remainder is not heard by the congregation at all, or is heard only insofar as one or another verse is quoted or alluded to in sermons, without, however, offering any understanding of the entire context, which is nevertheless of the greatest importance. . . .

It should therefore be considered whether the church would not be well advised to introduce the people to Scripture in still other ways than through the customary sermons on the appointed lessons. . . . It would not be difficult for every housefather to keep a Bible, or at least a New Testament, handy and read from it every day or, if he cannot read, to have somebody else read. Then a second thing would be desirable in order to encourage people to read privately, namely, that where the practice can be introduced the books of the Bible be read one after another, at specified times in the public service, without further comment (unless one wished to add brief summaries). . . .

For a third thing it would perhaps not be inexpedient (and I set this down for further and more mature reflection) to reintroduce the ancient and apostolic kind of church meetings.

In addition to our customary services with preaching, other assemblies would also be held in the manner in which Paul describes them in 1 Cor. 14:26-40. One person would not rise to preach (although this practice would be continued at other times), but others who have been blessed with gifts and knowledge would also speak and present their pious opinions on the proposed subject to the judgment of the rest, doing all this in such a way as to avoid disorder and strife. This might conveniently be done by having several ministers (in places where a number of them live in a town) meet together or by having several members of a congregation who have a fair knowledge of God or desire to increase their knowledge meet under the leadership of a minister, take up the Holy Scriptures, read aloud from them, and fraternally discuss each verse in order to discover its simple meaning and whatever may be useful for the edification of all. . . .

2

Our frequently mentioned Dr. Luther would suggest another means, which is altogether compatible with the first. This second proposal is the establishment and diligent exercise of the spiritual priesthood. Nobody can read Luther's writings with some care without observing how earnestly the sainted man advocated this spiritual priesthood, according to which not only ministers but all Christians are made priests by their Savior, are anointed by the Holy Spirit, and are dedicated to perform spiritual-priestly acts. Peter was not addressing preachers alone when he wrote, "You are a chosen race, a royal priesthood, a holy nation, God's own people, that you may declare the wonderful deeds of him who called you out of darkness into his marvelous light." . . .

Every Christian is bound not only to offer himself and what he has, his prayer, thanksgiving, good works, alms, and so forth, but also industriously to study in the Word of the Lord,

with the grace that is given him to teach others, especially those under his own roof, to chastise, exhort, convert, and edify them, to observe their life, pray for all, and insofar as possible be concerned about their salvation. If this is first pointed out to the people, they will take better care of themselves and apply themselves to whatever pertains to their own edification and that of their fellow men. . . .

3

Connected with these two proposals is a third: The people must have impressed upon them and must accustom themselves to believing that it is by no means enough to have knowledge of the Christian faith, for Christianity consists rather of practice. Our dear Savior repeatedly enjoined love as the real mark of his disciples (John 13:34-35; 15:12; 1 John 3:10, 18; 4:7-8, 11-13, 21). . . . . Indeed, love is the whole life of the man who has faith and who through his faith is saved, and his fulfillment of the laws of God consists of love. . . .

For this purpose, as well as for the sake of Christian growth in general, it may be useful if those who have earnestly resolved to walk in the way of the Lord would enter into a confidential relationship with their confessor or some other judicious and enlightened Christian and would regularly report to him how they live, what opportunities they have had to practice Christian love, and how they have employed or neglected them. This should be done with the intention of discovering what is amiss and securing such an individual's counsel and instruction as to what ought now to be done. . . .

4

Related to this is a fourth proposal: We must beware how we conduct ourselves in religious controversies with unbelievers and heretics. . . .

We must give them a good example and take the greatest pains not to offend them in any way, for this would give them a bad impression of our true teaching and hence would make their conversion more difficult. . . . If God has given us the gifts that are needful for it, and we find the opportunity to hope to win the erring, we should be glad to do what we can to point out, with modest but firm presentation of the truth we profess, how this is based on the simplicity of Christ's teaching. At the same time, we should indicate decently but forcefully how their errors conflict with the Word of God and what dangers they carry in their wake. All of this should be done in such a way that those with whom we deal can see for themselves that everything is done out of heartfelt love toward them, without carnal and unseemly feelings, and that if we ever indulge in excessive vehemence, this occurs out of pure zeal for the glory of God. Especially should we beware of invectives and personal insinuations, which at once tear down all the good we have in mind to build. . . .

5

Since ministers must bear the greatest burden in all these things that pertain to a reform of the church, and since their shortcomings do correspondingly great harm, it is of the utmost importance that the office of the ministry be occupied by men who above all are themselves true Christians and then have the divine wisdom to guide others carefully on the way of the Lord. It is therefore important, indeed necessary, for the reform of the church that only such persons be called who may be suited and that nothing at all except the glory of God be kept in view during the whole procedure of calling. . . .

However, if such suitable persons are to be called to the ministry, they must be available, and hence they must be trained in our schools and universities. . . . The professors could themselves accomplish a great deal here by their example (indeed, without them a real reform is hardly to be hoped for) if they would conduct themselves as men who have died

unto the world, in everything would seek not their own glory, gain, or pleasure but rather the glory of their God and the salvation of those entrusted to them, and would accommodate all their studies, writing of books, lessons, lectures, disputations, and other activities to this end. . . .

It would be especially helpful if the professors would pay attention to the life as well as the studies of the students entrusted to them and would from time to time speak to those who need to be spoken to. The professors should act in such a way toward those students who, although they distinguish themselves in studying, also distinguish themselves in riotous living, tippling, bragging, and boasting of academic and other preeminence (who, in short, demonstrate that they live according to the world and not according to Christ) that they must perceive that because of their behavior they are looked down upon by their teachers, that their splendid talents and good academic record do not help by themselves, and that they are regarded as persons who will do harm in proportion to the gifts they receive. On the other hand, the professors should openly and expressly show those who lead a godly life, even if they are behind the others in their studies, how dear they are to their teachers and how very much they are to be preferred to the others. In fact, these students ought to be the first, or the only, ones to be promoted. The others ought to be excluded from all hope of promotion until they change their manner of life completely. . . .

6

In addition to these exercises, which are intended to develop the Christian life of the students, it would also be useful if the teachers made provision for practice in those things with which the students will have to deal when they are in the ministry. For example, there should be practice at times in instructing the ignorant, in comforting the sick, and especially in preaching, where it should be pointed out to students that everything in their sermons should have edification as the goal. I therefore add this as a sixth proposal whereby the Christian church may be helped to a better condition: that sermons be so prepared by all that their purpose (faith and its fruits) may be achieved in the hearers to the greatest possible degree. . . .

The pulpit is not the place for an ostentatious display of one's skill. It is rather the place to preach the Word of the Lord plainly but powerfully. Preaching should be the divine means to save the people, and so it is proper that everything be directed to this end. Ordinary people, who make up the largest part of a congregation, are always to be kept in view more than the few learned people, insofar as such are present at all.

As the catechism contains the primary rudiments of Christianity, and all people have originally learned their faith from it, so it should continue to be used even more diligently (according to its meaning rather than its words) in the instruction of children, and also of adults if one can have these in attendance. . . .

179. Letter to a Foreign Theologian concerning the *Collegia Pietatis* (1677)

Soon after Spener began to hold his conventicle meetings in Frankfurt, some clergy and civil magistrates charged that they were a threat to the unity of the church and the maintenance of social order. Rumors spread that people neglected family responsibilities and church meetings to attend and women in particular were being allowed to preach. In 1677 Spener attempted to dispel such rumors by writing "A Letter to a Foreign Theologian," which contains the following description of the origins and activities of the conventicles.

From Philip Jacob Spener, *Sendschreiben an einen Christeyffrigen außländischen Theologum* **(Frankfurt: Zunner, 1677), 44–53, 62–64, 72–75.**

Now as for concerns about my house-practice or what is commonly called the *collegium,* I need nothing more that an opportunity to tell about the way in which it came to be held. It had its beginning in 1670 in August as a result of the following occasion. Some godly friends . . . had complained to me for some time about how all conversation and talk in ordinary life was so corrupt that one could seldom come away from social gatherings without a violated conscience. Even when those wanting to claim the name of Christ and be called Christians came together, one never heard anything spoken about except things belonging to this world, for the most part merely frivolous and sinful things, criticisms of other people, buffoonery, unseemly jokes, and other such things that go under the name of pastimes and amusements, without any concern that one might thereby be falling into sin. . . .

They wished to have the opportunity to come together occasionally with others of a godly disposition to speak with each other in simplicity and love and to find in such conversation among themselves what they sought for in vain elsewhere.

I could not contradict the complaint of those whose conduct was well enough known, nor could I rebuke or devalue their desire, which I recognized to be consistent with the Word of God and the nature of godliness. Therefore I praised such an undertaking and encouraged them, but due to the suspicion that other unseemly things might arise, I offered to be present myself and to make my study room and house available.

I also discussed the matter with one of my colleagues who shared their concerns, and he no less than I sanctioned the cause. (It did not seem necessary for us to bring the matter before an assembly of all of my clerical colleagues because it concerned a private practice.) . . . We also did not explicitly consult any magistrate since no private practice needed a public confirmation. . . .

Now concerning the nature of this gathering, our plan was that when we got together, which ordinarily happened to be two times a week, I would first give a short prayer, calling upon God and asking for his grace. Then I read something from a book, after which we spoke together about it, observing everything in the reading that was useful for the upbuilding of life and the strengthening of simple faith. We observed no special order among us and did not consider that to be necessary. As ordinarily happens among friends, it was left that one speaker was allowed to continue until he stopped, after which another could speak. . . .

We lived in hope that through such means we would receive among us not only wholesome knowledge of God and zeal for godliness but also that when all became more accustomed to speaking about good things, they would be able to converse in an edifying manner on other occasions among other people. It was also the intention that such a holy and close friendship would be established among these Christian souls that one could learn from another how far he had come along in his Christianity so that the fire of love would blaze more and more among us, and from this a more ardent desire would be kindled to upbuild each other at every opportunity and to stimulate others around us.

In this way, we read through the blessed Dr. Lütkemann's *Foretaste of Divine Goodness,* Bayly's famed *Practice of Piety,* and the reliable theologian Nikolaus Hunnius's *Epitome of Beliefs.*[2] After two years we set aside the books

by human authors that we read at the beginning and in childlike fashion simply read the Bible. . . .

Now, because we came together twice weekly, on Monday I started by repeating the content of the publicly held sermon from the day before so they would hear it a second time and so better bring it into their understanding. At the same time, it was possible to offer more explanation, and if someone felt uneasy about something, there would be an opportunity to ask a question about it. After that, we turned to the reading of the Gospel as far as we could get. When we came together on Wednesday, we spent the whole hour or time on the text dealing with it in the following way. I went on from where we left, also mentioning related texts, parables, and stories. I read one verse after another, observing the simple meaning of the words or what seemed to be useful for edification in it. When I stopped, I waited awhile in case someone wanted to call something to mind. This provided a good opportunity for some edifying discussion of the material. But if all were silent, I would go on to the next verse. We focused on the simple literal understanding of the text or considered its use in the practice of Christianity, noting especially any life rules we found in the text that were not generally observed. We also considered how the same should be endorsed and how they could be put into practice with the help of divine grace. . . .

Now, as for the people who attended these house gatherings, at the beginning there were few of us and mostly learned people. But now there are people from many different classes and ages, learned and unlearned, noble and common, students of theology, lawyers, doctors, merchants, craftsmen, simple people. . . . There were also quite a few Christian women, wives and unmarried young women, but they were separated from the others so that one could not see them, although they could hear everything. It was not granted to them to interject or to ask questions, and at no time would any of them have dared to do this. Thus in the house fellowship we conformed to the apostolic command in 1 Corinthians 14 and 1 Timothy 2. Now, as for the others, namely, the men, they mostly listened, though a few among them also spoke or shared something with the group. Those who talked along with me were almost all students of theology or people who had studied. There were others who had not studied, but their contribution consisted mostly in asking a question or mentioning the attraction of some words in Scripture that they considered useful. . . .

I also ask those who might consider such practices to be foreign or improper in the Lutheran church or dangerous to consider again what our dear and worthy Luther wrote (in "The German Mass" [cf. doc #73]): "The third kind of service that a true Evangelical Church Order ought to have should not take place publicly among all sorts of people, but among those who earnestly want to be Christians and profess the gospel with hand and mouth. They would perhaps meet by themselves in some house in order to pray, read, baptize, receive the sacrament, and do other Christian works. In this manner those who do not lead Christian lives could be identified, reproved, reformed, expelled, or excommunicated, according to the rule of Christ in Matthew 18. . . . In short, if one had the people and persons who truly wanted to be Christians, the arrangements and method could quickly be made. But right now I cannot and do not desire to set up such a congregation or assembly because I still do not have the people or persons to accomplish it, nor do I see many who insist upon it. But if it comes about that I am urged to do this and I cannot in good conscience refuse, then I will gladly do my part and help as best I can." Lest one think that the dear man was hasty here and only said this

once, we should know that he repeated this thought at other times.

Here we see that the dear man proposed to do more than we do or desire to do, and was prepared to do whatever was necessary where he had competent people. I admittedly confess that I was worried about the possibility of a schism or separation in such a case, so I considered it to be necessary to do whatever I could to prevent this from happening in the church. On the other hand, I ultimately hope that if this proposal can be practiced without separation from the church, it will be accepted and it will be recognized that Luther would at least not be against it. . . .

I also do not see how such practices can be opposed when unwarranted fears about various dangers can easily be avoided. The church has no need to be anxious about those who remain pure in the simplicity of Christ and desire more and more to become children of the Lord and only prepare themselves to do what almost all religious groups consider to be necessary.

August Hermann Francke

180. Sermon on Renewal (1709)

Francke preached this sermon in 1709 in Halle on a lectionary text for the seventh Sunday after Trinity. It reveals the Pietists' preoccupation with sanctification more than justification and shows Francke's concern for an ongoing process of spiritual growth, not just with a decisive conversion event.

From August Hermann Francke, *Schreiben und Predigten*, Bd. 10: *Predigten II*, ed. Erhard Peschke (Berlin: DeGruyter, 1981), 374–97.

TEXT: ROMANS 12:1, 2

Beloved in the Lord! When Holy Scripture teaches us that we should once more be renewed by Christ to the state that we lost through the Fall into sin, this word, "renewal," takes in a very broad concept that includes all of these parts: call, illumination, rebirth, justification, union with God, and sanctification. And when these parts of the entire work, which is commonly called renewal of the image of God, are mentioned, then the last part, namely, sanctification, has a special significance. By this it is understood that when a person is called through the Gospel, illumined with the gifts of the Holy Spirit, reborn, and united with God through faith, then this person must also steadily and unremittingly apply himself to sanctification so that he might from day to day be more and more cleansed from every defilement of the flesh and the spirit and carry on with sanctification in the fear of God, as it is stated by Paul in 2 Cor. 7:1. For this occasion we should comment on this topic out of our text for the day.

De Studio Renovationis or On Renewal and How a Faithful Christian Should Apply Himself to It

First Part

If now, beloved in the Lord, our task for today is to treat the *Studio Renovationis,* or the Study of Renewal, and how it must be found 1) in the intention of the heart and then 2) in steadily continuing practice, we discover that what the first entails is expressed in the first verse of our text: "I admonish you, dear brothers, by the mercy of God, that you present your bodies as a living sacrifice, holy and acceptable to God, which is your reasonable worship." This little verse contains much within itself, and everyone should diligently consider and take notice of these words of Paul so that they might be

August Hermann Francke

thoroughly understood. Once this is done, he is more able to go into his own heart, examine it, and find out whether he has such an intention of the heart that is called for and expressed by Paul in this verse. . . .

[Editor's note: Each phrase is discussed, and the first part then concludes with the following summary.]

Paul wishes that everyone who finds consolation in the truth of Christ and proposes to gain eternal salvation should truly consecrate himself to God the Lord and offer himself entirely to his possession. His goal in this world should no longer be to seek after his own interests, his own honor, his own riches, profit, or needs, his own pleasure, ease, or the like, but rather the intention of his heart must be directed in such a way that all he does in word and deed he does in the name of our Lord Jesus Christ, giving thanks to God and the Father by him; whether he eats or drinks or whatever he does is done to the honor of God. These are all the explicit words of Paul, the former in the Epistle to the Colossians 3:17 and the latter in 1 Cor. 10:31. Now that is the true intention of the heart that everyone must find in himself who devotes himself to renewal.

If this fundamental intention does not exist and consequently the person has not truly consecrated and offered himself to the Lord, he is not a righteous Christian, and if he deeply examines himself, he will see that he is nothing other than a hypocrite. . . .

Christ has purchased him by giving his own blood as a ransom, but the purchased servant wants to live according to his own will, to serve another lord, indeed the old lord, namely, the devil, the world, and sin, from which Jesus so dearly purchased him by his own blood. How iniquitous and disgraceful this is! Each person, if he inspects himself and examines his intention, will find out that in associating himself with Christ he speaks a judgment against himself, that his character is not upright. No one should doubt this because it is expressed here in such clear words, and Holy Scripture itself makes this expectation of us. Otherwise one might imagine that the teacher only demands so much and that it is enough if one only does something good, without offering himself entirely to the service of God the Lord. To the contrary, Holy Scripture so clearly lays down that we should present our bodies as a living sacrifice that is holy and acceptable to God. It discloses that worship consists not in going to church, not in going to confession and the Lord's Supper, not in reading a prayer book or occasionally in the Bible, but rather in consecrating oneself entirely to God and offering oneself to his glory such that in all one's living and doing one desires to belong to God and wishes nothing to be found within, not even a drop in the veins, which is not consecrated to God as his possession. Yes, one so earnestly hates to find that one's flesh and blood wishes another way, that one also seeks to overcome this through God's power, so that one might be found to be a true sacrifice to God. . . .

Second Part

Now let us also consider, as a second part, the steadily enduring practice of renewal that Paul expects, as it is now explained to us in the following verse: "And do not conform yourself to the world, but be transformed through the renewing of your mind, so that you might discern what is the good, acceptable and perfect will of God." . . .

"Do not conform yourself to the world": This does not mean that the world eats and drinks and so we should not do that because the world does it; for those are things belonging merely to outward life. Rather, Paul wants to direct us more deeply and show that we should shun those things that stand against the kingdom of God, and surely not only in external form or outward shape and in external representation (which many today tend to think is what these words mean) but rather also from the bottom of the heart, as Peter says: "you should not be conformed to the desires that you had when you lived in ignorance" [1 Pet. 1:14]. . . .

Further on, Paul says: "Be transformed through the renewal of your mind." This is the second thing that is expected in the practice of renewal. It is called μεταμορφῶσθε, "be entirely changed through the renewal of your mind." We certainly see that it is not doing enough for Paul if one is simply not conformed to the world in outward matters. Rather, he demands much that is greater, higher, and deeper in a person's heart, namely, that one should "be entirely changed," for that is the teaching here of Paul. One might perhaps think that if he says "be transformed," this should be in outward matters. So that one might not conclude that it only concerns outward matters, he says here "through the renewal of your mind." The mind should be entirely other, or it should be thoroughly changed in the person. . . .

Furthermore, Paul says, "So that you might discern what is the good, acceptable, and perfect will of God." This is the third matter that Paul associates with the practice of renewal. He wants a person to investigate and seek to know, and also hunt for that which is the acceptable and perfect will of God. For when one has consecrated and offered himself to God the Lord or has sought from the heart to devote all the powers of his body, soul, and mind to the service of God, and to apply himself rightly to God's glory, it results from this that the man, according to the same inward ground and intention of his heart, will seek in all things whatever is in conformity with God's will. For him, this involves more than knowing and understanding how to differentiate between what is and is not the will of God. Rather, because he has offered himself to the service of God, he also seeks, now that he knows the will of God, to do and practice it. . . .

Now, when the Holy Spirit fills the heart of a person more and more with his gifts and there is consequently a steady practice of goodness, then it is easy to discern that a person does the will of God more perfectly than he did in the beginning and that he is more and more equipped for all good works, as Paul also says in 2 Tim. 3:17 "that the man of God" (who not only rightly grasps the will of God from Scripture but also lets it lead him farther and farther through divine truth) "might be perfect, equipped for all good works." But this does not mean that this person would no longer have any temptation to sin, as if he were no longer *peccabilis* and could not sin, as if he could not be taken advantage of by his own flesh and blood. All these inclinations are present in a person as long as he abides in this earthly dwelling. But this is the meaning, stated in a comparative way: one who is said to do the will of his Lord can have another above him who does it still better, just as one can be a master but still have many masters above him, while in comparison with an apprentice and journeyman he is called a master because he has a superiority over them. Thus it also is with Christianity within which someone is called perfect, not in the sense that sin has been completely taken away from him and out of his

mortal flesh so that he no longer has to deal with temptation, but rather because he is more practiced in the way of God than a beginner. So speaks the Holy Scripture. . . .

Yes, in Christianity the strongest and most stalwart person should also still grow in power and strength as long as he lives, and there is no goal in sanctification set before him, until the end of his life, which cannot and should not still be surpassed. Insofar as this goal is in keeping with the acceptable and perfect will of God, the greatest virtues one receives from God are always used for greater growth. That is also the understanding of Paul in our text, that all of a person's spiritual powers must increase; his faith must always become stronger, his love purer, more ardent, and upright, his hope for eternity more and more firm, and the fear of God, which is the beginning of Christianity or of true wisdom, as the Scripture says, must also always increase. . . .

When a sailor propels his ship against the current, his arms must certainly be stretched out in order to row well, and all necessary work must be applied earnestly so that the ship can break through the power of the current and reach the intended harbor. But if he lets down his arms and gives up on the work, the ship will soon be driven back by the current and moved downstream. So it happens also with a person because sin always adheres to him and makes him sluggish, according to Heb. 12:1. A special and unremitting earnestness is needed for a person to move forward and become more closely united with God. Nevertheless, a person has this consolation that he does not effect this by his own powers but rather by the Holy Spirit, who strengthens him. . . .

If someone wants to blow a feather upwards, as long as this feather is kept up in the air, the easier it is to make it go higher. But if one decides to rest a little and lets the feather fall to the earth, it picks up an impurity that makes it difficult to raise it upwards again and, by one's breath, to drive it heavenwards. So it is also with the spirit of a person. If the spirit or mind of a person strives for what is heavenly and eternal, the heart will be more heavenly and spiritually inclined, and it will also be ever easier for him to hold to God and to be more closely united with God. . . .

O Lord, . . . give us the powers of your Holy Spirit such that we may be truly metamorphosed and so reshaped in our hearts, Jesus, that you establish your own form within us and henceforth we do not live but you live in us. May we actively and powerfully experience without ceasing, in the ground of our hearts, the godly life that you lead, sitting at the right hand of the majesty of God. . . .

181. The Footsteps of Divine Providence (1709)

The following text shows that Francke did not start out with a master plan when he began to develop the charitable and evangelistic institutions at Halle. He was convinced, however, that God had been continuously at work to help establish them and make them succeed.

From August Hermann Francke, *Segensvolle Fußstapfen des noch lebenden und waltenden Gottes entdecket durch eine Nachricht von dem Wäysen-Hause und übrigen Anstalten zu Glaucha vor Halle* **(3d ed.; Halle: Waisenhaus, 1709), 2–3, 5–9, 12–16, 19, 2, 101, 104, 105.**

CHAPTER ONE

1. It was formerly the custom in Halle and its suburbs for people to specify a particular day during which the poor should come at the same time every week to their doors to request alms.

Since Thursday happened to be the day in my neighborhood (being pastor at Glaucha), the poor frequently assembled before my door on that day for this purpose, and for some time I had bread distributed to them. But it soon came into my mind that this would be a desirable opportunity to help the souls of these poor people as well through the Word of God, since they, being for the most part grossly ignorant, are in the habit of getting involved in much evil.

One day, as they waited at my door for alms to satisfy their physical needs, I let them all come into the house, and, placing the adults on one side and the youth on the other, I began in a friendly manner to question the young people from Luther's Catechism about the principles of their Christian religion. The older persons only listened as I spent about a quarter of an hour in this catechetical exercise. I concluded with a prayer and then, according to custom, distributed the gifts among them, telling them in addition that in the future they should receive both spiritual and physical provisions in the same way at my house, which they accordingly did. The practice was begun about the beginning of the year 1694.

2. Since I found such gross and shocking ignorance among the poor, I scarcely knew where I should begin to impart to them a firm ground for their Christian faith. I was troubled for some time by thoughts about how I might more forcefully help them, considering that a very great harm arises for a Christian commonwealth when many people go about like cattle without any knowledge of God and divine things. This is especially the case when so many children, on account of their parents' poverty, are never sent to school and so never get any education to speak of. They grow up in the grossest ignorance and surrounded by such evil that in their later years they are good for nothing and so betake themselves to stealing, robbing, and other evil deeds. . . .

5. [A little while later, I] fastened a box in the living room of the parsonage, with these words written over it: 1 John 3:17, "If any one has worldly goods and sees his brother in need and closes his heart before him, how does the love of God remain in him?" And under it: 2 Cor. 9:7, "Every man must act according to his own will, not reluctantly or under compulsion, for God loves a cheerful giver." This was intended to remind those who went in and out or came to me from other places to open their hearts toward the poor. The box was put up in the beginning of the year 1695. . . .

7. About a quarter of a year after the poor box was set up in the parsonage, a certain person put into it, at one time, four thaler and sixteen gröschen. When I took this into my hands, I said, with the joy of faith, "This is now a considerable fund with which some important undertaking should be established; therefore I will begin a school for the poor with it." I did not confer with flesh and blood about this affair but acted in faith and the very same day made arrangements that books be bought for two thaler. Then I got a poor student to teach the children two hours a day. . . .

8, 9. Around Easter 1695, this charity-school was begun with the small provisions. . . . Soon after Pentecost some of the citizens, seeing that particular care was taken for teaching the poor children, wanted their own children to be instructed by the same master and offered him a gröschen weekly for each child. This obliged the master to teach five hours a day. . . .

Several people from outside heard about this undertaking and sent money to support it, and others sent linen to have shirts made so that the students could be persuaded by such benefits to receive instruction more easily.

And so our charity school was held throughout the summer and the number of poor and citizens' children who were taught in it was about fifty or sixty. . . .

13. At the beginning of the winter . . . I divided the children and gave the children of the citizens one instructor and appointed another one especially for the poor children. Each of these masters taught four hours a day. . . .

14. But now I saw that the children for whom one had the most hope were to all appearances accomplishing nothing because whatever was accomplished in the school was destroyed again when they left the school. This made me plan to single out some children for fuller care and instruction. This was the first occasion that it came into my mind to attempt to set up an orphanage, even before I knew of any fund to make this feasible.

When I informed a good friend of this endeavor, his Christian spirit moved him to bequeath five hundred thaler, the interest from which, amounting to twenty-five thaler, would be paid out each year at Christmas. This has been done ever since. When I saw this blessing of God, I wanted to select one orphan to be maintained by this yearly revenue. But it happened that four fatherless and motherless sisters were presented to me from whom I was to choose one.

16. I ventured, trusting in the Lord, to take all four. . . . The following day, after I had provided for the aforementioned four orphans, two more came in, and the next day, another; two days after this, one more; and eight days later, another was taken in. And so about the sixteenth of November, there were already nine who were committed to the care of several Christian people. For these I appointed a student of theology, whose name was Georg Heinrich Neubauer, to be their overseer, who was entrusted with all things necessary for their maintenance. . . . And thus we had poor orphans brought together even before we had built or bought a house for them. . . .

17, 18. As the undertaking was begun in faith, so it was now to be advanced in the same way, without letting rational concerns about future shortages hold it back. . . . I removed the twelve orphans (for that is what their number had become) from the three different houses in which they were lodging and brought them together in the house we bought and expanded. The student who was their overseer soon made arrangements to get beds and other household necessities for them, provided for their food and drink, and saw to it that they were kept clean and in good order. . . .

22. As the first beginning of this work was occasioned by the beggars coming to my door, so afterwards special care was constantly taken not only for children but also for incapacitated old people. And while in the beginning only Thursday was fixed for distributing alms, so afterwards Tuesday was added. They were catechized at the midday hour and then received their charity.

24. Another school was set up in September 1697 for those boys whose parents wanted them to be instructed in the fundamental points of learning. But in the year 1699, on the eighth of May, this school was united with that class of orphans who were taught languages and sciences. To manage them better, they were divided into three classes, each served by a different teacher to instruct them in Latin, Greek, and Hebrew as well as history, geography, geometry, music, and botany. . . .

31. After the Lord had thus provided for the orphans, and given many demonstrations of his fatherly providence over them, he further inclined the heart of an eminent and well-disposed gentleman to make a settlement for the maintenance of some poor widows and to entrust me with the management of this. . . . For these aged widows there is not only appointed a chaplain, of good and pious behavior, to go to prayer with them twice a day, but also a maid . . . to serve them, to buy such things as are necessary for them, and to nurse them if they happen to fall sick. . . .

Chapter Five

1. As for the spiritual benefits that may be expected to result from such endeavors, they may easily be deduced from the main purpose of the whole undertaking, which is the salvation of souls to eternal life. Now, as the soul is greater than the body, so the outward care of the body is in no way the chief intention but is used as the means to maintain the soul. . . .

7. In further consideration, cannot these foundations be thought of as schools and seminaries set up for the general good of the whole country? For good workmen are trained in all trades, good schoolmasters, so also, good preachers and counselors who afterwards will think themselves the more obliged to be of service to everyone because they have experienced the special care of God in their childhood and have been educated with all diligence. And the high authorities of the land cannot only hope that they will be loyal and desirable subjects but can also expect that through such well-educated subjects many others will be led away from a criminal life.

8. The country will also be cleared of stubborn beggars, thieves, murderers, highwaymen, and the whole mob of loose people who, for the most part, arise because institutions for the care of the poor and the education of youth are so inadequate. An undertaking of this sort may in some measure actually get rid of this problem, and so the land can expect many benefits, both spiritual and temporal, from its existence.

182. Instructions of King Frederik IV of Denmark to the First Pietist Missionaries (November 17, 1705)

Tranquebar, on the southeast coast of India, had been a Danish colony since 1624. When King Frederik sought missionaries to convert the native population to

Christianity, his court preacher referred him to Francke. This document relates to the commissioning of one of the first two German missionaries.

From J. F. Fenger, *History of the Tranquebar Mission*, trans. Emil Francke (Tranquebar: Evangelical Lutheran Mission, 1863), 309–11.

We, Frederik IV, King of Denmark and Norway and so forth, do in our royal favor desire that Mr. Henry Plütschau, born in Mecklenburg, whom we have resolved to send to Eastern India as a missionary, should with all submission conduct himself on his voyage out to and there in India, until our further royal orders.

1. He shall, on the whole voyage out, betake himself with all diligence to those on board ship who have been in Eastern India, ere this, and who are somewhat acquainted with the native language in order that he may learn from them something of that language.

2. Having by the grace of God safely arrived in the country, he shall, in the name of Jesus, heartily calling upon the same, at once begin the work for which he is sent out and shall labor among the pagans, as existing circumstances shall make it practicable.

3. Although it is of some help to improve the little rest of the knowledge of God, which men still have by nature, and thus to lead them to the knowledge of God that he has revealed in his Word—and it is left to the missionary himself to judge when and in what manner this may be done with advantage—yet he shall always specially betake himself to God's Word, not doubting that God will make the power laid therein prove effectual among the heathens.

4. He must hold and handle there in Eastern India nothing besides the holy doctrine as it is written in God's Word and repeated in the symbolic books of this realm after the Augsburg Confession and teach nothing besides it. And as Christ himself began his prophetic ministry by preaching repentance and commanded his disciples to preach repentance and remission of sins, so also he must follow the same course.

5. He has to instruct the ignorant in the first principles of the Christian doctrine with all possible simplicity, so that the needful foundation may be laid the earlier.

6. In order that the poor blind heathens may understand that the missionary himself has in his heart what he teaches, he must always show himself a pattern of good works, so that also by this his conduct they may be won over.

7. He shall not forget daily to pray for the cooperating grace of God and for everything required that he may perform his office faithfully and carefully and to call upon God in the name of Jesus, that he would bless our Christian undertaking with abundant and happy successes to the salvation of many souls, and that he would grant to our whole royal house the reward of this pious work with every needful blessing for this life and the life to come.

8. He shall keep good friendship also with the Evangelical pastors of the place and shall gather from them, as from men acquainted with the country, all kinds of useful information.

9. He shall be content with what we in our royal favor have granted him for his annual pay and support and not take any money from the people for the performance of his official duties.

10. Whenever a ship leaves India for this country, he shall send letters therewith, reporting to us according to his Christian conscience with all submission concerning his office, its successes, and its hindrances. In the same way, he may add his proposals suggesting how this new undertaking, which cannot be perfect at once, might perhaps be better arranged in future.

11. And finally he shall bind himself by a truthful promise as in the presence of God to obey this instruction, and with that intent he shall subscribe to a copy of it in his own handwriting.

JOHANN ALBRECHT BENGEL

183. *Gnomon of the New Testament* (1742)

Johann Bengel's philological research was an important step toward the development of modern biblical criticism. Having published a more reliable Greek text of the New Testament in 1734, Bengel worked on his *Gnomon* (Pointer), an extensive commentary published in 1742. In this book he was both scholarly in his exegetical analysis and practical in his concern to make the Bible a guide for daily living.

From Johann Albrecht Bengel, *Gnomon of the New Testament*, trans. James Bandinel, ed. Andrew Fausset (Edinburgh: T. & T. Clark, 1866), 9, 10.

Human selection of sayings and examples, taken from Scripture, have their use; the study, however, of the sacred volume, should not end here; for it should, both as a whole and in its several parts, be thoroughly studied and mastered, especially by those who are occupied in teaching others. In order fully to accomplish this, we ought to distinguish the clearly genuine words of the sacred text from those that are open to doubt or question, from the existence and authority of various readings, lest we should either pass by and thus fail to profit by the words of the apostles, or treat the words of copyists as if they were those of the apostles. . . .

Most learned men entirely neglect the spirit and, consequently, do not treat even the letter rightly. Hence it arises, that up to the present

Johann Albrecht Bengel

time, the most confused and contradictory opinions prevail, as to the mode of deciding between conflicting readings and on the method of combining such decisions with the received text. One relies on the antiquity, another on the number of manuscripts, nay, even to such an extent, as to exaggerate their number; one man adduces the Latin Vulgate, another the Oriental versions; one quotes the Greek Scholiasts, another the most ancient fathers; one so far relies upon the context (which is truly the surest evidence) that he adopts universally the easier and fuller reading, another expunges, if so inclined, whatever has been once omitted by a single Ethiopic—I will not say translator, but—copyist; one is always eager to condemn the more received readings, another equally determined to defend it in every instance. Not everyone who owns a harp can play upon it. We are convinced, after long and careful consideration, that every various reading may be distinguished and classified, by due attention to the following suggestions:

1) By far the more numerous portions of the sacred text (thanks be to God) labor under no variety of reading deserving notice.

2) These portions contain the whole scheme of salvation and establish every particular of it by every test of truth.

3) Every various reading ought and may be referred to these portions and decided by them as by a normal standard.

4) The text and various readings of the New Testament are found in manuscripts and in books printed from manuscripts. . . . We include all these under the title of "codices," which has sometimes as comprehensive a signification.

5) These codices, however, have been diffused through churches of all ages and countries and approach so near to the original autographs that, when taken together in all the multitude of their varieties, they exhibit the genuine text.

6) No conjecture is ever on any consideration to be listened to. It is safer to bracket any portion of the text, which may haply appear to labor under inextricable difficulties.

7) All the codices taken together should form the normal standard by which to decide in the case of each taken separately.

8) The Greek codices, which possess an antiquity so high that it surpasses even the very variety of reading, are very few in number; the rest are very numerous.

9) Although versions and fathers are of little authority, where they differ from the Greek manuscripts of the New Testament, yet where the Greek manuscripts of the New Testament differ from each other, those have the greatest authority, with which versions and fathers agree.

10) The text of the Latin Vulgate, where it is supported by the consent of the Latin fathers or even of other competent witnesses, deserves the utmost consideration, on account of its singular antiquity.

11) The number of witnesses who support each reading of every passage ought to be carefully examined, and to that end, in so doing, we should separate those codices that contain only the Gospels from those that contain the Acts and the Epistles, with or without the Apocalypse, or those that contain that book alone; those that are entire from those that have been mutilated. . . .

12) And so, in fine, more witnesses are to be preferred to fewer; and, what is more important, witnesses who differ in country, age, and language are to be preferred to those who are closely connected with each other; and what is most important of all, ancient witnesses are to be preferred to modern ones. . . .

13) A reading that does not allure to too great facility but shines with its own native dignity of truth is always to be preferred to those that may fairly be supposed to owe their origin to either the carelessness or the injudicious care of copyists.

14) Thus, a corrupted text is often betrayed by alliteration, parallelism, or the convenience of an ecclesiastical lection, especially at the beginning or conclusion of it; from the occurrence of the same words, we are led to suspect an omission; from too great facility, a gloss. Where a passage labors under a manifold variety of readings, the middle reading is the best.

15) There are, therefore, five principal criteria, by which to determine a disputed text. The antiquity of the witnesses, the diversity of their extraction, and their multitude; the apparent origin of the corrupt reading; and the native color of the genuine one.

16) When these criteria all concur, no doubt can exist except in the mind of a skeptic.

[Editor's note: #17–27—minor criteria and comments on the format of his text edition and commentary.]

184. Exposition of the Apocalypse (1740)

Bengel wrote several books about eschatology. The following excerpt from his interpretation of the book of Revelation, published in 1740, shows his interest in establishing a precise chronology of the history of salvation and the importance he attached to the early leaders of the Pietist reform movement.

From Johann Christian Friedrich Burk, *Dr. Johann Albrecht Bengels Leben und Wirken* **(Stuttgart: Johann Friedrich Steinkopf, 1832), 278–94.**

The whole book of Revelation breaks down into three parts: 1) the introduction, 2) the exposition, and 3) the conclusion. The first three chapters form the introduction, and their content is a preparation for what follows. First, the preparation takes place with regard to John. . . . Next, we have the preparation regarding the seven angels (or overseers) of the churches and then at the seven churches themselves. . . .

After these preparations, the Lord speaks anew to John, saying that he would "show him things that must take place after this" (4:1), and here now begins the exposition that opens with the manifestation that all power in heaven and in earth is given to Christ. This is made apparent, first in a general way in chapter 4 and then by the seven seals [chapter 6], the first four of which relate to visible events that commenced soon after the communication of the revelation.

The riders on the horses (6:2, 4, 5, 8) are not exactly particular people but rather representations of events taking place soon thereafter in the four regions [of the Roman Empire]. . . . *[Editor's note: The first four seals are associated with military victories and natural disasters during the reign of the Emperor Trajan, 98–117 A.D.]* The three last seals relate to the invisible world, which is likewise under the governance of Christ. First [under the fifth seal, 6:9] appear the martyrs, whose lives were taken by the Roman emperors. . . . Under the sixth seal (6:12) appear the wicked who have died and wait in terror for the Day of Judgment. . . . The

sealing of the elect in chapter seven may be regarded as a preparation for the all-important seventh seal (when, once again, representatives of the invisible world, namely, angels, appear). . . . The angels (ch. 8) now equip themselves for the full execution of the great commissions given to them, which they then carry out not altogether but one after the other. The trumpet of the first angel (8:7) relates to the Asiatic "earth" and signifies the dreadfully raging revolts of the Jews, which commenced during the reign of Trajan but took place mainly under his successors, especially at the instigation of the false messiah, Bar Kochba. . . . The second, in chapter 8:8, relates to Europe . . . and signifies the invasions of the Goths and other barbarian nations into the Roman Empire. The third, in chapter 8:10, relates to the heretic Arius, who "fell from" the "heaven" of the church through his blasphemous teachings, especially in Africa. . . . The fourth, in chapter 8:12, embraces the whole world, as then known, and signifies the downfall of the old Roman Empire, which in 395 was divided between Arcadius and Honorius and which Alaric, Attila, Genseric, and Odoacer then ravaged, one after another. . . .

The fifth trumpet, in chapter 9:3, relates to the false zeal of the heathen in Persia for their dark teachings because of which they persecuted the Jews severely for seventy-nine long years. . . . The sixth trumpet signifies the slaughter by the Saracens, which began on a small scale under the caliphs Abu Bakr, Omar, Osman, and Ali, but became more and more dreadful, until it was broken up before the city of Rome in 847. . . . In chapter 10 an angel appears who solemnly swears that although the three enemies—Satan, who is now thrown down to the earth; the Beast that rises up out of the sea; and the other Beast that rises out of the earth—will now bring about the third woe, yet, with the impending trumpet of the seventh angel, no further period of IIII 1/9 years will elapse until the consummation of the mystery of God, which was so often foretold by the prophets of the Old Testament [10:7].[3] . . . Along with the trumpet of the seventh angel, one hears, in chapter 11:17, the hymn of praise sung by those in heaven concerning the goal and end of the tribulation that is coming upon the earth at that time.

Then a new scene of very important things is disclosed. First, there appears, in chapter 12:1, "the woman clothed with the sun," that is, the church of God and of Christ as it originally took root mainly in Israel and then as it was planted, raised up, spread abroad to the east and the west, and preserved among the Gentiles. It will appear much more glorious in the future, especially when the natural branches (the Jews) will be grafted back again into their own olive tree. . . . The woman's pregnancy intimates that it began to be evident in the age of Charlemagne that all nations will become her inheritance, and her cries signify the anxious yearnings of the saints for the imminent consummation of the kingdom of God. The great red dragon with seven heads, ten horns, and seven diadems, who sets himself in violent opposition to this approaching consummation, signifies the devil in all his wrath and power [12:3]. His drawing after him of a third of the stars denotes the apostasy of many teachers from the true faith in the years 847–947, when the Manichaean heresy and the reckless life of the church brought about great harm. . . . The flight into the wilderness refers to the movement of Christianity from Asia to Europe, especially to its northern parts, which had, until then, been a spiritual desert in comparison to the lands that belonged to the old Roman Empire, where Christianity had long been upheld [12:6]. . . . The river that the serpent shoots out of his mouth [to sweep away] the woman signifies the Turkish power that

was delimited in the Asian "earth" by the crusades and subsequent events [12:16]. . . .

The Beast that is mentioned in chapter 13 has a twofold appearance: the first out of the sea and the second out of the bottomless pit. The first appearance is evil and continues for a long while, but the second appearance, though shorter, is worse. This Beast is a spiritual-worldly power that began not long after the second woe, . . . apparently nothing other than the papal hierarchy, which arose above all under Gregory VII and has, in principle if not always in actuality, claimed dominion over all the lands of the earth. . . . The "war with the saints" [13:7] may be seen in the history of the Albigensians and Waldensians in the thirteenth century, of the Wyclifites and Hussites in the fifteenth, and of the Protestants in the sixteenth and later centuries. . . . The Beast out of the sea lasts for 42 prophetic months or 666 6/9 years [13:5]. . . . I have attempted various calculations: for example, marking the start of this period in 1073, the beginning of the reign of Gregory VII, or 1077, the humiliation of Emperor Henry IV through this pope, or 1080, when Gregory VII named Rudolph as emperor, according to which the end of this period would fall around 1740–50, when the papacy sustained considerable diminution. . . . But I have not reached any precise certainty about this. . . .

The other Beast (13:11) rising "out of the earth" (apparently Asia) is the false prophet, the weapon-bearer of the first who appears at or after the end of 666 years. It is that power that upholds and defends the power of the pope intrinsically as well as out of its own interest. In the beginning it may be a party or order, but in the last time it may be an individual person. . . . Time will tell whether or not this is the Jesuits (who correspond with the characteristics very well) or perhaps the Freemasons. . . .

The tyranny over conscience that the Catholic church has exercised until now is only the prelude to a far worse religious tyranny that will arise when the mark [of the Beast, 13:6] must be accepted, partly as a marking on the body or clothing and partly perhaps as an [authorizing] signature.

The three angels who next appear (chapter 14) particularly signify three great messages and also the instruments through whom the messages are brought. The instruments are men who perhaps have special help from the invisible ministry of angels. The first is apparently [Johann] Arndt [14:6]. . . . The importance of Arndt is evident from the extensive circulation of his writings in many lands and in many languages and from the diligent use of them by all true Christians. The second angel is [Philip Jacob] Spener, through whom the study of New Testament prophecy came into fashion [14:8]. The third angel will not be far off. His commission is to warn, with threats of severe punishment, against the inward or outward honoring of the Beast. In his way of thinking, he appears to be nearly related to Arndt and Spener. . . .

The images of a harvest in chapter 14:14-20 represent two visitations before the outpouring of the seven bowls [in chapter 16]. In the crop harvest, the righteous are brought into the granary of heaven, and in the vintage harvest, the scornful are brought into the wine-press of wrath. . . . How long it will be until this period takes place cannot be exactly determined. It is enough to know that it will be near. . . .

In chapter 15 now follows that sign by which the wrath of God will be accomplished. Up to this point, he had looked upon the enemies with great forbearance, but now he shows his wrath to the utmost. It comes forth swiftly and whatever it strikes, it strikes completely. . . .

In chapter 18 the angel appears who most emphatically describes the fall of Babylon. The great debates about the nature of the fulfillment of this prophecy prove that it has still not happened. . . . However, all the traits mentioned in this chapter make it completely clear that no other city can be intended than Rome, the city that has most profusely shed blood, first under the heathen emperors and afterwards under the popes. . . .

Chapter 19: After the awful destruction of Rome, there follows another joyful hallelujah in heaven, and John catches sight of the Son of God in the triumphant perfection of his power, who now appears to utterly destroy his enemies upon the earth. . . . A conflict now begins between the Beast, the false prophet, and the Son of God that ends with their being thrown into the lake of fire. . . .

The devil now arrives at the third stage of his punishment. First, he lost his principality; under the seventh trumpet he remained awhile in heaven and was then thrust down to the earth. Now he will be cast for a thousand years into the bottomless pit. . . . After the termination of this thousand years, Satan will be loosed again for a short time, but when this time is completed and Satan's last attempted attack through Gog and Magog is repelled, he will come to the fourth stage of his punishment in the lake of fire. . . .

Chapter 21 describes the eternal glory and blessedness of the new universe, where now the New Jerusalem appears. . . . That the New Jerusalem will be a spatial place is entirely certain because we will have bodies that must occupy a space. But whether the numerical descriptions of the size of the city are to be taken literally or to be understood with reference to the number of the elect, I will not attempt to determine. . . .

ACCOUNTS OF SPIRITUAL EXPERIENCES

The Pietists frequently collected and published accounts of conversion experiences. Although there is considerable variety among them, certain patterns often reappear. The individual becomes aware of his or her sinful state, goes through a difficult period of struggle with guilt and despair (a *Busskampf*), and then experiences a breakthrough *(Durchbruch)* and the beginning of a new life. We see all of these elements in the following account, which was reported in the form of an interview.

185. The Conversion of the Peasant Farmer Jacob Schneider (1697)

From *Fortgesetzte Sammlung Auserlesener-Materien zum Bau des Reichs Gottes*, vol. 5, ed. Joachim Wilcke (Leipzig: Walther, 1736), part 36, 462–65.

How did your conversion come about?

Our preacher at Arensfelde, named Herr Richler, was very zealous and gave precise warnings to all hearers. As soon as he noticed someone absent from the church service, we would go to visit him at his house after the sermon and ask him why he had not been in church. Now it happened that once when my servant had skipped the sermon, Herr Richler asked me where my servant was. I said he was at the mill, though I could not remember whether or not this was true. When I went to confession the next Saturday, Herr Richler took me to task on the confessional stool and chastised me before all the people, saying that I had lied to him, that my servant had not been at the mill, and that I and my people were Sabbath-breakers. It annoyed my old Adamic nature that he had chastised me publicly before all of the people and considered me evil, so,

although I had gone to confession, I did not partake of communion that Sunday. After the sermon, Herr Richler came to me and chastised me more sharply, saying that I was a scorner of Holy Communion and the Word of God. He wanted to inform the authorities about me so that they would chase me out of the town because I hindered all blessings and worked on Sundays.

What happened after that?

O, my dear God faithfully followed me and sought my poor soul. Once when I was plowing in the fields, it became so bad for me that I had to put the plow away and go home. When I came home, I lay on my back on my bed, and as I lay there I saw before me a deep abyss and round about it a barren mountain. Then it seemed as if someone spoke to me: "Jacob, if you do not truly repent and convert yourself, you will go down into the deep abyss." Because of this I was very anxious and afraid. I told my wife about this and sought consolation from her. My wife went to a neighbor and asked him to come and comfort me in my despair. He came running with his Bible, but it was like a blind man showing others the way. Finally, I had to be silent and say no more.

What happened then?

Once when I was coming from the fields and wanted to go home, our preacher, Herr Richler, met me at the bridge and spoke to me, saying: "Now, Jacob, how does it stand with you, do you persist in your evil mind? Do you not want to get better and convert to God?" Just as the man said this to me, it became entirely different for me. I could truly feel that my spirit was different, and my hate and anger was all at once changed into such heartfelt love that I would have gladly given him all that I had.

How did you conduct yourself after this?

I began to pray, and dear God sent me great joy and sweetness and a true foretaste of eternal life so that a thousand times I wished to die right away.

Did you remain long in such joy?

O, no! I entered into a long repentance-struggle *(Busskampf)* through which I had to sweat for a long time. First I came under the law, and for over a year I truly felt the anguish of hell. Now if the least unrighteous thing remained in me, I had to give it up ten times over. Afterwards, I came into the hardest struggle, namely, with disbelief, and this again endured for a year. I could not imagine anything other than that I would be eternally lost and damned. In such great anguish, I once stood under an apple tree in my garden and thought: "Why don't I go back to the world and live as before, like others who still have hope that they will become holy and do not have such anguish as I have?" But then I thought about what someone once said to me: "Turn back to the world and you will be ten times more chastised." And so I made a firm determination that I would not go back again, whatever the cost might be. In such anguish, when I felt pure anger and disgrace, I went back to Arensfelde to the preacher to cry out my need to him. While I was under way, I fell to my knees in a field and cried earnestly to God, remonstrating with him about why he had created and upheld me for so long, why he had so dearly redeemed me if I still was so lost.

Were you long in this state?

I must have spent a year in such anguish until finally dear God brought me into the gospel. I received assurance and certainty that I had forgiveness for all my sins and was a child of God. I still remain this way up to the present time through God's grace.

What was the nature of your former life?

O, God have mercy. I lived in such blindness; you can count on that. I went to confession, church, and communion, indeed I was truly zealous about that, and I also led an honorable life. I was diligent in my calling and in my work, but only out of avarice. I respected the authorities, such that they were always at peace with me. However, I was unconverted and not yet reborn. Therefore, I cannot thank God enough that he put up with me so long in my blindness and still rescued me out of my blindness in my advanced years. . . .

How does it go with you now that you have begun a different life?

I must suffer much. They want to stone me out of the village. As long as I am silent about their way of life they can put up with me, but when I see that their unrighteousness, their hard-drinking, and their dances are not right and no longer participate in such activities, they take offense at me, and if they had it in their power, they would often beat me up. When the preacher criticizes this or that sin of theirs from the pulpit, they always say, "The prayer-knave *(Bett-Schelm)* has been informing on us again." . . .

Most people hold back from true repentance and true Christianity because they would have to suffer mockery and scorn. But if we want to obtain a crown, we must be willing to suffer. Therefore, we can rejoice at what our Lord Jesus said in Matt. 5:11, 12: "Blessed are you when men revile you and persecute you and utter all kinds of evil against you falsely on my account. Rejoice and be glad, for your reward is great in heaven." All mocking names will one day become pearls in our crown. I have suffered much. Prayer-Knave was my best title, but God never leaves us in suffering without consolation. . . .

Has God also shown you a special grace?

Yes, God led me once into the bridal chamber of the Lord Jesus, where I saw, heard, and tasted very much. But I should not speak about that. One must always remain in humility. . . .

186. Petersen: Dreams and Revelations (1719)

Eleanor von Merlau Petersen was one of the most influential women in the early development of Pietism. She and her husband, John Petersen, lived in Frankfurt and were married by Spener in 1680. Later, however, they became promoters of Philadelphianism, a movement begun by Jane Leade in England that disassociated itself from all existing churches and nurtured apocalyptic expectations about the eventual restoration of a pure, spiritual church.

From *Der deutsche Pietismus*, ed. Werner Mahrholz (Berlin: Furche-Verlag, 1921), 236–45.

. . . The following secrets were disclosed to me during the years of my marriage. In the year 1685 I received for the first time a disclosure about the holy Revelation of Jesus Christ that I had never had thoughts about before, having always passed by such a great book thinking I would understand nothing in it. But as I went one time into my little room and took the Bible into my hand, a phrase from it jumped out at me. I received into my eyes, the words of Rev. 1:3: "Blessed is he who reads and hears the words of prophecy and keeps what is written there, for the time is near." These words went very deeply into my heart, and I thought to myself, "You have neglected and bypassed the book of holy Revelation, and there are still such great things in it." And although I excused myself for having passed it by because I thought I would not understand the content, it came into my mind if there were such great promises in such books and also such threats, God would faithfully give me the grace to learn to understand what I should do so that I might participate in such promises and flee what could cast me into such judgment. With this

expectation, I fell down before God, imploring him with inner sighs to open the eyes of my understanding for me so that I might know his most holy divine will and he might always find me to be a true doer of his word. As I now rose up from prayer and took before me this blessed book to read, I did not have the least thought that it would be immediately opened to me, but as I began to read I did not feel well, as if my heart were pierced with the light of God, and I understood all that I read. Many Scripture passages that relate to the holy book of Revelation came to mind, and as I looked them up I was very moved and humbled before God that he let such grace happen to me, his lowly maid. I took a piece of paper and wrote down the passages in order to harmonize them with what I found in the Apocalypse, thinking that they might escape my memory, and when I had written them down, I went to my dear husband and said, "See what our dear God has opened up for me from holy Revelation." He took the sheet in his hand to read and was shocked. He also handed me his own written page, still moist, for it was written just that hour. He said to me, "The Lord has truly disclosed to you what he has done to me. Go now; we will show each other again in a little while what the Lord has further revealed to us." So it happened that when I showed him something the Lord opened up to me, the same was also opened up to him, and similarly when he brought me something, I had also already received it. Then we remembered a vision I had had in a dream in the year 1662, when I was eighteen years old, in which I saw the number 1685 in large golden numerals up in the sky. The first two numbers were quickly covered by the clouds, but both of the other numbers, 85, remained standing. To my right I saw a man standing who pointed to the numbers and said: "See, at that time great things will begin to happen and something should be revealed to you." This also truly came true, for in the year 1685 great unrest and persecution came about in France, and in the very same year, the blessed one-thousand-year reign of Jesus Christ from holy Revelation was opened to me.

PIETIST HYMNS

187. Freylinghausen: Who Is There Like Thee?

Johann Anastasius Freylinghausen (1670–1739) served as assistant to August Hermann Francke for many years and eventually succeeded him as pastor of St. Ulrich's Church in Halle and director of the Francke Institutions. In 1704 he published the *Spirit-Rich Songbook*, which went through several editions and became the most widely used hymnbook among the Pietists of northern Germany. He wrote forty-four hymns himself, which have often been considered among the best produced within the Pietist movement. The following "Jesus hymn" (the original German version has fourteen verses) has also circulated widely in the English-speaking world in a freer translation by John Wesley as "O Jesus, Source of Calm Repose."

From James S. Stallybrass, trans., in *Sabbath Hymn and Tune Book*, ed. John Curwen (London: n.p., 1859).

Wer ist wohl wie du
Who is there like thee,
Jesus, unto me?
None are like thee, none about thee,
Thou art altogether lovely;
None on earth have we,
None in heav'n like thee.

Love that warmly glowed,
Blood that freely flowed;
Life that stooped to death to save me,
And a deathless being gave me,
Bore my guilty load,
Brought me back to God!
Plant thyself in me,
I will learn of thee,
To be holy, meek, and tender,
Wrath and pride and self surrender:
Nothing shouldst thou see
But thyself in me.

188. Laurenti: Rejoice, All Ye Believers

Laurentius Laurenti (1660–1722), who served for many years as cantor and director of music at the cathedral church in Bremen, is usually associated with the Pietist movement, but his hymns are free of the thematic peculiarities and overindulgent expressions of emotion to which many non-Pietists objected. The following Advent hymn (the original German version has ten verses), composed in 1700, is based on Matt. 25:1-13, the same text that, a hundred years earlier, inspired Philip Nicolai's famous chorale, "Wake, Awake, For Night Is Flying."

From Sarah Borthwick Findlater, trans., in *Hymns from the Land of Luther*, 1st series, ed. Jane Borthwick (Edinburgh: Kennedy, 1854).

Ermuntert euch, ihr Frommen
Rejoice, all ye believers,
And let your lights appear!
The evening is advancing,
And darker night is near.
The Bridegroom is arising,

And soon he draweth nigh.
Up, watch, and pray, and wrestle,
At midnight comes the cry!

Ye saints, who here in patience
Your cross and sufferings bore,
Shall live and reign forever
Where sorrow is no more.
Around the throne of glory
The Lamb ye shall behold;
In triumph cast before him
Your diadems of gold!

Our Hope and Expectation,
O Jesus, now appear;
Arise, thou Sun so longed for,
O'er this benighted sphere!
With hearts and hands uplifted,
We plead, O Lord, to see
The day of earth's redemption,
That brings us unto thee!

189. Hiller: O Son of God, We Wait for Thee

Philip Friedrich Hiller (1699–1769), the most productive hymnwriter among the south German Pietists, has been called a poetical exponent of the practical theology of his teacher, Johann Albrecht Bengel. He wrote 1,075 hymns, 297 of which were inspired by the prayer book of Johann Arndt. The following hymn (the original German version has four verses) expresses a sense of world-weariness and a longing for bliss, feelings that were often part of the Pietist frame of mind.

From Joseph A. Seiss, trans., in *The Story of Christian Hymnody*, ed. E. E. Ryden (Philadelphia: Fortress Press, 1959), 124.

Wir warten dein, O Gottes Sohn
O Son of God, we wait for thee,
We long for thine appearing;
We know thou sittest on the throne,
And we thy name are bearing.
Who trusts in thee may joyful be,
And see thee, Lord, descending
To bring us bliss unending.

We wait for thee, 'mid toil and pain,
In weariness and sighing;
But glad that thou our guilt hast borne,
And cancelled it by dying.
Hence, cheerfully may we with thee
Take up our cross and bear it,
Till we the crown inherit.

We wait for thee; soon thou wilt come,
The time is swiftly nearing;
In this we also do rejoice,
And long for thine appearing.
O bliss 'twill be when thee we see,
Homeward thy people bringing,
With ecstasy and singing!

190. Von Bogatzky: Awake, Thou Spirit of the Watchmen

Carl Heinrich von Bogatzky (1690–1774) was born into a noble Hungarian family. His father, a high-ranking army officer, disowned him when he enrolled as a student of theology at Halle instead of pursuing a career in the army. Limited by poor health, he devoted his life to writing, including the composition of more than four hundred hymns. The following hymn (the original German version has fourteen verses) reveals the strong Pietist interest in evangelization and foreign missions.

From Winfred Douglas and Arthur Farlander, trans., in *The Story of Christian*

Hymnody, ed. E. E. Ryden (Philadelphia: Fortress Press, 1959), 118.

Wach auf du Geist der ersten Zeugen
Awake, thou Spirit of the watchmen,
Who never held their peace by day or night,
Contending from the walls of Sion,
Against the foe, confiding in thy might,
Throughout the world their cry is ringing still,
And bringing peoples to thy holy will.
O Lord, now let thy fire enkindle
Our hearts, that everywhere its flame may go,
And spread the glory of redemption
Till all the world thy saving grace shall know,
O harvest Lord, look down on us and view
How white the field; the laborers, how few!

The prayer thy Son himself hath taught us
We offer now to thee at his command;
Behold and hearken, Lord; thy children
Implore thee for the souls of every land:
With yearning hearts they make their ardent
    plea;
O hear us, Lord, and say, "Thus shall it be."

191. Woltersdorff: Come, My Heart, No Longer Languish

Ernst Woltersdorff (1725–61) was a pastor in Silesia and founder of an orphan asylum. The following communion hymn (the original German version has thirteen verses) is notable for its graphic description of the redemptive suffering of Christ. Such meditations on the blood and wounds of Jesus were even more commonplace in the writings of Count Nicholas von Zinzendorf, the Pietist leader who was involved in the formation of the Moravian church.

From J. Salyards, trans., in *Collection of Hymns for Public and Private Worship from the Evangelical Lutheran Joint Synod of Ohio* (8th ed.; Columbus: n.p., 1872).

Komm, mein Herz!
Come, my heart, no longer languish,
Jesus feeds thee on his anguish:
Blood of life divine is flowing,
Cool the thirst within thee glowing.
Joy is through my spirit streaming;
Lo! a God, my soul redeeming,
Robes me for a nobler station,
Bathes me in his free salvation.

Bread most holy! let me bless thee!
For he mingles as I press thee,
Flesh divine, all rent and riven,
Wounds my guilty race has given,
As the bliss I feel suffusing,
I will taste it, deeply musing
How for me my Savior dying,
Lowly in the grave was lying.

Wine most holy! Let me bless thee!
In my kindling soul confess thee:
For that blood is in thee glowing,
Once for guilty mortals flowing.
Quick'ning all my barren spirit,
Moves the Savior I inherit.
Is there here mysterious seeming?
Yet his blood within me streaming!

Bibliography of English-Language Resources

General Readings on Lutheran History and Theology

Bergendoff, Conrad. *The Church of the Lutheran Reformation: A Historical Survey of Lutheranism*. St. Louis: Concordia, 1967.

Bodensieck, Julius, ed. *The Encyclopedia of the Lutheran Church*. 3 vols. Minneapolis: Augsburg, 1965.

Gritsch, Eric W. *Fortress Introduction to Lutheranism*. Minneapolis: Fortress Press, 1994.

Gritsch, Eric W., and Robert Jenson. *Lutheranism: The Theological Movement and Its Confessional Writings*. Philadelphia: Fortress Press, 1976.

Lueker, Erwin, ed. *Lutheran Cyclopedia*. Revised edition. St. Louis: Concordia, 1975.

Schlink, Edmund. *Theology of the Lutheran Confessions*. Translated by Paul F. Koehneke and Herbert J. A. Bouman. Philadelphia: Muhlenberg, 1961.

Chapter One: Crises and Controversies during Martin Luther's Lifetime (1483–1546)

Primary Source Materials

Hillerbrand, Hans J., ed. *The Reformation: A Narrative History Related by Contemporary Observers and Participants*. New York: Harper & Row, 1964.

Janz, Denis, ed. *A Reformation Reader: Primary Texts with Introductions*. Minneapolis: Fortress Press, 1999.

Lull, Timothy F., ed. *Martin Luther: Basic Theological Writings*. Minneapolis: Fortress Press, 1989.

Pelikan, Jaroslav, and Helmut Lehmann, eds. *Luther's Works*. 55 volumes. Philadelphia: Fortress and St. Louis: Concordia, 1955–86.

Luther Biographies

Brecht, Martin. *Martin Luther: His Road to Reformation*. Translated by James Schaaf. Philadelphia: Fortress Press, 1985.

———. *Martin Luther: Shaping and Defining the Reformation*. Translated by James Schaaf. Minneapolis: Fortress Press, 1990.

———. *Martin Luther: The Preservation of the Church*. Translated by James Schaaf. Minneapolis: Fortress Press, 1993.

Edwards, Mark U., Jr. *Luther's Last Battles: Politics and Polemics, 1531–1546*. Ithaca: Cornell University Press, 1983.

Gritsch, Eric W. *Martin: God's Court Jester*. Philadelphia: Fortress Press, 1983.

Kittelson, James M. *Luther the Reformer*. Minneapolis: Augsburg, 1986.

Lohse, Bernhard. *Martin Luther: An Introduction to His Life and Work.* Translated by Robert Schultz. Philadelphia: Fortress Press, 1986.

Oberman, Heiko A. *Luther: Man between God and the Devil.* Translated by Eileen Walliser-Schwarzbart. New Haven: Yale University Press, 1989.

von Loewenich, Walther. *Martin Luther: The Man and His Work.* Translated by Lawrence W. Denef. Minneapolis: Augsburg, 1986.

Wicks, Jared. *Luther and His Spiritual Legacy.* Wilmington, Del.: Michael Glazier, 1983.

Luther's Thought

Althaus, Paul. *The Theology of Martin Luther.* Translated by Robert C. Schultz. Philadelphia: Fortress Press, 1966.

———. *The Ethics of Martin Luther.* Translated by Robert C. Schultz. Philadelphia: Fortress Press, 1972.

Ebeling, Gerhard. *Luther: An Introduction to His Thought.* Translated by R. A. Wilson. Philadelphia: Fortress Press, 1970.

Headley, John M. *Luther's View of Church History.* New Haven: Yale University Press, 1963.

Lienhard, Marc. *Luther, Witness to Jesus Christ: Stages and Themes of the Reformer's Christology.* Translated by Edwin H. Robertson. Minneapolis: Augsburg, 1982.

Loeschen, John R. *Wrestling with Luther: An Introduction to the Study of His Thought.* St. Louis: Concordia, 1976.

Loewen, Harry. *Luther and the Radicals: Another Look at Some Aspects of the Struggle between Luther and the Radical Reformers.* Waterloo, Ont.: Wilfrid Laurier University Press, 1974.

McGrath, Alister E. *Luther's Theology of the Cross: Martin Luther's Theological Breakthrough.* New York: Blackwell, 1985.

von Loewenich, Walther. *Luther's Theology of the Cross.* Translated by Herbert J. A. Bouman. Minneapolis: Augsburg, 1976.

General Works on the Reformation

Bagchi, David V. N. *Luther's Earliest Opponents: Catholic Controversialists 1518–1525.* Minneapolis: Fortress Press, 1991.

Blickle, Peter. *Communal Reformation: The Quest for Salvation in Sixteenth-Century Germany.* Translated by Thomas Dunlap. Atlantic Highlands, N.J.: Humanities, 1992.

Bossy, John. *Christianity in the West, 1400–1700.* Oxford: Oxford University Press, 1985.

Brady, Thomas A., Jr., Heiko A. Oberman, and James D. Tracy, eds. *Handbook of European History, 1400–1600: Late Middle Ages, Renaissance, and Reformation.* 2 vols. Leiden: Brill, 1994.

Cameron, Euan. *The European Reformation.* Oxford: Clarendon, 1991.

George, Timothy. *Theology of the Reformers.* Nashville: Broadman, 1988.

Greengrass, Mark. *The Longman Companion to the European Reformation, c. 1500–1618.* London: Longman, 1998.

Grell, Ole Peter, ed. *The Scandinavian Reformation: From Evangelical Movement to Insti-tutionalisation of Reform*. Cambridge: Cambridge University Press, 1995.

Hillerbrand, Hans J., ed. *The Oxford Encyclopedia of the Reformation*. 4 vols. New York: Oxford University Press, 1996.

Lindberg, Carter. *The European Reformations*. Cambridge, Mass.: Blackwell, 1996.

McGrath, Alister E. *The Intellectual Origins of the European Reformation*. New York: Blackwell, 1987.

———. *Reformation Thought: An Introduction*. 2d edition. Cambridge, Mass.: Blackwell, 1993.

Ozment, Steven. *The Age of Reform (1250–1550): An Intellectual and Religious History of Late Medieval and Reformation Europe*. New Haven, Conn.: Yale University Press, 1980.

Reardon, Bernard M. G. *Religious Thought in the Reformation*. 2nd edition. New York: Longman, 1995.

Scribner, Bob, Roy Porter, and Mikulas Teich, eds. *The Reformation in National Context*. Cambridge: Cambridge University Press, 1994.

Guides to Reformation Research

Aland, Kurt. *Hilfsbuch zum Lutherstudium*. 3d edition. Witten: Luther-Verlag, 1970.

Bainton, Roland H., and Eric W. Gritsch. *Bibliography of the Continental Reformation: Materials Available in English*. 2d edition. Hamden, Conn.: Archon, 1972.

Maltby, William, ed. *Reformation Europe: A Guide to Research II*. St. Louis: Center for Reformation Research, 1992.

Ozment, Steven, ed. *Reformation Europe: A Guide to Research*. St. Louis: Center for Reformation Research, 1982.

CHAPTER TWO: THE DISSEMINATION OF THE REFORM MESSAGE

Chrisman, Miriam Usher. *Lay Culture, Learned Culture: Books and Social Change in Strasbourg, 1480–1599*. New Haven, Conn.: Yale University Press, 1982.

———. *Conflicting Visions of Reform: German Lay Propaganda Pamphlets, 1519–1530*. Atlantic Highlands, N.J.: Humanities, 1996.

Edwards, Mark U., Jr. *Printing, Propaganda, and Martin Luther*. Berkeley: University of California Press, 1994.

Matheson, Peter, ed. *Argula von Grumbach: A Woman's Voice in the Reformation*. Edin-burgh: T. & T. Clark, 1995.

Russell, Paul A. *Lay Theology in the Reformation: Popular Pamphleteers in Southwest Germany 1521–25*. Cambridge: Cambridge University Press, 1986.

Scribner, Robert W. *For the Sake of Simple Folk: Popular Propaganda for the German Reformation*. Oxford: Clarendon, 1994.

Strauss, Gerald. *Luther's House of Learning: Indoctrination of the Young in the German Reformation*. Baltimore, Md.: Johns Hopkins University Press, 1978.

Chapter Three: The Implementation of Reform Proposals

Hsia, R. Po-chia. *Social Discipline in the Reformation: Central Europe, 1550–1750.* London: Routledge, 1989.

Karant-Nunn, Susan. *Luther's Pastors: The Reformation in the Ernestine Countryside.* Transactions of the American Philosophical Society, vol. 69. Philadelphia: American Philosophical Society, 1979.

Reed, Luther D. *The Lutheran Liturgy: A Study of the Common Liturgy of the Lutheran Church in America.* 2d edition. Philadelphia: Fortress Press, 1975.

Senn, Frank C. *Christian Liturgy: Catholic and Evangelical.* Minneapolis: Fortress Press, 1997.

Steinmetz, David C. *Reformers in the Wings.* Philadelphia: Fortress Press, 1971.

Tolley, Bruce. *Pastors and Parishioners in Württemberg during the Late Reformation, 1581–1621.* Stanford, Calif.: Stanford University Press, 1995.

Chapter Four: The Church's Struggle for Survival (1546–1648)

Gagliardo, John G. *Germany under the Old Regime, 1600–1790.* London: Longman, 1991.

Holborn, Hajo. *A History of Modern Germany.* 3 vols. New York: Knopf, 1959–69.

Lau, Franz, and Ernst Bizer. *The History of the Reformation in Germany to 1555.* Translated by Brian A. Hardy. London: Black, 1969.

Manschreck, Clyde L. *Melanchthon: The Quiet Reformer.* Westport, Conn.: Greenwood, 1975. Reprint.

Stupperich, Robert. *Melanchthon.* Translated by Robert H. Fischer. Philadelphia: Westminster, 1965.

Vierhaus, Rudolf. *Germany in the Age of Absolutism, 1648–1763.* Translated by Jonathan B. Knudsen. Cambridge: Cambridge University Press, 1988.

Chapter Five: Factionalism in the Late Reformation (1546–80)

Bente, Friedrich. *Historical Introductions to the Book of Concord.* St. Louis: Concordia, 1921. Reprint, 1965.

Jungkuntz, Theodore R. *Formulators of the Formula of Concord: Four Architects of Lutheran Unity.* St. Louis: Concordia, 1977.

Klug, Eugene F. A., and Otto F. Stahlke. *Getting into the Formula of Concord: A History and Digest of the Formula; Historical Notes and Discussion Questions.* St. Louis: Concordia, 1977.

Kolb, Robert. *Andreae and the Formula of Concord: Six Sermons on the Way to Lutheran Unity.* St. Louis: Concordia, 1977.

————. *Confessing the Faith: Reformers Define the Church.* St. Louis: Concordia, 1991.

Kolb, Robert, and James A. Nestingen, eds. *Sources and Contexts of the Book of Concord.* Minneapolis: Fortress Press, 2001.

Kolb, Robert, and Timothy J. Wengert, eds. *The Book of Concord: The Confessions of the Evangelical Lutheran Church.* Minneapolis: Fortress Press, 2000.

Lentz, Harold H. *Reformation Crossroads: A Comparison of the Theology of Luther and Melanchthon*. Minneapolis: Augsburg, 1958.

Raitt, Jill, ed. *Shapers of Religious Traditions in Germany, Switzerland, and Poland, 1560–1600*. New Haven, Conn.: Yale University Press, 1981.

Rogness, Michael. *Melanchthon: Reformer without Honor*. Minneapolis: Augsburg, 1969.

CHAPTER SIX: THEOLOGY IN THE AGE OF ORTHODOXY (1580–1700)

Clouse, Robert G. *The Church in the Age of Orthodoxy and the Enlightenment: Consolidation and Challenge from 1600 to 1800*. St. Louis: Concordia, 1980.

Elert, Werner. *The Structure of Lutheranism*. Translated by Walter A. Hansen. St. Louis: Concordia, 1962.

Preus, J. A. O. *The Second Martin: The Life and Theology of Martin Chemnitz*. St. Louis: Concordia, 1994.

Preus, Robert D. *The Theology of Post-Reformation Lutheranism*. 2 vols. St. Louis: Concordia, 1970–72.

CHAPTER SEVEN: SEVENTEENTH-CENTURY DEVOTIONAL LITERATURE AND HYMNODY

Erb, Peter C., ed. *Johann Arndt: True Christianity*. Classics of Western Spirituality. Mahwah, N.J.: Paulist, 1979.

Lund, Eric. "The Second Age of the Reformation." In *Christian Spirituality: Post-Reformation and Modern*. Edited by Louis Dupré and Don E. Saliers in collaboration with John Meyendorff. New York: Crossroad, 1989.

———. "The Problem of Religious Complacency in Seventeenth-Century Lutheran Spirituality." In *Modern Christian Spirituality: Methodological and Historical Essays*. Edited by Bradley C. Hanson. Atlanta: Scholars, 1990.

Sattler, Gary R. *Nobler than Angels, Lower than a Worm: The Pietist View of the Individual in the Writings of Heinrich Müller and August Hermann Francke*. Lanham, Md.: University Press of America, 1989.

Senn, Frank C., ed. *Protestant Spiritual Traditions*. New York: Paulist, 1986.

CHAPTER EIGHT: LUTHERAN PIETISM (1670–1750)

Brown, Dale W. *Understanding Pietism*. Revised edition. Nappanee, Ind.: Evangel, 1996.

Erb, Peter C., ed. *Pietists: Selected Writings*. New York: Paulist, 1983.

Fulbrook, Mary. *Piety and Politics: Religion and the Rise of Absolutism in England, Württemberg, and Prussia*. Cambridge: Cambridge University Press, 1983.

Gawthrop, Richard L. *Pietism and the Making of Eighteenth-Century Prussia*. Cambridge: Cambridge University Press, 1993.

Lindberg, Carter. *The Third Reformation: Charismatic Movements and the Lutheran Tradition*. Macon, Ga.: Mercer University Press, 1983.

Sattler, Gary R. *God's Glory, Neighbor's Good*. Chicago: Covenant, 1982.

Stein, K. James. *Philipp Jakob Spener: Pietist Patriarch*. Chicago: Covenant, 1986.

Stoeffler, F. Ernest. *The Rise of Evangelical Pietism*. Leiden: Brill, 1965.

————. *German Pietism during the Eighteenth Century*. Studies in the History of Religions. Leiden: Brill, 1973.

Notes

CHAPTER ONE

1. Aristotle, *Ethics* 2.1: "We become just by doing just acts."

2. Gabriel Biel, *Sententiarum* 2, dist. 28k: "Man can by his own nature, through free will, fulfill divine precepts according to the substance of the act but not according to the intention of Him who gave the precept, which is a consequence of our salvation."

3. John Duns Scotus (c.1265–1308), an English Franciscan philosopher, and Gabriel Biel (c.1420–95), an important defender of the *via moderna* (nominalist scholasticism) in Germany.

4. A dualistic sect that began in Persia but was prominent in north Africa during the early centuries of Christianity.

5. The Elector had a passion for collecting relics and displayed about 19,000 fragments of the saints at the All Saints' Foundation in Wittenberg. He had received a papal privilege to offer those who came to visit the collection up to 1,900,000 days of indulgence.

6. A story circulated among the Lutherans that Johann Tetzel had been asked by a knight whether a person could receive a letter of indulgence for a future sin. Tetzel supposedly agreed to this. Soon thereafter the knight came back and robbed him of all the money he had collected.

7. The Council of Konstanz (1414–17) ended the late-medieval papal schism that had prompted the Bohemian reformer Jan Huss to criticize abuses of papal power. Huss received a safe-conduct to attend the Council to defend his views, but, once there, he was declared a heretic and burned at the stake.

8. The Greek Orthodox Church and the other churches of the East rejected Western claims about the unique authority of the bishop of Rome. As a result the two branches of Christianity repudiated each other in the Great Schism of 1054.

9. If a serf died, the other members of his or her family were obligated to compensate the lord for the loss of this person's labor services.

CHAPTER TWO

1. One sermon for Epiphany is 173 pages long in the Weimar edition or 128 pages long in the American edition. Any attempt to deliver the entire sermon from which the excerpt in this chapter was taken would have required at least an hour and forty-five minutes. Luther's own evaluation of the postil is found in WA 23:279, lines 13–14 (*LW* 37:147).

2. "A Brief Instruction on What to Look for and Expect in the Gospels," trans. E. Theodore Bachmann, *LW* 35:123.

3. Hans-Joachim Köhler, "Die Flugschriften der frühen Neuzeit," in Werner Arnold et al., eds., *Die Erforschung der Buch und Bibliotheksgeschichte in Deutschland* (Wiesbaden: Harrassowitz, 1987), 325.

4. Paul Russell, *Lay Theology in the Reformation* (Cambridge: Cambridge University Press, 1986), 6; Mark U. Edwards Jr. *Printing, Propaganda and Martin Luther* (Berkeley: University of California Press, 1994), 17; Miriam Chrisman, *Conflicting Visions of Reform* (Atlantic Highlands, N.J.: Humanities, 1996), 2–4; Steven Ozment, "Pamphlet Literature of the German Reformation," in *Reformation Europe: A Guide to Research* (St. Louis: Center for Reformation Research, 1982), 85–98.

Chapter Three

1. "Quadragesima" is the name given to the first Sunday in Lent (so-called because it is almost forty days before Easter). Cross Week is also called Rogation Week and refers to the days between Rogate Sunday and the feast of the Ascension, forty days after Easter. On Rogation Days, special prayers were traditionally recited to promote spiritual renewal. These included the three days before the Ascension. St. Bartholomew was commemorated on August 24.

Chapter Five

1. See *The Book of Concord*, ed. Theodore Tappert (Philadelphia: Fortress, 1959), 222.

2. Johannes Cochlaeus (1479–1552) was a prominent Catholic controversialist whose works included the extensive, critical biography of Luther noted in chapter two. Georg Witzel (1501–73) became a Protestant through Luther's influence but reverted to Catholicism when he concluded that the Protestants lacked true piety.

3. Amsdorf based this claim on passages such as the following from Luther's 1535 lectures on Galatians (*Luther's Works*, vol. 26, trans. Jaroslav Pelikan [St. Louis: Concordia, 1963], 36):

> Because my sins are so grave, so real, so great, so infinite, so horrible, and so invincible that my righteousness does me no good but rather puts me at a disadvantage before God, therefore Christ, the Son of God, was given into death for my sins, to abolish them and thus to save all men who believe.

4. Origen (185–254 CE) was one of a number of theologians from the early church whom the Philippists cited in support of their mild synergism. The Gnesio-Lutherans also respected these early writers but were not averse to pointing out their errors on this issue.

5. Flacius has in mind the sermon on Luke 2:21 in Luther's Church Postil, WA 10/I:1, 508.

Chapter Six

1. Quenstedt calls all of the Swiss Reformers "Calvinists," ignoring some differences in their thought. Ulrich Zwingli (1484–1531) was the first reformer of Zurich.

2. Erasmus (1469–1536) was the leading Christian Humanist of the sixteenth century. Francisco Suarez (1548–1617) was a prominent Jesuit philosopher of the Counter-Reformation. Theodore Beza (1519–1605) was successor to Calvin as leader of the Reformation in Geneva.

3. Hollaz gives the standard definition of the communication of majesty: "The Son of God truly and really communicates the attributes of his own divine nature to the assumed human nature in consequence of the personal union, for common possession, use, and designation."

4. Peter Martire Vermigli (1500–1562) was an Italian monk who converted to Calvinism and wrote extensively on the Eucharist.

Chapter Seven

1. Kaspar Schwenkfeld (1489–1561) was a Silesian Spiritualist who questioned the value of Baptism and believed that the Spirit of God could guide individuals apart from the Scriptures. Andreas Osiander (1498–1552) was an associate of Luther who taught that sinners are not only declared righteous by imputation but also made righteous by the indwelling of the righteousness of Christ. Valentin Weigel (1533–88) was a Lutheran pastor who became controversial because of his criticisms of the church and his mystical theology. He emphasized the internal testimony of the Spirit more than the record of revelation in the Scriptures.

2. Johann Gerhard, *Schola Pietatis* (Nürnberg: Endters Tochter, 1736), 223, 224.

Chapter Eight

1. Martin Statius (1589–1655) was a pastor in Danzig who was best known for producing volumes of selections from the writings of other people. In addition to his selections from Luther, he published a very popular volume of excerpts from the devotional writer Stephan Praetorius (1536–1603).

2. Joachim Lütkemann (1608–1655) was a disciple of Johann Arndt. See chapter seven. Lewis Bayly was an English Puritan. His *Practice of Piety* was the most widely read English devotional book after John Bunyan's *A Pilgrim's Progress* and was very influential in German Pietist circles. On Nicholas Hunnius, see chapter six.

3. Bengel associated a precise number of years with certain terms in the book of Revelation as a result of calculations derived from the importance of the numbers 666 and 1000 in the book. He decided that a prophetic month is 15 and 6/70 years, a "time" (καιρος) lasts III 1/9 years, and a "period" (κρονος) equals IIII 1/9 years.

Index

✣